Property Rights and Changes in China

Qiren Zhou

Property Rights and Changes in China

北京大学出版社
PEKING UNIVERSITY PRESS

Springer

Qiren Zhou
National School of Development
Peking University
Beijing, China

ISBN 978-981-15-9884-5   ISBN 978-981-15-9885-2 (eBook)
https://doi.org/10.1007/978-981-15-9885-2

Jointly published with Peking University Press
The print edition is not for sale in China (Mainland). Customers from China (Mainland) please order the print book from: Peking University Press.

Translated by Wang Qiong, Proofread by Luo Xiaoping

This Springer imprint is published by the registered company Springer Nature Singapore Pte Ltd.
The registered company address is: 152 Beach Road, #21-01/04 Gateway East, Singapore 189721, Singapore

Preface

This collection is based on *Property Rights and Institutional Changes* published by China Social Sciences Press in 2002 and its revised and expanded version published by Peking University Press in 2004. With several articles added and another several dropped, this edition is renamed as *Property Rights and Changes in China* per the suggestion of the editor, so the readers will have a "new" book.

This edition includes five new articles. The first and also the most recent one, "System Costs and China's Economic Growth", was published in *China Economic Quarterly*, Volume 16, Issue No. 3-2017. Based on several re-straightened concepts, it expounds on the economic logic behind China's rapid economic growth and its institutional changes. The core concept, of course, is still "transaction costs" as proposed by Coase; however, for a non-market economy that once prohibited market transactions, the concept of "transaction costs" must be appropriately extended so as to be applicable to mandatory economic activities; hence the concept of "institutional costs" soon emerges and becomes widely accepted. However, the institution, as a crucial constraint on economic behaviors, is not a single, isolated variable, but an interwoven "system". From this perspective, Arrow's interpretation of Coase's transaction costs as "the costs of running the economic system" is more relevant. This article calls "a series of systematic institutional costs" as "system cost", which might cope better with China's experience. The reform in the words of Chinese people is "system reform", isn't it? Based on this premise, this article explains the trajectory of China's economic growth and its challenges in recent years with the drop and then the rise of its system cost, and concludes with a discussible argument: if the system cost cannot be constantly and significantly reduced, it will be difficult for the "China miracle" to sustain.

The second new article, "Monetary System and Economic Growth", discusses a popular topic, monetary policies, and the fundamental monetary system. The monetary system also an institutionalized system that is closely correlated to the systems on fiscal affairs, market access, and property rights and their protection. To understand and analyze monetary phenomena, all these factors must be put together in the same big picture.

The third one, is about an analysis to the new round of China's healthcare reform. This article aims to draw a line between the role of the government and the market mechanism in the healthcare service. The argument is that to address the severe supply/demand imbalance of medical services, the market mechanism must be allowed to play a decisive role in market access and drug pricing. The government must take full responsibility for public health, and can appropriately subsidize low-income patients as allowed by the fiscal conditions; however, it must eliminate the improper controls over general medical services in terms of market access and pricing. Otherwise, China's new round of healthcare reform will end up embarrassedly like "half-cooked rice".

The fourth, "The Theory of the Firm and China's Reform" was written in 2008 to review China's reform in the last three decades. According to Lenin's conception at that time, to build the socialist planned economy in a country with relatively backward productivity like Russia is nothing more than operating the whole national economy as a super firm. As the state power left little room for legitimate market activities, it seems that the planned economy is immune from "transaction costs"; however, the super state firm is still constrained by another type of cost—organizational costs, proposed by Coase in his theory of the firm. From this perspective, how to save the enormous organization costs of the super state firm is the driving force for the reform of the planned economy.

The three articles on the telecommunications reform were deleted from the previous edition. Viewed across the globe, China's telecom system reform initiated in the 1990s can be seen as a pioneer. After many years of efforts, tremendous progress has been made as compared against the exclusive administrative monopoly by one single SOE that blurs the government and the enterprise; nevertheless, in terms of basic telecommunications the reform still cannot go beyond the "market" with limited competition between only several state controlled corporations, and strong barriers are still there for private players. This industry is still behind advanced international level both in rates and quality of services. The fact that the Chinese premier had to directly call for the telecommunications to lower the rates and improve service speaks for the necessity for deeper reform.

The previous articles on empirical studies of the reform of public-owned enterprises (POE) stay in the collection, a new paper, "Property Rights of Human Capital" is added. The basic idea was also reflected in other articles chapters. The concept is also the pivot for observation and analysis of the POE reform, namely at the end of the day the capabilities of humans are at the disposal of the person, and this holds true under any system. The difference is, a system not acknowledging the property rights of human capital will fail to fully leverage people's talents and eventually will be forced to change the system by the pressure of competition. Economic growth in modern society ultimately has to rely on giving full play to people's talents and capabilities. From this point of view, stagnation of the POE reform will not last very long.

On the topic of rural reform and land reform, the article on China-Russia comparison was deleted, because it seems that bench-marking against "the Big Brother" (nickname for USSR in China) never helped China that much in the reform. However more generally, it is worth watching what kind of role the previous strategy of "promoting the reform through the opening-up" will still play in the context where many developed countries are opting for trade conservatism in their policy. It seems that it is increasingly important for China to push forward the system reform based on its actual conditions.

Lastly, "Real-World Economics: Coase's Methodology of Economics and its Application in China" is moved from the last paper in the previous two editions to the opening paper of this new edition. The author believes it is necessary to give some explanations at the very beginning if sticking to this unfashionable and unpopular methodology.

The original Preface is kept right after this Foreword to help readers understand the intention of this collection when it was first published.

Last but not least, I would like to express my heartfelt thanks to all the editors. They are TANG Zongkun, QIAO Tongfeng, DENG Zhenglai, YIN Lian, LIU Guoen, and HAO Xiaonan, without whose meticulous editing, coordination, and accountability, it would be impossible to present these articles to the readers as they are today.

Beijing, China
June 2017

Qiren Zhou

Preface to the Original Edition

Except for one article on research methodology in economics, all articles included in this collection study the reforms and changes of the central planning economic system and the public ownership structure based on China's actual experience. This is the focus of my economic research in the past 20 years. I am delighted to take this opportunity of the publishing to share the background with the readers.

One

Milton Friedman said economic problems are always linked to choices.[1] However, when I started to show interest in economics, the only observable economic system at the time there seemed to offer no opportunities for people to make choices at all. Under the central planning and public ownership system, production and investment were controlled by government commands, no one could choose their desired careers or jobs, and non-human factors of production could not freely flow or be reorganized. Not to mention the choice of the form of economic organization, as it was a matter of "direction and road", which could not be touched by ordinary people. In that era, "choice", private choice in general, was not legitimate in the system.

It takes very close observation and experience to discover that even the economic system does not allow free choice, private choices still exist tenaciously. Take for example what I saw when I was assigned as an "educated youth" to the countryside of Heilongjiang Province between 1968 and 1978. The same farmer worked like two totally different persons on his private plots vs on collective land. Wasn't he making a choice? With the same weather, same acreage, and same number of people, the efficiency between piece rate pay and time wage was totally different; wasn't this the choice by laborers, or anything else? Not to mention the arbitrary, inconstant and sometimes even ridiculous "production and investment decisions"; were they attributable to the "education level" or "personal disposition" of the managers of the

[1]Friedman, Milton. 1962. *Price Theory*. Aldine Publishing Company, Chapter 1.

public economy? If yes, then why didn't we see the same absurdity in their own private consumption?

Hence, this is the first thing I have learned about economic behaviors: people still make choices even under a system that seemingly does not allow choices. I was then unable to ask the question: under the property rights system where all assets are publicly owned, why can individuals—farmers, workers, and managers alike—still make their de facto choices about production? When everything is determined by the "collective unit" as to what, how much and how to produce, why can individuals still decide de facto the amount of efforts that they provide to the public production system? My real question is: how does this seemingly illegal and trivial "right" take root in the public ownership system for so many years?

Two

Before I was able to straighten out the question, the remarkable reform of public economy already started in China. Since late 1970s, the household responsibility system (HRS) has been widely adopted in rural areas, untying, contracting, and restructuring of state-owned enterprises (SOEs) have taken place in cities, private enterprises re-emerged as self-employed and other forms, and foreign-invested companies cropped up in coastal cities. Private property rights, wiped out by state power decades ago, now comes back thriving. And *the Constitution of the People's Republic of China* has been amended four times since the 1980s to accommodate the new structure of property rights.

By chance, I began to participate in the survey of rural reform guided by Mr. DU Runsheng when I was still a college student, and the survey lasted for nine years.[2] The survey aimed to provide policy recommendations to the central government's rural reform; therefore, in addition to the economic behaviors of farmers, state behaviors also came into my research. The basic concept that I have obtained from the observation and participation, is that the HRS reform is a result of bottom-up practice, which is different from many hymns to the reform. What I observed is that long before the upper leadership made any policy, the HRS as a reform of property rights of the collective land had already started in the countryside. What intrigued me was how the driving force for the reform was generated from within the system where everything was owned by the public. Or to put it generally, how did private property rights arise from within the public ownership system maintained by the state?

It seems easy to answer the above questions with the hypothesis of human nature in economics. Since it is human nature to pursue self-interest, private ownership, of course, survives and thrives. However, if this hypothesis explains why the reform of the public ownership system started, how can it allow for the establishment of public ownership system in the first place? Later, I figured out that the focus of the

[2]I reviewed this valuable experience in the Preface to *Rural Reform and China's Development 1978–1989*, Oxford University Press, Hong Kong, 1994.

economics hypothesis on human nature is not that human will chase self-interest, but that "human will try his/her best to pursue self-interest under constraints". Therefore, self-interest has little explanatory power. I think what matters is to understand the constraints on economic behaviors. Again, I keep on asking: under the same human nature hypothesis, why has the economic system, namely the ownership structure, changed significantly? What are the constraints on the re-establishment of private property rights under the public ownership system?

Long investigative work enables me to realize that the following three constraints cannot be ignored. The first constraint is the state behavior. The state apparatus in the era of the planned economy aimed to "destroy and transform private property". Unlike Thatcher's cabinet and Yeltsin's administration, the Chinese government never put forward any clear privatization program even after entering the reform, but repeatedly and expressly opposed privatization. Second, the planned public economy, like other economic systems, shapes up its own vested interest. When the economic system is changed at the ownership structure level, these vested interests will inevitably be hurt. For example, the abolition of the work point system will all at once dispel the opportunities to profit from expertise of such a system. Third, the planned public ownership means that all the properties nominally belong to not only the entire existing population, but also to the entire future population that includes those to be born legally. Yes, under the collective ownership of land, every member of the community, including the future members to be born legally, are entitled to share the land rights and interest; and it goes without saying that the ownership by the whole people should take care of everything for its citizens from cradle to grave, and it has committed to provide everyone with a job for the future incremental labor. Therefore, the inherent rights of all people, including those to be born, will be impacted by the reform.

These three constraints should help explain why public ownership can sustain a long period once it is established; why it is very difficult to establish private ownership under the public ownership system; and why ownership change is easily ignored in ideology and delayed in practice in the process of the reform. Paradoxically, under the above-mentioned triple constraints, the ownership structure reform, marked by the re-emergence of the private ownership, still took place. People may have different comments and views, but there is no question about the basic fact.

The question therefore becomes more challenging. In private ownership systems, it is easy to see, in the market economy, all sorts of shared use rights and even joint ownership established by free contracts. If the state takes resolute actions—such as the experience of large-scale nationalization by the former Soviet Union, China, and other countries—it would not be so difficult to make all private properties public-owned. The question is, while the state is eliminating de jure any private ownership and adamantly opposing privatization, property rights reform still occurs, and private ownership gets rebuilt in China. How did this happen, and why?

Three

As Theodore Schultz pointed out, thought eventually is subject to the language of economics.[3] Therefore, to understand property rights reform, ideological and academic openness is decisive. I came to know of Schultz's theory on *Transforming Traditional Agriculture* (later I read an abstract in Economic Science Translation Series) at a course by Prof. LI Yining. Later then, a book of American neoliberal economics written by a Frenchman, was translated into Chinese and published to introduce to us the concept of property rights in common language. Around 1985, I got a photocopy of *The Future of China* and *A Revisit to China* by Prof. Steven N. S. Cheung of the University of Hong Kong from the development department of a private company. Then, I got the original version of *The Orange Seller's Words* from a close friend during my visit to Xiamen University in the fall of 1986. These three books, together with other articles by Prof. Cheung become the enlightenment works for me to learn the theory of property rights. According to this theory, property rights are not automatically deduced from the hypothesis of self-interest human nature as so believed by many who are for or against the theory. The property right is an institutional social constraint on individual's pursuit of self-interest. This constraint can explain the economic behaviors of people and the achievements of economic growth, because different property rights constraints have a decisive impact on the transaction costs of an economy.

The second half of *The Future of China*, contains the Chinese translation of one article written by Steven Cheung for the Institute of Economic Affairs. In this 1981 paper, Cheung predicates in black and white that "Over time China will adopt an ownership structure similar to private ownership."[4] What impressed me most was that Cheung came up with the prediction, rather than a forecast from a succinct theory. He first extended Ronald Coase's "transaction costs" into "institutional costs" and split it into two pieces: the costs to maintain the economic system and the costs to change it. Cheung then explained that the planned system sustained for a long time despite the high institutional costs only because the costs to change it was even higher due to the information cost and the opposition from the vested interests. However, DENG Xiaoping's opening and reform policy significantly brought down the costs to change the system. Watching from Hong Kong, Cheung saw this point clearly and therefore reasoned that the planned system would be fundamentally changed.

The opening-up has reduced the costs to reform the planned public ownership and made it impossible to maintain the prohibitive system. I believe this is a very solid basic ground for Cheung's prediction. The only thing that I feel that needs to be explored further is that the high institution costs itself—to save it will generate some income—will motivate people to look for possibilities to save it. Take the household contracting responsibility system (HRS) as I know for example. It first took place in Yongjia, Zhejiang Province in 1956, when China was clearly far from being opened

[3]Schultz, 1980. "Economics for Agriculture Productivity in Low-Income Countries", published in *Origins of Increasing Returns*, Peking University Press, 2001:234.

[4]Cheung, *The Future of China, Hong Kong Economic Journal Press,* 1985:206.

up. Doesn't it show that the driving force for reform has long been born from within the system?

More importantly, I realize from Cheung's reasoning that economics theory—of course the good ones—is a fantastic assist for us to explain the perplexing real world. In 1987, XIAO Geng, a direct student of Prof. Harold Demsetz at UCLA visited the Rural Development Center of the State Council where I worked, I asked him to bring us more literature on property rights and transaction costs—especially those highly recommended by Cheung. I remember that the literature brought by XIAO included four pages of manuscript by Armen Alchian as the entry of "property rights" in *The New Palgrave Dictionary of Economics.* The opening sentence reads "A property right is a socially enforced right to select uses of an economic good." Alchian's straightforward statement awakened me: since to select is a right, doesn't the de facto private selection observable under the public ownership system suggests that "private property" has never been fully eliminated even within the public ownership system?

Four

I believe the answer can be found in the academic tradition of property rights economics. In the next two or three years, we read and discussed the papers of Coase, Alchian, Cheung, Demsetz, Douglass North, etc., brought by XIAO Geng or found by ourselves, at a book club organized by the Industry and Enterprise Research Office of our institute. I still fondly remember the life in those days: we put the books in our backpacks to go to the countryside and spent our time reading and discussing after finishing the investigations, observations, interviews, and meetings. The travel time was great for our roaming thoughts. At that time, I wasn't able to read English, a few colleagues helped to translate for me. A few years later, these translations were published by Shanghai Joint Publishing House, which should be the very first translation collection on property rights and new institutional economics in Mainland China.[5]

In the fall of 1990, thanks to the recommendation of Prof. Gare Johnson, I went to University of Chicago and served as a visiting scholar at the Department of Economics. For about a year, I spent most of the time reading in the library apart from attending an undergraduate microeconomics course and Prof. Gary Becker's introductory courses for graduate students. What influenced me most was certainly Schultz's theory on the transformation of traditional agriculture and the human capital theory developed therefrom. It is said that since Schultz put forward the concept of human capital in his speech in 1960 when he was the president of the American Economic Association, for decades, three-quarters of doctoral dissertations of the Department of Economics at the University of Chicago alone are related to this

[5]*A Collection of Economics Papers on Property Rights and Institutional Change.* Translated by LIU Shouying et al., Shanghai Joint Publishing House, 1992.

topic. This is not surprising; as capital has always been the foundation for classical economics, and the theory of human capital has obviously become the core of the new growth theory.

Schultz's theory of human capital derives from Irving Fisher, whom he referred to as a great American economist. So, I went upstream to read Fisher's books and really enjoyed the fascination of the inheritance and development of the important thoughts by generations of scholars. According to Fisher, capital is a stock that has value as a source of current and future flows of output and income. Therefore, all resources that may generate future income should be regarded as assets—and of course, it should include human labor and knowledge; capital is but the present value of assets in the market. At the time I was awakened by the thought: with Fisher's concept, the "capital and labor" analysis framework is no more needed; to say "capital and labor" is like to say "capital and capital"?

Tied up by the focus of my own question, I am not so interested in other applications of the theory of human capital, for example, measuring the contribution of education, training and technology in economic growth. I was fascinated by such propositions as "the private rights of capital are not just limited to property… human capital also entails rights."[6] And so, I found very meaningful inspiration from Sherwin Rosen, another professor of the Department of Economics at the University of Chicago and a leading light of the New Labor Economics. He pointed out: "Differences in the form of human and non-human capital are of less import for analysis than are differences in the nature of property rights between them. The ownership of human capital in a free society is restricted to the person in whom it is embodied."[7]

The biggest reward for me at the University of Chicago library, is perhaps reading Yoram Barzel's papers. His definition of transaction costs as the costs associated with the capture, protection, and transfer of property rights is very special, as it is broader than that by Coase (costs incurred from market transactions) but narrower than that of Cheung (institutional costs). What's more special is that Barzel insists on studying abstract property rights with carefully verified historical and empirical examples. Each of his paper is remarkable, and for me, the most significant one is "An Economic Analysis of Slavery"[8] written in 1977. Why in the slavery system in southern United States and the West Indies occasionally some slaves, who were the legal property of their owners, could redeem themselves and become freemen? Barzel's answer is that the costs for slave owners to exercise the legal ownership rights is based on an important fact—the productiveness of slaves is up to themselves; to reduce this costs, some slave owners use the quota system to incentivize slave labor and reduce the monitoring and policing cost; under the quota system, some capable slaves accumulate money that was finally enough to redeem themselves.

---

[6]Schultz, Theodore W. 1997. "On Economic History in Extending Economics", *Economic Development and Cultural Change* 25 (the Supplement): 245–250.

[7]Rosen, Sherwin, 1987. "Human Capital". *The New Palgrave*: *A Dictionary of Economics*, Vol. 2. Palgrave Macmillan, 681–690.

[8]Barzel, Yoram. 1977. "An Economic Analysis of Slavery", *Journal of Law and Economics,* 20 (1): 87–11

Relatively speaking, Barzel's research is closer to my question: how is private property defined peacefully under the oppression by the coercive opposition force. I've read other studies on the origin of private property,[9] and their common feature is there is no such constraint as coercive opposition force; therefore, private property may spontaneously react to changing economic opportunities. However, even in the slavery case study by Barzel, the slave owner who favors the quota system can still take the move and sign the private contracts where there is still no strong state power that has a direct conflict of interest with private property.

It is in North's research on longer-term institutional changes that the state has formally become an important force in the rise of emerging and effective property rights. According to North, in the seventeenth century, the Netherlands and Britain successfully completed the transformation from public land ownership to private ownership and grew from there into strong and wealthy countries; whereas Spain was dragged down in regards to the land system reform by the interest group—sheep herders, and was left behind. North argues that the different attitudes of the state toward emerging property organizations can explain this significant historical divergence. Reading North's paper, I focused my thoughts on the question: what factors determine the attitude of the state—the only organization that can legally use coercion as put by North—toward effective property organizations? A more general question is: without the protection by the state, the emerging property rights cannot become common practice; but what forces can compel the state to vigorously protect property rights and make further infringements difficult? I jotted down "North Puzzle" in my notes. Although North has developed his theory into a sophisticated system, I don't think this question is answered.

I have learned a lot from the readings when I studied at the University of Chicago and subsequently at UCLA. The most important learning is that human capital, one of the basic factors of economic growth, along with its various manifestations is an inherent asset attached to the individual that embodies it. The individual is the de facto controller of the provision of human assets under any economic system. What is different from system to system is whether the laws (including habitudes which is informal) and informal institution acknowledge—and how they acknowledge—the private property rights in human capital, which is controlled by the individual. Correspondingly, the use and effectiveness of human resources differ from system to system. I believe this is a pivot for understanding, as it helps explain various behaviors under the public ownership system which I am familiar with, and the reform of public ownership; more importantly, it helps explain how and in what environment the private property, a right to select uses of an economic good, gets

[9]Such as Knight's analysis of the acquisition of public roads in 1942, Demsetz's study of the conversion of Beaver habitat in Montagnes from public ownership to private ownership in 1967 and John Umbeck's study of California gold rush in 1977 which finds that private property was defined by private-created law, especially, the rights of human capital and personal ownership of firearms, and Barzel's study of rights delineation of oil resources in the North Sea. See Barzel, Yoram. 1989. *Economic Analysis or Property Rights*. Cambridge University Press, Chapter 5.

re-built after the private property ownership system is mandatorily deprived and eliminated by the state.

When I re-read Coase's work, I had already read his lecture notes on the formation of his academic thoughts.[10] So, I studied his theory on the firm as the theory on the state.[11] Yes, the theory proposed by Lenin used to be the basis of the planned public ownership: in terms of economy, a socialist country can organize social production like a super firm, and all members of the society will become employees of the state. It is said that the conclusion after very hard thinking by the young Coase is: in order for the state to operate like a firm to command, plan and coordinate all social production to eliminate the massive transaction costs as a result of market activity elimination, this only firm that exists has to pay exorbitant "organization costs". Coase's theory explains why firms exist in the market: firms exist because they can save transaction costs, but they have to pay organization costs for it; when the two costs equal at the margin, the boundary of the firm is determined. As for me, the important thing is that we can use organization costs (or institutional costs as put by Cheung) to analyze economic behaviors of the planned public ownership system of countries eliminating all market relationships.

Five

Let me summarize. My academic life is closely related to two types of selections: on the one hand, I keep on observing various choice behaviors by people under the planned public economy; on the other, I keep on selecting economic theories to explain these behaviors. Perhaps because my mind was preoccupied with phenomena in the real world to be explained, I had little interest in learnings that present superb intelligence with imaginary constraints. In hindsight, this "question-oriented" study mode has a benefit: the academic tradition and theories available for selection are very concentrated. Given the unique experience of our generation (in mainland China): the mis-alignments of time sequence between formal schooling, observation and participation in social practice, the above methodology helps us to leverage our strengths and avoid our weaknesses. Since everyone acknowledges the role of division of knowledge, to choose a narrow topic for my research and try to come up with my personal views makes sense.

Next let me briefly cover the topics of the papers collected in this book and the questions for further study. "China's Rural Reform: A Review of Changes in Economic Institutions" was written in 1993 and 1994 as a theoretical summary of

[10]Coase, Ronald. 1988. "The Nature of the Firm, 1. Origin, 2. Meaning, 3. Influence", *Journal of Law, Economics, and Organization*. 4:3–47.

[11]"The transaction-cost approach to the analysis of economic organizations can be extended upward from a few participants to the 'government' or even the country itself." See Cheung, Steven N. S. 1987. "Economic organization and *transaction costs*", The *New Palgrave*: *A Dictionary of* Economics, Vol. 2. Palgrave Macmillan, 55–58.

the rural reform investigation that I participated. The paper argues that the bigger-than-North-Puzzle difficulty in the socialist property rights reform is "how to re-establish the order of property rights under the condition of abused state functions". I tried to answer this question by explaining the experience in changing the collective land ownership. The main findings are: under the people's commune system where everything is nominally owned by the public, private property has, however, never completely disappeared. The "partial exit right"—meaning, human capital, although de jure public-owned, can invest the labor and management efforts into non-collective activities—increases the institutional costs of the collective land system controlled by the state, and forces the state to adjust, at the grass-root and local level first, its policy and retreat from its previous policy until the private land tenure and the farmer's private property formed by the HRS have re-gained recognition across the country.

It seems now that there are two shortcomings of this study: First, there was information exchange and interaction between the state and farmers on the choice of property right system, but I did not know how to name it; so I used such inappropriate concepts as "transaction" and "negotiation". Yet obviously there was neither the "transaction" in its real sense nor "negotiation" between farmers or farmers' organizations and state agents. What actually happened is that farmers spontaneously adopted a new form of property rights, such as private plots and the contracting system, etc.; and then the state decided whether or not and how to recognize the legitimacy of these new forms of property rights. Second, as the private land tenure has been re-established, I optimistically predicted—though not very sure—land reform would continue and move forward based on the same logic, but failed to see another possibility: the land income right and transfer right can be delayed for a long time after the reform of the land use right has been put in place.[12]

"Farmers, Market and Institutional Innovation" was written in 1986. The inclusion into this collection is to record the changes in my understanding of rural property rights reform. The focus of this research report is on property rights, reflecting that we did not miss the point in our observations and theoretical selection. In addition, based on an analysis of the difficulties encountered by reform of the unified purchase and marketing system (UPMS), the report concludes that the re-establishment of private land tenure of farmers will require a fundamental change to the planned economy—property rights and organizations of industries and commerce. This problem has not been completely solved yet and is obviously a good subject to apply "transaction costs/institutional costs" for analysis. In addition, there is another point worth mentioning. This report proposes that farmers' land tenure needs to be manifested legally. It even points out that without legal recognition of the ownership innovations, it would be difficult to punish backpedaling (The embarrassing fact is that there is still no sound law to protect the rural contracting economy, which involves

[12]Last year, I re-visited the issue of farmers' income and found that the rural land property rights reform has stagnated after the farmers' private land tenure was more or less universally established. See "Farmers' Income is a Series of Events", China Center for Economic Research (CCER) at Peking University, and a series of articles published in *21st Century Business Herald*.

the fundamental interests of several hundred million people). This point was raised several years earlier than de Soto and his Peruvian colleagues, who emphasized the significance of formal legal expression of property rights on the genesis of capital.[13]

"Property Rights Reform and New Business Organizations" was written in 1996. It is based on my tour to Uzbekistan, which used to be part of the former Soviet Union; I was commissioned a year before by the World Bank to share the experience of China's rural reform. This tour gave me the opportunity to observe directly and think about the agricultural economy of the Soviet Union. My understanding of the "great agriculture" of the Soviet Union is based on my field trips, literature review and my own experience in Northeast China's state-run farms. This way I obtained a foundation to analyze the difficulties facing the "big market" reform versus the experience of China's rural reform. The conclusion of this article sings a very different tune from the popular statement that "The gradualist reform was a success while the radical reform was a failure."

"The Firm in the Market: a Special Contract between Human Capital and Non-Human Capital" is based on my reading notes taken at the lectures by Prof. Demsetz on the theory of the firm at UCLA; it is sort of a summary of related theories. Demsetz has a clear explanation of the concept of transaction costs, but he does not agree with Coase in using transaction costs to explain why there are firms in the market.[14] After close comparison, I decided to select Coase's contract theory plus my readings on property rights in human capital at the University of Chicago and UCLA to obtain my understanding of "the firm as a special contract". These notes also served as an outline of my research of firms after I returned to teach at Peking University, although I knew that public-owned enterprises (POEs) under the planned system are not based on contracts. To me, a theory is not only a good tool to explain things, but also a guide to the observation of the much more complicated real world.

The Enterprise Control Incentive and the Entrepreneur-Controlled Enterprise was written in 1997; it is a case study of the ownership of Hengdian Group (HG) in Zhejiang Provence—a township enterprise. From this research, I learned that the information filled in the "ownership" form does not necessarily tell you what is really going on with property rights. Under the same name of public ownership, the property rights of private human capital—I mainly study the entrepreneur's human capital—can be completely different. Under the "HG mode" which I studied—although its founder refers to it as "community ownership"—the company is actually controlled by the entrepreneur as an individual rather than by the community government. The entrepreneur obtains company control, but does not share the corresponding residual claims—this special arrangement provides what I call "the enterprise control incentive". I believe the success of some POEs in the transition period can be explained by "the enterprise control incentive" mechanism, just in the same way as it can be used

[13]De Soto, Hernando. 1989. *The Other Path*. Basic Book Press; 2000. *The Mystery of Capital*. Basic Book Press.

[14]Demsetz, Harold. 1997. *The Economics of the Business Firm*. Cambridge University Press. For the Chinese edition, see translation by LIANG Xiaomin, China Social Sciences Press, 1999.

to explain what longer-term institutional challenges these entrepreneur-controlled enterprises will face.

"Reform of Enterprise Property Rights System and Entrepreneurs' Human Capital" continues the study on POEs, but shifts its focus to the experience of their restructuring. Obviously, I have drawn on my previous understanding of the reform of the collective land system, but I also noticed the following two characteristics of non-land assets: First, because of the sensitivity to the "smallest economic scale", the enterprise restructuring cannot simply copy the experience of collective land system reform. The latter adopts average contracting based on the population/labor force and such an issue as entrepreneurs does not exist. Second, because the quality of corporate assets is way more difficult to measure than the land; therefore, the experience of land reform—to maintain nominal public ownership but contract the land use rights to individuals—cannot be duplicated in the POE reform. Under these new constraints, the delineation of the property rights of human capital, which are naturally private owned, has become the real starting point for the POE reform.

The research puts all its observed rich experience of POE restructuring onto this same pivot and finds that the logic of the reform is very natural: As the competition in product markets gets transmitted to factors markets, the relative price of entrepreneurial human assets increases; with the corporate control shifted from the administrative authority to the entrepreneur, the reform to delineate the residual claims between the government and the entrepreneur as an private individual is finally put on the agenda. As we can see later, whether we like it or not, in order to incentivize and restrict the enterprise control that is already in the hands of the entrepreneur, the entrepreneur's human capital property rights have been changed from covert to overt, from illegal to legal, from valueless to valuable, from current to long-term, and from non-transferable to transferable. It is no exaggeration that POEs are undergoing a property rights revolution.

However, I also know from the research that it is difficult to see, in the capacity of a researcher, the sensitive details about the POE restructuring, yet these details are very critical for research on institutional change. After trying many different ways, which I elaborated in the preface of another book,[15] I had worked part-time as an adviser at the Department of Investment Management at Stock Exchange Executive Council, spending about three years there and participating in the survey, consulting, financing, and restructuring of nearly 20 companies. As a diehard empiricist who started the career with economic investigation, I learned a great deal of solid knowledge about companies during this period. Unfortunately, these surveys involve trade secrets for which I have followed business practice and signed the confidential commitment; so, of course I will honor the non-disclosure agreements and not disclose them in my report. Fortunately, according to Coase, the descriptive material waits for a theory or a fire. With appropriate abstraction and simplification, the cognition from these cases can be generalized.

"The Nature of the Public-Owned Enterprise" was published in 2000 as an abstract summary of many case studies. As I often try to match the name with the reality,

---

[15]ZHOU Qiren, Preface to *Real-world Economics*, China Development Press, 2002, Pages 5–8.

this article aims to get to the bottom of the question: The traditional socialist public ownership has no traceable private property, nor is it built on market contracts. These two points are fundamentally different from firms in the market. Therefore, I don't think the once-popular "separation of ownership and management" mode and the currently prevailing "principal-agent" modes are the best frameworks to analyze this kind of economic organizations. I selected the inconsistency between the de jure and the de facto ownership as the basic mode to study the POEs. Faced by the de facto private ownership of human capital, POEs are forced to look for systems to restrict the pursuit of self-interests. However, since private property no longer legally (and ideologically) exists, POEs have to use state rent to replace the "private property + contract" system. As a result, enormous POE resources are in the "public domain", leading to a variety of capturing behaviors. One conclusion of this paper is that whether or not to recognize the legal status of private property is an inherent systemic problem with the POEs.

Lastly, "Real-World Economics" is a book review written in 1996 for *Case Studies in China's Institutional Change (Volume 1)* published by Unirule Institute of Economics. Encouraged by this outstanding research project, I took the opportunity to share my take on Coase's research methodology. At that time, I already knew that to distinguish the methodology of Coase Theorem from that of Positive Economics—to verify the hypothesis with observable facts, would be controversial. However, the three points proposed for economic research in this paper—to find questions from the fascinating real world, to focus on constraints, and to generalize—have always been my own lodestar guiding my research on property rights and economic institutional changes in China by leveraging the experience of China's reform.

The papers in this collection, except for one, have been published in *China Social Science Quarterly (Hong Kong), Economic Research* and *International Economic Review*. I would like to take this opportunity to thank the editors of these journals and my readers as well as the editors at China Social Sciences Academic Press as the publisher of this collection.

Beijing, China
April 2002

Qiren Zhou

Contents

Chapter 1
Real-World Economics: Coase's Methodology of Economics and Its Application in China

Volume 1 of *Case Studies in China's Institutional Change*,[1] a research project by Unirule Institute of Economics (UIE) has been published. A notable feature of these fruits, i.e. the application of many new economics developments since the emergence of Ronald Coase to China's recent institutional evolution, has drawn wide attention. The research also systematically applies the methods of Coase Economics to China, yet this point has so far not been noticed by critics. This paper discusses the methodological approach for this research and shares the author's take on the methods in Coase Economics.

1.1 Coase's Methodology of Economics

What's fascinating about Coase is that his research findings never had immediate effect. As readers must know, his *the Nature of the Firm*, published in 1937, didn't impress economists that much until some twenty or thirty years later. The later prevailing concept of "transaction costs", according to his recollection, was formed in 1932 when the young guy was just an assistant lecturer at a British school of economics and commerce who was worried about his lecture preparation. The paper was published five years later, with some colleagues and friends coming to congratulate him, yet no one discussed about his new insight. At that time, it seemed that the only person optimistic about the great potential contribution of this paper to the development of economics was Coase himself.[2] The paper was collected into an

[1]Zhang (1996).

[2]One friend of Coase recalls that he wrote to him in the early 1940s, "I can't believe that I have done such important work in my life" (Coase 1988: 23).

This article was originally published in *China Social Sciences Quarterly* (Hong Kong), Issue No. 2 (1997).

Q. Zhou, *Property Rights and Changes in China*,
https://doi.org/10.1007/978-981-15-9885-2_1

important selected works of price theory in the United States in the 1950s and cited in footnotes in the 1960s. People started to discuss about it in the 1970s, and then, citations and discussions suddenly shot up so steeply in the 1980s and outnumbered the total figure over the previous four decades.[3] Coase was already an octogenarian when he was presented the Nobel Prize for Economics in Stockholm in November 1991 for his contribution to economics from transaction costs, property rights, and business contracts.

However, even after Coase made his mark in academia, his contribution to research methods for economics was seldom mentioned. Putting aside agreement or disagreement from experts, we all see that Coase Theorem has been widely "considered". "Transaction costs" gets elaborated, applied, and criticized by various people, and the concept has been widely, or even too widely "considered". His idea of "social costs", along with its application in property rights, commercial disputes, environment protection and the use of public properties, and its far-reaching impact on all contracts with "externalities", becomes even more obvious to us all. But how has Coase accomplished these achievements that influence or even change the landscape of contemporary economics? What is so unique and great about his research methods? These questions are less followed. One possible reason: there seems to be no profound methods at all for studying economics in his plain, prose-style essays and it seems that the crowd would rather be carried astray by adoring "profound" things. It may take another 40 years for his plain approach to examine the "real-world" to get its due attention.

As a matter of fact, Coase's 1937 paper opens exactly with the methodological approach for economics. In the very first paragraph, he points out that "Economic theory has suffered in the past from a failure to state clearly its assumption", and criticizes "Economists in building up a theory have often omitted to examine the foundation on which it was erected". In the first paragraph, the central point Coase makes is that the assumption on which an economic theory stands should not only be "manageable", but also, more importantly, "realistic".[4]

In a speech delivered in 1987, Coase himself inferred that most readers have neglected this viewpoint on methodology and skipped this paragraph during reading (in fact, an editor named Putterman even deleted the whole paragraph when the article was re-published).[5] We certainly don't know how many Chinese readers have skipped it. As for myself, I read this paragraph, but neglected his unique insights. I once mistook it as a polite reference to and an agreement with the argument of Joan Robinson, who was very well-known in the UK in the 1930s. Later on, I didn't realize that Coase and Robinson have opposing opinions on economics methodology until I read the script of the 1987 speech! In *Economics Is a Serious Subject* (1932), Robinson's main argument happens to be that the assumption for economics must be manageable; and that if the assumptions we can manage are unrealistic, we have no choice but to adopt them. In those days Coase already opposed sacrificing "realistic"

[3]Cheung (1983).

[4]Coase (1937: 33).

[5]Coase (1988: 24).

in pursuit of "manageable" for economics research, and he clearly expressed that his goal is to find an assumption that is both realistic and manageable.

"Manageable" means it is easy to apply accumulated economics knowledge and analytical skills to deal with the matter in question. This is definitely important, because in the division of knowledge structure, the accumulation of analytical skills and knowledge in a special discipline is significant for improving cognitive efficiency. If economists of each time all choose "original" assumptions that cannot be built on the readily-accumulated economics knowledge, and carry out their research with these assumptions, it would be impossible for economics to form any tradition of knowledge accumulation and to develop as an academic discipline. Coase does not object to the proposition that assumptions should be "manageable". What he opposes is simply to regard "manageable" as the sole criterion for assumptions, and especially to put it before "realistic." In Coase's view, this tendency of giving up "realistic" for the sake of "manageable" has led to the following bad practice: "When economists find themselves unable to analyze what is happening in the real world, they replace it with an imaginary world that they are capable of handling."[6] If all economists produce papers and books in such an "economical" way, would they really help to understand the questions and relationships in our real world?

Coase's choice is the opposite: to use real assumptions to replace the imaginary world. What he is looking for is an assumption that is "both real and manageable". His own work sets a good example. Before him, economics had already accumulated a wealth of knowledge and analytical skills about market transactions and the price mechanism. However, one of the self-evident assumptions in previous economics was that market transactions and price mechanism themselves were cost free. Under such assumptions, people were not only unable to understand some of the complex organizations and contracts (such as firms) in the real world, but also turned a blind eye to these increasingly important phenomena in the modern market economy. Coase first revises the assumption of "zero cost for market transactions", and replaces it with the real assumption that "transaction fee is positive". Then he uses analysis to connect organizations (firms) with (transaction) cost. At this point, firms and other complex contracts from the real world becomes "manageable" in economics because now it is possible to use the previously accumulated economics knowledge and analytical skills (especially marginal analysis) to probe into the large numbers of organizations and contracts that exist in the real world but have been neglected by previous economics.

1.2 How to Achieve "Both Realistic and Manageable"?

We would further chase the question and ask: how to obtain an assumption that is both "realistic and manageable"? Coase did not disclose anything in 1937. It was not until 50 years later when he detailed the origin, significance, and implications of

---

[6]Coase (1988: 24).

the paper, we began to understand his approach.[7] The following three points, I feel, are the key:

First, seek knowledge from the real world. According to Coase himself, his economics training was mainly accomplished in the business school. One of the features of business schools is that they focus on case studies, which is, to explore theory through what happens in the real world. Therefore, as Coase studied price mechanism under Professor Plant, he also worked a lot on economic questions of the British public utilities and accumulated essential knowledge (such as commercial law, industrial organization, finance, and accounting) needed to study real firms. Perhaps it was precisely this "two line learning approach" (one is theory, the other, real cases) that the young Coase "was hit heads-on" with the question: if price mechanism automatically allocates resources, why do we still have different organizations? As we clearly see it today, it was really a blessing for economics development for Coase to "run into" such a question. Probably some incidental factors played a role, but one thing for sure: if he had not studied real firms, he would not "encounter" this question, or he might have come across but missed it. In fact, his sense of mission made him not only encounter the question, but also seize it although this kind of questions didn't get discussed at all by the then "renowned economists", nor was this question treated as an economics question by any existing literature. Then, how to find the reasons for the existence of enterprises in the real world where the price works? I believe that the following sentence is commendable: "I try to find the reason for firms to exist from the office of factories and companies rather than from the writings of economists".[8] This was Coase's attitude. For this reason, he went to the United States in 1932 using the travel scholarship from London School of Economics to study firms and organizations across the Atlantic Ocean. He spent most of his time interviewing factory and company management. He tried to find answers to the lingering questions by talking to these "real guys". Coase spent lots of time doing this and he was not afraid to "get his hands dirty" as he dived deep to collect real information. As a young scholar, Coase certainly also visited universities and bookstores, but he only spent a little time attending lectures. Even for courses given by the most well-known Professor Frank Hyneman Knight at the University of Chicago, the guest student only attended a couple of times. The problems that Coase studied were not found from books by senior scholars, nor had he hoped to find readily-available answers from existing publications. Just as expected, this US tour in 1932 enabled him to find out, from factory and company offices, why companies exist in the market. After returning to the UK, he wrote the draft in 1934. Three years later, the paper was published almost unrevised, and this is the world-renowned *The Nature of the Firm*.

Second, focus on constraints of the question. As the real world is complex, it is definitely not easy to seek knowledge from it. Coase's secret is to focus on investigating the factual constraints of the issue. While studying American companies, what Coase had in mind was the question of why enterprises exist, what he asked was not

---

[7]Coase (1988: 1–3).

[8]Coase (1988: 24).

such confusing questions as "why does your firm exist?"; but rather he kept on asking the interviewees, "When do you make, and when do you buy?" This, in essence, is to investigate the constraints for existence of firms in the market. As we know, Coase prefers real cases to hollow cases. Hollow cases, such as "Robinson Crusoe on the isolated island" as frequently adopted by many economics books, are simplifications of the imaginary world. The good thing about hollow cases is that they are "manageable", and, if well used, help to explain complicated theories; but the danger is that they may not at all reflect the true conditions of the question. Just imagine: if the question itself becomes hollow, how can the answer help to understand more about the real world?

In this regard, real cases have an obvious comparative advantage. As simplifications of the real world, real cases always contain true constraints. However, some important constraints might also get simplified when what is happening in the real world is simplified. Therefore, Coase prefers not only real cases, but also the real cases that he has worked on himself. Were the British lighthouses in history built by the government or the private sector, how did the US Federal Communications Commission (FCC) centralize the power through allocating channel resources, and the degree of integration of Ford and its parts factories, to name just a few of such solid questions that became well-known later. On the one hand, Coase uses lots of first-hand and second-hand information to find out the ins and outs of the facts, on the other, he simplifies the facts himself to obtain "qualified" cases that serve the purpose of economics research.

Third, generalize the study of real cases. The real case contains elements for the answer, but it does not automatically answer the question. To go from studying real cases to obtaining the understanding of the economic institutions, organizations, and human economic behaviors in the real world requires a jump in thinking, namely to generalize what has been learned from these real cases. Coming back to Coase's research on firms: He not only studies the real cases of the American companies regarding "when to make and when to buy", but also generalizes the different factual circumstance into the following judgement: "If the firms find it cheaper to purchase material and make the products than to buy them, they will make, and vice versa." This generalization is a leap in thinking, from which Coase extracted a general concept in economics—transaction costs. This way, now "enterprises" and all the complicated contracts become "manageable", just like "products and labor". Previous economics ignores transaction cost or automatically assume it to be zero, so it becomes impossible to analyze different organizations in the market. Coase generalizes the transaction costs from the analysis of real cases, expands rather than abandons the framework of economics analysis, and enables it to "handle" questions related to firms. Therefore, we will be no longer astonished when reading "At the margin, the cost of organizing within the firm will be equal to transaction costs by price mechanism.", as this has now become a standard economic proposition. This illustrates that Coase's study of the real cases does not stop at "a massive of descriptive materials waiting for a fire", rather, he "digests" the cases and generalizes the embodied logic and rationale into a theory.

The above discussion shows at least three key words are important in the Coase's methodology: the real world, constraints, and generalization. They also serve as several proper indicators as to if Coase's approach is adopted or not. Next, we will, accordingly, comment on the case studies by UIE on institutional change, and we will be able to see the pros and cons of the research through the discussion around these key words.

1.3 The Fascinating Real World

The works of UIE demonstrate that stories from the real world, elaborated by economists, can be fascinating. Each and every one of the first nine cases is inviting although different readers may find them attractive to different degrees.

Thinking deep, we can conclude that what makes real stories attracting is that what happens in the real world seems to go against the "well-accepted" logic. In such cases, what everybody believes will come does not happen, yet, in contrast, what everybody believes will never come does. Of all these unreasonable stories, the most interesting are those that differs from the predictions or assertions by "authoritative people". Anyone who likes to explore just can't help asking why? This kind of questions is definitely enchanting.

Let's take some examples from UIE's research. Such as, it was once agreed by all that a socialist country's government will not (or should not) legalize the trade of any kind of quota (coupon). The justification of this consensus is that the planned quota (coupons) as a certificate of allocation is issued by the government, not "created by labor", and carries "no value" in itself. If the government allows the trade of planned quota, wouldn't this pamper "getting benefit without work"? As of today, the above well-recognized logic is still valid in most cases as the authorities have always banned, attacked or cracked down the underground trading of many kinds of planned quota (coupons). However, there is one exception: foreign exchange (forex) quota trading. Sheng Hong seizes this exception, explores its origin, and studies how it changed from illegal to legally-allowed trading, and evolved into a transitional form of China's forex management system reform.[9] Under which conditions will the government accept and protect the "trading of rights"? Such a story is, of course, intriguing.

Moving on to another example. It is widely accepted that "repetitive construction" and "repetitive importation" is a waste of resources. From promoting the superiority of the planned economy several decades ago to criticism on current malpractices in economic development over the past few years, the "waste resulted from competition without government regulation" has always been a basic argument. However, the investigation into the refrigerator industry by Liu Shijin and Jiang Xiaojuan shows that it is this waste-accompanied competition that drives the quality improvements and economies of scale of the industry, and effectively reduces time to market. More

[9]Zhang (1996: Chapter 3).

interestingly from the story, the so-called "industrial policies" which get rid of competition and seem more optimum by calculation, are either unfeasible to implement or will lead to even more waste. These realities goes so much against our common sense that more attention will be surely paid to these "shouldn't happen" facts.[10]

The most enchanting case study in the book is about the stock market in Chengdu and Shanghai. These two stories are the best as they, in the first place, note down an important progress of China's reforms in the 1990s; and secondly, they explain very well how the support systems needed by complicated trading forms can be established in an "abnormal" way in China. Many scholars believed that advanced markets (e.g. stock market and futures market) cannot be developed until the primary market reform (such as the liberalization of the product market) is solidified, until SOE restructuring starts to see effects, until a series of relevant laws and regulations have been formulated and improved, and until the government has made considerate and well-scheduled arrangements. However, Yang Xiaowei's outstanding research on the spontaneous "Hongmiaozi" stock trading market in Chengdu tells us: under certain circumstances (expected strong returns, relaxed government regulation, etc., among other things), individuals or voluntary civil societies may also take the leading role in the provision of public goods which seems available only from the government and requires defining property rights constantly for the purpose of complex trading.[11] What happened in "Hongmiaozi" market is truly like climbing the ladder upside down: when primary trading is still chaotic and disorderly, advanced trading such as the trading of symbolized products like stocks is already achieved by spontaneous efforts. The beauty of this story lies in that it is illogically true. Look, when the regulations, the services, and everything are not sound, or even in existence at all, these Sichuanese, surprisingly are buying "paper"—the early form of stocks. There are about 100,000–300,000 participants per day and the turnover reaches 10 million yuan!

Relatively speaking, the story of Shanghai's stock market by Chen Yu is not as dramatic as Hongmiaozi, but equally real and interesting. No matter how hard the government tries to "regulate" over-the-counter transactions and curb transactions, the "private contract" nature of the trading, e.g. free trading, never gets changed. (What gets changed is only the trading costs to deliver the private contract under "legal," "illegal," or "semi-illegal" conditions). The game between the regulation and the profit-seeking shareholders didn't come to an end until the establishment of Shanghai Stock Exchange (SSE), an organization to institutionalize free bidding for stocks.[12] Chen Yu's story shows that "regulations" trying to "eliminate" investors' "humble" profit seeking motive do not create order at all, because they are never enforceable. In comparison to Chengdu Hongmiaozi spontaneous stock market, the overt and/or covert OTC stock trading in Shanghai ended up surviving and evolving into a longer-term result from the institutional arrangement. But this is not important because the history of institution evolution doesn't care about such success or failure.

---

[10]Zhang (1996: Chapter 7).

[11]Zhang (1996: Chapter 1).

[12]Zhang (1996: Chapter 2).

What is important, though, is that these two stories come together to reveal the dynamics of institutional and organizational change in the real world. London, New York, and Hong Kong become global financial centers as a result of multiple factors. But if we try to find the answers only from written norms, we will definitely get lost. Because behind the lines of the written norms lies the voluntary profit-driven effort, innovative attempts, and the superficial craze of "guys". Anyone who does not comprehend spontaneity at all and claim to understand market economy is doing nothing but murmuring to himself.

These fascinating stories do not come easily. The colleagues at UIE seem to have inherited Coase's work style: looking for questions and answers regarding the institutional change "from factories and company offices, rather than from books of economists".[13] This, where ever performed, is no easy job. The work becomes even more challenging for the following reasons. First, it is more difficult to make observations to the research subject—institutional change, as compared to other research projects. Second, cumulative reports on any aspect, field or from any organization are very rare in China, plus such limited data is very fragmented because of the silos between different departments and regions, and "confidentiality". Third, the evaluation system does not particularly encourage research that includes lots of realities. Therefore, looking back to the work of UIE to organize such a large-scale real case-based research, it probably takes great perseverance and efforts to practice one's own chosen methodology. We can feel this kind of momentum reading Zhang Shuguang's "Project Plan": "This study not only fills in the gaps in case study, but also attempts to explore the way to modernization for China's economics."[14] Hereby, I would like to send my congratulations and shout out loud: "Please keep up the good work!" as I certainly hope to read more fascinating stories like these.

1.4 "Invisible" Constraints

Every fascinating story can pose at least one attractive question. How do we open up the questions after seizing them? As mentioned earlier, Coase's way is to focus the investigation on the real constraints to unfold and solve question. As for such "social software" as institutional constraints, Coase starts with the consequence from economic behaviors to explore impact from the "invisible" institutional constraints. In the work of UIE, as we can see, there are many excellent cases of institutional change. Next, to what extent have the researchers revealed the constraints of these "not-supposed-to-happen" stories and helped with our understanding of the real world? My comment on these first jobs of UIE is that some jobs are good while some, not good enough.

---

[13]Coase (1988: 24).

[14]Zhang (1996: 311).

Take the China Unicom case[15] by Zhang Yuyan as an example. He poses an extremely important question: Why to relax control of the telecom industry, such an important and sensitive sector with "natural monopoly", and allow Unicom to break the monopoly of the Ministry of Posts and Telecommunications? Zhang Yuyan's report, at least in two aspects, shows that he has the capacity and potential to answer this significant question. First, he clearly and succinctly describes the full picture for telecom to move from monopoly (by one single entity) to duopoly. This is no easy job as this study involves not just the telecom sector, but also three relevant ministries, the military, and high-level decision-making at the State Council. Second, his mastery of theories helps him directly hit the point—the state has issued more telecom licenses to weaken the government's monopoly. Unfortunately, the study does not progress any further when it comes to the central question: under what constraints did the state "abnormally" relax its regulation over the telecom sector? ZHANG uses a "basic judgement" to replace further study: "the deregulation of China's telecom industry was directly attributable to the financial distress".[16] In fact, the basis of his judgement is not sufficient: "At least from the surface, we see the industry's deregulation and financial difficulties happened at the same time, and behind this coincidence there might be an inevitable connection."[17] This, of course, is just a guess, because two events taking place at the same time do not necessarily have "inevitable connections". Guess is certainly needed, and even essential for science. Yet the guess must also become a topic for further study and verification. The problem is, the author does not try to verify the link in his guess. Instead, he cites North and Hicks' comments on King of England's solution in the seventeenth century to the financial distress by selling concessions and rushes to his assertive "basic judgement".

Qin Hai, a commentator who is versed with the telecom sector, pointed out that this judgement by Zhang Yuyan is "arbitrary".[18] Zhang Shuguang, the executive editor of this book, after introducing the theoretical and practical significance of this paper, also pointed out that "it is not appropriate to attribute the telecom deregulation to financial difficulties."[19] However, neither Qin nor Zhang gave a better explanation. Qin's conclusion is that the deregulation is the result of changing productivity of the telecom industry,[20] and Prof. Zhang believes "the directly reason is the attraction by high profits from huge market demand'.[21] Without knowing the reader's response, I would see the two alternative conclusions as potentially less convincing than Zhang Yuyan's guess. But that is not the point here. My point is that they fail to criticize Zhang Yuyan from the perspective of methodology, nor do they suggest that the author investigate further. My criticism is that they, just like the author, have underestimated the importance of investigating real constraints. The question of "Under

15 Zhang (1996: Chapter 6).

16 Zhang (1996: 167).

17 Zhang (1996: 157).

18 Zhang (1996: 182).

19 Zhang (1996: 19).

20 Zhang (1996: 182).

21 Zhang (1996: 19).

which circumstances does the state relax its control over the telecom sector", just like the "when to buy and when to make" for enterprises, is the key that cannot be underestimated. For such a key point, guessing and existing literature by earlier economists, are both meaningful, but still they cannot replace down-to-earth site investigation.

Interestingly, in "Why Only Forex Quota Trading was Allowed" by Sheng Hong and "How China Liberalized Grain Prices and Canceled Grain Coupons" by Zhang Shuguang, the inspiration of both authors comes from North's view that "financial considerations determine government policies".[22] This is not surprising, because it is almost impossible, after North's emergence, to ignore his viewpoint to explain the driver of the government in institutional change. However, under the same pressure from financial subsidy, why the government chose to legalize forex trading and opted for a different approach for the question of grain coupons—reducing planned government purchase and sale and expanding the free grain market? Putting the two cases together, we cannot get a clear answer to this question. The weakness here, I feel, might be that the authors have not spent sufficient efforts on "pick and throw" when they investigated the restraints. Just imagine, when Ford decided to make some parts and buy others, there must be many factors at play. Coase must have done a lot of work to pick from all these factors, otherwise he would not be able to come down to the central and critical constraints of "factory organization cost" and "the cost to buy from the market".[23] Of all the real constraints, some are more general, more important, and more fundamental than others. In the study, it is not only necessary to pick out these essential constraints but also drop the irrelevant ones. Otherwise, it would be difficult to move on into the next step—"generalization".

In contrast, the study on the constraints of the spontaneous institution innovation in this book is impressively concise and clear. The central question of the Hongmiaozi case is, "under what conditions can the spontaneous stock trading reach a sizeable scale?" In answering this question, Yang Xiaowei probably also has made some guesses, but he "focuses" on investigating one object—the copy of the shareholder's ID card. The central clue of the investigation is "is transfer of names achievable if you hold both the bearer's stock and a copy of the original shareholder's ID card?" If the answer is yes, then the spontaneous stock trading—a kind of trading of rights—is secured; otherwise, the spontaneous trading in pursuit of profit loses its institutional basis. The "tiny-thriving-fall" trilogy of the Hongmiaozi spontaneous stock market, not surprisingly, corresponded to what happened to the copy of shareholder's ID: not accepted—accepted (accepted by enterprises with no objection from local government)—expressly prohibited.[24] We all know that it is a terrifying leap in institutional change to go from the establishment of property rights to making the property rights transferable. New Institutional Economics (NIE) contains complicated information in the discussion on exclusivity and transferability of property rights. We (at least myself) can never imagine, deduce, or design that the most essential institution

[22]Zhang (1996: Chapters 6 and 9).

[23]Coase (1937).

[24]Zhang (1996: Chapter 1).

to support the complicated trading of one kind of rights could be so "simple". The capability to minimize cost of this scattered spontaneous innovation is truly amazing. Chen Yu moved further in the investigation. He discovered that during the spontaneous stock trading stage in Shanghai, some "agents" (who specialize in helping with transfer of names) were even capable of transferring the ownership of the "lowest rated" stocks, i.e. those without the original shareholder's ID card, therefore the large-scale private stock trading was realized through a kind of "division of labor".[25] Economists usually use "spread" to explain trade. They believe trade will take place, being it stocks, coupons, certificates, or the like, if the price difference is big enough. However, to convert the spread into the income of the parties requires the institutional support—the "invisible system". Yang Xiaowei and Chen Yu have very sharp eyes. One saw the "ID card", the other spotted the "agent", helping us a lot to understand the constraints for trading of rights in the real world.

1.5 Generalization

The biggest weakness of the first batch of UIE's research work, in my opinion, lies in the generalization of real cases. I am not saying these case studies lack theoretical depth. On the contrary, many previous collections of reports cannot be compared to them in theoretical intensity, novelty, and coverage; and even quite a few "theoretical monographs" are not their match. For example, "the Unanimous Administrative Consent in the Absence of Constitutional Rules"[26] by Tang Shouning, is, I am afraid, too abstruse even for an economics PhD candidate. In this regard, I believe the research discusses the subject but does not only stay with the subject, thus has fulfilled its aim of achieving "innovation in economics theory".

The problem is, there is sufficient theory in the forepart yet inadequate generalization in the last. Why this comment? At least six of the nine articles resort to the theory of institutional economics to pose the question in their Preface or Introduction. Posing the question, describing the case, making analysis and discussions, testing the assumptions, all the way to conclusion. Reading the conclusions of most of these papers, one may find it discouraging that authors do not spend much energy generalizing their cases.

Looking for evidence? Readers interested in this comment can just follow me and skim through the Conclusion of the nine papers. The two papers by Fan Gang, Liu Shijin and Jiang Xiaojuan[27] conclude with policy discussions; Kong Jingyuan and Zhang Shuguang focus on the direction of institutional evolution (one forward, the other backward).[28] Policies and outlooks are, admittedly, important, but they are not the result of generalization obtained from the abstraction analysis of economic

[25]Zhang (1996: Chapter 2).

[26]Zhang (1996: Chapter 5).

[27]Zhang (1996: Chapter 4 and 7).

[28]Zhang (1996: Chapter 8 and 9).

behaviors or institutional change in their cases. The theoretical elements of Zhang Yuyan's case study are quite strong, but in the Conclusion there is a classical kind of Chinese style ambiguity: "To strengthen or weaken state monopoly, to expand or narrow the concession, the judgement seems to be, at least from a historical perspective, very much dependent on time."[29] The case by Tang Shouning becomes more and more like realistic writing, the library case is put in the Appendix, and the whole paper is about stories and concludes with the summary of such stories, leaving no room for extraction.[30] In Chen Yu's Conclusion, the "Summary of Experience" is also a wrap-up of the story. And the concept in his "Summary of Theory", just as Zhang Jun, his commentator, criticized, "was not reflected and adopted in the previous case analysis."[31] In other words, the generalization is not about the cases in question, but comes from outside.

In my reading, in the Conclusion of all the nine papers, only the two papers by Yang Xiaowei and SHENG Hong make real efforts to abstract the behavior and the process in their cases. As mentioned earlier, YANG tells a best story. His Conclusion also goes up to the general principles for "institutional innovation", but it seems that his Conclusion seems to be restrained too much by existing "framework" of economists. The Hongmiaozi story actually shows that the so-called "spontaneous" stock trading contains not only the pure voluntary efforts of "individuals and groups", but also encompasses the acquiescence of the local government as well as the inaccessibility and the unseeing eyes of the central government for some time. The thriving of Hongmiaozi was the result of a tacit agreement between profit-seeking individuals and groups and the interests of the local government. Later, when this tacit agreement collapsed, the Hongmiaozi market also fell. Therefore from this we might come up with more institutional innovation paradigms that goes beyond the "spontaneous institutional innovation" and the "mandatory institutional innovation"[32]—the innovation might go beyond the level of pure individual spontaneity, but still it's not the result of government mandatory guidance. As long as the efforts by individuals "seduce" a no-objection or acquiescence from the government, institutional innovation can also take place. Yang's Conclusion does not go beyond the discussion on "spontaneous innovation" and "mandatory innovation" paradigms although he throws deep doubt on the mandatory government innovation model. In my own study of rural reforms, I also find that the legalization of Household Responsibility System (HRS) was achieved by neither purely private efforts nor mandatory innovation by the central government, but it was the result of the interaction between the peasants and the government (local government at first).[33] I would like also to bring up this point and hope to get some insight from my colleagues Xiaowei and Yifu, as well as other readers.

---

[29] Zhang (1996: 172).

[30] Zhang (1996: Chapter 5).

[31] Zhang (1996: 53).

[32] Lin (1989).

[33] Zhou (1995).

Sheng Hong's Conclusion offers a good generalization as for under what circumstances the trading of rights in a planned economy can be legalized. From his Conclusion, we can obtain a more generalized understanding which goes beyond the forex quota trading case during the transformation of the planned system. I am not saying that his Conclusion is flawless, but from the perspective of Coase's methodology, I have no criticism on it. By the way, it seems that Sheng Hong doesn't have not much theoretical discussion in the first half of the paper, and saves his energy for extraction to the last part, e.g. generalization of the real cases.[34] Among all the colleagues at UIE, only Sheng Hong has visited the Law School of the University of Chicago and received Coase's instruction face to face. Perhaps Sheng Hong's research style was "infected" by Coase, but it is a slight pity that he is not contagious enough to infect more people.

We do not know all the reasons for the common weakness of generalization in the fruits of the first batch of studies by UIE. Only their own summarization will be more reliable. But I would like to venture to point out the frequently mismatched and improper allocation of resources (i.e. funding and time) for research work. To my observations, almost no project under the research fund will underestimate facts—finding and data collection. However, by the time the data has been collected, you are running out of energy, funding, and time and researchers have to rush to the finish and move on to the next project. The result: before the hard-earned raw materials get well processed, chewed and digested, the products already get launched and exported. When I made my first visit to UCLA in 1991, two professors at the University of Southern California were studying Chinese township enterprises. We talked a few times and collected some data. Soon after that, they wrote a 200-page project proposal, with contents covering background, question description, literature review, hypotheses, modelling, data source description, and preliminary validation results, and everything. This project proposal looks more like "a research fruit" than many research fruits in China. Later on, I figured out that it is quite common in the United States to apply for research funds with "semi-finished products" or "nearly-finished products". I am not qualified to give full-ranged comments on the pros and cons of this "international practice" as regard to scientific research. However, this practice has at least one advantage: once the resources are in place, refining of the "semi-finished products" or "nearly-finished products" become possible. Admittedly, a lot of resources have been put on the re-processing of these fruits from UIE, which can be seen from the executive editor's recommended revisions to the authors and the comments by the commentators; but there is still tremendous "untapped value" in this research. I would encourage the organizer, if interested, to provide more resources to these authors who have worked hard on real-world cases so that they can re-edit, refine, and re-digest the materials. In this way, they will be forced to go back and think harder and more quietly to come up with better-quality generalized understanding of institutional changes in China.

34Zhang (1996: 80–81).

1.6 Beyond "Positive Economics"

After commenting on UIE's institutional change case studies using the key words from Coase's methodology, I would like to conclude this article by addressing a "misunderstanding" of this methodology. The real-world economics advocated by Coase is often called "Positive Economics". In a broader sense, all studies on the real world are called "positive economics". For example, Zhang Shuguang, the executive editor of this book, regards case study as "an important method for empirical analysis".[35]

Influenced by the philosophy of positivism, positive economics has a long history. Classic positive economics emphasizes that the accuracy of the theory can be fundamentally tested by the consistency between assumptions and facts.[36] But since the publication of Friedman's "the Methodology for Positive Economics" in 1953, this methodology for economics research has become distinctive and exerted far-reaching impact.[37] The central argument of Friedman's essay is that the quality of competing theories should be measured by the "predictions" they generate. As for Friedman, the prediction (hypothesis) that can be tested by empirical facts is the core for economic research. If an economist proposes a prediction that is "amazingly consistent with facts", then it doesn't matter whether or not this prediction is realistic or not. In Friedman's view, if succinct and imaginary predictions can be validated, it means theory can be used to explain many things with just a little investment, and this is the very "economic" effects of the theory. Although this Friedman's positive economics was later criticized by many, it is still quite a popular practice for economists to try to "guess" a prediction method that is consistent with data.

However, Coase is not satisfied with this approach. He emphasized that the assumptions must first and foremost be real for positive economics, which centers on testing the consistency between assumptions and facts. Commenting on Friedman-style empirical economics, Coase asserted that "economists cannot, and should not choose their theory based on the accuracy of their assumptions."[38] In this regard, Coase sees eye to eye with Hayek, challenges whether economists are more capable than others to propose a "prediction".[39] He does not believe that the main job of an economist is to make predictions and test them. The sole job for economists to choose theories is to understand and explain the real world. Of a myriad of theories, the only reliable choice, in Coase's view, is the one with assumption that is both "realistic and manageable". In fact, his lifetime job is to look for and identify such assumptions. As we all know, he found one—"that the real world market transaction cost is not zero." Based on this point, my view is that Coase's methodology to study real-world economics is different from positive economics. There are two fundamental differences: First, according to Coase, assumptions must be both realistic and

[35]Zhang (1996: 6).

[36]Robbins (1932).

[37]Friedman (1953).

[38]Coase (1988: 24).

[39]von Hayek (1952).

manageable. Second, Coase believes the main mission (of economics) is to discover the logic behind people's economic behaviors, thereby improving our understanding of the behaviors in the real world, rather than making and testing predictions. Just as what he says when receiving the Nobel Prize, he did not contribute any advanced theory to economics, but his work—finding more realistic assumptions—changed the foundation of economics.

Can the real-world economics be more far-reaching than positive economics among younger scholars? Can it generate more research fruits than positive economics? Can it make up for the defect of "avoiding the reality" of positive economics? We don't know. But we don't need to be bothered too much by these kind of questions, which will be determined by the "market of thoughts". What matters is that we know that there is a methodology different from positive economics, and that a small number of economists have started to practice the real-world economics. As Chinese readers, we are particularly delighted to know that we have such practice in China, too. UIE's work is not flawless, but what's important is that they have embarked on the journey in a systematic way.

References

Cheung, Steven N.S. 1983. The Contractual Nature of the Firm. *Journal of Law and Economics* 26 (1): 1–21.

Coase, R.H. 1937. The Nature of the Firm. *Economica* 4: 386–405.

Coase, R.H. 1988. The Nature of the Firm: 1. Origin, 2. Meaning, 3. Influence. *Journal of Law, Economics, and Organization* 4 (1) (Spring): 3–47.

Friedman, Milton. 1953. The Methodology of Positive Economics. In *Essays in Positive Economics*. Chicago: University of Chicago Press.

Lin, Justin Yifu. 1989. An Economic Theory of Institutional Change: Induced and Imposed Change. *The Cato Journal* 9 (1): 1–33.

Robbins, Lionel. 1932 (1935, 2nd ed.). *An Essay on the Nature and Significance of Economic Science*. London: Macmillan.

von Hayek, Friedrich August. 1952. *The Counter-Revolution of Science: Studies in the Abuse of Reason*. Glencoe, IL: The Free Press. For translated Chinese version, see translation by Feng, Keli, Yilin Press, 2003.

Zhang, Shuguang (ed.). 1996. *Case Studies of Institutional Change in China*, Vol. 1. Shanghai People's Press.

Zhou, Qiren. 1995. Rural Reform: a Retrospective of an Institutional Change. *China Social Science Quarterly (Hong Kong)* (6).

Chapter 2
Property Rights of Human Capital

Human capital theory, as many readers know, extends the economics concept of and theory on "capital" to the analysis of "human resources". Exploring why the output growth outpaces the factor input growth in economic growth, some pioneers in economics discover that health, education, training, and more effective economic accounting capabilities have become an increasingly important source for modern income growth. With the generalization of this understanding, human capital economists look at human health, physical strength, production knowledge and skills as a kind of capital stock, which serves as a source for current and future output and income growth.

Many people believe that the property rights characteristics of "capital" are, just like the same for other "goods", very clear. If fact, when people talk about property rights, they usually refer to products, money, and other goods; and when they talk about capital, they usually refer to machines, equipment, factories, sites, working capital, roads, bridges, and so on. The so-called property rights of capital are, naturally, the bundle of rights of the "property" that can be invested into production and generate returns, that is, the right to income and the right of alienation on the capital products enjoyed by the owner of the capital.

Here, the owner of private capital is often called capitalists. In an economy, if the economic status is defined by the size of the property rights from capital, and the social status also determined by the amount of property rights from capital, which then results in economics activities of the society also led by capitalists, it would be inevitable for this kind of society to be called "capitalism".

Despite the fact that many economic historians and economists since the time of Braudel point out that the concept of "capitalism" is very ambiguous, "capitalism" still prevails.[1] For us Chinese, even without the reform and opening up, the terms would sound very familiar even to farmers in very remote villages. The reform and

[1] Braudel (1997).

This paper was written in September 1996.

Q. Zhou, *Property Rights and Changes in China*,
https://doi.org/10.1007/978-981-15-9885-2_2

opening up has changed the judgement of some people on the value of the "property right of capital" and "capitalism" (the judgement of others was unchanged, hence the debate over whether the reform is socialist or capitalist). There are also changes in the outlook of the general public. For instance, it was always believed in the past that socialism and "property rights of capital" are contradictory. Now things are different, a part of the mainstream ideology is that "preservation and appreciation of state-owned assets is related to the fate of the country". Needless to say, property rights of individuals, associations, enterprises, the state, or whomever, in the sense of seeking value addition from resource utilization every minute of every day, are protected not only by routine property policies but also by the constitution. Therefore, the property rights of assets and its characteristics are very lucid.

2.1 Human Capital Is Indivisible from the Individual

The property rights of human capital is a different story. First, "Does human capital have property rights?" is a question in itself. Interestingly, the difficult part is not about if a good answer can be found, but rather the questions itself cannot be brought up in a crystal clear way. The right is always linked to "exclusivity". The human capital as defined by economists, includes human health, appearance, physical strength, energy, skills, knowledge, capabilities and any other mental strength with economic significance,[2] which naturally belongs to natural persons. Not a single element of human capital can be independent from the natural person, which makes it different from the assets in the form of "physical properties". Machines can be moved around; factories can be dismantled and re-built; and the legless monetary capital can travel to every corner of the world. Roads are paved on the ground; and bridges are built over the river. But roads are not naturally affiliated to the ground, just as bridges are not naturally affiliated to rivers. Therefore, when we try to ask the question of "the property rights of human capital", are we really asking "to whom the property rights of human capital belong?", or "to whom the person belongs"? As human capital inseparably belongs to the natural person, why still ask this question? As to the question of affiliation of humans, it does not make much sense except for the slavery society, and I guess no one would ask such a question. No question means no answer. That is why most literature on human capital either focuses on the economic significance of human capital or measures its impact on economic growth, but generally does not touch upon the "property rights of human capital". The number of scholars is very limited who are well versed in human capital theory on the one hand and interested in property rights on the other.

The first economists running into the question of property rights of human capital are those studying slavery. In 1977, Yoram Barzel published a paper in *the Journal of Law and Economics*, raising an interesting question on the slavery economy. Under the slavery system, slaves belong to the slave owner in the sense of right, and they are

---

[2]Rosen (1987).

part of their master's property. So the slave owners have the full power to arrange the labor for slaves and take away all their output. Then how come in American history some slaves accumulated their own wealth, and eventually bought themselves and became free people? Barzel found that as a full-fledged property, slaves not only escape, but also actually control the supply of their labor. Slave owners do have the "right" to force them to work, but because of the nature of slaves as full-fledged property, it seldom works for the slave owners to enforce the scheduling of the slaves' degree of labor or physical efforts even if they pay high "supervision and policing" costs.[3] In order to save the costs for maintaining the operations of the slavery system, some slave owners had to not only treat their slaves well (as found by Fogel[4]), but also adopt a quota system, which allowed slaves to keep the beyond-quota output to themselves. Hence some capable slaves started to have their own private property, accumulated sufficient wealth, and eventually had enough money to buy back their freedom.

Barzel was a colleague of Prof. Steven N. S. Cheung at the University of Washington. According to Cheung's recall in 1984, when Barzel proposed the concept of "full-fledged property", Cheung told him that previously he was unable to explain the economic reason for slaves' liberation because he couldn't think of the "full-fledged" feature. Now with the establishment of this concept, Cheung made terrific improvisations: "Both labor and knowledge are assets. Everyone has brains, and makes his own choices and decisions." The important feature I'd like to highlight is that "the person who makes the choices and the assets are physiologically integrated into one and controlled by the same nerve center, and they are indivisible. Integrated with the asset, the person can work hard, rely on himself, and develop himself, or he can disobey instructions, go against the order even if it means death."[5] The feature of human capital being indivisible from the person, as mentioned above, originates from here.

2.2 Human Capital Is Private Property

However, Cheung does not explore from the perspective of property rights of human capital. He does not go further and ask: "Since human capital is integrated with the person, what are the features of the forms of its property rights?" No question means no answer. So his viewpoint is not adequately convincing when used to explain some phenomena. This can be seen in his argument with Theodore W. Shultz, a Nobel Prize winner in economics, and founder of human capital theory. In 1982, Cheung wrote a booklet about China's future, arguing that manpower and knowledge at that time were not private property in China, and that this non-private nature would affect their utilization in economy. Schultz read the book and wrote to criticize him:

[3]Barzel (1989).

[4]Fogel and Engerman (1995).

[5]Cheung (1988: 181).

"How could manpower in China not be private property?" Cheung responded: How could Schultz's conclude that human capital, which includes knowledge, is private property in China? "He (Schultz) has lectured in China, how could he not know that the Chinese people do not have the freedom to choose and to assign their jobs? By definition, private property rights entail the freedom to transfer and to enter into contracts. In terms of manpower and knowledge, these rights are absent in China. Therefore, these assets cannot be regarded as private property in China."[6]

Cheung's rebuttal is indeed very reasonable. Yet perhaps he didn't realize that his logic contradicts with the aforecited feature as "Human capital naturally combines itself with the person". If the statement is true, then human capital, legally, can only be owned by the person unless the law protects the slavery system. Sherwin Rosen uses a constraint, "free society" when he explains that the property rights of human capital can only belong to the person. What he means is that this statement can be true only when slavery is prohibited.[7] But after reading Barzel's research on slavery economics, we can argue that due to the uniqueness of human capital, even if the constraint of "a free society" is removed and the slavery system becomes legal, human capital in fact still can only belong to the person. After all, as a natural private property, human capital, actually cannot be disregarded even under the legal framework of the slavery system. In other words, due to its characteristics as a resource, human capital has to be private property, or at least, has to be de facto private property!

Back to the disagreement between Shultz and Cheung. Schultz is not as familiar with China as Cheung, but his "surmise" is probably based on logic. Imagine: all elements of human capital naturally belong to the person and the institutional cost of its "forced use" is unbelievably high—this kind of asset has to be naturally private. This is universally true as it is determined by its nature and has nothing to do with the specific condition of any country. As the founder of human capital theory, Schultz has indeed studied more about various forms of human capital. He doesn't analyze property rights that much, but when it comes to the property rights of human capital, he makes the "surmise" and his "surmise" hits right to the point: human capital actually can only be private property also in China.

2.3 Without Freedom to Choose, Human Capital Is Still "Private Property"

However, we simply cannot neglect Cheung's observations of the facts. Under the planned system, it is true that Chinese people did not have the freedom to choose or transfer their jobs. At that time, jobs of urban people were assigned; rural people were not allowed to move into cities freely; more physical labor didn't mean more reward; skills, technical expertise, and production knowledge were not valuable; inventions, not patented; and innovations legally unprotected; let alone entrepreneur

[6]Cheung (1988: 173).

[7]Rosen (1987).

capabilities, whoever "discovered a market" was despised as a capitalist. None of the elements and forms of human assets were freely tradable, and there was no market price whatsoever. Admittedly the factors of human capital were "attached" to the person, the person was still not allowed to trade with the factors of his/her own human capital, or to have the freedom to enter into contracts for these factors. So how can it be called a private property? Property rights, is "a right realized through social enforcement to make choices among the multiple purposes of economic goods".[8] Now, Prof. Cheung would be puzzled by his reasoning why Schultz still regards the institutional constrained human capital and knowledge as "private property" if the person does not have adequate freedom to use his/her own human capital?

Schultz is reasonable, so is Cheung. What to do for us younger scholars? Generally, if free trading in the market is restricted, human capital, like its non-human counterpart, will inevitably have truncations in its property rights as described by Harold Demsetz. In other words, some of the rights out of the complete bundled rights of the human capital for use, for choosing contracts, for income and transfer, etc., get restricted or deleted. When the truncation gets severe and reaches a certain extent, the private property only exists in its name, becomes legally empty and thus has no economic use at all. This explanation sounds nice, but we have to ask a further question: in the case of truncation of property rights, is the response from human capital the same as from the non-human capital (if it can respond)?

Of course not. Human capital is a "full-fledged property" naturally embodied in individuals and can only be controlled, initiated, tapped, and utilized by its natural owner. Therefore, when the bundle of property rights of human capital is partially (or fully) restricted or removed, the owner can "shut off" the corresponding part of human capital as if it does not exist. When people are unhappy, even the most gorgeous could look ordinary, and an ordinary could give you an unsightly face that would become negative asset. The resources of physical labor also become difficult to manage. For the simplest work of farming, the super immortal can do nothing with him if the illiterate peasant is unwilling to work: he can just show up and not make any efforts, and fool the supervisor. The intangible factors as skills, expertise, and production knowledge are even more difficult to manage. As the supervisor even though you have absolute authority and want to show power, but you don't know where to start. In all parts of the world, the most powerful boss would be running out of his wits when asked "show me how you do it" by his angry employees with unique expertise. Intellectuals are a big problem for many leaders, although they do not provide physical labor, they mix up different grain crops, they are physically weak, and they just read books and have some knowledge. It is hard to categorize intellectuals into bourgeois or petty bourgeoisie, and even more difficult to categorize them into proletariats. Most of them may be timid when knocked down, but it then would be extremely difficult for them to create, invent, or provide innovative products. The common logic for all these phenomena is that the "full-fledged" property feature of human capital enables it to have a special weapon to counter the "truncation of property rights".

---

[8] Alchian (1987).

2.4 Automatic Devaluation Due to "Truncation of Property Rights"

What's more special about the restricted or deleted property rights of human capital is that they cannot get centralized into the hands of other owners to achieve the same purpose. A piece of confiscated land can be immediately transferred to a new owner with the same area and fertility, a workshop or machines, after confiscation, can still be used by another production process without losing the value or efficiency. A pile of "non-stinky" money is worth the same value whoever uses it. Yet a "confiscated" person, even in the hands of a slave owner, can still be disobedient, "lazy and stupid", or "would rather die than obey the order" as described by Cheung. In other words, human capital is a special asset that might automatically devalue immediately with the truncation of its property rights, and it is the "full-fledged" characteristics that makes the economic value of such assets plummet or even down to zero.

Because of this special mechanism, the private nature of human capital stands in any society. Even in the envisaged socialist society where all means of production (that is, all non-human capital) are public owned, human capital is still owned by the person, meaning a private property. It is Karl Marx rather than the so-called "bourgeois economists" who clearly explains this point. In his *Critique of the Gotha Program*, the little book believed to be "a mature works on Marxism", Marx tacitly agrees that in his ideal socialist society, that "it is a natural privilege for workmen to have unequal individual endowment, and thus unequal productive capacity", and that the "bourgeois legal jurisdiction" stipulating that "distribution of consumption goods should be based upon the actual work provided by the workmen" must still be maintained.[9] As of today we see it is impossible to realize such an idea (because when all production materials are public owned, and the production of commodities is eliminated, it is inoperable to measure the contribution of each individual's work of based on working hours except in a very tiny and simple "society"). This means, even if non-human capital is pushed into a currently impractical high degree of public ownership, human capital remains private, solid and unchanged. The pre-reform planned economy in China cannot get rid of commodity currency in any way, how could it be possible to have human capital owned by the public?

2.5 "Discovering the Market" and Realizing the Market Value

There is another characteristic of human capital: it always tries everything possible to find opportunities to realize its own value. Couldn't we see those "lazybones" sleeping on the collective land yet laboring and sweating on their private plots? The stone-faced salesclerks of state-owned shops become energetic and enthusiastic

[9]Marx (1875).

when "going through the back door", and in terms of "service quality" they never would lose to their western counterparts with "professional smiles". Ordinary people could teach themselves and find various ways to gain benefits through so called "taking the path of capitalism". The tricks of "Intellectuals" are even more innumerable. What do these stories tell? Human capital or asset, as natural private property, has never been "cleanly and thoroughly" eliminated. It either "disappears" when the right is completely not allowed, or tenaciously manifests itself and tries to discover its markets regardless of the market color: white, grey or even black. "As long as the person survives, this desire remains", that is, human capital always tries to realize its own market value.

From the above discussion, we can see the three features of property rights of human capital: First, human capital naturally belongs to the person. Second, in the case of truncation of its property rights, human capital may immediately devalue or even vanish. Third, human capital always spontaneously looks for market to realize itself. Without knowing anything about the characteristics of the property rights of human capital, it would be extremely difficult to understand the popular "incentive" theory in today's economics. Why the incentive mechanism is not needed for land and other natural resources, workshops, equipment, and bank loans, but it is needed for human capital and is a must? The reason lies in the nature of property rights of human capital.

References

Alchian, A. 1987. Property Rights. In *The New Palgrave: A Dictionary of Economics*, Vol. 2. London: Macmillan.

Barzel, Yoram. (1989). *Economic Analysis of Property Rights*. New York: The Press of University of Cambridge.

Braudel, Fernand. 1997. *Ecrits Sur Le Capitalisme*. Central Compilation and Translation Press.

Cheung, Steven N.S. 1988. New Labor Economics. In *The Orange Seller's Words*. Sichuan People's Press.

Fogel, Robert William, and Stanley L. Engerman. 1995. *Time on the Cross: The Economics of American Negro Slavery*. New York: W. W. Norton. Reissue edition; first published in 1974.

Marx. 1995. Critique of the Gotha Program (1875). In *Selected Works of Marx and Engels*, Vol. 3. Central Compilation and Translation Bureau.

Rosen, Sherwin. 1987. Human Capital. In *The New Palgrave: A Dictionary of Economics*, Vol. 2. London: Macmillan.

Chapter 3
Rural Reform: A Review of Changes in Economic Institutions

China's economic reform is extensively changing the form and efficiency of property rights for resource utilization. The background of this significant reform is the failure and slackening of the previous socialist economic model. This article discusses the experience of rural reform, the beginning of this great change.

The rural reform in China in the 1980s witnessed, on the one hand, the weakening of the centralized government control over rural economic activities, and on the other, the growth and development of villages and private property of farmers. Based on a review of the rural reform, this article tries to explain the government behaviors from the perspective of the establishment, enforcement, and changes of farmers' property rights. The central argument is that the government's protection of efficient property rights policy is the key to long-term economic growth. However, the government usually does not automatically provide such protection unless farmers, proxies of emerging property rights and rural elites extensively participate in the formation of the new property rights systems, communicate and bargain step by step, and enters into covenants with the government. China's experience shows that effective private property rights can be gradually established in the original public ownership system.

This article is composed of five parts: the first part discusses the theory regarding the relationship between government and property rights; the second outlines the characteristics and the origin of the pre-reform rural property rights systems; the third studies the transformative factors in the people's commune system; the fourth analyzes the experience of rural property rights reform in the 1980s; and the last is summary and comments.

Q. Zhou, *Property Rights and Changes in China*,
https://doi.org/10.1007/978-981-15-9885-2_3

3.1 Literature Review: Property Rights and the Government

3.1.1 Property Rights Paradox

When people discuss property rights, the often-used concepts usually include contracts, incentives, supervision costs, exclusive income rights, risks, opportunism, organization costs, and asset specificity, etc. Basically, all these concepts are about the considerations of individual social members and their relationships.[1] This shows that since the pioneering work by Coase and other economists, economic theory has by far deepened the understanding of the real world with a positive transaction cost and asymmetrical and incomplete information.[2] In today's world, property rights arrangements are no longer insignificant for economic development. But the further question is: if we do not bring in the behaviors of the government and its agents, will we be able to truly understand the policy arrangements on property rights and their changes?[3]

If property rights is purely the contract between individuals which can be fulfilled by the creditworthiness of individuals, then the government does not become a constituent element of property rights arrangements.[4] Unfortunately, no such world exists in reality where there is any big scale of transactions.[5] Therefore, when economists on property rights elaborate on the "exclusive income right" of property, they usually emphasize that the property rights are usually enforced; so the

---

[1]This mainly refers to the work of Coase (1937, 1960), Alchian and Demsetz (1972), Cheung (1969a, b), North and Thomas (1973, 1981, 1990) etc. Most of this literature has been translated into Chinese by Sheng and Chen (1990), Liu and Hu (1990) and North (1991). The article by Yang et al. (1993) introduces the recent developments in property rights economics and its mathematical models as well as his own work in this area. For criticism by the school of "imperfect information" on the inadequacy of above-mentioned school of "transaction cost" the other school in the new institution economics, see the article of Bardhan (1989).

[2]The concept of "transaction cost" proposed by Coase (1937, 1960) challenges some of the seemingly self-evident assumptions of neoclassical economics, the central point of which is that the cost of maintaining a fully competitive market is zero. As a result, just as Schultz (1953) sharply criticizes, "economists often leaves people with an impression that as long the market, enterprises, and families are there, the economic system will operate and work.

[3]Furubotn and Pejovich (1972) point out that although the property right is exclusive, but we cannot count on this point and hope it to be an unrestricted right. Because most of the restrictions are imposed by the government, the theory on property rights cannot be completed without covering the government.

[4]The Coase Theorem seems to emphasize the importance of private mediation of disputes over rights, but this is only based on the assumption of zero transaction cost. When the cost is positive, although the property rights arrangement is essential, the institutional and ideological arrangements related to its enforcement are even more so. Sheng and Chen (1990) divide the Coase Theorem into two parts, the first theorem and the second theorem, which helps us understand this point.

[5]The discussion of the origin of property rights always involves the topic of government. Cooter and Ulen (1988) built a model to illustrate this point.

intensity of property rights has to involve the effectiveness of protection provided by the government.[6]

The government would certainly not protect property rights for free. The resources it spends on the protection at the end of day derive from the "tributes and taxes" of property rights. In other words, property rights are, from the outset, not so entirely independent, and are bound to be "entangled" by the government. Of course, the property rights can buy government protection by paying taxes, in which case the government is the sole and only organization that can lawfully use coercive power and also enjoys the "economy of scale". The relationship between the property rights and the government seems to be no different from any other equal contractual relationships.[7]

The question is, why can't the government ask for a higher price since it enjoys the sole monopoly over the legitimate use of coercion? If the government and its agents are self-interested, given their unique status, what stops them from asking for a higher rent for its services or even completely depriving private property to collect wealth for themselves? As we can see in economic history, government breach of property rights can lead to long-term recession, yet the lesson is not bad enough to keep the government and its proxies off from the temptation of higher short-term rents. After all, the life, tenure, and rationality of any proxy of the government have a limit. Perhaps that is why when Demsetz proposes the important concept of "the truncation of ownership", he has to mention the government in particular. He points out that the truncation of property rights means that part of the complete bundle of property rights has been deleted, and this happens because "the position that controls the abolition of the bundle of property rights has been assigned to or has been taken by the government".[8] It is clear that this truncation of property rights is the result of government infringement and it is completely different from the government services bought by private property owners for their equivalent value. Demsetz does not discuss this further because he believes that the economic theory on the government has not evolved enough to enable us to fully understand the behaviors of the government and its members.[9] Now we can see what I call the "property rights paradox" logic. On the one hand, property rights cannot be effectively enforced without the government; on the other, the introduction of the government is very likely to lead to truncation of property rights, such that even if in theory we can assume that there is a rational government, the consequence of invalid property rights still cannot be fully avoided.

---

[6] Alchian (1965: 243).

[7] Cooter and Ulen (1988). This is also the argument of Buchanan and Tullok (1962). But there are other ways to analyze government behavior, see Justin Yifu Lin's quote (Lin 1989: 23–24).

[8] Demsetz (1988: 18–19).

[9] Demsetz (1988: 19).

3.1.2 North Puzzle

North and his collaborators once made a concise conclusion on the economic growth of the modern western world, namely effective economic organization (property rights) is the key to economic growth.[10] However, he later discovered that an effective property rights arrangement is just one of many possible outcomes of the interaction between the government and the private actors, rather than the inevitable and only outcome under the conditions of relative factor price changes.[11] When North later tried to answer a more important question of why a large number of inefficient economic organizations exist long term in the economic history, he proposed an analytical framework about the government. According to this framework, the government is believed to have the motive to maximize the rents for the ruler but is also willing, within this premise, to reduce transaction costs so as to increase tax revenue. However, North noted that the above two objectives of the government are not always consistent, because "there is a long lasting conflict between the property right structure that enables the maximization of the rents to the ruler (and his group) and an efficient system that reduces transaction costs and facilitates economic growth".[12] It is this basic tension that explains why many economies are unable to achieve long-term growth. This way, it seems that the success in the early days of Netherlands and UK, i.e. the consistence between the maximization of government rents and the effective reduction of transaction costs, was on the contrary, a mere coincidence. Why are these two countries so lucky and so different?[13]

Habermas's research into the structural transformation of the early modern Western society may help us understand this question. The central concept that he abstracted from the history of the seventeenth century UK and the eighteenth century France is the "bourgeois public sphere", namely a public sphere composed of the assemble of the class of the private bourgeoisie, which functions include not only to coordinate various private authorities, but also to act on behalf of the civil society to supervise, restrict, suppress and confront possible government aggression into the society.[14] According to Habermas's research, the key to the success of the transformation of the early Western European society into modernization lies in the fact that the "bourgeois public sphere" maintains a check and balance mechanism between the civil society and the government. However, Habermas's theory is too philosophical and seems to be difficult to be applied to the empirical studies of

[10]North and Thomas (1973).

[11]North and Thomas (1981, 1990).

[12]North and Thomas (1981: 25).

[13]"The existence of government is the key to economic growth, but the government is also the source of the man-made economic recession" (North and Thomas 1981: 20). This amazing wrap-up of North means every nation has a fair share of opportunities for either growth or recession.

[14]Habermas (1989: 14–26).

non-Western European societies.[15] One problem is that many civil societies have emerged in early modern history, but not every such society has the capability or opportunity to reach the balance with the government power.[16] In addition, it seems that Habermas's logic cannot explain the differences between the British and French economies. In Britain, both the civil society and the government had matured to the point where they can reach a compromise, while in France, the situation was more like continuous conflicts. Therefore, we may be able to generalize the above discussion into the following: only when the collective action of the owners of emerging property or their proxies is strong, and strong enough to force the government and its proxies to effectively protect the property rights as the only way to meet their own interests, can the win-win result be reached. Under this principle, the government power pursues rent maximization, and property right becomes the norm to regulate profit-seeking behaviors.

This does not mean that the relationship of rights between the government and the civil society can be clearly defined once for all. On the contrary, it means we have entered a new era of continuous institutionalized bargaining between the government and the civil society. Michael Mann defines "infrastructural power" as the power of government to penetrate into the civil society, but it must and will increasingly rely on institutional negotiations with the civil society for the implementation of political decisions.[17] He points out that the primary trend of political modernization is the strengthening of the infrastructural power, because only the infrastructural power can mobilize public resources more effectively.[18] This is a good reflection of the characteristics of this new era.

3.1.3 A New Hypothesis

Now let's go back to the North Paradox. Why some governments opt for effective property rights protection that leads to long-term economic growth, while others end up getting only the short-term maximized rents from their power but being trapped by a long-term plight of an invalid system? This paper proposes a new hypothesis: only when the civil society and the government achieve a balance of power in dialogue,

---

[15]Huang (1993) comments that as a historian, Habermas reproduces the history of early Western Europe; but as a moral-political philosopher, he tries to generalize his concepts to comment on the reality and regulate the world accordingly.

[16]For example, Rowe (1984), Rankin (1986), and Strand (1987) found the public sphere composed of the urban bourgeoisie, local gentry, and citizens in Hankou before 1889, in Zhejiang in the second half of the nineteenth century, and Beijing in the 1920s. However, Wakeman (1993) found evidence from their own writings to show that these "public spheres" are different from those in early Western Europe.

[17]Mann (1984: 185–213).

[18]For example, not a single government does not wish to collect more tax. However, not even the most autocratic power in history managed to levy a tax as high as the 50% of today's North Europe.

consultation, and transaction, can it be possible to achieve an alignment between the maximization of government rents and the protection of effective property right innovations. In this process, sporadic emerging property rights may be spontaneously formed in response to the induction from relative price changes of resources, but they themselves alone cannot get the protection by the government. In addition, the government usually does not automatically provide protection because the rent maximization is often inconsistent with the protection of new property rights. The only possibility to break this deadlock is collective (rather than the individual) action by the owners of emerging property rights which raises the costs of the government to safeguard old property rights and at the same time protects the benefit from property right innovations, until a new constraint structure for the government to obtain rent is re-established, and the consistence is reached between maximizing the rents and protecting new property rights. In other words, the key to long-term economic growth is neither the isolated government power (no matter how smart the government is) nor the isolated emerging property rights (no matter how effective they are) alone, but the tacit agreement between the property rights and the government, which is randomized at first and then legalized by the institution.

Lots of details have been skipped in the above discussions. But this crude new hypothesis prevents us from cutting the most indivisible question into pieces. This is crucial for the study of large-scale institutional changes. Next we will validate and revise this hypothesis by reviewing the institutional changes in China's rural reform. Let us start with the characteristics and mechanisms of the pre-reform economic institutions.

3.2 Collective Economy Under the Control of Government

3.2.1 What Is Collective Economy?

Collectivizational economy is not a co-operation of farmers based on private property rights in rural communities, but in essence, a form of government control of rural economic rights. Following the literal meaning and interpreting the collective ownership as a kind of co-operative agriculture is not only misleading for the understanding of collective economy, but also leads to the wrong perception of the reform.

To cover how the government controls the operations of the rural collective economy may take up more text. Here, the author just would like to point out, that in fact the government has long made itself the first decision-maker, dominator and beneficiary of the economic factors (land, labor, and capital) controlled by the collective ownership system through various measures, such as mandatory production plans, unified purchase and marketing system (UPMS), prohibiting long-distance transporting and sales and restricting free trade (even if for a collective business), closing the rural factors market, and isolating the migration of people between urban and rural areas.[19] The collective is but the enforcer and implementer of the will of the government within the legitimate scope. At best, it only possesses economic resources, and more often is unable to prevent the government from infringing upon collective property rights. In fact, as early as in 1958, the "Resolution on the Establishment of the People's Commune in Rural Areas" by the Central Committee of the Communist Party of China (CPCCC) states: the people's commune has some ingredient of ownership by the entire people (state ownership), and this ingredient "will continue to develop and grow and gradually replace collective ownership".[20] Therefore, unlike the farmers' economic co-operative organizations, collective ownership economy is under the control of government power from its very beginning.

It should be noted that the government here no longer simply acts the role of external protector and arbitrator for property rights and their transactions. It has entered and controlled the rural property rights. Interestingly, when the government acts in the name of the whole people, it has eliminated not only the private ownership of traditional rural households but also the property rights in the general sense. As property rights economists have pointed out, the most important institutional arrangement for property rights is the exclusive income right and the right of transfer of economic resources.[21] The "whole people's economy" controlled by the socialist government makes all exclusivity institutional arrangements unnecessary (in China). With the rights exclusivity gone, market transactions of resources are also eliminated. This point, in my opinion, is the key to understand the counter-market tendency of the traditional socialist economic institutions.

In terms of institutional characteristics, the rural collective ownership in China is the same as government ownership. Also, collective ownership does not necessarily mean that it is a loose form of government control. The real difference between collective ownership and the whole people's ownership is that the government exerts control over the former but does not directly bear the financial responsibility for the consequences of such control. However, in the latter case, the government guarantees the employment, wages, and other fringe benefits with its fiscal income. Therefore, the government's control of and intervention in the collective ownership is more likely to be overwhelmed by romanticism, or "blind commands" and even become arbitrary.[22] The collective economy does not have the full decision on its own as to what, how much and even how to produce, let alone the right to sign contracts in the market for the purchase of production factors and the sale of products. All these decisions are made by the government, and implemented top-down. Of course, the collective needs to bear the economic consequences of all these top-down orders, which is to determine the amounts of final distribution, comprised of collective retention and the amount corresponding to the work points of commune members. At this time and only at this time collective economy is worthy of the name.

[19]Task Force of Development Research Institute (1988).

[20]Quoted from Bo (1993, Vol. 2: 746).

[21]Demsetz (1988).

[22]Almost the entire history of the people's commune supports this argument. Most of the most ridiculous actions took place between 1958 and 1959. See Bo (1993, Vol. 2: Chapters 26 and 27).

In a nutshell, the collective ownership is neither a "jointly-owned co-operative private property" nor a purely public property of the entire people. It is a rural socialist institutional arrangement controlled by the government with the collective to bear the outcome of such control. In general, it is not suitable to analyze collective economy with the Western "co-operative economy" theory, because the foundation of such institutional arrangements is not at all a spontaneous contract between private individuals who own property rights.

3.2.2 *Government's Industrialization Faces Equal Distribution of Land Rent*

To understand China's rural collective economy, the first question is to find out the driving mechanism that brought the government control down to the village level after the 1950s (which was never achieved at any time in China before). And then we need to figure out why the vast number of peasants (farmers) have accepted such a non-contractual institutional arrangement.

The unprecedented penetration of government control into rural society is closely related to the target of industrialization by the government. The main reasons summarized by the 1949 Revolution for China's poverty and weakness since the nineteenth century: first, there was no strong government machine; second, there were no developed industries. Therefore, strengthening the government's centralized mobilization and utilization of economic resources, and accelerating industrialization, especially the development of heavy industries, have become the economic priorities of the new regime. Government's industrialization, a term that frequently appeared in Chinese official documents in the 1950s, not only means industrialization was a pressing goal of the national economy but also means that the government should play a decisive leading role in the process.

The capital accumulation of the government's industrialization was mainly from the agricultural surplus of the country.[23] Some scholars estimate that the surplus provided by China's farmers through land taxes and rents before the revolution accounted for about 30% of the total agricultural output,[24] indicating that China had not been an economy with inadequate surplus since quite early in the old days.[25] The problem is that only a small part of the agricultural surplus was used for modern industrial capital accumulation. After the revolution with the re-establishment of a unified national government and the social order, the new regime now had the possibility to transfer the agricultural surplus into industrial capital accumulation.

[23]Song (1982) is the first scholar to provide an analytical framework to understand this issue, which was published by the China Rural Development Research Group (CRDRG) (1985, Vol. 1).

[24]Lippit (1974).

[25]Mark Elvin believes that traditional China was trapped in a "high-level equilibrium trap". When illustrating the concept by graphing, he points out that the pressure from the increasing population consumed the surplus beyond the essential subsistence needs of the people (1973: 313).

However, to this end, the government must first centralize the agricultural surplus into its own hands to the greatest extent possible. This means that the post-revolutionary regime would not only replace the old government to control the land taxes, but also replace the landlords to centralize the control and the use of the land rents.

As for taxes, the agricultural tax rate in the early 1950s has reached 11% of the total production,[26] higher than the Ming and Qing Dynasties and the *Kuomintang* (the Nationalist Party) administration before the War Against Japanese Aggression, but lower than that for China's regions under the Japanese rule and the rate after the same war.[27] From this perspective, the new regime is already the most effective tax collector during peacetime throughout history, but it does not seem to be content with it.

However, the main part of the Chinese agricultural surplus, namely the rent (plus interest), was equally distributed to the entire rural population in the Land Reform. Based on the 30% of the agricultural surplus estimate, after the land reform, at least about 20% of total agricultural products, after taking away the agricultural tax, fell into the hands of farmers. This equal distribution of land rent to the farmers has enhanced their political support to the new regime. However, the established national strategy to accelerate industrialization could not tolerate to have 20% of the agro-produce transformed from surplus (which would otherwise be possible industrialization accumulation) to private consumption and investment. The tension between the government and the farmers[28] starting from 1953 was, in phenomenon, the reluctance of the farmers to sell grains and other agricultural products leading to difficulties for government purchase, but, in essence, the misalignment between the small peasant economy after the equal rent distribution and the government's ambitious industrialization goal.

The government tried to get back some of the lost rent by increasing taxation, however several increases in the 1950s caused collective protests by farmers. This shows that 15% of tax plus surcharges[29] is the threshold for agricultural products. Beyond this limit, the cost of taxation will rise so much that it will outweigh the gains. After all, it is much more difficult to collect some rent into the state treasury from all rural households than to do the same from just landlords and owner-peasants. The conclusion is clear. If the government continues to act as a traditional tax collector,

---

[26]See Wang and Zhang (1993), Gao and Xiang (1992), and Cui (1988). However, there is a record showing a 30% tax rate after the Land Reform in South China (Yang 1959: 56–57, 155–156), and see Huang (1993: 170–171).

[27]The tax rate in the Ming and Qing Dynasties accounted for 2–4% of land output (Wang 1973). The same by the *Kuomintang* government in North China before the War Against Japanese Aggression was 2–5% of the income of farmers (Huang 1985: 290–292). During the Japanese puppet period, the rural tax rate climbed up rapidly, it rose sharply from the 1941 rate of 6–8% for North China; the figure for some sub-Yangtze regions was recorded to be up to 50% (Huang 1993: 172). For the same period, the actual tax rate for the regions under the *Kuomintang's* rule was about 20% and that in the Shaanxi-Gansu-Ningxia Border Area was about 13% (Selden 1971: 181–183).

[28]Bo (1993, Vol. 1: Chapter 12).

[29]Cui (1988).

it is impossible to concentrate the already-equally-distributed land rent and use it for industrialization.

3.2.3 Reforming Private Property System of Small Peasants

Therefore, the new government had to go beyond the norms of traditional government behavior. It not only went deep down into the village level, but also interfered in the decision-making of rural households and clans. It not only re-organized the rural political and spiritual life, but also controlled the production, trading, and distribution of agricultural products. In particular, it must control urban-rural relations. In short, the government, after the 1950s, was no longer unable to reach the grass-roots. It is true that the ubiquitous government control and influence on society stemmed from the ambition of the new regime to transform the entire old society, but from the economic perspective, re-centralizing the land rent which was already equally distributed to the small peasants became a more practical and urgent goal for that time. Since the equal distribution of land rent was the result of equal distribution of land to the farmers, to achieve the goal of re-centralizing the land rent, the system of small peasant private ownership had to be changed fundamentally.

Government power gradually infringed upon the farmers' property rights. In the first phase, government policies only restricted the farmers' private property right, but not legally erased it. For example, the government set the grain and cotton production quota for each household; brought the output under the uniform purchase and sale system; banned people hiring, land tenancy and loan offering; and closed the village fairs to cut off the link between farmers and private merchants. All these measures although did not change the farmers' nominal property rights, but imposed certain restrictions, control, and interventions on its use, income and transfer. In the words of property rights economists, the government caused the "truncation" of farmers' property rights. What is important is that the "truncated" farmers' property rights were now in fact concentrated in the hands of the government and constituted the source of the non-tax agricultural surplus.[30] The government obtained taxes by establishing and protecting the private property rights of farmers, and moved further to receive partial land rent by infringing their land property rights. In the hands of a centralized authority, the tax and the rent were integrated into one.

Collectivization further erased the already-truncated private rights of the farmers. The Mutual Aid Group Movement put together the production activities of farmers. The Elementary Co-operative combined farmers' main assets. The Advanced Co-operative eliminated the dividends from land and livestock. And the people's

[30]We used to call the mandatory unified low-price purchase by the government as a "hidden tax" (Comprehensive Task Force of Development Research Institute 1988). Now "hidden rent" seems to be a more appropriate name.

commune promoted public ownership on an even larger scale.[31] So far, the government has removed the fence surrounding the property rights of the rural society, and the administrative power has made its way to every aspect of the village life. A system with a very high level of centralization of agriculture surplus has finally been established. This collectivized public ownership integrating the government and the co-operative shapes up a distinctive foundation for rural area institution and organization which is very different from China's tradition.

3.2.4 Property Rights Created by Government

Now let's discuss from the farmer's perspective why they would allow the government to change and deprive them of their property rights. With the theory of seeing the government as an institutional arrangement under potential coercive force, we can, of course, assume that socialist agricultural collectivization is just a result of government coercion. But in reality, China's agricultural collectivization is at least less coercive than the former Soviet Union. On the other hand, private land property rights were seen as the main economic driver to guide the farmers towards supporting the revolution. Therefore, the farmers would, sure enough, see the private land property rights as their lifeline. The real difficult question to answer is what measures the government adopted to deprive the small peasants of their land, and yet they were widely accepted by peasants.

The crux of the issue lies in the nature of the private property rights of the farmers, rather than the radical actions during the so called "surpassing period" of collectivization. We will see that it is the former that provides the basis for the large-scale occurrence of the latter.

The property right system established by the Land Reform is undoubtedly private ownership of the land by farmers. However, this kind of private ownership was not a product of long-term spontaneous transactions in the property market, nor was it the result of restrictions on property rights transactions imposed by the government, but rather it was the result of direct re-distribution of land as the outcome of a large-scale class struggle organized by the Party and the government. As the organization and leadership of the government and the Party played a decisive role in the hitchhiking of landless or almost landless farmers (the majority) during the movement of equal land distribution, and also the result of equal land allocation became quickly legalized because it was ratified by the government, the government that led the land privatization movement cast its own will into the private property rights of farmers. Therefore, when the will of government changes, the farmers' private ownership must also change accordingly.

[31] Du (1985: 10–18).

3.2.5 Three Types of Private Land Ownership

The argument above is very important for this paper, so it is necessary to elaborate on it. Let's compare the three possible ways for a landless or almost landless farmer to acquire the private property right on land. In the traditional land market, the farmer can purchase the land. He may not be able to afford it all at once, so he may rent it first and buy it later, or he may get a mortgage. The buying power of the farmer may come from his family's savings, his own incomes, or maybe an unexpected bumper harvest or some windfalls. To acquire the property rights on the land, he may need formal legal services from the government, or he may simply rely on the local custom and a middleman in the village. In any case, he acquires the property rights through a free exchange contract.

The second way is through a government-interfered land market. The government may only regulate the land price. For example, the CPC government for the revolutionary base during the War Against Japanese Aggression and the Taiwan *Kuomintang* authority in 1950 respectively restricted the land rent rate not to exceed 37.5% of the total output. This time it perhaps is easier for the farmer to accumulate the principle for the deal, but he must also accept the same intervention from the government when he rents out the land later. The government can also further intervene in property rights transactions, such as the land reforms in Japan, South Korea, and Taiwan after WWII. The land beyond the specified acreage was purchased by the government or authorities at a specified price, and then sold to landless farmers or farmers with minimal land. In this case, the farmer in question still obtains the pro forma property rights of the land, but he knows it would be impossible for him to become the owner of the land under the same purchasing conditions without government intervention.

The last way, this farmer obtains the land without going through a transaction at all. He participates in the political movement which deprives the landlords of their land, and gets his share of the lands based on the number of people in his family. Such deprival is organized and legally endorsed by the government. The farmer's land ownership is not bought, even in form, but distributed to them. He benefits from the government-led political movement, as it is impossible for him to only rely on his own individual efforts and get an equal share out of the landlords' property.

The above-mentioned three types of private land ownership lead to a completely different relationship between the property rights and the government. In the first case, the farmer has an independent negotiating power. He can evaluate the quality of government services and then decide to pay (tax). Or when he determines that the deal is not worthwhile, he completely gives up the ownership, which means he no longer needs to buy the government services. This independent negotiating power is compromised in the second case and almost totally lost in the third case. Therefore, it is completely possible to have different types of private land ownership, which have different intensity, different stability, and totally different logic for further change.[32]

[32]Therefore, as Alchian says, different hardness of property rights perhaps can reflect a totally different relationship between property rights and the government.

The farmers' private ownership established by China's Land Reform is the outcome of direct land re-distribution by a social political movement. Therefore, the farmers' private ownership system formed in the Land Reform already contains all the possible forms of private ownership for the future collectivization, because the government creating the property right by a political movement can also change it by political movements. One of the facts supporting this judgment is that in the first half of the 1950s when the government's policy-makers at the upper level debated whether or not to continue with the new democratic economic policy, and whether or not to retain the farmers' private ownership,[33] the farmers themselves did not have the right to voice their opinion before the decision was made, or the right of to choosing after the decision was made. This provides a good case for the idea of "dependent path" (meaning the preceding choice often affects subsequent developmental trajectories) in the institutional change theory (North and Thomas 1990). At the same time, it also supports a long-held viewpoint of the author: the ultimate issue of the socialist property rights reform is not the confirmation of certain form of ownership (even it is the purest private ownership) by the government, but first the definition of the limit of the government power in the property right reform.[34] In an environment where the government has the power to arbitrarily specify property rights and change property rights contracts without consulting the society, even if it fully duplicates the most effective property rights system, it is still unable to achieve long-term economic growth.

3.2.6 *Why Is Collective Economy Inefficient?*

We have seen why and how the government created collective ownership. However, the government cannot guarantee that its "institutional products" will work. The inefficiency of collectivized agriculture is an indisputable fact. According to calculations by Wen (1989), except for the 1952–1957 period, which witnessed a slight increase in the total-factor agricultural productivity, the pre-1983 productivity of agricultural collectivization was obviously lower than the level of private owned agriculture in 1952. This is a diametrically opposite result against the expectations of the initiators of the collectivization movement.

One explanation has been widely accepted: in rural production, there is inadequate supervision and measurement of the labor of its members by the collective

[33]In 1951, the CPC Shanxi Provincial Committee submitted a report proposing to weaken and even abrogate the farmers' private ownership system, meanwhile to expand the socialist elements in the agricultural mutual aid groups, and to convert them into collectivized agricultural organizations. LIU Shaoqi criticized the report and said that it represented a dangerous imaginative agricultural socialism. However, Mao Zedong endorsed the proposal, criticized Liu's view, and launched the Agricultural Cooperative Movement. According to Bo Yibo, there were altogether three debates on the question of rural areas at the top decision-making level between 1950 and 1955 (1993, Vol. 1: 184–203).

[34]Zhou (1988), see Li (1990: 711).

organization, which led to insufficient incentive to the efforts of the members.[35] This explanation takes note of the loss of efficiency caused by the low enthusiasm of workers in co-operative production but may neglect another type of efficiency loss, that is, the inefficiency caused by insufficient incentive to the managers.

Any production team faces measurement, supervision, and management. Effective supervision is, therefore, a necessary condition for members of collective economy to pull adequate efforts. But how to motivate managers of collective production to provide adequate and effective supervision? Alchian and Demsetz (1972) demonstrate the economic significance of property rights in this regard. They point out that the property right of economic organizations is actually a kind of residual claim, which incentivizes the owner to supervise. The property owner of an economic organization can assume the full responsibility of supervision himself and take the residual claims all to himself. Or he can pay the residual claim on supervision to specialized managers and have them assume the responsibility of supervision. In any case, the effectiveness of supervision in collective production is guaranteed by the residual claims enjoyed by the supervisors. When the property rights are eroded, the incentive mechanism for residual claims is bound to be weakened. If collective production does have economies of scale (i.e. the total output of co-operative production is greater than the sum of individual producers' output combined), then property rights, i.e. residual claims, will constitute an institutional assurance for such economies of scale. Therefore, the difficulty of supervision in collective production stems on the one hand from technical factors, namely the difficulties in collecting and processing information, and on the other from the institutional factor, namely insufficient incentive to supervisors as a result of truncation of property rights.

3.2.7 Administrative Hierarchy Replacing Residual Claims as Incentive

Collective economy eliminates the mechanism of residual claims in its institutional arrangements, but it cannot eliminate the need for economic incentives to supervisors of collective production. The fact that the government-controlled public economy has to resort to the bureaucratic hierarchy shows that the socialist system still needs to motivate its economic management cadres. For example, the prospect of promotion is the main positive incentive while demotion and dismissal constitute the main

[35] Lu and Wang (1981), Du (1985), CRDRG (1985) all identified from field investigations and underscored the uncertainties of agricultural production and the difficulty of labor measurement, and explained why accordingly organizations in the form of families (households) enjoyed very low supervision costs, and did not affect efficiency even with inadequate measurement and supervision, while the collective production organizations failed. Lin (1988) proposed a model for the Agriculture Production Team, analyzing that under the production team system, the managers chose a lower level of supervision because of the supervision difficulties, while the workers chose to be lazy because of inadequate measurement and unreasonable compensation. Therefore, the failure of the production team system can be explained by insufficient incentive for the workers' efforts.

negative incentive. In this sense, the official-as-the-core idea in the administrative hierarchy of the economic institution can be seen as an alternative to the property rights systems.

However, the use of administrative promotion mechanism to replace the residual claim system in China's rural collective economy faces a special problem. Due to its vast territory and large population, the formal administrative system for rural areas under the central authority can only practically reach the township (commune) level. Below the township, cadres of villages (production brigades) and production teams are informal bureaucrats, and there is an insurmountable status gap between them and formal government cadres. In reality, throughout the entire collectivization period, most of the village and production team cadres were not included as the candidates for the government bureaucracy system.[36] In other words, the administrative promotion mechanism did not work for the grass-roots cadres of the people's communes. At the same time, because there is no hope for promotion, the negative incentives of the system also lose the punishment function on them. Yet these grass-roots cadres are the direct supervisors of collective production activities. The failed incentives on them makes it impossible to achieve the effects of collectivized scale economies of scale. This explains why the rural collective economy is even more inefficient than the state ownership (or whole people) economy, and why the reform, namely the introduction of residual claims, starts with the countryside.

In summary, the government-controlled collectivized economy was inefficient due to the lack of incentives to supervise the collective production activities, which makes the already-existing measurement and supervision problems in agricultural production even worse. The original agricultural system now suffers from dual loss of enthusiasm for both supervisors and farmers. The key is a severe truncation of property rights caused by government behaviors. However, viewed from another perspective, the low-efficiency institution encompasses great potential effects from its correction, and makes property rights reform into something that brings substantial institutional benefits. But will the government be willing to change its own institutional product just because of the inefficiency of collective economy?

3.3 Famine, Retreat and Make-Shift

3.3.1 The Primary Driver for the Institutional Change

The efficiency of economic systems can only be estimated afterwards. When we estimate it in various ways, we assume that there is a direct interaction between institutional efficiency and institutional change. However, this assumption is theoretically

[36]With very few exceptions, for instance, the cadres of the Dazhai Brigade, Xiyang County, Shanxi Province, became government leaders during the Cultural Revolution.

troubled,[37] because different stakeholders have different welfare evaluations on the efficiency of the same system, yet we cannot add up the welfare function of every individual and treat the aggregate as the sole social welfare function.[38] If different social welfare function (or more accurately, group welfare functions) means different attitudes of stakeholder groups towards institutional change and causes different behaviors, the question of the primary driver for institutional change will be complicated into the relative strength of different groups.

However, the nature of collectivized ownership simplifies this question. The government control by the people's commune and the dominant position of government determine that the government can "dictatorially" use its own evaluation of the welfare for the people's commune as the sole social welfare function. Thus correspondingly, we must first look at the changes in the cost-benefit structure of the government-controlled collective economy to look for the root of institutional change.

3.3.2 Cost and Benefit of Government-Controlled Rural Economy

What directly pushed the initial changes in the people's commune system was the gradual change in its cost-benefit structure. The government, according to North, as an entity monopolizing the coercion power, can, indeed, create any form of property rights. In a certain period of time, it can even do whatever it wants. But after all the government lives in a world where organizational costs are positive. The government itself and the economic organizations it creates are, still at the end of day, subject to transaction costs and the rules revealed by property rights economics.

Figure 3.1 shows the cost and benefit trend of the government-controlled rural economic system between 1952 and 1982.[39] First, we can see that for most of the years, namely 23 out of the 30-year period between 1952 and 1982, the cost index for government control of the rural areas grew faster than the benefit index. Admittedly, this does not mean that the rural institution was always a "loss" in absolute terms to

---

37. This is to say, the efficiency of the institution can be measured and used to evaluate the outcome of policy and institutional changes, but it cannot fully explain the driving mechanism and process of such changes.

38 This is the idea expressed by the Impossibility Theorem (Arrow 1963).

39 The benefit index of government-controlled rural economy is the weighted average of agricultural tax, agricultural and sideline products purchase (including the spread in rents and taxes in unified government procurement), foreign exchanges earned by agro-products, savings of farmers in government banks, and farmers' recognition of the institution and political support (indirectly measured by the growth rate of agriculture total output value and the per capita net income of farmers from the collective business operation). The cost index is the weighted average of the government fiscal fund for supporting agriculture, subsidies for sales of agricultural production materials, government administrative expenses, overhead of collective economy, government banks' loans to rural areas, and ideological investment to win farmers' support (measured by the net income of farmers from family sideline business). See Tables 3.2 and 3.3 and their notes for data and interpretation.

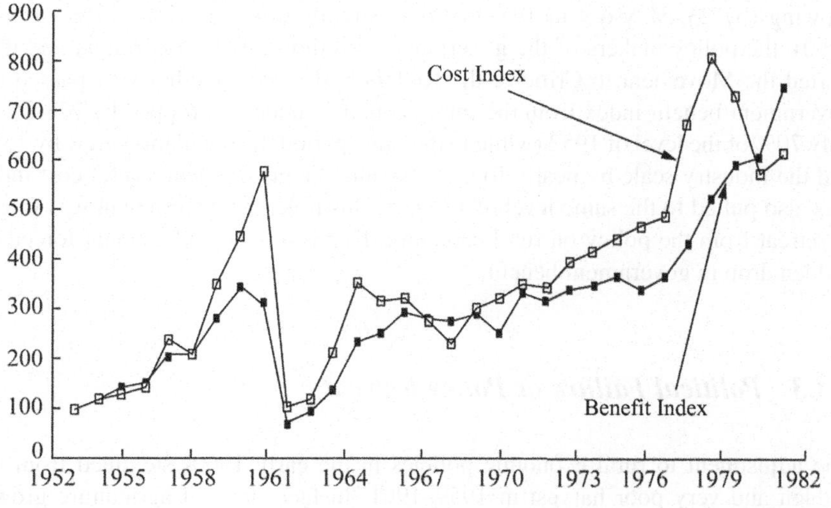

Fig. 3.1 Cost and benefit index of government-controlled rural economy, 1952–1982 (*Note* For data and description, see the Appendix Tables 3.2 and 3.3)

the government, but it does show that the government was under pressure in most years from rapidly increasing institutional costs.

For this period, there are two obvious peaks for the cost index growth to outpace the benefit index growth. The first one is between 1957 and 1961, with the tip being 1960; and the second, between 1972 and 1981, with the tip being 1979. It is precisely around these two tips that some major adjustments were made by the government to its rural economic policy. Based on the analytical framework of this paper, this is certainly no coincidence. These two tips illustrate when (under which circumstances) the government will consider changing its economic policies, and disregard the existing power structure, the ideological coherence, and the negative impact of new government policies on the authority of the original policy-makers and even the legitimacy of the government.

The remaining subsections of this part will discuss how the first peak for the cost-outweighing-benefit structure in the chart caused the adjustment to rural policies in the early 1960s and created conditions for the subsequent reform. The examination of the second peak will be discussed in the next section.

As shown in Fig. 3.1, the decisive factor between 1957 and 1961 was that the sudden dive of the government benefit index had threatened the minimum need of government survival. The government's efforts in increasing public ownership for agriculture since 1957 caused continuous steep institutional cost growth, which also outpaced the government benefit index growth year after year. In 1958, the composite government cost index increased by 66.82% year on year, 33.8% percentage points higher than the benefit index growth of 33.02% (see Appendix Table 3.2, and the same for subsequent descriptions); two years later the cost index went up to the peak of 582 points (the index for 1952 = 100), but because the benefit index was still growing (by 23.4% y-o-y in 1959) or only slightly dropping (by 9.77% y-o-y in 1960), the policy makers of the government still didn't make any retreat and they started the Movement to Criticize the Rightists. However another year passed the government benefit index from the rural economy suddenly dropped by 77.42% to only 70% of the level of 1952 (while in the same period the population grew by 15%, and the industry scale by nearly four folds), and the government's rural cost index was also pulled to the same level of 1952. At this time, the government was forced to retreat from the policy on rural economy. This is a policy adjustment forced by sudden drop in government benefit.

3.3.3 Political Failure or Policy Retreat

The adjustment to rural economic policies in the early 1960s stemmed from the sudden and very poor harvest in 1959–1961. In fact, the real agriculture growth index in 1958 already dropped about 5 percentage points from 1957. The index fell by another 15.9 percentage points in 1959 from the previous year, by 22 percentage points in 1960, and then by 51 percentage points in 1961.[40] Grain production in 1959 dropped by 15% from the previous year, and for the next two consecutive years, the grain production was only 70% of the level in 1958.[41] Due to the lag of government decision-making, the agricultural tax, agricultural exports, and the hidden tax incurred in the purchase of agricultural and sideline products continued to rise in 1959, so the government benefit index in 1959 still increased by 66% over the previous year.[42] This delay in policy adjustment left the grain ration for some rural population below the subsistence needs, and about 30 million people died from the famine.[43] Since the agricultural crisis of 1959–1961 was an absolute food shortage, it could not be alleviated by issuing additional currency. And as China was a closed economy, it could not be resolved by importing from international market. Because the agricultural surplus at that time still accounted for a considerable part of government revenue, the sharp decline in rural income was bound to affect the overall situation. Last, the proliferation of the severe famine has escalated the economic crisis into a political crisis that challenged the power of the decision-makers and the legitimacy of the government.[44]

---

[40]See Column 4 in Appendix Table 3.3 and divided by the market price index in column 13 to eliminate the price effect.

[41]Quoted from Lin (1990: 17).

[42]The data is shown in Columns 6, 9, and 2 of Appendix Table 3.3.

[43]Ashton et al. (1984), Lin (1990). The number of deaths in this famine was more than that of other natural disasters in China in the twentieth century. The abnormal deaths even exceeded that in the 1920s famine of the former Soviet Union after the collectivization movement (MacFaquhar and Fairbank 1987: Chapter 8).

[44]A Chinese saying goes, "Food is of paramount importance." Here the food does not mean the food per se or agriculture. It means that after the government controls the people's livelihood, the last boundary of the legitimacy of the government is the subsistence of the people.

All of the above-mentioned factors worked together in 1961 to force the government to choose between a political failure and policy retreat. The precarious economic situation left the government with no choice but to adopt all possible policy measures to mobilize farmers to increase production and save themselves. This teaches us a valuable lesson that even 100% government controlled social and economic system is very dangerous, even to the government itself.

3.3.4 The Long-Term Impact of the Short-Term Adjustment

The 1960 adjustment included two distinct elements. The first, is to maintain the institutional framework of the people's commune, but with substantial policy repairs, such as shrinking the scale of people's commune and establishing a production team-based ownership system, restricting the bureaucrats from arbitrarily allocating the properties of their inferior units and of the farmers (i.e. criticizing over-egalitarianism), dissolving public canteens, improving the work-point system and the internal management of the production teams. The second, is to recognize the status of household operations in collective economy (private plot, private livestock and family sideline business were allowed), open up free markets in the urban and rural areas, and allow to contract production to households or even allow to contract land to households. These two policy combinations with completely different directions indicate that the government has to make a full-scale retreat from its rural economic policy. However, the retreat, made by the government under the pressure of sharp drop of the benefit curve, was short-lived. By the time the total agricultural output returned to its original level (1964–1965), many effective policies were called off as make-do compromises. The short-term total income decline did not fundamentally shake the structure of protection for the original institutional arrangements. The people's commune, as an organization, via which the government exerted control over the rural economy, was retained and continued.[45] The government benefit index from controlling the rural economy began to recover and rise since 1962. Although the cost index also went up, the two indices basically maintained the same trend until the early 1970s. When the crisis was resolved, the policy retreat was over, although after the adjustment, the total factor productivity of agriculture, at its best, only reached 87.8% of the 1952 level.[46]

---

[45]Between 1961 and 1962, 80% of communes and production brigades in Anhui adopted the household responsibility system, the figure was 74% for Linxia Prefecture in Gansu, 70% for Xinchang County in Zhejiang and Jiangbei County in Sichuan, 42.3% for Longsheng County in Guangxi, 42% for Liancheng County in Fujian and 40% for the entire Guizhou, the national coverage of the household responsibility contracting system was about 20%. In the meantime, the CPC's Central Committee debated over whether or not to legalize the household responsibility system, and in the end, Mao Zedong's opinion to criticize the play solo (namely household responsibility) practice won the debate. See Bo (1993, Vol. 2: 1078–1090) and see Du (1985: 14–15).

[46]See the calculation by Wen (1989).

But the short-term policy adjustments in the 1960s also left some long-term effects. From an institutional point of view, recognizing the legal status of the family sideline business and establishing a production team-based system are the two most important points. The former serves as a safety valve to prevent the recurrence of the famine, and the latter was a compromise between the farmers' objection to the communist style of sharing everything and the government's purpose to maintain the people's commune institutional framework.[47] Unexpectedly, these two pivots strengthened the farmers' bargain power against the collective, and the same of the collective against the government, thus creating conditions for the reform.

3.3.5 *Make Voice, Exit and Slack-off*

Farmers had no say in the creation of the people's commune economy, so they had no institutionalized bargaining power for changes in the collective economic system. With the denial of their property rights, the "Hukou" (permanent household residence registration) and the grain coupon systems used to isolate cities and the countryside, along with the ration and work point system within the commune, became well established.[48] Farmers could not take back their land and livestock and withdraw from the commune, nor could they even take back themselves to exit the commune system. In Hirschman's (1970) terms, farmers under the commune system had neither "exit right" nor the freedom to "make voice". They stayed in the system not out of loyalty, but simply because they had no choice.

However, farmers could still express their dissatisfaction with the commune system. A common lawful way was to reduce the quantity, or more commonly the quality, of labor contribution to collective production; or they could do other things that increased the supervision costs. As we all know, in collective labor, the opportunistic attitude of one member is contagious to others. As a result, after the spreading for "laziness to drive out diligence", the labor productivity of collective economy declined, and the per capita income stagnated for a long time.[49] Finally, when the "right to subsistence", as put by Scott (1976), of some commune members were

[47]The principle of "production team-based three-level ownership" attempted to protect the property rights of production teams on the premise of administrative obedience. However, from the perspective of the exclusivity of property rights, it is full of contradictions. Yet, in the policy environment of rural China at that time, the contradictions in the policy often provided a legal basis for different forces to compete for the right to subsistence. In this example, the commune and production brigade could underscore the "three-level ownership" while the production team could underscore "production team-based."

[48]Qiu (1988).

[49]Huang (1993) found that even the Yangtze River Delta—the richest rural areas in China, after decades of collectivization, were still trapped in "growth without development", which means despite increasing agriculture output and yields, per capita income did not increased. He refers to this phenomenon as "collectivist involution" (16–17).

threatened, the government was compelled to choose between disregarding sacrificed legitimacy, increasing financial relief, and changing systems. In short, since the farmers who have lost their property rights could neither exit nor vote to change the collective system, the only thing they could do was the passive method of dragging down the productivity to ask the government to make concessions.

3.3.6 Partial Exit Right

The above mechanism has played a fundamental role in the reform of the entire socialist agricultural system. However, we need to further understand the conditions under which this mechanism works.

If the degree of public ownership is so high that all the income of the farmers' families comes from collective production, we have reasons to believe, the possibility for slackness is minimal. Logically speaking, a few commune members can get more leisure by reducing their labor contribution, but this kind of leisure is worthless to farmers struggling for survival. In addition, no rational members would reduce their labor contribution just to punish their lazy teammates, as it would lead to declining living standards for themselves and their families. Therefore, the more reasonable assumption seems to be that the higher the degree of public ownership for the collective economy, the lower the tendency toward slackness might be for its members. At least once the opportunistic behavior reaches a certain threshold (that will threaten the survival of farmers), it will tend to converge, because at this point, the spontaneous mutual monitoring mechanism of the laborers will kick in.

The real problem of a high-degree public economy is about the management of economies of scale, because even if labor measurement and supervision are not needed, the collective economy faces a series of complex questions such as "corporate strategies". When a large-scale production rejects the residual claims incentive and only follows the stimulus of the administrative hierarchy, the manager may guide the originally-not-so-low spirit of labor towards the irrational direction, causing economic failure. For example, between 1958 and 1959, when the people's commune reached its highest degree of public ownership, the enthusiasm and momentum of commune members for farming, irrigation and water conservancy and other infrastructure construction and industrial production were misused by the commune leaders who wholeheartedly followed the utopian fantasy of their leaders, and even of the central government and the chairman of the central committee (For example, tens of millions of labors were mobilized to make steel rather than harvest their crops).[50] Therefore, in addition to the dented enthusiasm of laborers, we may need to look for factors at the micro-level for the fall of agricultural production in 1959 and the

[50]In 1958, the number of rural laborers working in small-scale industries (mainly coal mining and steel-making) reached a peak of over 60 million (Bo 1993, Vol. 2: 708), which seriously compromised the autumn harvest of the year (ibid.: 714).

famine for the next couple of years.[51] In short, the author maintains that in a highly collectivized economy, there is very little possibility for the farmers to exercise the veto power to the institution even through slackness.

However, when the degree of collectivization decreased, especially with the introduction of self-retaining economy for farmers families, their above-mentioned veto power became much stronger. First, the farmers now had some sources for livelihood under their own control, they no longer had to fully rely on the collective economy for a living. Second, their reduced labor input caused by dissatisfaction with the collective system could now be invested into their own family operation and become economically meaningful. Third, they now could implement the strategy of "punishing slackness with slackness". Although they may still not be allowed to exit completely from the people's commune, they could partially exit from collective labor. It is precisely this partial exiting right that enabled the farmers to express their dissatisfaction by slacking off under the circumstances of inadequate supervision and measurement and poor management of the collective economy, and to compete with their small family operations against the large yet inefficient public ownership economy in the overall public ownership system. Chinese farmers are still worthy of their reputation of being hardworking.[52] But now how to make them work hard on the collective land, became the number one question in the government's economic strategy.

This was exactly what happened after the policy was adjusted in the early 1960s and the farmers family sideline business got recovered and developed. By 1978, the sideline business already contributed to 26.8% of the total net income of farmers, close to the level of 1957.[53] Of course, since the proportion of family operations out of the total rural economy between 1960 and 1978 was less than a quarter, the positive impact on total productivity from this effective labor was not enough to offset the negative impact from the ineffective labor in collective production, the total factor agriculture productivity for this period was never brought back to the pre-1957 level.[54] However, during this period, when family operations were allowed (1961–1967 and 1972–1973), the total agricultural productivity increased; otherwise

---

[51] This is not to say that there was no problem with the enthusiasm of the members under the people's commune system, but rather to emphasize the correlation between the initiative of the workers and the institutional arrangement, especially the supervisor incentives and the exiting right.

[52] Anyone having visited the farmers' private plots will agree with this. The yield of the private plots is estimated to be 5–7 times that of the collective field. See Comprehensive Task Force of Development Research Institute (1988: 5).

[53] In 1957, the net income of farmers from family sideline production accounted for 29.4% (NJZ 1983: 523). Since there are no data from 1958 to 1961, the figure for this column in Appendix Table 3.2 is calculated using the annual average growth rate of this period, and it presents an upward trend. A more reliable estimate is that the income of the farmer's family sideline business declined from 1958 to 1959, but came back quickly after 1960.

[54] The family operations within the collective economy may have a complex impact on overall productivity. On the one hand, the higher efficiency of family operations may push up the total efficiency; on the other, with partial exiting right, farmers could be even lazier in collective labor and thus drag down the total efficiency.

it would decrease.[55] In short, by introducing the concept of "partial exit right" we can explain all the changes in total factor agriculture productivity after 1960.[56] More importantly, the results of family operations indicated a possible direction for collective economic reform, namely to treat households as the basic unit of agricultural production and save all the supervision costs. This model trades reduced economy of scale for increased in incentives. If the loss of benefits from reduced economies of scale can be offset by the gain from the incentives to labor, then the overall productivity can be improved by reforming the collective economy into a household operation model. Finally, the partial exit right helps us understand how farmers gradually established their bargaining power in the fully government-controlled collective economy. This point is decisive for future property rights reform.

3.3.7 Reverse Substitution

In previous text we propose that the government-controlled collective economy is a model of replacing the residual claims with the administrative promotion mechanism. However, for cadres of production brigades and teams who were below the formal bureaucratic system, such inadequate alternative incentives led to poor supervision and low enthusiasm of work in collective economy which is based on compulsory co-operation. Before 1962 with the obscure prospect for the people's commune to be upgraded to whole people's ownership, grass-root cadres still had, more or less, some expectation for being promoted,[57] but after the collective ownership of the commune was emphasized and the production teams were announced to be its base, such expectation lost its institutional foundation. Now the question becomes whether or not these de facto supervisors of the collective economy will reconcile to the embarrassing status without both promotion opportunities and residual claims.

Observations show that the supervisors of collective economy were not willing to assume the huge responsibility of supervising surplus production simply because of a meager "subsidy for lost work time". Although unable to change the hierarchical

[55]For data, see estimates from Wen (1989) and the graphs developed by Lin (1990: 37) using the data from Wen (1989).

[56]This concept explains why after the 1960s when farmers still had no right to exit, the Great Famine of 1959–1961 did not happen again. Lin (1990) uses the abolishment of the farmer's exiting right to explain the Great Famine of 1959–1961. He proposes that co-operative agriculture can also be successful, but the success can only be obtained under the precondition that the members of the co-operatives reach a tacit agreement to discipline themselves. This kind of self-enforcing contract can only sustain if the members have the right to exit when other members violate the contract. Lin uses this viewpoint to explain why the productivity of co-operatives increased from 1952 to 1957 when farmers had the right to withdraw, but the efficiency collapsed and became stagnant after the right was abolished. Also, see the collection of articles by James Kung, W. Bentley MacLeod, and Dong and Dow, published in *the Journal of Comparative Economics 17* (1993) on discussion of this paper.

[57]The author believes that this is the root cause for many abnormal ridiculous phenomena in 1958–1959.

system under the central authority so as to increase their incentives,[58] they actually controlled the production and primary distribution of the surplus of rural economy, so they leveraged their residual control to get a share of the residual claims for themselves,[59] and balanced their supervision efforts according to the amount of real gains. This is to say, the supervisors of collective economy would spontaneously and unstoppably chase the residual claims and lead to a "reverse substitution" mechanism, meaning to replace promotion incentives with de facto right to share the surplus.

3.3.8 *Supervisor's Privilege*

One form of residual claim is the supervisor's privilege, namely the grass-root brigade and team cadres leverage the managerial positions to acquire personal benefit. As the people's commune is a system integrating government administration with commune management, the supervisors of collective economy undertook not only the management functions of the production team, such as dispatching labor, labor measurement, distributing work-points, money, grains, firewood and so on, but also many government public administrative functions, such as household Hukou registration, conscription, marriage approval, family planning, dispute mediation, public security and local politics. It was difficult for the government to effectively monitor the actual exercise of this highly concentrated power at the rural grass-roots level because the cost of information was simply too high; it was also difficult for the farmers to effectively counterbalance this power because of lack of foundation for independent economic and political rights. Therefore, the supervision power at the rural grass-roots level easily mutated into a regulatory privilege, which gave supervisors the additional intangible, physical, and monetary benefits. This part of residual claims took the form of corruption, and originated from infringement of the welfare of the farmers and the collective, and the vested interest of the government. It is quite difficult for us to measure the total amount of encroachment by this privilege, but we can tell that the infringement was very common because the call for each and every rural political movement between 1960 and 1978 was to clean up the economic mistakes of grass-roots cadres.[60] The privilege of the supervisors is unproductive,

---

[58]Production brigade cadres have some chance of being promoted to a clerk at the commune or county level, and a limited few of them may even get an urban Hukou or become government cadres. Competition for transferring from agricultural to non-agricultural status is extremely fierce nationwide, which constitutes a focus of the political fight at the brigade.

[59]In one Cui Zhiyuan's his papers, he emphasizes the differences between "residual claim" and "residual control" (Cui 1993). He points out that due to insufficient information and incomplete contracts, the "residual claim" cannot be clearly defined in advance. Therefore, what is important is to control the production process of the surplus (residual), which is usually the result of multi-party co-operation. He uses "joint ownership" to interpret the organizational characteristics of Chinese township enterprises.

[60]For instance, in 1962, Liu Shaoqi estimated that rural grass-roots cadres were severely corrupted. He even proposed to dispatch tens of thousands of government cadres to each county to take over the rural grass-roots administration (Bo 1993, Vol. 2: 1118–1136).

so it will not increase the total amount of wealth. However, it is precisely this kind of privilege, the non-institutionalized residual claim that compensated the insufficient incentives of the people's commune system, thus maintaining the operation of the system. No matter how the government and the society morally condemn it, this privilege was actually an indispensable part of the people's commune system. It shows that it doesn't work to replace the residual claim with other institutional arrangements unless the government has an uncapped budget and full supervision capabilities.

Now we come to understand why the government resorted more often to political movements and officialdom cleanups in the mid-1960s to mobilize the rural economy. This is because when the positive incentives were weakened, the government had to rely more on the punishment mechanism to maintain the economic efficiency of the people's commune. However, no mechanism as efficient as the residual claim was invented. The political movements, one after another, not only consumed economic resources, but also impaired the legitimacy of the government machine, the convincing power of the ideology, and the reasonable expectations of the officials. The central government at the very top finally found that neither positive nor negative incentives could help to obtain the full loyalty and efficiency from grass-root rural supervisors unless their privilege was recognized in a tacit manner.[61] Here, the problem with institutions, organizations, and mechanisms now became a tangle of ethical problems of individual cadres and led to endless political fight.

3.3.9 "Collective Capitalism"

There is a more positive form of residual claim: the collective industry and sideline businesses actively developed by the collective economy supervisors and controlled by themselves rather than by the government, with the purpose of creating more disposable residuals. The early forms of such collective industry and sideline businesses were enterprises under the commune, or production brigades, which can be dated back to the late 1950s, but it was not until the 1970s that they became very common.[62] This was the fastest-growing sector in the rural collective economy.

[61] In the "Four Clean-ups" Movement, a serious disagreement between Mao Zedong and Liu Shaoqi was how to deal with the corrupt rural cadres. Liu advocated clean-up by severe punishment, but Mao asked to set free those with embezzlement of only several hundred RMB, and guides the lancehead towards the "the capitalist leadership" at the upper level. Later, in his talk with American journalist Edgar Snow, Mao says that Liu's mistake in "being a leftist in form but rightist in nature" was one of the reasons to make him determined to get rid of Liu (Bo 1993, Vol. 2).

[62] Extensive literature can be cited on the development history of production brigade/team-based enterprises. Systematic studies can be found in the work by the China Rural Development Research Group, CRDRG (1985) members such as Sun and Bai (1983), Li (1990: 422–451), and Byrd and Gelb (1988), Huang (1993: especially Chapter 12). In addition, the former Development Research Institute of the Rural Development Research Center of the State Council and the Rural Sample Survey Group have been conducting a continuous sample survey of large township enterprises in ten provinces since 1986, which

Based on the constant price of 1970, the total output value of commune and production brigade/team-based enterprises (PBEs) in 1978 (38.2 billion yuan) increased by 3.9 times as compared to 1971 level (7.79 billion yuan), with an average annual growth rate of 25.5%, much higher than the 4.25% average annual growth rate of agricultural output.[63] This part of the economy beyond the planned system responded to the stimulus of the very high profits of the processing industry under the original system and broke the monopoly of the state-owned sector. Therefore, from an orthodox view from the planned economy, the businesses of the PBEs were always seen as aliens that differs from the government control over the rural economy.[64] In the era of the people's commune, the repeatedly-criticized "collective capitalism" exactly refers to this kind of economic activities which were organized by the collective, breaking through the government-plan control and obtaining the surplus. In this sense, if we see farmers' family operations as an individual breakthrough in the government-controlled rural system, then the PBEs is a collective breakthrough.[65]

The capital for the collective industry and sideline businesses was mainly from their own savings and bank credit, so it was still a collective public asset.[66] However, if we compare such collective asset with the land property of the people's commune, we find that the two are distinctly different. Production of the former is market-oriented, thus the surplus can be acquired by the community while the surplus of the latter is all taken by the government. The asset of the former is liquid and can be re-organized while the land in the latter case is not tradable or rentable. The former is controlled by cadres of production brigades/teams and the entrusted community elites, while the latter is almost completely controlled by the government. These differences reveal a primary driving force for the rapid growth of the PBEs. That is, the rural communities tried their best to control their own resources so as to share the economic surplus from the rural economy, which was originally fully claimed by the government.

---

provides most systematic data for this field. For the introduction and analysis of this survey, see Li (1990: 265–288), Li (1990: 625–646), Qiu (1987, 1988) and Li (1990: 816–840), all published in the compilation by Li (1990: 265–288, 293–322, 482–511, 625–646, 744–768, 816–840).

[63]For the output value of enterprises under the people's commune system, see ZTN (1983: 215); for the output value of industrial enterprises under brigades, see National Statistics Bureau (1991); for the statistics of total agricultural output value, see National Statistics Bureau (1991).

[64]Today's urban citizens commend township enterprise for rising from elsewhere, for leader of the rural communities, the rise was from their home base.

[65]To say that the production brigade/team-based enterprises are the results of government policy is only a compliment after these enterprises become successful. Nearly all the founders of these early enterprises were condemned for "damaging government plans". In terms of resource utilization, these enterprises have long been discriminated by the system and policies.

[66]Less than 10% of the funding for the establishment of these businesses was from government fiscal appropriations and low-interest government loans. The main part was from collective savings (accumulation) (23.6%), and credits (61.13%) guaranteed by the collective. See Li (1990: 265–288), published by Li (1990: 265–288, same below).

The cadres of communes and production brigades/teams played a decisive role in establishing the early enterprises. Under the people's commune system, the supervisors of collective economy played dual roles: both proxies of the state power in the countryside and representatives of collective economy. After a long-term rural socialist reform, only this class has the legitimacy of organizing economic organizations beyond the household size in rural areas. Therefore, the earliest rural entrepreneurs mainly grew out of rural grass-roots cadres.[67] Despite the ambiguity in final ownership of the collective enterprises, the control always stayed in the hands of the cadres. In the early days, the surplus of the enterprise was mainly used to support agricultural expenses (purchasing agricultural machinery, constructing irrigation and water conservancy facilities, and aiding poor teams), community welfare, and enterprise accumulation. The cadres could only get a little bit of monetary income for themselves. However, the power to control these assets, especially to control non-agricultural employment opportunities, meant lots of power and high social status in an agricultural community. In other words, although the early entrepreneurs could not fully enjoy the surplus of the firm for themselves, they control its use. More importantly, all these monetary and non-monetary benefits did not come from direct giveaway by the government, but from the efforts and talents of the cadres to establish the business. This constitutes an effective incentive mechanism to transform rural community elites to entrepreneurs in the early days.

The second possibility for rural enterprises to improve efficiency is to retain economies of scale while introducing the residual claim-based incentive mechanism to improve supervision efficiency. The existing literature has not given enough attention, although the change in this direction has actually played a significant role in the future reform of collective economy.

Interestingly, once the communities have their own businesses, they need no more to bow down to the government as they used to; just as when the rural households have their own family businesses, their bargaining power is significantly enhanced against the collective unit. From the perspective of the community, the allocation of economic resources faces two directions: one is towards agriculture to satisfy government taxes and rents and farmers' subsistence, and the other is towards the industrial and sideline sectors to create jobs and maximize profits. Obviously, it is more difficult for the government to control such a dual system. The government has to exercise its control through rural grass-roots cadres, but the implementation system in the rural areas have its own "private piece". In the context of diminishing marginal effect of the administrative control, the government has to relax its exclusive control over the rural surplus. A telling example is the fact that the government increased investment into agriculture since the late 1970s when township enterprises enjoyed rapid development.[68]

---

[67] Of the early founders of rural enterprises, 55% were cadres of communes and brigades and teams, and 21% were craftsmen.

[68] In the 1970s, the government's fiscal expenditure on agricultural aid was 10.86 billion yuan per year, an increase of 82.02% over the 1960s. See Appendix Table 3.2.

In any case, the residual claim now has been partially introduced into the rural collective economy. Though not yet institutionalized or even legalized, its existence has changed the rigidity of the people's commune system that does not allow trading. We can find the origin of the institutional evolution from the trade of interest in the people's commune system before 1978.

3.4 Property Rights Generated by Contracts

The rural reform of the late 1970s was the recurrence of the first large-scale of the short-term policies and arrangements in the early 1960s. The old logic for property rights formed and changed by the government-led political movement now finally give way to a new logic, namely a new effective property rights formed through interactions between the government and the farmers and between the farmers themselves. In an interactive environment that can be formed and changed based on the policy, the government took big backward steps from the ubiquitous control of the rural economy in exchange for stable taxation, low-cost control, and political support from the farmers; while the farmers guaranteed the hand-in produce and took up the responsibility for operation in exchange for long-term land-use rights and transfer rights, private property rights of the beyond-quota resources, and partial or full property rights of non-agricultural resources. A property rights systems composed of multiple forms of residual claims has been established in the multi-step progressive reform. Most importantly, the government has gradually begun to protect the new and effective property rights, because it can no longer unilaterally change the property rights without negotiating with farmers. In this section will discuss how new property rights of the farmers was formed in the context of full government control over the economy.

3.4.1 The Second Government Retreat

We can see different characteristics of the second peak from the first peak in Fig. 3.1. Throughout the 1970s, the government's benefit from rural areas grew stably. Except for the small fluctuations in 1972 and 1976, the government's income index increased by 121.6% in 1979 as compared to 1970, with an average annual growth rate of 8.74%. However, the government expense index rose even faster during the same period. It increased by 152.17% from 1970 to 1979, with an average annual growth rate of 10.82%. Especially after 1976, the government expense index increased so significantly that the gap between the expense index growth and the income index growth continued to widen and form another long-lasting peak with a big spread. We can see that the driver for the government to adjust rural economic policies was the constraint from its administrative costs. When the government was unable to increase its administrative costs, the policy retreat got started.

Looking at the expenses item by item, we can easily see that the fastest growing during this period were the government fiscal aid to agriculture and the sales of agricultural production necessities (growing by 186.96 and 112.66% respectively in 1979 as compared to 1970).[69] After the 1970s, the Chinese government has become more and more like a national agricultural "manager" who needs to take care of the agricultural input and output in person. Facing their grass-root proxies who are enthusiastic about collective capitalism or their supervisor's privilege and farmers who now has partial exit right, the government has to invest more to maintain the revenue growth. The government continues to launch political campaigns, but it has learned that the government's rural income just cannot increase automatically without tangible incentives.

This does not mean that the government will immediately make purely economically rational responses to the adverse changes in the cost-benefit structure of the people's commune system. It still has to consider the ripple effects of changing policies, especially the image of government authority and the coherence of ideology. However, precisely in the late 1970s, the political structure of the central government has completely changed from 20 years ago. First, the government's absolute authority has been weakened a lot by the long-term wrong economic policies, the abuse of power and authority by leaders, and the succession crisis of the top leader. Second, the challenge for legitimacy of the rule and the "potential threat of being replaced" not only comes from the outside (such as the Taiwanese *Kuomintang's* counter attack on the mainland in the 1960s), but also from within the institution.[70] Third, the less hostile international environment reduces the external pressure to strengthen centralization.[71] In this context, the government once again makes big adjustments to its rural economic policy.

---

[69]See columns 5 and 11 of Appendix Table 3.3 for the nominal value.

[70]For example, within the CPC, the pragmatists and Maoists had the potential to replace each other in the leadership.

[71]When analyzing the international situation in December 1977, Deng Xiaoping predicts that it was possible for China to stay in peace for a longer time, because the United States adopted a conservative global strategy after the failure in Southeast Asia, and the Soviet Union was not ready (Deng 1983: 74). Few people have explored the impact of this more conciliatory international situation on China's decentralization reform policy adopted since then. But this is a very important point if we look at the economic institution evolution. For instance, in the seventeenth century, Britain's taxation right was controlled by the Parliament composed of merchants and middle and upper-class landlords. Their interest was to restrict the king's power and to put an end to restrictions so as to protect private property rights and competition. However, in Spain and France, the royal family held unrestricted taxation rights and earned royalties by transferring monopolies to the guilds. One reason for this difference is that England, as an island country, faced less threat from invasion than continental Europe, and did not have good reasons to centralize property rights and taxation rights, nor did they have reasons to establish a mega central government (North and Thomas 1981: 155–156).

3.4.2 *Bottom-Level Reform*

At the rural grass-roots level, that the government's income index growth outpaces the growth of agricultural output value and farmers' net income growth, this means the allocation to the government was rising and to the farmers was declining. From 1970 to 1979, the national agricultural output value increased by 79.21%. The per capita net income of farmers obtained from the collective operation increased by 40.24%; after deduction of price impact, the growth was 60.39 and 21.42%, respectively, which was significantly lower than the above-mentioned increase in the government's income index (112.6% in real terms). This proves that the people's commune system that had undergone institutional adjustment in the early 1960s did not eradicate the government's infringement to property rights.[72] The poverty of the farmers and rural areas remained astounding.

The reactive response from farmers is to slack off in collective labor, and their active response, to work hard and expand their family operations. WEN (James) Guanzhong's data indicates that in the mid-to-late 1960s, as an inevitable result of the "criticize-capitalism" campaign in rural areas launched by the "Cultural Revolution", the total factor agricultural productivity continuously dropped and reached a record low in 1972.[73] After a brief recovery from 1972 to 1973 (during this period, the "extreme leftist" policy was denounced), it fell again between 1974 and 1977 when the policy tendency was to denounce the bourgeois legal rights. The productivity index was 74.2% in 1977, even lower than in 1961.[74] In the same year, farmers in some extremely poor and seriously disaster-afflicted regions were no longer satisfied with investing the "surplus" resources from the collective production into their family operations, because this was still insufficient for subsistence. They asked to take up all the land resources for family operations, but in return they would contract and commit the output. This was the origin of waves and waves of household responsibility system (HRS) reform.[75]

With the experience from the 1960s, to contract the output quota to households cannot be seen as institutional innovation, but rather propagation and popularization of the institution. Farmers in Fengyang County, Anhui Province, took a step further and changed the HRS from contracting the output quota to contracting the land,[76] changing the farmer contracting object from the output to operation of the land

[72]Yang et al. (1992) points out several forms of government infringement of property rights during the people's commune period.

[73]The total factor agricultural productivity index in 1972 was only 72.22% of that in 1952, 5.8 percentage points lower than that in 1961, see Wen (1989).

[74]Wen (1989).

[75]The three principles of contracting production to the household proposed by farmers demonstrate their considerations about dealing with the government and the collective. This also shows that the household production contracting system is a tri-party contract involving the government, the collective, and the farmers.

[76]See the field investigation report of the CRDRG (Zhou 1993).

property.[77] The farmers came up with a new institutional arrangement where "all the rest belong to themselves after handing in enough to the government and the collective". That is to say, all the available land resources is to be first put into family production, and the farmers can keep all the incremental output as long as they can guarantee that the vested government and collective interest is not harmed. This plain invention by farmers at the bottom layer shows that to save the operating costs of the system, the question on forms of property rights arrangements simply cannot be avoided. The important thing here, is that the move from output-based to land-based HRS in Anhui, Sichuan, Guizhou, Inner Mongolia, and Guangxi were taken between 1977 and 1978,[78] namely before the famous Third Plenary Session of the 11th CPCCC. As we will see, it is the bottom layer that pulled the policy of the upper layer from adjustment towards a reform.

The production-based HRS or the land-based HRS is but an expansion of the private plot economy. However, the former differs from the latter in a key point. The former involves at least making choices for the public at the production team level, such as balancing different opinions, facilitating the contracting agreements, formulating and safeguarding new rules of the game, and keeping the common secrets confidential. Production team leaders enjoy a natural comparative advantage in supplying public goods that are essential for institutional innovation.[79] Therefore, backward regions became the birthplace of rural reforms in the 1970s. The farmers there were so poor that they want to change, meanwhile the collective industries and sideline businesses were either too weak or non-existent at all, which drove the production brigade/team leaders to become the leaders for the HRS reform. This is also a non-negligible condition.

3.4.3 Challenges of Land Privatization

After decades of socialist transformation in the agricultural sector, China's farmers still had the dream of having private family land.[80] Where collective economy was not enough to feed the farmers, the desire for land was even stronger. Every time

[77]The unified planning and unified distribution still remain there for production teams adopting the household production contracting system. The farmers contract the output and perform production, and get a share of the beyond -quota output as an incentive. Contracting the land to households saves the measurement and supervision cost for the contracted output and extra output, with the precondition to satisfy the hand-into the government and the withholding by the collective unit.

[78]See the CRDRG (1981).

[79]For example, in Xiaogang Production Team, the first in Anhui Province to implement the production-based HRS, the HRS was completed under the leadership of its chief surnamed Yan. See Chen Xiwen and Ma Suyuan's field investigation report (CRDRG 1984, Vol. 1).

[80]"The land is there; you can see it every day. The robber cannot take it away. Thieves cannot steal it. Men die, but the land remains." "Money will be used up but land never." These views of farmers' on the land in the southern Jiangsu province were recorded by FEI Xiaotong in the 1930s (FEI 1939: 182). Understanding this, you will understand why the farmer revolution occurred and why private plots was effective.

the top-down control was relaxed, the call for privatization would emerge first at the grass-roots level. In fact, when the production-based HRS was still carried out secretly, some farmers already proposed to re-privatize the land, that is, to "let the land and forest go back to the original home", namely to go back to the post-Land Reform land distribution system.[81] These farmers have actually seen the land rights allocated from the Land Reform as the sole lawful basis for land re-distribution.

The first opponent against the above-mentioned privatization was not some conservative officials (because the leadership in office, whatever their political tendency, didn't know what happened in the village), but another group of farmers in the village who believed the Land Reform, after all, was something implemented 30 years ago. Since then, the rural population increased by 300 million and the number of rural households by about 100 million. How could it possible that these younger and more productive population and labor with more strength to contend for resources be deprived of everything? Therefore, at the village level, even without political or ideological pressure, radical privatization would not work.

A feasible approach after revision was to distribute the land equally according to the current population. But the trouble with this approach is whether or not the different rights of labors and non-labors should be accepted during the distribution. If yes, the labor gets more than the non-labor; then the next trouble comes: is it necessary to re-distribute the land after the labor population ratio changes in the farmers' families. If re-distribution happens, it equals that there is no privatization and result in "privatizing every year". To reject the re-distribution, the new private property system will have to withstand the pressure from the changes in labor population ratio of all the families.

Or let's step back and do a one-off land distribution: to treat everyone the same way and equally distribute all the land to all the people with the land property certificate, and then allow them to trade or rent the land freely. There is no problem with the simplicity of this scheme, but how to set the cutoff date? No matter which date you pick, the households which give birth to babies the next day will surely oppose it. You may claim that the majority overwhelms the minority, but on issues like this the minority is always tougher than the majority.[82] You may suggest a democratic vote, but there will definitely be another vote in the future. You may suggest authoritarianism by the brigade leader or the president, but then the farmers who suffer a loss will do everything possible to overthrow them as long as it is cheaper than buying land. The crux lies in two aspects: First, different households in different stages of the

[81] Such incidents between 1977 and 1982 were seldom publicly reported. This is because reporting was not allowed, also because farmers were not willing to share the details of the secrets with outsiders. However, from some local government circulars and investigation reports, we may indirectly see such phenomena. Examples include the Circular in 1980 by Fengyang County, Anhui Province, and the Investigation Report in 1980 by the Policy Research Office of Qinghai Provincial Party Committee. For both, see CRDRG (1981: 222–330, 322–333).

[82] Because if one household in a village of 30 households is about to have a new-born, and if the benefit it can possibly get is 1, the other 29 households might face a loss of one 29th. But it takes organization costs for these other 29 households to joint hands.

family, with different labor population ratios, have different and changing requirements on land distribution.[83] Second, the population-based distribution cannot set a stable boundary for property rights in any case. The first point entails the procedural trouble of land privatization, and the second entails a real trouble. During the early days of the reform, many villages had lots of sleepless nights facing the difficulties of making the above-mentioned common choices. The new contracting agreements not only should not disrupt the continuous agricultural production but also must be signed before farming starts.

There are some profound reasons for the household output responsibility system rather than the once-for-all land privatization to become popular at the village level. As we will see later, no matter how close the land contracting right become to private property or quasi-private property, certain measures by the village community as the ultimate owner still remain there so as to respond to the pressure from changing demographics. The HRS arrangement recognizes the private property rights of the produce after hand-in quota, which opens up a way for farmers from within the collective system to have private property without being entangled by the tradition of population-based equal distribution. This point will be discussed later, the imperative task for now is the legalization of HRS.

3.4.4 Decentralized Decision-Making

It is undeniable that in the late 1970s there was a big gap between the rural economic policy that the central government intended to implement, and the already-occurred household contracting reform at the grass-root level. Literature shows that the main message of the newly formulated rural policy at the end of 1978 was to "rehabilitate and invigorate" and to strengthen grass-roots autonomy. The measures for the first aspect included raising the government's purchase prices of agricultural and sideline products, reducing mandatory government purchase, and importing more agricultural products. For the second aspect, the autonomy of the production team was highlighted again. However, there was no intention from both aspects to initiate institutional reforms in rural areas.[84]

As a result of implementing the "recuperate and invigorate" policy, government access to agricultural surplus has fallen to roughly the same level as traditional agricultural taxes.[85] At the same time, the government's support policy for agriculture

---

[83] Based on this view, Chayanov (1986) believes that the differentiation of farmers in rural Soviet Union was not a differentiation between different classes, but simply it was because of the economic differences of rural families during different stages of the family life cycle.

[84] The resolution on agricultural issues by the famous Third Plenary Session of the Eleventh Central Committee explicitly prohibits the HRS. The statement was kept in the revised resolutions of the Fourth Plenary Session one year later. Both documents were published in the *China Agriculture Yearbook* (1980: 56–62).

[85] In 1980, the total agricultural accumulation was 36.074 billion yuan. If excluding the government's expenses on rural areas, the net outflow of agriculture was 27.862 billion yuan (Feng and Li 1993),

led to an all-time high of cost index in 1979 (see Fig. 3.1) and continuous fiscal deficit.[86]

The autonomy of the production team is even more complicated. First, to what extent is its operations allowed to go beyond the government plan. Second, the production team has the right to change its own forms of property rights or not. The simple slogan on autonomy almost breaks up all the illusions of the collective ownership. The HRS introduced by Xiaogang Production Team in Anhui was a unanimous decision of all the farmers. But was it legal?

Nobody can directly answer this question, because there is no law to record the right of the production team and the procedures for its adjustments and alterations. Although habitually scholars on institution comparison conclude that the degree of control by planning in China was much lower than in the Soviet Union, the level of central authority was very high in terms of economic organization and forms of property rights. In particular, when it came to the issue of rural property rights, it could only be determined by the CPCCC and the chairman thereof.[87] According to the latest resolution of the Party at the end of 1978, as mentioned above, the HRS was still clearly banned. It was simply impossible for the central government to complete the legalization for the HRS on a national basis.

Property rights arrangements affect people's economic behaviors through their expectations,[88] so legalization is an inherent requirement from the very beginning. If the property rights are not legally recognized, or if they are expected to be canceled at any time, then it would not be surprising to see opportunistic behavior from the person in question. The problem is that illegal property rights innovation may lead to resources plundering, but it's even more impossible for resource-plundering "property rights" arrangements to be legalized. This is the real difficulty of the socialist property rights reform.[89] Neither farmers nor rational community elites can completely solve it.

The main experience of China's rural reform is to delegate decision-making to the provincial level, which means each province can use its provincial political resources and decide whether or not to legalize HRS through the provincial political procedures. The legal basis for the province-by-province decision-making is the new thoughts set by the Third Plenary Session of the 11th CPCCC to strengthen local enthusiasm

accounting for 12.78% of the 218 billion yuan total agricultural output value (ZTN 1983: 13) (The figure for 1977 and 1978 is 15.73% and 14.05% respectively). This is already lower than the figure in 1955 (12.83%) and only slightly higher than in 1952 (11.49%, same source above).

[86] At that time, the purchase prices of agricultural and sideline products increased, but the sales prices to the urban residents remained unchanged. The government financed the gap. This growing expenditure in the 1980s is not included in the government's rural expense index in Fig. 3.1 and Appendix Table 3.3, because it reflects the relationship between the government and urban residents.

[87] In the early and late 1950s, DENG Zihui and PENG Dehuai were leaders of the Central Committee and the State Council respectively. However, they both lost their say in policy issues because of their differences with Chairman MAO Zedong on rural issues.

[88] Demsetz (1988: 104).

[89] That the socialist property rights reform is very likely to move towards radicalism may have a lot to do with this.

and uphold the principle that practice is the only standard to test truth. In addition, the seniority of provincial leaders and their relationship with the central leadership have a big impact on the intensity of provincial decisions. As we all know, the first provinces to provide political protection to and legalize HRS were poor and heavily agricultural provinces such as Anhui, Sichuan, Guizhou, and Inner Mongolia.[90] This is not accidental. In China, the distribution of natural disasters is uneven, and the proportion of rural population and economic development are also different from one province to another. That is to say each province faces different probability of famine, disaster relief pressure and accordingly political risks and responsibilities. Developed provinces may find it not worth the risks to go first in HRS, yet less developed provinces would see it as an answer to their pressing problem, just like less developed provinces wouldn't be as keen on legalizing township enterprises as the developed provinces. In short, each province has different constraints structures on the spontaneous grass-root innovation, and so they might provide different political protections.

The decentralized decision-making completes the legalization of new property rights arrangements on a local basis. To China's farmers, the county government—not to mention the provincial government—is certainly authoritative. This significantly enhanced farmers' confidence with the implementation of the new property contracts, thereby reducing the risks of policy changes on property rights, increasing the demonstrative effect of local successes and the possibility of institutional reform competition between different regions.[91] Experience has shown that decentralized decision-making is a key step in the change of the property rights system for such a huge country like China.[92]

---

[90]Taking Anhui for example, the Xiaogang Village HRS model caused a huge debate in Fengyang County. Finally, the Standing Committee of the Anhui Provincial Party Committee made a field visit to the village and decided to give it the green light.

[91]The gradualistic character of China's reform is not only manifested in the continuity in time, but also in the uneven spatial distribution.

[92]The decentralization reform was criticized by some famous economists in China after 1989. The representative work is an article published by Wu Jinglian in December 1989. This article systematically criticizes erroneous economic reform measures by the former State Council leader. One important mistake was to confuse "administrative empowerment" with "economic empowerment", which led to segmented markets, decentralized macro control and "Vassal Economy". Written in an academic and consultative style, the articles carries great ethical courage to challenge super authoritative persons although it is now impossible for the criticized to make openly any response to such criticism. (The author's note says that "This article was based on the author's reports delivered on June 9, 1987, July 1, 1988, and January 11, 1989, at the Central Party School" [Wu 1989: 51].) After the publication, many domestic and overseas Chinese language newspapers continued to attack the "Vassal Economy". The representative work with opposite view is the article by Li Xianglu published in 1990 in *the American Intellectuals* magazine. He believes that the reform of the bureaucratic system has to start in a piecemeal manner because there is no way to rely on the bureaucracy for central planning to mobilize and promote reform. Only the decentralized policy can launch the socialized mechanism for the reform within the system of totalitarianism. The experience of the rural reform shows that, we luckily had the "wrong economic reform measures" of decentralization; otherwise we might still live under the people's commune system today.

3.4.5 Local Governments Promote Central Policy

Local legalization is not yet equal to national legalization, and this difference embodies certain risks.[93] Therefore, after the HRS produced preliminary success, the provinces taking the lead in reform pushed for nationwide legalization of the HRS. On this point, the local political interests were highly consistent with new property rights arrangements. The central government held a meeting attended by the First Party Secretary of each province to revisit the HRS in 1980, in less than one year after the previous plenary session of the CPCCC which expressly banned the HRS.

Western political scientists who study China's decision-making process notice that the central working conference attended by officials from all provinces is of great significance.[94] But most of previous meetings did not change the top-down decision-making mechanism.[95] The 1980 conference had a new feature, namely all provinces were eager to incorporate their local experience into the central policy, that is, to strive for the national legalization of their models. However, due to the wide gap and disparate positions between different regions, it was difficult to reach consensus.[96] Finally, the policy document adopted by the meeting allowed the production team/brigade to implement multiple responsibility contracting arrangements, including the HRS.[97] This is equivalent to revising the original position of the central government and legalizing the HRS on a nationwide basis.

The most important contribution of the decision-making model in 1980 was not so much in its content as in its procedures. Divergent local interests and propositions can be negotiated and bargained in the central decision-making process and finally be synthesized into a new central policy. Based on this innovation, the original transaction between the central government and the farmers around the property rights has developed into multiple-level negotiation, communication, and "transaction" between farmers, rural communities, local governments, and central government.

---

[93]In 1961, the HRS in Anhui obtained the approval of Zeng Xisheng, the First Party Secretary of the Province, and the acquiescence of the central leaders, including Mao Zedong. However, after the famine was over, Zeng was criticized and dismissed because of this policy (Bo 1993, Vol. 2).

[94]Lieberthal and Oksenberg (1988: 29, 152).

[95]The 7000-people conference held in 1962 was an exception, which summarized the bad lessons of 1959–1961 at various decision-making levels.

[96]The heated debate even extended from the venue to the eating table. Chi Huaqing, the First Party Secretary of Guizhou, who supported the HRS, once said during the meal to Yang Yichen, the First Party Secretary of Heilongjiang, who was against the HRS, "You go your sunny big road, I will take my single-log bridge". Unexpectedly, this remarks provided the idea for the solution with coexistence of multiple modes.

[97]This is the Central Document No. 75 in 1980. For background for the formulation of this new policy document, see Du Runsheng's speech at the meeting to formulate this policy document attended by First Party Secretaries of All Provinces, Municipalities & Autonomous Regions (Du 1985: 1–9) and the article by Wu (1980).

We do not need to over-estimate the degree of institutionalization of this decision-making model, but from a long-term perspective, it contains the elements that re-build the relationship between the government and the society.[98]

3.4.6 *Step-by-Step Incremental Transaction*

Next, farmers demanded to make this new policy long term, as they feared that this policy adjustment would just be a short-term "expediency", like what happened in the early 1960s.[99] Farmers and rural community elites actively increased production on the one hand in response to the government's purchase price increase and permission to the HRS, on the other, they made voice and exercised their exit right alternately to force the government to make this reform policy long term. A key fact here is that the average annual fertilizer usage growth was 14.4% (ZTN 1993: 349) from 1978 to 1982 nationwide, which seems to substantiate the report by many journalists, local officials, agronomists, and policy investigators saying that farmers were depriving the land fertility due to concern about policy changes. Short-sighted behaviors are often denounced, but why don't we see such peasants' behaviors as a rational response to a short-term institutional arrangement? More importantly, such short-term behaviors point at the short-term constraint and compel it to change its structure.[100] Then at the beginning of 1984, a central policy document expressly specifies that the land contracting period should be 15 years and above, and it also allows the paid transfer of land contracting rights.[101]

3.4.7 *Property Rights Generated by Transactions*

With the HRS legalized and becoming long term, farmers accumulated increasing amount of economic resources at their own disposal. This part of the surplus beyond the hand-in to the government and the collective, was initially only enough to feed themselves, but over time, it grew into economic resources that can be used for investment for some of the farmers in some regions. If the government is to nationalize or collectivize this part of the surplus and impose government plan and control on it, it is unilaterally breaching the HRS contract; the farmers may, conversely not to honor their commitment to hand in the quota to the government and the collective. Such a

[98]See Ji (1993) for the importance of procedures in the process of reform.

[99]Historical experience shows that if the government still dominates the rural society, then the reduced government rent and tax can be raised again after the economic recovery, and the empowered authority can be reclaimed for various reasons.

[100]This argument also applies to the analysis of other rent-seeking behaviors in the reform process. Many people condemn rent-seeking but completely ignore the role of rent-seeking in institutional innovation.

[101]For the notice of the CPCCC on rural work in 1984, see Ma (1992: 133).

result was not affordable to the then political structure (otherwise, the government would not accept the HRS in the first place).

Another possible option is to accept the farmers' arrangement to "their own" resources in the same way as to their private property, which can be traded on the market. This way the incentives to farmers under the HRS can be ensured, and at the same time the efficiency of utilizing the farmers' own resources in the society can be improved. Throughout the 1980s, after the government's confirmation of the HRS, the basic direction of the rural economic policy, pushed by the farmers' spontaneous institutional innovation, was to admit the farmer's own resources as their private property. During this period, the government repeatedly reduced the varieties and quantity of planned acquisitions (1983–1984); replaced the unified procurement and distribution with the contract-based acquisition (1985–1987); announced that after government acquisition surplus agricultural and sideline products could be freely traded (1979–1985); allowed long distance trafficking and cross-region sales (1980); allowed farmers to do business in cities (1984–1985); announced to reform of the rural supply and marketing co-operatives and rural credit co-operatives by restoring its private nature, and re-introducing the share-holding and dividend system (1983); the government allowed private investment in large-scale production materials and the creation of private capital invested enterprises (1983); gave tacit agreement to and then formally recognized the lawful status of private enterprises with more than eight employees (1981–1987); encouraged farmers to engage in non-agricultural activities (1979–1984); opened up employment and business venturing in small towns and small to medium-sized cities (1984–1985); reformed the recruitment system of SOEs in large and medium-sized cities, and opened the urban labor market to rural migrant workers (1986–1987).[102] During this period, "collective capitalism", i.e. the PBEs, gained full legitimacy.[103] The government still restricted individuals from financial equity investment or using land as equity, but for the collective this kind of activities were opened up. Most importantly, the collective unit can "sell its licenses" to individuals, so that those having misgivings about government policies can still be engaged in private capital activities with a collective hat. Roughly by the end of the 1980s, China's rural areas has completed perhaps the greatest ever business revolution in history. The institutional foundation is the household contracting system of the collective land, "collective capitalist" enterprises, and the private property system for households and individuals. In short, the fully-transformed residual claims

[102]The policies and legal documents mentioned here can be found in the *Chinese Agricultural Yearbook*. Yang et al. (1992) made an excellent review of these rural reform policies and laws of this period in English. Except that their measurement of the policy system environment is totally based on the documents, which seems to me could be improved because the documents sometimes lag behind the reality and sometimes are not fully implemented. Therefore, the documents are not fully equal to the factual institutional constraints.

[103]The local political establishment of developed regions, under the Contracted Fiscal Responsibility System, provided fullest protection to their township enterprise and worked hard to obtain the recognition from the central policy. What they did was consistent with what the less developed areas did to protect the HRS.

mechanism back in the 1950s, now gets re-built in rural society in many different forms.

3.4.8 Full Exit and Stability

New policies and institutional arrangements have strengthened farmers' right to exit. Now farmers not only control the production and primary distribution of agricultural products but also can exit from production of some agricultural products and join the same for others or move to industry, construction, transportation, and service sectors. They can also fully withdraw from unsatisfactory market transactions and produce only for the consumption of their own families.[104] Last, the most productive farmers can also leave the countryside and move to towns and cities. That is to say, the farmers partial exit right now has developed into full exit right, which has strengthened their bargaining power. Now we can see that farmers are making voices everywhere in the property rights markets, just as they shout out the price in the products and factors markets.

By the same token, the bargaining position of rural communities with the government has also improved. With a large starting scale and strong human capital, rural communities are well positioned to defend their property rights and have more methods to counter infringement. Since the fiscal interests of local governments are closely related to township enterprises, the local political establishment of developed provinces always becomes the protection layer for township enterprises, just as the less developed provinces were keen to protect family operations in the early days. In developed villages, the community economy constitutes the backbone of the rural society.

In the context of changed government-rural society relations, the new property rights arrangements include a mechanism for self-protection. Indeed, the legalization and protection of the new property rights is still a government function that cannot be replaced, but now when the government effectively does so, it is rewarded by the society with long-term increased fiscal contributions. Conversely, if the government repeats the mistake of infringement, it will definitely face backlash from the communities and suffer financial losses. In short, it is no longer easy for the government to unilaterally transform the society, especially property rights as it pleases.[105] So far, the adjustment of rural economic policies that began in the late 1970s has evolved into an irreversible reform on property rights. This is neither unilaterally because of the wise vision of government, nor entirely due to the spontaneous efforts of farmers

[104] For example, if each rural household, on the average, decides to reserve an additional of 100 kg of grains, the supply to the national market will be reduced by 18 billion kg. This fact constitutes the basic driving force for the reform of the grain purchase and sale system since 1985.

[105] A recent evidence is that between 1990 and 1991, certain officials of Beijing initiated a new version of rural socialist education movement, which ended up nowhere.

and community elites. In fact, it is a mutually beneficial deal derived from a decade-long stepwise trade-off in the framework of decentralized decision-making for the re-construction of an effective property rights institution between the government and the farmers.

3.4.9 The Big Picture

Since the reform, the property rights structure in rural China has undergone fundamental changes. Table 3.1 lists the author's estimate of the current total rural assets based on data published by the National Bureau of Statistics (NBS) in 1993. If this estimate is acceptable, then 77.29% of the total assets of rural China (95,196.12 billion yuan, 1992) is collective land property (farmland and mountains) and enterprises assets, and 22.71% is farmers' private property. Of all collective assets more than 95% is contracted to households or individuals by long-term contracts, and less than 4% are still managed by the collective.

This newly formed property rights structure contains some important features. First, the collective assets operated by rural households and individuals under long-term contracts account for more than 70% of the total rural assets, constituting the most important institutional form of rural production activities in today's China.[106] The institutional feature of this contracted economy is that it is a contract between the community as the collective and rural households on the use of collective assets. The ultimate property rights belong to the collective, and the right to use and control goes to the farmers and individuals. However, the HRS is sort of a case-by-case system for different regions, different businesses and different people, because what it follows is the balance of power between different local interests holders, rather than a consistent institutional norm.

Second, the property rights contracts of operation contracting themselves are changeable. Important changes have taken place or are taking place to both the land contracting system established in the early 1980s and the collective enterprise contracting system established in the mid-1980s. For example, the land contract system has changed from short-term to long-term (recently the central government has announced that the contract can be extended up to 30 years),[107] and in some less developed areas, the early arrangements for the continuous re-distribution of contracted land to include new population have been discontinued.[108] The right

---

[106]Coase (1992) stresses that the institutional structure of production is what he and other institutional economists are studying.

[107]Quote from Du and Yuan (1993).

[108]The early HRS system did not exclude the possibility of land reallocation due to population changes, which caused the endogenous instability of land contracting. Meitan, Guizhou was the first place to carry out institutional innovation to eliminate such rights. The Meitan approach is to provide low-interest loans by the local government to support farmers to develop barren hills and slopes so as to accommodate the demand of the increased population. The author once saw this as the most important institutional innovation since the HRS because it solved a long-standing dilemma

Table 3.1 China's rural asset structure in 1992

(1)	(2)	(3)	(4)
Rural assets	Quantity	Estimated value (Billion RMB)	Ratio (%)
I. Total rural assets		951,961.2	100.00
II. Collective-operated collective assets		343.416	3.61
2.1 Cultivated land[a]	4.1931 mm ha	220.159[b]	2.31
2.2 Forest land	1.8231 mm ha	27.789[c]	0.29
2.3 Enterprise fixed assets	≈ 300,400[d]	51.718[e]	0.54
2.4 Enterprise working capital		81.276[f]	0.85
2.5 Enterprise debt		36.786[g]	−0.39
2.6 Collective net deposits[h]		−0.740	−0.01
III Collective assets contracted to farmers		7013.825	73.68
3.1 Cultivated land	120.9619 mm ha	6351.099	66.72
3.2 Forest land	18.2309 m ha	277.894	2.92
3.3 Enterprise fixed assets	≈ 1.216 mm	206.872	2.17
3.4 Enterprise working capital		325.104	3.42
3.5 Enterprise debt		147.144	−1.55
IV Private assets of farmers		2162.371	22.71
4.1 Agricultural fixed assets[i]		111.432	1.17
4.2 Enterprises	19.272 m	100.782[j]	1.06
4.3 Private housing[k]	1.2681195 b	1434.903	15.07
4.4 Net deposits		3107.80[l]	3.26
4.5 Cash and other financial assets		2044.7[m]	2.15

Notes

[a]According to National Bureau of Statistics, the total area of cultivated land in China was 95.4258 million hectares (i.e. 1.43 billion *mu*) in 1992, but a note says that this number was smaller than the actual (ZTN 1993: 332). According to the same book (ZTN 1993: 356, 357), on average for every household, the per capita figure was 0.1373 hectares (2.06 *mu*) of cultivated land and 0.022 hectares (0.33 *mu*) of forest land (ZTN 1993: 356, 357). Based on the total rural population of 911.544 million (ZTN 1993: 329), the total cultivated land was 125.155 million hectares (1.877 billion *mu*) and the forest land was 20.054 million hectares (300 million *mu*). This table is based on the statistics of the latter

[b]The valuation method of cultivated land is as follows: The land rent rate is assumed to be 40% of the total agricultural output value. In 1992, the total rent was about 363.38 billion yuan (ZTN 1993: 333). Based on the loan rate to self-employed in rural areas that year was 11. 23% (ZTN 1993: 671), after deducting the price index of 5.4% (ZTN 1993: 199, 237), the real interest rate is about 5.53%, so the total land value was about 6.571212 trillion yuan with a total area of 125.155 million hectares (see Note a), so the average land value was of 522,505 yuan per hectare or 3500.33 yuan per mu

[c]The valuation method of the forest land is as follows: The land rent rate is assumed to 40% of the total forestry output value (42.261 billion yuan in 1992, ZTN 1993: 335), so the total value of forest land was 16.904 billion yuan. The real interest rate was calculated at 5.53% (see Note b). The total value of forest land is 305.678 billion yuan, and the total cultivated forest area was about 20.054 million hectares (see Note a), so the average land value was of 15,243 yuan per hectare or 1016.2 yuan per mu
[d]There was a total of 1.52 million township/village collective enterprises (ZTN 1993: 395). It is estimated that less than 20% were still under collective operation; the rest were either contracted to individuals or just collective in the name
[e]The net value of fixed assets of township/village collective enterprises was 258.59 billion yuan (ZTN 1993: 397), where collective operation accounted for 20% and contracted operations 80% (see same column for item 3.3)
[f]The working capital of rural collective enterprises was 406.38 billion yuan (ZTN 1993: 397) at the end of the year, based on collective operations accounting for 20% of the total
[g]The balance of bank loans of rural collective enterprises was 183.93 billion yuan (ZTN 1993: 397); 20% is recorded here, and the remaining 80% is recorded in the same column of item 3.5
[h]Collective net deposits equal the balance of collective agricultural deposits at the end of the year, minus the balance of loans. The statistics only include net deposits from the credit co-operatives (ZTN 1993: 667), but not from government banks namely the Agriculture Bank, because the latter did not have a breakdown for rural households and the net amount in 1992 was almost zero (ZTN 1993: 664). Item 4.4 (net deposits of rural households) uses the same method of calculation
[i]This includes draft animals and commercial livestock, large and medium-sized iron or wood farm tools, machinery for farming, animal husbandry, fishery, and transport (ZTN 1993: 35)
[j]There were no statistics for the assets of enterprises below the village level. Here, it is calculated as the sum of machinery, workshops, and other items of the producers' fixed assets (ZTN 1993: 354). It can be argued that although it records the original value instead of the net value, the estimated total assets of the farmers' household enterprises were lower than actual (here the average value of fixed assets of each enterprise was only 5688.92 yuan)
[k]See ZTN (1993: 323)
[l]The net deposits of rural households in rural credit co-operatives were 210.78 billion yuan in 1992 (the balance of farmers' deposits was 286.73 billion yuan, and the loan balance was 75.95 billion yuan, ZTN 1993: 667). The balance of farmers' deposits in government banks was not published separately. The only data available were rural deposits of 140.942 billion yuan) and agricultural loans of 144.872 billion yuan (ZTN 1993: 664), the amount of net deposits balance of farmers was not clear. The national private savings deposits for the year was 1.15447 trillion yuan, of which 40–45% was estimated from farmers. Therefore, the amount of net deposits balance of farmers was estimated here to be the sum of the net deposits of farmers' households in credit co-operatives (210.78 billion yuan) plus 100 billion yuan
[m]The total cash in hand for all residents was 340.79 billion yuan (ZTN 1993: 602); rural households' cash in hand was estimated to account for 60% of the total

to transfer land contracts (land tenure) has been legalized, and a market for land contracts has been developed in some localities.[109] The contracting system of rural enterprises has developed into a co-operative shareholding system,[110] which, combined with the rural community fund, may lead to further innovation in rural

between population and land use (Zhou and Liu 1988). This approach aroused much interest and has been followed by many other places (Du and Yuan 1993).

[109]Such as the experience of Pingdu County, Shandong Province. See the investigation report of the Land System Research Group of the Rural Department of the Development Research Center of the State Council (print version, 1990).

[110]Du and Yuan (1993).

property rights systems. It is expected that with a better liquidity for rural economic factors, the property rights contracting will further evolve.[111]

Third, the assets of rural households and their freely-formed alliances already accounted for 23% of all rural assets. The majority of private property of farmers was private housing (accounting for 66.4%), and the assets available for production and investment were still rather limited. However, of all the types of rural property, the private property of farmers was growing fastest,[112] which was mainly generated from the incremental surplus of the contracting operations, namely the part after handing in the quota. Therefore the formation of farmers' private property sees the contracting system as its historical precondition. In addition, in actual operations, the farmers' private property and their contracted economy were usually integrated, with the decision-making, control and dispatching for both being performed by the same farmer or individual, and the only difference in product distribution which follows different contracts. These two points determine that China's rural private property is closed related to the community public property, and vice versa. However, the farmers' private property, in the sense of legal power, is not dependent on the collective public property, but has an independent status. For instance, today, a farmer can completely withdraw from the contracted operation without giving up his private property.[113]

Finally, the new forms of property rights in rural China, including the contracted operation and private property of farmers, are a kind of rights structure that has

[111]These actual changes are mutually dependent and mutually promoting with the farmers' call for "policy consistency" and the government's promise. The latter ask to prevent property rights from being created or changed again by top-down political means, while the former express the need to adjust the property right contract based on the changing transaction environment. What is important is that after the late 1980s, institutionalization and legalization of the new structure of rural property rights have been put on the agenda of the reform. This, of course, does not mean to write down the most perfect forms of property rights into the law and task is finished, but rather it means to record, in a legal form, the property rights that have been established through transactions, to adopt more measures to effectively protect the property rights and increase infringement costs, and then based on that, to formulate procedures for amending property rights contract between the parties.

[112]The author once estimated the rural asset structure in 1985. At that time, the rural households private property uncounted into private firms was about 700 billion yuan, plus the total assets of 22 billion yuan from various individual's enterprises, the total was 722 billion yuan. At that time, the valuation of agricultural land was based on nominal interest rates rather than real interest rates, so the land prices were undervalued. Based on real interest rates, the value of agricultural land would be about 5 trillion yuan, and the total rural asset would be about 6 trillion yuan. Therefore, the private property of farmers accounted for about 12% of total rural assets that year (see Comprehensive Research Task Force of the Institute of Development Studies 1988: 65–80). Since then, the private property of farmers has increased by nearly three times, with an average annual growth rate of 16.97%, 12 percentage points faster than the average annual growth rate of public property.

[113]Because he doesn't get the private property for nothing, he makes efforts to completes the hand-into the government and the collective, and undertake risks and responsibilities to obtain such property. In this sense, the private property of Chinese farmers today is different from what was formed by the Land Reform. Since the private property is not a gift from the government through large-scale political movements, the government is not entitled to change the contract arbitrarily.

developed with the development of its implementation and protection systems.[114] The reality is, the formation is not the result of a unilateral efforts of the government to provide a set of systems for implementing and protecting effective property rights, nor is it just the result for rural communities and farmers themselves to follow village customs or any other paid arrangements. It is, rather, the outcome of a series of step-by-step interaction between the central government, local governments, rural communities and farmers, which first rules out, to the maximum extent possible, government's infringement of the contract on rural private property rights, and secondly enhances the exclusivity for the utilization of internal resources of the rural community. This exclusive institutional arrangement with dual significance was realized not by written laws or some reinforcement agencies, but mainly by the yet-to-be-legalized communication, negotiation and bargain, especially by farmers' de facto exit right. Therefore, unlike the property rights generated by political movements, the above-mentioned new property rights generated by transactions can only be enforced and protected by checks and balances between the parties. A good transaction will make neither party lose. Only no-one-loses transactions last long, and long lasting transactions require to have, and can possibly supply institutionalized rules.[115] Therefore, only after more than a decade of reform, can people safely predict that the demand for legal service from contracts with multiple forms of property rights in rural China will increase substantially.

3.5 Conclusion

This article regards China's rural reform as an institutional change centered on the re-construction of property rights. Classic socialist agricultural transformation, in its theory and practice, attempts to remove the farmers' property rights namely the residual claim incentive mechanism so as to accelerate industrialization. The failure of this model is manifested not only in the low efficiency of the economy and stagnation of living standards, but also more in the high costs of system operation, and the ossification of its self-adjustment function. Under this model, the government invades into all areas of rural life, and directly controls and directs all rural economic organizations. This not only suffocates rural vitality but also impairs normal government functions and the legitimate authority of political organs.

---

[114] Or, in the words of Alchian and Demsetz (1972), the hardness of rural property rights is gradually increased with the growth of its protective structure.

[115] Many people are accustomed to the idea that institutions or rules are free of charge. For example, Bater (1990) provides a game theory model to illustrate the order for the property rights relationship between cattle farmers in the upper reaches of the Nile. In this model, the two cattle-raising households, in the absence of an arbitrator, always rationally choose the strategy of attacking the other family. The consequence of this resource-wasting "prisoner's gaming" doesn't get changed until a third party is introduced to punish attacks. The problem with Bater's model is that this third party does not consume any resources, yet in real life, it is impossible for institutions, order, and norms to be free.

The time when the socialist rural institution needs to be reformed is usually when it finds itself trapped in trouble—the result of compounding between a long-term chronic disease of the systemic, a random sudden disaster, and an upper-level political crisis.

The question here is not about how the two cattle-raising families in the upper reaches of the Nile River can find a middleman to mediate with or without pay so as to avoid wasting resources from mutual attacks. It is also not like how the hunting tribes in eastern Canada define the hunting ground when fur price goes up to avoid the too fast extinction of "public animal resources". Also indeed different from the United States, where the great principles on private property have long been well established into its laws and its customs, China needs to resolve the disputes over the rights not written or impossible to be written in prior contracts on property rights, just like the noise from the aircraft after its invention.

The socialist property rights reform faces a North's Paradox, to say the least, namely, why and how the government who has the legitimate coercion strictly protects the boundary of property rights contracts; or conversely, why and how individuals can prevent government from crossing the boundary.

But this is not all. Because the real problem is that this war-tested powerful government, with the great ambition of government industrialization and transforming the old China, has made its way into the rural society, with long track records of creating, changing and depriving farmers' property rights. In this case, the problems faced by the reform include: on the one hand, why and how the government should change its policy on property rights; on the other, why and how farmers can expect the new government policy to be stable and long-term, and treat it as a binding foundation for themselves to fulfill contracts with other individuals. Simply put, the problem here is how to re-construct an order for property rights, especially such order during the transition period under the constraint of government functions being abused before.

This is where the problem lies. China's rural reforms have created some plain but valuable experience. As we see, the embryo of the property rights reform already took shape during the people's commune period in the forms of production team autonomy, household operations, and the PBEs. In the early days, they could only rely on partial exiting right to protect themselves and stay away from the storms of political movements. These elementary rights were so tenacious that they affected the cost-benefit structure of the government-controlled rural economy, and forced the government to adjust and retreat from the previous rural economic policies with the assistance from natural disasters and other sporadic factors. Then the farmers expressed that they will warmly uphold the reform which was actually initiated by themselves. They contracted almost all the public property, and established their own private property from the surplus after handing in the prescribed quota. Most property rights innovations were legalized first locally. When institutional innovations proved to be notably effective for economic growth, these locally-created rights became solidified, thus changing the political balance in the central decision-making and obtaining nationwide legalization. It is under such a structure that a one-time, short-term transaction developed into multiple long-term transactions. And it is in these multi-party transactions that people exchanged information, balanced their interests, developed their expectations, and corrected contractual behaviors. In less than a decade, the landscape for collective property rights has changed over from the government-controlled mode to a new mixed structure between the contracting system and private ownership system. That is the main institutional foundation for rural economic growth and structural changes since the 1980s. Based on constant prices, the total rural output value increased by 14% per year between 1980 and 1992, and the per capita net income, by 6.16% per year. During the same period, every year about 5 million rural labors resettled in non-agricultural sectors.[116] Given that this is an economic activity involving more than 900 million people, or about 1/6 of the world's total population, the experience of China's rural reform is worthy of attention.

Perhaps what's most important in China's experience is that its reform takes into account the new property rights contract, and the co-ordination between its enforcement system and its assurance system so as to avoid the property right innovation fighting alone. Different from the path in early Western Europe, the protection mechanism of new property rights in rural China is not to use the "individual – bourgeois public sphere" to counter balance the government. But rather it leverages a large number of formal and informal transactions between the central government and the "households-rural community-local government" alliance so as to change the government-society relationship, creating conditions for protection and enforcement of the preliminarily defined property rights contracts. Next, many more complex forms for property rights contracts are being created. As we have seen, China's rural areas have not only completed the re-construction of the community public property contracting system and farmers' private property system, but also witness the flourishing of joint-stock system, co-operative shareholding system and other types of property rights contracts that were not even heard of in traditional times. We cannot say for sure what further changes may take place in China's property right structure in the next decade, but it is likely to carry on its reform tradition formed in more than a decade, e.g. it will rely more on the balance of power between the government and the society, rather than only on the balance of this or that kind of upper political power. In any case, the experience of China's institutional changes and the experience of Eastern Europe and Russia constitute a comparison worthy of continuous observation and comparison.

Appendix

[116]For rural total output value, see ZTN (1993: 333); for price, see ZTN (1993: 238); for farmers per capita net income, see ZTN (1993: 312). For labor data, see ZTN (1985: 224) and ZTN (1993: 330).

Table 3.2 Cost and benefit of the state controlled rural economy, 1951–1982 (in RMB Yuan)

Year (1)	AG 100 MM (2)	APG 100 MM (3)	ATAX 100 MM (4)	CMF 100 MM (5)	CR Per Person (6)	DTAX 100 MM (7)	EXPORT 100 MM (8)	GEA 100 MM (9)	GEM 100 MM (10)	PFR Per Person (11)	RL 100 MM (12)	RS 100 MM (13)
1952	461.00	14.10	31.11	0.00	0.00	24.55	27.10	9.04	72.30	0.00	3.20	0.00
1953	510.00	19.20	31.21	0.00	0.00	36.19	34.80	11.84	93.90	0.00	5.80	1.10
1954	535.00	25.00	37.70	0.00	2.43	43.41	40.00	13.51	76.40	56.39	6.90	4.30
1955	575.00	28.20	35.11	0.00	10.24	41.80	48.70	14.99	83.70	30.98	9.20	6.10
1956	610.00	37.00	34.21	1.70	43.01	51.31	55.70	26.99	85.40	17.02	28.50	8.00
1957	537.00	32.60	34.17	4.90	40.54	49.32	54.50	23.50	76.80	21.46	25.80	17.90
1958	566.00	66.80	37.53	4.70	41.39	91.62	67.10	43.86	71.60	24.08	40.10	27.80
1959	497.00	81.50	38.05	7.20	37.60	114.46	78.10	58.23	84.60	27.01	39.50	48.20
1960	457.00	101.50	32.26	7.20	41.25	127.29	63.30	90.52	86.00	30.30	56.90	49.90
1961	559.00	70.00	24.95	9.10	48.12	70.54	47.80	54.88	76.80	33.99	57.80	56.20
1962	584.00	60.30	26.14	10.00	46.06	73.94	47.10	38.23	78.60	38.15	61.00	31.60
1963	642.00	59.70	27.56	9.00	46.16	88.75	50.00	55.60	89.90	35.65	68.40	34.60
1964	720.00	65.50	29.74	8.10	47.52	110.05	55.40	67.16	98.10	35.72	70.40	45.60
1965	833.00	80.20	29.63	16.57	52.28	122.31	63.10	54.98	112.10	33.29	76.50	50.10
1966	910.00	100.00	34.06	17.36	53.64	149.48	66.00	54.39	126.90	32.58	76.10	62.90
1967	924.00	91.40	33.32	18.20	55.04	125.38	58.80	45.82	105.80	31.88	79.60	69.30
1968	928.00	88.10	34.48	19.08	56.48	106.26	57.60	33.47	117.00	31.19	78.80	83.30
1969	948.00	103.30	34.04	19.99	57.96	127.18	59.80	48.03	151.00	30.53	80.90	78.40
1970	1058.00	129.20	18.71	20.96	59.47	83.03	56.80	49.40	170.60	29.87	82.30	83.30
1971	1107.00	152.30	35.51	22.26	62.94	178.63	68.50	60.75	200.40	29.23	48.10	93.50

(continued)

Table 3.2 (continued)

Year (1)	AG 100 MM (2)	APG 100 MM (3)	ATAX 100 MM (4)	CMF 100 MM (5)	CR Per Person (6)	DTAX 100 MM (7)	EXPORT 100 MM (8)	GEA 100 MM (9)	GEM 100 MM (10)	PFR Per Person (11)	RL 100 MM (12)	RS 100 MM (13)
1972	1123.00	169.80	32.61	15.87	61.77	185.94	82.90	65.13	194.00	28.60	52.40	91.40
1973	1226.00	189.00	35.05	15.65	65.36	205.50	116.90	85.17	181.00	27.99	54.20	107.30
1974	1277.00	196.20	34.59	18.85	65.76	199.22	139.40	91.21	170.30	27.39	59.19	123.40
1975	1343.00	224.70	33.86	22.02	63.22	223.78	143.00	98.96	181.10	26.8	68.50	136.90
1976	1378.00	240.40	33.52	26.46	62.80	207.24	134.80	110.49	175.50	26.23	85.30	136.70
1977	1400.00	258.50	33.60	27.51	64.98	228.14	139.70	108.12	192.30	32.81	93.00	143.20
1978	1567.00	293.70	32.68	28.43	74.00	253.99	167.70	150.66	216.80	35.79	109.20	154.40
1979	1896.00	324.00	33.83	31.98	83.40	261.64	211.70	174.33	279.60	44.00	129.90	203.70
1980	2180.00	346.00	31.75	33.87	85.93	300.14	272.40	149.95	260.60	62.55	166.50	239.80
1981	2460.00	347.50	32.66	35.02	101.32	280.19	371.20	110.21	238.90	84.52	175.80	278.40
1982	2785.00	388.50	33.71	49.51	208.63	282.87	420.00	120.49	258.00	102.80	192.60	389.90

Notes

1. AG: total agriculture output calculated in the then price (ZTN 1983: 13); APG: sales of means of agricultural production calculated in the then price (ZTN 1993: 611); ATAX: agricultural taxes and surtaxes (based on 15% taxation) (ZTN 1983: 446); CMF: management cost of collective economy of people's commune, represented by non-productive cost out of the total cost, generally this is underestimated (NJZ 1983: 510); CR: net income of people's commune from collective economy (NJZ 1983: 517); DTAX: price differential for state purchase of agricultural and sideline products (Feng and Li 1993/9: 63); EXPORT; the annual export of agricultural and sideline products, raw and processed (ZTN 1983: 420); GEA: fiscal fund to support agriculture (ZTN 1993: 225); GEM: state administrative and military expenses (ZTN 19831983: 448); PFR: farmer's net income from household sideline activity (NJZ 1983: 523); RL: rural loan balance (NJZ 1983: 321); RS: rural savings (NJZ 1983: 321)

2. Of all the above items, AG, ATAX, DTAX, EXPORT, CR and RS are seen as state benefit from rural areas because they bring direct or indirect benefit to the country; while APG, CMF, GEA, GEM, PFR and RL are calculated as state costs although some of the items are indirect. In order to reasonably estimate the state cost and benefit from rural areas, all the above items are converted to the index where the figure for 1952 = 100 to remove the impact from prices and then weighted to arrive at the state benefit and cost index (see Appendix Table 3.3)

Table 3.3 Cost & benefit index of state controlled rural economy, 1952–1982

Year (1)	State benefit index (2)	State cost index (3)	AG (4)	APG (5)	ATAX (6)	CMF (7)	CR (8)	DTAX (9)	EXPORT (10)	GEA (11)	GEM (12)	FMP (13)	PFR (14)	RL (15)	RS (16)
1952	1.00	0.95	100.00	100.00	100.00	100.00	100.00	100.00	100.00	100.00	100.00	100.00	100.00	100.00	100.00
1953	1.17	1.19	110.63	136.17	100.31	100.00	100.00	147.43	128.41	130.97	129.88	104.82	100.00	181.25	100.00
1954	1.42	1.31	116.05	177.30	121.18	100.00	100.00	176.83	147.60	149.45	105.67	107.27	100.00	215.63	390.91
1955	1.51	1.45	124.73	200.00	112.87	100.00	421.40	170.27	179.70	165.82	115.77	107.09	54.94	287.50	554.55
1956	2.03	2.41	132.32	262.41	109.96	100.00	1769.96	209.01	205.54	298.56	118.12	106.91	30.18	890.63	727.27
1957	2.12	2.11	116.49	231.21	109.82	288.24	1668.31	200.89	201.11	259.96	106.22	109.91	38.06	806.25	1627.27
1958	2.82	3.52	122.78	473.76	120.64	276.47	1703.29	373.21	247.60	485.18	99.03	118.55	42.70	1253.13	2527.27
1959	3.48	4.52	107.81	578.01	122.31	423.53	1547.33	466.25	288.19	644.14	117.01	120.09	47.90	1234.38	4381.82
1960	3.14	5.82	99.13	719.86	103.69	423.53	1697.53	518.51	233.58	1 001.33	118.95	137.82	53.73	1778.13	4536.36
1961	0.70	1.04	121.26	496.45	80.21	535.29	1980.25	287.35	176.38	607.08	106.22	496.27	60.28	1806.25	5109.09
1962	0.92	1.20	126.68	427.66	84.03	588.24	1895.47	301.19	173.80	422.90	108.71	322.55	67.65	1906.25	2872.73
1963	1.36	2.11	139.26	423.40	88.59	529.41	1899.59	361.51	184.50	615.04	124.34	243.36	63.22	2137.50	3145.45
1964	2.35	3.56	156.18	464.54	95.59	476.47	1955.56	448.27	204.43	742.92	135.68	169.36	63.34	2200.00	4145.45
1965	2.50	3.15	180.69	568.79	95.24	974.71	2151.44	498.19	232.84	608.19	155.05	174.82	59.04	2390.63	4554.55
1966	2.94	3.22	197.40	709.22	109.49	1021.18	2207.41	608.89	243.54	601.66	175.52	176.91	57.78	2378.13	5718.18
1967	2.74	2.77	200.43	648.23	107.10	1070.59	2265.02	510.70	216.97	506.86	146.33	179.91	56.53	2487.50	6300.00
1968	2.76	2.28	201.30	624.82	110.82	112.35	2324.28	432.82	212.55	370.24	161.83	179.91	55.31	2462.50	7572.73
1969	2.90	2.99	205.64	732.62	109.43	1175.88	2385.19	518.04	220.66	531.31	208.85	179.73	54.14	2528.13	7127.27
1970	2.46	3.22	229.50	916.31	60.13	1232.94	2447.33	338.22	209.59	546.46	235.96	179.73	52.97	2571.88	7572.73

(continued)

Table 3.3 (continued)

Year (1)	State benefit index (2)	State cost index (3)	AG (4)	APG (5)	ATAX (6)	CMF (7)	CR (8)	DTAX (9)	EXPORT (10)	GEA (11)	GEM (12)	FMP (13)	PFR (14)	RL (15)	RS (16)
1971	3.33	3.49	240.13	1080.14	114.13	1309.41	2590.12	727.62	252.77	672.01	277.18	195.45	51.84	1503.13	8500.00
1972	3.11	3.41	243.60	1204.26	104.81	933.53	2541.98	757.40	305.90	720.46	268.33	211.55	50.72	1637.50	8306.09
1973	3.36	3.97	265.94	1340.43	112.68	920.59	2689.71	837.08	431.37	942.15	250.35	222.73	49.64	1693.75	9754.55
1974	3.45	4.15	277.01	1391.49	111.20	1108.82	2706.17	811.50	514.39	1008.96	235.55	26.82	48.57	1846.88	11,218.18
1975	3.61	4.39	291.32	1593.62	108.83	1295.29	2601.65	911.54	527.68	1094.69	250.48	235.91	47.53	2140.63	12,445.45
1976	3.35	4.68	298.92	1704.96	107.75	1556.47	2584.36	844.14	497.42	1222.23	242.74	245.27	46.52	2665.63	12,427.27
1977	3.65	4.83	303.69	1833.33	108.00	1618.24	2674.07	929.29	515.50	1196.02	265.98	239.36	58.18	2906.25	13,018.18
1978	4.30	6.75	339.91	2082.98	105.04	1672.35	3045.27	1034.57	618.82	1666.59	299.86	223.64	63.47	3412.50	14,036.36
1979	5.23	8.12	411.28	2297.87	108.75	1881.18	3432.10	1065.75	781.18	1928.43	386.72	213.55	78.03	4059.38	18,518.18
1980	5.91	7.32	472.89	2453.90	102.04	1992.35	3536.21	1222.55	1005.17	1658.74	360.44	217.82	110.92	5203.13	21,800.00
1981	6.07	5.70	533.62	2464.54	105.00	2060.00	4169.55	1141.30	1369.74	1219.14	330.43	230.45	149.88	5493.75	25,309.09
1982	7.52	6.15	604.1215	2755.319	108.36	2912.35	8585.60	1152.21	1549.82	1332.85	356.85	238.09	182.30	6018.75	35,445.45

Notes

1. FMP: comprehensive price index for consumer products at village fair (ZTN 1992: 81), and all other items in Columns 4–16 are converted to growth indices where the figure for 1952 equals 100

2. The state benefit comprehensive index is derived as a weighted average of six sub-items, all indices are based on real term prices to remove the impact from price movement (with FMP as the representative), and the calculation formula is: State Benefit Index = (ATAX × 0.4 + DTAX × 0.4 + EXPORT × 0.1 + AG × 0.05 + CR × 0.025 + RS × 0.025)/FMP, the weight of each sub-item is estimated according to the degree of importance to state benefit

3. The state cost index is derived as a weighted average of six sub-items, the price impact is removed using the same method, and the calculation formula is: State Cost Index = GEA × 0.65 + GEM × 0.1 + CMF × 0.03 + APG × 0.15 + PFR × 0.01 + RL × 0.01)/FMP where the weights are also the estimate by the author

References

Alchian, Armen. 1965. Some Economics of Property Rights. In *Economics Forces at Work* (1977), A. Alchian, 127–149. Indianapolis: Liberty Press.

Alchian, Armen, & Demsetz, H. (1972). Production, Information Costs, and Economic Organization. *American Economic Review, 62,* 777–795.

Arrow, Kenneth. 1963. *Social Choice and Individual Values.* New Haven: Wiley Press.

Ashton, Basil, Kenneth Hill, Alan Piazza, and Robin Zeitz. 1984. Famine in China, 1958–1961. *Population and Development Review* 1 (4): 613–645.

Bardhan, Pranab. (1989). The New Institutional Economics and Development Theory: A Brief Critical Assessment. *World Development, 17*(9), 1389–1395.

Bater, Robert H. (1990). Capital, Kinship and Conflict. *Canadian Journal of African Studies, 24*(2), 151–164.

Bentley, Mac Leod W. (1993). The Role of Exit Costs in the Theory of Cooperative Teams: A Theoretic Perspective. *Journal of Comparative Economics, 17,* 521–529.

Bo, Yibo. 1993. *A Review of Several Major Decisions and Events,* Vol. 2. Beijing: CPC Central Party School Press.

Buchanan, J., and G. Tullok. 1962. *The Calculus of Consent.* Ann Arbor: University of Michigan Press.

Byrd, William A., and Alan Gelb. 1988. Why Industrialize? The Incentives for Local Community Governments. In William A. Byrd and Qingsong Lin (eds.) (1988), Chapter 16.

Chayanov, A.V. 1986. *The Theory of Peasant Economy.* Madison: The University of Wisconsin Press.

Cheung, Steven. 1969a. *The Theory of Share Tenancy.* Chicago: University of Chicago Press.

Cheung, Steven. 1969b. The Structure of a Contract and the Theory of a Non-exclusive Resource. *Journal of Law Economics* 13 (April): 12.

China Rural Development Research Task Force. 1981. *Selected Information on Household Responsibility System,* Vols. 1–2. Internal Printout.

China Rural Development Research Task Force. 1984. *A Systematic Study of Rural Economic Reform.* Beijing: China Social Sciences Press.

China Rural Development Research Task Force. 1985. *Countryside, Economy, and Society,* Vol. 1. Knowledge Publishing House.

Coase, R. H. (1937). The Nature of the Firm. *Economica, 4,* 386–405.

Coase, R. H. (1960). The Problem of Social Cost. *Journal of Law and Economics, 3,* 1–44.

Comprehensive Research Task Group of Development Research Institute. 1988. *The Reform Faces Institutional Innovation.* Shanghai Joint Publishing Company.

Cooter, R., and T. Ulen. 1988. *Law and Economics.* New York: Harper Collins.

Cui, Xiaoli. 1988. *Unified Purchase and Unified Sales and China's Industrialization.* Development Research Report No. 5. Development Research Institute of Agriculture Research Center under the State Council.

Cui, Zhiyuan. 1993. A Schumpeterian Perspective and Beyond. In *China: A Reformable Socialism*?, ed. Yang Gan and Zhiyuan Cui. Oxford: Oxford University Press.

Demsetz, Harold. 1988. *Ownership, Control, and the Firm.* Oxford: Basil Blackwell Inc.

Deng, Xiaoping. 1983. *Selected Works of Deng Xiaoping (1975–1982).* The People's Press.

Du, Runsheng. 1985. *Rural Economic Reform of China.* China Social Sciences Publishing House.

Du, Ying, and Chongfa Yuan. 1993. Reform and Development of Rural China: Retrospective and Prospective. A Keynote Report delivered at the International Academic Seminar on the Reform and Development in the 1990s in China's Rural Areas, Rural Economic Research Center of the Ministry of Agriculture.

Elvin, Mark. 1973. *The Pattern of the Chinese Past.* Redwood City: Stanford University Press.

Sun, Fangming, and Bai, Ruobing. 1983. Team-based Enterprises: The Pillar of Regional Rural Development. *Outlook* (1): 26–28.

Fei, Hsiao-tung. (1939). *Peasant Life in China.* New York: E.P. Dutton & Company.

Feng, Haifa, and Li, Wei. 1993. Research on the Amount of Capital Accumulation Provided by China's Agriculture to Industrialization. in *Economic Research* (9): 60–64.

Furubotn, E., & Pejovich, S. (1972). Property Rights and Economic Theory: A Survey of Recent Literature. *Journal of Economic Literature, X*(4), 1138–1162.

Gao, Xiaomeng, and Ning Xiang. 1992. *Analysis of China's Policy on Agricultural Prices*. Zhejiang People's Publishing House.

Habermas, Jurgen. 1989. *The Structural Transformation of the Public Sphere*. Cambridge: MIT Press.

Hirschman, Albert O. (1970). *Exit, Voice and Loyalty*. Cambridge: Harvard University Press.

Huang, Philip C.C. 1985. *The Peasant Economy and Social Change in North China*. Stanford: Stanford University Press.

Huang, Philip C. C. (1993). 'Public Sphere'/'Civil Society' in China? The Third Realm Between State and Society. *Modern China, 19*(2), 216–240.

Ji, Weidong. 1993. On Procedures. *Papers of Contemporary China Research Center* 4 (3).

Kung, Kaising James. (1993). Transaction Cost and Peasant's Choice of Institutions: Did the Rights to Exit Really Solve the Free Rider Problem in Chinese Agriculture? *Journal of Comparative Economics, 17,* 485–503.

Li, Guodu (ed.). 1990. *Development Research*, Vols. 1–2. Beijing Normal University Press.

Lieberthal, Kenneth, and Michel Oksenberg. 1988. *Policy Marking in China*. Princeton: Princeton University Press.

Lin, Justin Yifu. 1988. The Household Responsibility System in China's Agricultural Reform: A Theoretic and Empirical Study. *Economic Development and Cultural Change* 36 (4): S199–S224.

Lin, Justin. (1989). An Economic Theory of Institutional Change: Induced and Imposed Change. *Cato Journal, 9*(1), 1–33.

Lin, Justin. 1990. Collectivization and China's Agricultural Crisis in 1959–1961. *Journal of Political Economy* 98 (6): 1228–1252.

Lippit, Victor. 1974. *Land Reform and Economic Development in China*. New York: International Arts and Sciences Press.

Liu, Shouying, and Zhuangjun Hu. 1990. *Selected Papers on the Theory of Property Rights and Institutional Change*, trans. Jianbo Chen and Jicheng Qiu. Shanghai Joint Publishing Company.

Lu, Xueyi, and Xiaoqiang Wang. 1981. *The Origin of Household Production Contracting and its Future Development*. China Rural Development Research Task Force, 166–196.

Ma, Kewei (ed.). 1992. *Encyclopedia on China's Reform, the Volume for Land Institution Reform*. Dalian Publishing House.

MacFarquhar, Roderick, and John K. Fairbank (eds.). 1987. *The Cambridge History of China (1949–1965)*. Cambridge: Cambridge University Press.

Mann, Michael. (1984). The Autonomous Power of the State: Its Origins, Mechanism, and Results. *Archives Européennes de Sociologie, 25,* 185–213.

National Statistics Bureau. *China Rural Statistical Yearbook (ZNTN) for 1985*. China Statistical Press.

National Statistics Bureau. *China Statistical Yearbook (ZTN) (1983, 1992, 1993)*. China Statistical Press.

National Statistics Bureau. 1991. *The Outline for National Economic Statistics (GJTY) (1949–1984)*. China Statistical Press.

North, Douglass. 1991. *Structure and Change in Economic History*, trans. Yu Chen and Huaping Luo. Shanghai Joint Publishing Company, 49–65.

North, Douglass, and Thomas, Robert. 1973. *The Rise of the Western World: A New Economic History*. Cambridge: Cambridge University Press.

North, Douglass, & Thomas, Robert. (1981). *Structure and Change in Economic History*. New York: W. W. Norton.

North, Douglass, & Thomas, Robert. (1990). *Institutions, Institutional Change and Economic Performance*. Cambridge: Cambridge University Press.

Planning Department of Ministry of Agriculture, Animal Husbandry and Fisheries. *Information on Rural Economy (NJZ) (1949–1983).* Ministry of Agriculture, Animal Husbandry and Fisheries.
Publishing Committee of China Agriculture Yearbook. *China Agriculture Yearbook (1980–1987).* China Agriculture Press.
Qiu, Jicheng. 1988. Township Enterprises: Basic Clues from Community (Government) Management Mode. In *Development Research*, ed. Guodu Li, 744–768. Beijing Normal University Press, 1990.
Rankin, Mary Backus. 1986. *Elite Activism and Political Transformation in China.* Stanford: Stanford University Press.
Rowe, William. 1984. *Hakow: Commerce and Society in a Chinese City 1796–1889.* Stanford: Stanford University Press.
Schultz, Theodore W. 1953. *The Economic Organization of Agriculture.* New York: McGraw-Hill.
Scott, James C. (1976). *The Moral Economy of the Peasant: Rebellion and Subsistence in Southeast Asia.* New Haven: Yale University Press.
Selden, Mark. 1971. *The Yenan Way in Revolutionary China.* Cambridge: Harvard University Press.
Sheng, Hong, and Yu Chen. 1990. Preface to Translation. In *Enterprises, Market and Law.* Shanghai Joint Publishing Company.
Song, Guoqing. 1982. *Economic Growth and Economic Structure.* Encyclopedia of China Publishing House.
Strand, David. 1987. *Rickshaw Beijing: City People and Politics in the 1920s.* Berkeley: University of California Press.
Wakeman, Frederic, Jr. (1993). The Civil Society and Public Sphere Debate: Western Reflections on Chinese Political Culture. *Modem China, 19*(2), 108–138.
Wang, Yeh-chien. 1973. *Land Taxation in Imperial China, 1750–1911.* Cambridge: Harvard University Press.
Wang, Gengjin, and Xuansan Zhuang. 1993. *The Research on China's Agriculture Modernization and Accumulation.* Shanxi Economic Press.
Wu, Xiang. 1980. Bright Broad Road and Single-Log Bridge. *People's Daily*, November 5.
Wu, Jinglian. 1989. Review and Thoughts A Decade of Development and Reform. *Learning Materials for Economic Workers* (59): 51–88.
Wen, Guanzhong James. 1989. The Current Land Tenure System and Its Impact on Long Term Performance of Farming Sector: The Case of Modern China. Ph.D. Dissertation, University of Chicago.
Yang, C. K. 1959. *Chinese Communist Society: The Family and the Village.* Cambridge: MIT Press.
Yang, Xiaokai, Jianguo Wang, and Ian Wills. 1992. Economic Growth, Commercialization, and Institutional Changes in Rural China, 1979–1987. *China Economic Review* 3 (1) (Spring): 1–37.
Yang, Xiaokai, Jianguo Wang, and Ian Wills. 1993. Economics of Property Rights and Chinese Reform. The Hainan Conference Papers.
Zhou, Qiren. 1988. Land Institution: Effective Property Right, Long-Term Tenancy and Paid Transfer. In *Economic Reference Information.*
Zhou, Qiren (ed.). 1993. *Rural Reform and China's Development (1979–1989).* Hong Kong: Oxford University Press (China).
Zhou, Qiren, and Shouying Liu. 1988. *Change in Land Institution in Meitan, a Traditional Agricultural Region.* Development Research Report No. 7. Development Research Institute of Agriculture Research Center Under the State Council.

Chapter 4
Farmers, Market, and Institutional Innovation: Deep Reform Faced by Rural Areas After Household Responsibility System

It has been eight years since the re-launch of the household responsibility system (HRS) in 1978 in Anhui, Sichuan, and some other places. With simple motive and approach, this reform has reversed the rural economic and political situation that was deeply mired in the "socialist impoverishment" and contributed to the remarkable great liberation of China's rural productivity.

Like many great reforms in history, the problems sparked by the HRS reform are more extensive and profound than the ones it directly solved. While domestic and overseas public opinions are applauding the success of China's rural reform, deeper-level reform tasks, along with their complexity, have all of a sudden sprouted from the reality of rural areas. More and more farmers, rural workers, and researchers have expressed their puzzlement about the new problems faced by the rural areas and the solutions thereof. This reality, which should not be concealed or evaded, indicates that to develop large-scale modern commodity economy, is to go beyond all previous experiences accumulated in rural China.

To face up to the task of deepening China's rural reform and explore the solutions is the best commemoration for the 8th anniversary of HRS. The task of the deep reform is initiated by the history of the reform. Therefore, a re-visit of the recent history can help us better understand the new task.

The first draft of this article was completed in October 1986, and the revision was completed in December 1986. DAI Xiaojing also participated in the writing. Many colleagues at the Development Research Institute have contributed to the discussion and revision, and the article was published in the name of "Comprehensive Research Task Force of the Development Research Institute" in *Economic Research*, Issue No. 1-1997.

Q. Zhou, *Property Rights and Changes in China*,
https://doi.org/10.1007/978-981-15-9885-2_4

4.1 Property Rights and Freedom of Identity: Dual Liberation for Farmers

Farmers are the main subject of the rural reform. The reform liberates productivity forces, but more importantly, it liberates the labor. The central clue of the chronicle for HRS is the changes in the status of farmers. The property rights are of fundamental significance in economic terms.

Before the reform, Chinese farmers only possessed a little property. In 1978, each rural household had an average of 3.64 rooms with an estimated value of no more than 500 yuan, a saving of 32.09 yuan at the end of the year; a small amount of savings in kind, such as grains and livestock and negligible number of simple farming tools. It is estimated that the total assets of all Chinese farmers was less than 80 billion yuan. Each household in the agricultural area had 0.5-0.7 *mu* (about 333–466 m^2) of private plot, which was still owned by the collective but used by the household to serve, in principle, only the purpose of supplying vegetable and some ration to the family. For the pastoral area, the family also had a few domestic animals. Considering the large amounts of debt owed to state banks, credit co-operatives, and production teams in those days, the pre-reform Chinese farmers were almost rural proletarians. This is the result of the cancellation of the land-based dividend system by advanced co-operatives more than 20 years before in 1956.

Back then, the only owner of the rural property was the people's commune as the collective. According to a sample survey, in 1978, the fixed assets of each commune was 3.059 million yuan, and the estimated national total was 161.46 billion yuan, and the valuation of China's total collective farmland was 1,266.5 billion yuan. In addition, there were 5.56 billion yuan of collective deposits and some public grain stocks. Minus the collective debts, the total assets of the people's communes was about 1.4335 trillion yuan, of which 88.4% was in the form of land property.

During the socialist transformation in the mid-to-late 1950s, almost all of the property belonged to the collective. The movement featured by "too demanding, too fast, and too rough" left a series of serious problems. As the theoretical masters of the collective economy, the farmers were never worthy of this name in regard to their actually relationship with collective property. The "integrating government with community" system resulted in the affiliation of property rights to administrative power. Due to the innate blurred boundaries between different levels within the system, even the subsequent so-called "three-level ownership" (communes, production brigades and production teams) did not work, and the institution became precisely the reason for "egalitarianism in distribution and unpaid appropriation from subordinates" widely practiced by the people's commune. Within each-level of the collective, no consistent and legally-assured norms were established for the formation and control of public property and the distribution of income therefrom. The stormy political movements also could never work to protect collective property, as at least proven by the massive "*Four Clean-ups" Movement* ("Four clean-ups" was a term for the socialist education movement—aimed at cleaning things up in the political, economic, organizational and ideological fields—which was carried out between 1963 and May 1966 in some rural areas and a small number of urban factories, mines, enterprises, and schools—notes by the translator). In fact, before the reform, the "collective public property relationship" was not the common true reality for the vast rural areas, and in many places the collective property publicly owned by the working farmers were very badly eroded. This naturally could not win the basic confidence with the collective economy from the farmers, who even didn't see the collective property as public property in which they themselves had a share. Very commonly in those days, farmers were low-spirited when working on the "collective property", the productivity of collective land was roughly only 1/7–1/5 of that of their private plots, and they had little interest in or sense of responsibility for community public affairs. Some farmers even participated as well in the encroachment of collective property whenever the chance allowed.

Before the reform, the rural economic system also imposed various restrictions on the freedom of farmers to choose jobs, migrate, and change their social status. Before the mid-1950s, farmers enjoyed considerable freedom in recruitment, relocating, and means of living, but things turned around soon after. The "Great Leap Forward" initiated in the late 1950s, moved nearly 20 million people back to the countryside in the early 1960s. Since then, the non-agriculturization of the rural labor force and urbanization became stagnated. The ration system, the work-points system, and the household residence registration (or Hukou) system of the people's commune were strengthened to prevent farmers from migration and to bind them to the farmland. By the era of "using proletariat dictatorship to run agriculture", farmers lost not only all the freedom to change their social status, but also to a great extent the freedom on how to farm. "Proletarian" as they were, they were never "as free as like birds" back then, generating far-reaching adverse impact on economic development and improvement of the quality of the population.

In 1978, the per capita annual net income of China's farmers was 133.57 yuan,[1] increasing by 60.62 yuan over 1975, with an average annual growth rate of only 2.9%.[2] About 200 million people could not feed themselves that year. A report from a provincial party committee of an impoverished region at that time says: "In the past we deprived the farmers of not only their property, but also their freedom. These are the two important root causes for their almost unchanged poverty in the past few decades. So far they have not yet risen to fight back mainly because our Party had a very strong "flesh-and-blood" relationship with them during the wartime, we then ended the war and established the people's regime, bringing them several decades of peaceful life. However, if we still do not make major adjustments to previous rural policies, the farmers will eventually take up their shoulder-poles and fight." These cautionary words was obviously applicable to not just poor areas.

For hundreds of millions of farmers, there was no basic protection to their property rights, and the freedom of identity was strictly restricted, and this cannot be fully explained just by the ideological "misunderstanding" of Marx's doctrine. Economically, it all comes down to the special difficulties faced by China's industrialization

[1]NBS (1984: 9).

[2]NBS (1984: 5–7).

and its choice of solutions. Industrialization requires huge amounts of capital. For a backward agricultural country, the main source of capital accumulation can only be "the tribute from farmers". The "tribute" can be overt, such as the heavy rents and taxes during the Meiji reign in Japan; it can also be covert, such as price scissors. China opted for the latter: The agricultural products were set by the country at low prices, uniformly purchased from the farmers, and uniformly sold also at low prices to urban residents and industrial enterprises so as to maintain low wage and low raw material costs for large enterprises to enable them to create excess profits. Finally, by collecting taxes and profits from these industrial enterprises, the construction fund for industrialization was centralized.[3] This is the economic substance of the unified purchase and marketing system (UPMS). However, the unified low-price purchases would always cause dissatisfaction from farmers. Hence, a series of supporting measures were adopted with inherent logic.

Regarding production, the farmers' independent land was merged and consolidated, land loss was strictly prohibited to prevent the price increase of agricultural products driven by land rent; the flow of agricultural labor was restricted to suppress the opportunity cost of labor so as to maintain the low wage cost for agricultural products.

Regarding distribution, on the one hand, farmers' produce was set at low prices and uniformly purchased, on the other, low-cost supply of agricultural production materials and free investment were provided as compensation. Urban residents were given low-priced food and other fringe benefits on the one hand, and paid with a low salary on the other.

Regarding circulation, the purchase and sales were monopolized by the state, markets were closed, inter-regional trading restricted, and long-distance selling banned.

The UPMS served the country's industrialization purpose and formed quite a complete system. Its organizational foundation in the countryside is the people's commune where government administration and commune management were integrated.[4]

This way, although the farmers' rights and status of freedom before the reform had pre-modernization features, they served the basic target of the modernization (industrialization) process. It is estimated that the total tribute from farmers hidden in the form of price scissors in the past 30 years is over 600 billion yuan, definitely a historic contribution to China's industrialization.

The problem lies not in the historical necessity of farmers' tribute, but in the efficiency of this approach. The general policy direction of the UPMS is to curb the development of the commodity economy in China; however, the industrialization of the backward country still felt the strong impulse from the commodity economy day in and day out. The original economic system had to be beefed up by iron hands of ideology and politics. Otherwise, the spontaneous development of the commodity economy would change the economic progress of the early stage industrialization.

[3]Song Guoqing and Luo Xiaopeng (1985).

[4]Gao Xiaomeng (1986).

The high-intensity resource mobilization has laid the material foundation for China's industrialization, but to absorb the products and improve the efficiency of industrialization has to rely on a full-fledged commodity economy.[5] In the countryside, it was already discovered during the introduction of the advanced co-operatives or the people's commune that productivity would be shackled by depriving the farmers of their property rights and restricting their freedom of identity. In the second half of 1955, the first wave of household responsibility system was initiated in Yongjia County, Zhejiang Province. For more than subsequent 20 years, the "capitalism" was denounced but didn't die out, and the "small production forces" were attacked but never knocked out. This conversely proves that the existing system was only a suppression of the inherent conflicts in economic life, but it could never be the solution. During this period, the direction of use of state power was inconsistent with, or even against, the needs of the social system, thus it was impossible for the reform to come true. Farmers' passive resistance to the people's commune system was reflected in the extremely low agricultural productivity: the shortfall in agricultural products supply, the poverty of farmers, and a confined domestic market—all becoming the bottlenecks for the country's economic development. The repeating realities seemed to suggest everything was already determined by the natural conditions: the weather is so, the land is so, the farmer is so, and the agriculture is so and so. Who could change this?

Reform has become a weather vane to change the unreasonable situation. At the end of the 1970s, the immediately-rewarding household responsibility system introduced first to the most poverty-stricken places turned out to suggest that there was another solution to all these problems. Encouraged by the thoughts and policies from the Third Plenary Session of the Eleventh CPCCC, it only took two to three years for the HRS to sweep across the country. Just like a thunder, it broke the darkness and revealed a basic fact: almost all farmers supported a fundamental reform to the people's commune system. By the end of 1984, only less than 2,000 out of the total 5.69 million production teams in China continued with the old unified operating model, accounting for only 0.04%, all the rest opted for yield-based or land-based HRS.

The HRS reform didn't uphold the flag of "reforming the ownership". However, since day one, a necessary prerequisite for HRS was to contract collective property (mainly land and agricultural machinery and tools) to individual households. The result dramatically stimulated the increase in total output and surplus products, which in turn enabled farmers to reinvest their portion of the surplus products and gradually obtain private property. The intrinsic link between the contracted collective property and the formation of the farmer's private property didn't attract any attention until quite late, but looking back, it was the starting point for the transformation of the relationship in rural property rights.

Subsequently, the forms of the original collective property were fundamentally changed. The changes can be seen in the following: (1) The collectively-owned property, mainly all the farmland, and a considerable part of water surface, pasture,

[5]China Rural Development Research Task Force (1987).

forest, mudflats, etc., were contracted to farmers for independent operation, with the income shared between the farmers and the collective, and the term had mostly been extended to more than 15 years after 1984. In 1985, the total value of farmland in China was 2 trillion yuan, and the average per household contracted was 10,500 yuan. (2) Other collective livestock and large to medium-sized agricultural machinery, etc. were sold to farmers, and the money went to the collective. As of the end of 1985, the collective assets sold to farmers amounted to more than 20 billion yuan. (3) As for the assets of rural enterprises, or PBEs, some were contracted to enterprise collective or the directors (managers), some were returned to production teams/brigades and farmers at discounted prices and turned into new enterprise entities after absorbing new shares, and still some, sold to individual farmers at a discount. As of the end of 1985, the total fixed assets (the original value) of China's township and village enterprises was 75.038 billion yuan, over 90% of which were contracted or converted into shares in various forms.

Reform has re-established farmers' private property rights. According to a survey, in 1985, the average total value of production fixed assets, private housing, cash in hand and saving deposit, and surplus grains owned per rural household was 3,821.77 yuan. The total assets of all rural households was estimated to be above 700 billion yuan. This part of the wealth was growing the fastest, increasing by 1.68 times in real terms as compared to 1981, representing an average annual growth rate of 27.37%.

To cope with the need to expand operations, a large number of property entities have been created based on partial ownership and moved beyond the scale of household operations and differed from the collective mode: new joint ventures, co-operative enterprises, and private enterprises, to name a few. In 1985, there were a total of 484,700 new joint ventures above the statistics cut-off line, with a fixed asset of 4.881 billion yuan. In the same year, the total asset of co-operative enterprises owned by commune members and other types of co-operative enterprises was 21 billion yuan. Meanwhile, rural private enterprises were also developing rapidly. According to the statistics in 1985 to a total of 1.293 million specialized households engaged in secondary or tertiary industries, 18,169 of them employed more than eight helpers or apprentices (on average, each employed 10. 97 people). These specialized households were the embryos of private enterprises, with a predicted total asset of about 1 billion yuan.

The above-mentioned changes interweave to draw up a new picture of relationships in China's rural properties. To get a global view, let us use the data with limited accuracy from different sources to draw a general picture for the current landscape: The total rural assets is 3 trillion yuan, of which 2 trillion yuan is collective land contracted to individual households. Productive fixed assets totals 270 billion yuan, 55% of which is owned by farmers, 1.78% by new joint ventures, 42.43% by original collectives, and 0.07% by private enterprises. The value of the non-productive housing assets totals 500 billion yuan, of which 90.6% belongs to farmers. Besides, there is over 200 billion yuan of savings in cash and in kind, over 60% of which is from farmers' households.

Now, most of the farmers' property is non-productive housing (62.42%), and productive fixed assets only accounts for 20.79%. Of the farmers' own productive assets, draft animals, large iron and wood farm tools and machinery for farming, forestry, animal husbandry, and fishery account for 57.4%, plus they have some cash and production materials. All of these must be combined with the contracted collective land to engage in production activities. Before the reform, the collective ownership of land and other properties was achieved through unified management and direct control over income distribution. Now it is achieved through the hand-in by the contracting farmers. In 1985, the average per capita hand-in to the collective from the contracting was 10.79 yuan, and the national total was 9 billion yuan. The total amount of hand-in to the collective plus the profit of township and village enterprises was 6.773 billion yuan in book value (the actual amount should be more). So, the total annual income generated for the collective from the property contracting was over 15 billion yuan, representing an increase of 45.6% over 1978 (10.3 billion yuan). Therefore, despite the unavoidable re-distribution of some of the properties, the mainstream of this property rights reform deeply participated by 800 million farmers is to create new property owners amongst the rapidly-growing total property.

Recognizing the property rights of farmers also means to expand their freedom in economic activities. China's total 2 billion *mu* (about 133 million hectares) of farmland seems to be inadequate to absorb its rural labor force of several hundred million. Therefore, to truly expand, their freedom of operation should not be limited only to the freedom to expand agricultural activities, but expanded to include the freedom to engage in non-agricultural sectors and further the freedom to change their social identities. Since 1978, the CPCCC and the State Council have promulgated a series of important policy documents, gradually removing the restrictions on farmers' freedom in economic operations from the previous system. The changes range from recognition of diversified forms of operations, clear positioning of PBEs, legalization of different ownerships and economic forms, allowing assignment of land contracting, promoting prosperity of small towns, and all the way to allowing farmers to migrate to cities for various industrial, commercial or tertiary industry activities, and even allowing them to register their permanent residence (namely Hukou) in cities without food rations. All these are directional changes that couldn't be even imagined in the previous few decades.

Between 1979 and 1985, 45.772 million rural labors in China transferred from agricultural and sideline sectors to non-agricultural sectors. In the same period, the urban population increased by 127 million, and there were another millions of farmers who made a living in various ways in cities as a migrating population. Every year about six million rural labors left their villages to become temporary workers. About one million jobs out of the new jobs in cities were taken by farmers every year. That is to say, over the past few years about one-fifth of the farmers have changed their employment, place of residence, and social identity, leading to substantial changes in their lifestyles, production methods, and ways of social interaction. In 1989, there were as many as 12 categories of labors from towns and villages, and 19% of them were engaged in sectors other than farming, forestry, animal husbandry, sideline, and fishery on a non-seasonal and temporary basis. These "farmers", who now actually played a new role in the society, are different from the urban residents under the previous system only in two aspects: (1) they are not entitled to enjoy the social welfare from the government; (2) they are still somewhat linked with the farmland. But obviously they are no more the farmers in the traditional sense. That indicates that the freedom of free trading, of jobs, and of social identity for China's farmers, or 80% of the country's population has been significantly improved to cope with the need from economic and social development.

Property rights and freedom of identity are the two magic weapons for HRS. These weapons evoked the love of hundreds of millions of Chinese farmers for land, their enthusiasm for work, and their vision for life. Between 1979 and 1985, the rapid growth of China's agriculture and rural economy was unusual not only for China in its own history, but also for all post-war major economies. There were many factors at play, including cumulative materials conditions, potential market size, and fiscal factors. However, all these factors could not function effectively without the enthusiasm of the farmers. The real secret behind China's extraordinary agricultural growth is the reform. This fact helps draw the lesson as to how to adopt the cause of socialism for countries with farmers being the majority of the population: in no case should the government use political power to deprive farmers of their property and restrict their freedom. If socialism attempts to reduce farmers to proletarians and then force them to participate in "socialist construction", then this proposition is bound to face passive yet insurmountable resistance from the farmers. Wherever this happens, the cost will be a stagnant rural productivity. Conversely, as long as the mistake is corrected for any place, it will be rewarded with enormous economic and political benefits even in a short time.

4.2 Conflicts and Frictions-Ridden Primary Development of Rural Commodity Production

The emergence of multiple types of owners, re-construction of rural property structure, and noticeable improvement in farmers freedom in social identity with the development of the division of labor, all require a large-scale development of the rural area commodity-currency relationship so as to meet the needs of the situation. From 1979 to 1985, the total amount of purchase of agricultural and sideline products in China increased by two folds. If the amount of village fair trading and the amount of non-agricultural products sales in rural areas are included, the total commodity rate in rural China has reached 63.9% in 1985, and the per capita cash income of farmers accounts for 65.3% of the total income. At present, more than 50% of the purchasing power is from farmers, and more than 60% of retail goods are sold to rural areas. At the same time, 60.42% of the total money stock in the society is also in the hands of farmers. Never before have Chinese farmers been associated with such large-scale commodity trading and currency utilization. This is indeed a historic leap.

Interestingly, the development of the rural commodity-currency relationship was driven even also by the fiscal pressure. In 1979, the government substantially increased the purchase prices of agricultural and sideline products, and this move played a significant role. However, the adjustment alone was not enough to solve the problem. The newly increased purchase prices still could not sensitively reflect the changes in the value of agricultural products and their market supply and demand dynamics; but on the other hand, the sales prices remained almost unchanged, and led fiscally to a massive reversed price gap between the purchase and the sales. Thus, the better the harvest, the more acute the problem with fiscal burden, currency and inflation. This unreasonable reality cast a shadow onto the overall reform in the making. At the end of 1984, the quantity of commodities and agro-produce from farmers reached a historical high, but the government, the largest buyer, was badly caught in the midst of a trouble: it could not buy, sell, store, or transport and transfer so much volume. The fiscal income, as the central nervous system of national economy, became so distressed that it would be unable to sustain if the mistake didn't get corrected.

The essence of the then problem was the progress made at the micro-level reform to the people's communes was in conflict with the overall system of the national economy. At the beginning of 1985, the CPCCC and the State Council announced a nationwide reform to the 30-year-old UPMS for agricultural products, put an end to the unified government purchase and sales for grains and replaced it with the contract-based purchase system (CPS) from that current year onwards. The foundation of this decision is a series of reforms to agricultural circulation after 1979: restoring the village fair, breaking the monopoly with multi-channel businesses, and gradually liberalizing the purchase and sales prices of most agricultural products. However, grain was, after all, the high-voltage line for China's economy. Therefore, it is fair to say that to reform the grain system was the most daring decision in the history of the reform.

This reform touched the foundation for China's economic system and previous development strategies. The fundamental feature of UPMS is that the commodity purchase and sales is only the phenomenon, but the essence is the direct distribution of national income, which was completed via exchange: every time farmers sell agricultural products, they hand in some contribution; every time workers buy agricultural products, they obtain some welfare. Now, for the superficial "buying and selling" to move into market-based exchange of equivalent value, the fundamental interests of all producers, consumers, and business owners will have to be involved, and the forms of organizations for the operation of the entire economy have to be profoundly changed.

From 1979 to 1984, the extraordinary growth of China's agriculture, especially in crop production, accumulated abundant reserve of agricultural products, which provided a favorable condition for reforming the UPMS. However, the necessity of reform is not rooted from "increased agricultural products". It is a common sense to all that China is short of agricultural resources as compared against its population, and its per capita agricultural products supply is far below developed countries and even lower than the world average. It is precisely the scarcity of China's land resources and the relative shortage of other agricultural resources that make this reform more urgent and more important than other countries. The reason is very simple, because after the problem of subsistence is solved, if we indulge low food prices which embed all sorts of subsidies and welfare to artificially stimulate the demand, and if the scope of mandatory supply extends from daily necessities to non-necessities (such as meat), then we will have big problems with mid to long-term development of the economy. The former Soviet Union and some Eastern Europe countries subsidized their meat supply, which led to excessive consumption; as a result, when the per capita GNP was 100 US dollars, the Engel coefficient of these countries was ten percentage points higher than Western countries at the stage of the same income level.[6] We should learn something from this lesson. China's land resources are scarcer than the former Soviet Union and Eastern Europe. Therefore, it is strategically meaningful for long term development to make the bold move and introduce the market mechanism into food (especially meat) supply and demand right after the need for subsistence is satisfied. Hence this reform will be launched sooner or later, and it cannot be avoided ever.

More importantly, subsidized welfare was realized through UPMS. Although it helped maintain low wages with cheap food and guaranteed hand-in of high profits with cheap raw materials, it also distorted the real prices for factors from agricultural production in the process of industrialization, thus weakening the adaptability of enterprises to price changes of factors. This is an important reason for the absence of cost awareness across the entire social and economic system and the low profitability. From 1952 to 1981, China's average annual growth for comprehensive economic factors input was as high as 6.3%, but its annual average growth rate for added value was only 6%, meaning the comprehensive factor productivity was decreasing by 0.3% every year. This shows that although China's original system had a strong economic resource mobilization capability, the efficiency was extremely low for these resources mobilized with intense efforts. If the original system is not reformed to fully turn around this hard-to-accept fact, China's modernization will not stand a chance.

The indisputable necessity of reform does not automatically guarantee its success. It must now be acknowledged that the complexity of the reform was underestimated. If we are to openly announce the general assessment of the UPMS reform which kicked off two years ago, it is fair to say that although the reform has generated a significant impact on the old system, its primary goal has yet to be reached, and the threat from backpedaling has not been eradicated.

In practice, two prominent kinds of problems may have a decisive influence on the success or failure of the reform: (1) The purchase and sales of some agricultural products were not truly liberalized, moving back and forth from time to time. (2) Some of the liberalized products faced drastic supply and demand volatility and caused market shake. Grain was a typical case for the first circumstances. The initial approach of the reform was to abrogate the UPMS and replace it with the contract-based purchase system (CPS). The method worked in 1984 when farmers found it difficult to sell grains and hoped that the government could buy more. The most critical condition back then was the gradual decline of grain prices in the (free) market to below the (government) purchase prices. But the real problem was that the main factors supporting the critical condition were changing: the burden of financial subsidies

[6]Liu Yunzhi (1985: 92).

was too heavy and needed to be alleviated; the prices of industrial products used for agriculture started to rise sharply; farmers naturally cut down their investment into farming and reduced the acreage of planting in response to several consecutive difficult years of selling grains; and some non-planting sectors were being identified to make money. These factors worked together to lead to, 10% contractual grain price drop in the spring of 1985 from the previous year on the one hand, and a recovery of free market prices that summer and autumn on the other. Purely from the perspective of grain supply and demand, the changes were normal, and they did not lead to grain supply crisis. The real crisis was with the reform: when the market price was higher than the contractual price, the farmers were not willing to enter into contracts, and the grain purchase volume actually became less guaranteed as compared against the previous year; yet the sales volume could not be reduced accordingly. Hence, the "panic" about "whether or not the new system can guarantee supply" appeared first in the sales regions and then spread to the production regions. To increase the contractual purchase price just by several fen (1 RMB yuan = 100 fen) per jin (weight measurement unit in China, 1 jin = 0.5 kg), the total amount would be too huge a fiscal hole for the authority at any level. To exchange with industrial products, was not very realizable. To subsidize agriculture with industrial profits from township enterprises, it would not work globally for China. The most uncertain factor was the grain price trend in the market. No one knew what short and medium-term impact the overall price situation would bring to grains. The boundary for the reform was guarantee that there should be no supply interruption. Therefore, the government had to announce to farmers that the purchase was mandatory and must be fulfilled even if they were not willing to do so. So to speak, "the UPMS was thrown out of the window but came back through the gate and climbed onto the back of CPS". The supporting measures were also readily available, namely restricting the village fairs within the region ("The grain market would not open until farmers fulfilled their contracts") and blocking inter-region grain transactions. The difference was that the volume under CPS was even higher, and the requirement on variety was even tighter than under UPMS. That is why from 1985 to 1986 many farmers were complaining that the CPS was even a more unified system than UPMS. This is the circumstance for "not truly liberalized".

The other circumstance was the drastic volatility in the supply and demand, which was quite common for liberalized agricultural products, such as pork, vegetables, poultry, eggs, fruits, fisheries, and hemp. Sharp price hikes and dips are often followed by steep production rises and falls, resulting in alternating cycles of severe excess and severe shortage for the same agricultural product. Products with high elasticity of substitution (e.g. aquatic products) were less affected by drastic fluctuations and converged more easily, and products with low elasticity were much more affected by excessive volatility and prone to market shock, bringing catastrophic consequences for both supply and demand.

From the above two aspects, we can see that the reform was hitting the wall, and needed to find a solution. At this point, the whole society was reflecting: Why should we introduce the market mechanism? Why should we suffer the pain? It seemed that all the prerequisites of the reform and the already-solved problems now come back like strangers in front of farmers, commercial organizations, consumers, and government agencies. If we cannot reach basic consensus in identifying the problem and seize the true root of deepening the reform, the enthusiasm for the reform will surely be dampened, and people may hear the laughter of the old system from the dark: "The market mechanism is like hell, come back!"

4.3 Market Presentation and Underlying Structure

The boundary to distinguish the elementary development of the commodity-currency relationship and market mechanism is a key. The market mechanism is usually described as follows: (1) Producers make independent choices and decisions based on different returns from producing different products; (2) Consumers' purchase behaviors are restricted fully by their income, credit, and consumption preferences; (3) The proportion of factor resource that each product consumes is subject to the demand structure of the purchasing power of the society; (4) The supply/demand conflict is reflected by price changes and regulated by the impact on economic behaviors of producers and consumers.[7] However, we should go further and think about the question: what underlying structures such as norms, common code of conduct and organizational vehicles must be created to enable the price signal to powerfully drive both producers and consumers to react as expected?

From the perspective of economic realities, the underlying structure of the market includes two main points. First, the interests of economic units of the society shall be independent and translated into clear property rights, which is the result of the joint effect of the development of the division of labor and the disintegration of various dependent social relations. Independent economic personality constitutes the primary driving force for the universalization of commodity exchange, and only the establishment of a property rights system with exclusivity protected by law can force all economic units of the whole society, without any exception, to seek their interests through fair competition, and to follow the rules and complete their exchange through equal transactions. Clear and independent ownership is the most basic structure of the market mechanism.

In order to avoid becoming a "legal fantasy", ownership must include a full range of specific economic behavioral norms, which constitute the second point of the underlying structure of the market: sound business laws and regulations. Any country with a developed commodity economy follows very sound civil and commercial laws and regulations as the basis for all of its economic activities. On this basis, most people are strictly trained to act in accordance with the principles of the contract. Without this condition, the primary commodity-currency relationship would only result in widespread infringements. It is off the topic to discuss "market mechanism" or "deepening of the market reform" without property ownership and systematic commercial laws and regulations.

---

[7] Virlyn W. Bruse (1983).

Therefore, the liberalized price and its powerful regulative role in resource allocation are not determined by its own form, but rather by the characteristics of the market's underlying structure. This abstract exposition may help to remind us that we should look into the underlying structure of the society for the real cause for both the distortion of prices and the distortion of their regulative functions.

At present, the basic units of rural areas in China include: farmers' households, multiple forms of enterprises run by farmers, governments at all levels and their economic and technological departments. Viewed from the pre-reform perspective, they all have mutated a lot since the inception of HRS. However, if we use another measure, namely the establishment of an underlying organizational structure that enables the price mechanism to fully function and to regulate resource allocation, we will find that the foundation for the success of the reform is not so solid. Why is the economic system reform starting with HRS trapped in difficulties when it comes to the point to solve the circulation problems by expanding the application of the price mechanism? Perhaps the following analysis will offer some insight. As mentioned before, with the introduction of HRS, the rebuilt independent property rights and the obtained freedom in decision-making for China's farmers has turned them into proactive commodity producers and consumers. Yet they still have two common notable features: First, they are still semi-self-sufficient with different stocks at different degrees. According to a national sample survey in 1985, 34.7% of the total income and 33.5% of the total expense of farmers were still not commoditized. Second, the scale of operations was rather small. The average farmland per household was less than 0.51 hectare, among the smallest in the world. Plus the majority of rural households operated on a variety of land products, industrial, commercial, and sideline businesses, and labor services too, and the scale of each product was very small. Even specialized planting households, which accounted for 1.67% of the total number of households, only had an annual income of 5379.3 yuan per household. Hence this became the restrictions for their economic behaviors as explained below: farmers were unable to make prompt responses and adjust their production and consumption according to price signals; most farmers were more sensitive to input market prices than to output market prices, and only a few very specialized and large-scale households were the opposite; the farmers had little strength to withstand price fluctuations. It was quite common that they could only afford to win but could not afford to lose, and it was very difficult for them to make "reverse adjustment" based on the cyclical price fluctuations; once the environment became too unfavorable, most farmers would simply defend themselves through buying less and selling less, and increasing self-sufficiency. These behaviors can all be regarded as rational, as they are the rational responses made by the farmers after the trade-off between long-term and short-term interests to seek the maximum benefit.[8] The "abnormal" behaviors are actually just the normal reactions to the abnormal environment.

With this we understand why the more are farmers driven by the independent property right to pursue monetary benefits, the higher requirements will they have on the business environment. Therefore, to maintain and develop an environment

[8]Huang Zongzhi (1986).

that continuously satisfies the increasingly complex needs of the farmers and gives them long-term incentives, has become the most important condition for sustained economic growth after the HRS reform.

Which organizations are responsible for meeting these requirements? First are the economic and technical departments (including production technology, commerce, finance, etc.) of governments at all levels in rural areas. This system is indeed the "main channel" for China's rural input and output. Serving the UPMS for a long time, this system had the following organizational characteristics: they are highly dependent on vertical administrative power and exercise control by fully following administrative orders. In order to assure supply, they did not need to respect any property rights or follow the principle of equal transaction. After the reform, primary monetization started to penetrate into the departmental system, making the interests of each chain and each unit relatively independent, and forming a complex driving structure to run after multiple objectives (ranging from completing the task assigned by higher authorities, expanding commercial services to getting more bonus for their own departments). The problem is not that different departments and localities have their own respective independent interests, but whether or not these interests can only be obtained by following the same rules. The actual current situation is that the interests of the "semi-marketized" localities and departments have both the power of administrative monopoly and the motive of pursuing self-interest. When things do not go their way, they have the luxury to over-ride the norms for ordinary commodity producers and adopt special methods such as mandatory orders, blocking markets, jacking up monopolized prices, arbitrary penalties, and even extortion. The organizational blur between the government and the enterprise leads to behavioral mixing-up of administrative activities and commercial activities. This way even the most formal organization becomes un-organized. A township tax office in Anhui, surprisingly, even ordered "big contributors" not to record some things in the accounting so as to line its own pockets. This is an important reason for such a phenomenon that "if producers' price goes up by one cent, the intermediary's price will go up by three" since the reform on agricultural product prices.

As a counterbalance, some farmers organized themselves and entered circulation. In 1985, there were a total of 147,000 farmers' commercial enterprises, plus 3.25 million self-employed businessmen from cities. However, regarding the effectiveness of farmers' self-organizations, once the premise went out of the local village fair, the external risks suddenly got much higher, and the farmers found their organizations unadaptable in terms of business scale, economic strength, and internal organizational characteristics, making them unable to secure a stable market share from the bigger commercial environment. The transaction costs for all self-organizations to engage in large-scale commercial activities were extremely high. This perhaps explains why most farmer circulation teams could only make a difference in high-profit businesses, but could not provide stable and large-scale pre-production and post-production services to farmers. In 1986 when the UPMS reform encountered obstacles, the spontaneous business organizations of farmers didn't became the main cornerstone, but their number shrank dramatically.

The problem does not end here. Farmers go to the market via "intermediaries" to serve urban residents and factories on the other side of the market. Along this long channel chain, the price regulation exerts an asymmetrical impact on the supply and demand sides. Previously there were already important differences between urban and rural systems, and their reforms didn't started at the same time, the degree of monetization of the relationship of the country with farmers went up first, and the same with urban residents and factories was still very low. Major agricultural products such as grains and cotton were still marketed at low prices by the state. Therefore, the sales volume and prices made no response to whatever producer prices. The prices of other products such as vegetables, pork, and certain industrial raw materials were liberalized; but as urban workers and residents were at a strong negotiating position, they could transmit the price pressure to enterprises and institutions, even bigger increases in industrial products prices, or to the government finance. The government finance is not the ultimate one to bear the final load, as it can take some measures to ease the pressure, such as internal sharing between central and local finance, over-drawing from banks, and shifting expenditures (such as reducing the financial support to agriculture when the produce prices rise). If these methods are still not enough, the government comes up again to reset the low prices for the supply from farmers. Behind this asymmetric price pressure transmission system are the enterprises attached to administrative power in the organizational structure of the urban economic system and the urban residents, of whom the government takes full care. This tradition has become a huge inertia for the vested interests, making the reform even harder than for rural areas.

The pressure of agricultural price reform is directly or indirectly transmitted back to the farmers who have just cheered for the reform. They are the ultimate one to bear the risks and pressure from China's economic reform. Farmers do have got some benefit from the price increase of some agricultural products, but these benefits are soon offset by bigger increase in industrial products prices and by all sorts of higher intermediary costs. Econometric studies have shown that after 1985, the coefficient between farmer-generated national income and their earned national income is reversed, which in turn has to degrade their interest in technological innovation and accumulation. According to sample surveys, the contracting households and their combinations (including private enterprises) have become the main investors for production in rural areas. However, the ratio of productive fixed assets investment by farmers to their total expenditures began to decline after reaching its peak (5.7%) in 1983: 4.7% for 1984, 3.8% for 1985, and 3.43% for the first three quarters of 1986. What is more noteworthy is that once the farmers, after their subsistence is resolved, go back to the self-sufficiency economy to avoid market risks, the traditional rural customs will easily devour their limited capabilities for accumulation. In 1985, every rural household in Jingzhou, Hubei Province, spent about 200 yuan on entertaining relatives and friends and gift giving. The costs of weddings and funerals in Fengyang County, Anhui Province, were almost 5–10 times higher than 5 years ago. Nationally, the market volatility in 1985 and the concurrent acute problems with agricultural input were by no means only a problem of quantity as indicated by superficial observations.

The relapse in the UPMS reform has even weakened the solidification and stability of the most important achievement of the current rural reform, e.g. the contracting economy, which is a hybrid system of rights that encompasses both public property (land and PBEs) and some private property of the farmers. However, to date, with the absence of clear legal regulation to govern the rights and obligations of both parties within the contracting economy, many of the most basic rights are often violated in various forms and degrees rather than solidly protected. For example, the farmland contracting right only enjoys non-standardized protection by its characteristics of following the "population-base equal distribution". Even so, the freedom to plant and the right to sell products, both closely related to the contracting, are often subject to a variety of arbitrary interventions due to the unsuccessful first step of the reform. The rising "taxes and fees" become too heavy for contractors. In addition, the demographic changes of rural households often put pressure on the long-term farmland contracting, leading to further distribution or re-distribution of land. This fatal difficulty has to do with the failure to establish transfer rules for land contracting rights. All this means the policy goal of "maintaining long-term land contracting without change" cannot be protected with an institution; and in turn, it will compromise the progress to adopt price mechanism to China's rural economy.

To make a succinct analysis of the difficulties of reform, our conclusion is that the productivity gain from HRS is being offset by the shooting-up transaction costs due to the lack of a thorough deep-level structural reform. People often wonder why with more supply, the prices are still getting higher. One of the important reasons is that although the physical supply (products) does have increased in recent years, "soft infrastructure" (the market organizations and rules that convert products and factors into commodities) are relatively "in short supply." The soaring transaction costs have significantly reduced the possibility of large-scale equivalent value transactions for agricultural products.

The relative strength obviously could not ensure the effectiveness of head-on attack in the rural product price reform. That led to the birth of the "dual-track system", with the original intention of gradually moving towards the objective of the reform, the full formation of price mechanism. The system used mandatory purchase and sales to maintain the stability of the overall economic situation, and push the rest to "being determined by the market" in the hope to develop new mechanisms and foster substituents. It was hoped that the full price mechanism would be established through the long-term change in relative strength. However, we should not evade from the deep contradictions of the "dual-track system". The parallel operation and safe compatibility like a rail track between the administrative mandatory plan and the market price mechanism is still, as of today, only a wishful assumption. The empirical facts from the agricultural products price reform show that the two of them tend to confront much more than co-exist. The township/village fair trading has long been in existence outside the UPMS, but the stable growth is hindered from time to time, and such markets are even closed up sometimes. Moreover, the administrative system can continuously expand its power under the pretext of securing the supply of agricultural products so as to enhance their negotiation power. At the same time, the system's responsibility in securing supply automatically shrinks as they can shift any market pressure towards government finance and the farmers. The "market track" is always a supplement that cannot grow into a substituent. Therefore, the key to the problem lies in whether or not to launch a timely, thorough deep structural reform during the dual-track transition; without such reform efforts, the dual-track system won't automatically evolve into the elixir for full price mechanism.

4.4 Redefining the Reform: From Organizational Innovation to Institutional Innovation

The difficulties encountered in the deep reform do not have quick fixes, because when we study the problems from the deep structure, we will find that there are no effective modern intermediary commercial organizations to continuously cut down the rising the transaction costs that comes along with the development of the commodity-currency relationship. Specifically, the agricultural price reform has encountered an organizational crisis, and unlike farmer household operations, there are no traditional organizational resources readily available.

China's historical heritage in terms of organizational resources is a bipolar structure: the centralized government and the family clans. In-between, there is neither the tradition or experience of community or local autonomy, nor have cities of free citizens emerged. The huge and complex administrative system is connected with scattered and isolated clans by the non-governmental and non-private village-level organizations. The lack of effective intermediary organizations makes it especially vulnerable. The great merits continuously achieved by the vertical administrative system via highly centralized national resources are always obtained at increasingly larger management costs. Once the tolerable limit of the clans is exceeded, the control will fail, and chaos will occur. The founding of the People's Republic of China has put an end to the loose-sand situation and achieved unprecedented unification. This is a favorable political condition that has never existed since the 19th century. Basically, by relying on its own strength, China has launched extensive and profound social reforms, carried out large-scale economic construction, and achieved outstanding achievements in industrialization. More than 30 years of history demonstrates that China has strong capabilities to mobilize social resources,[9] which is uncommon for developing countries. With the help of Party organizations, the state power has penetrated into the township and village level, destroyed the old landlord-based rural classes, and restrained, to a large degree, the clan and blood relations by establishing new organizations, achieving high intensity of local resources mobilization. However, this new organizational structure from the central government all the way down to the grass-root level is too reliant on the vertical administrative system. Apart from the setback of too centralized power, it also severely dampens the initiative and vitality of local and grass-roots organizations, driving up the co-ordination and regulation costs and dragging down the efficiency. On the other hand, this kind of control

[9]China Rural Development Research Task Force (1987).

leads to a monotonic organization structure for China. Although the structure has many levels, the interests of the intermediate levels are not independent, and there is no mechanism for functional differentiation within and between organizations, therefore, it is difficult for various organizations to improve the overall co-ordination capability and the efficiency of the society through the mutually coordinated self-organizing process. The relapse of the cycle of "liberalization-chaos-tightening" is not because of lack of determinations to deregulate, but because of severe shortage of existing organizational resources in China. To understand this point is of decisive importance to grasp the task of China's deep-level rural reform.

The requirement to have new organizations was born almost as soon as HRS was implemented. From connecting together the farm land pieces, swapping labor collaboration, sharing farm cattle and machinery to all sorts of new economic joint ventures, the self-organization process is always on the go. Previous rural economic and technological functional departments affiliated to the government have also started to separate the functions of government and enterprises and even go back to their non-governmental status. Adaptive restructuring of a series of economic organizations has been conducted to re-build them into large numbers of companies, associations, and centers of various forms. The inherent pressure of economic development has driven people into active organizational innovation. However, we have to see that, the existing organizational innovation to date in rural areas is mostly still limited to the renovation of informal organizations. By informal, it means that there is no clear code of conduct, and no guaranteed compliance with such code by the members through social coercion. In reality, this kind of organizations are dependent on primary social network, such as blood ties, neighbors, relatives and friends, and "connections', and are bonded together by special media such as "favor" (rather than by money and law). They are extremely flexible, easy to create, and thus almost ubiquitous. The limitation of this kind of organization is that the candidates in the choice are highly constrained by the endowments and cannot be optimized in a larger scope; the internal relationship of the organization is largely maintained by some elementary social norms, dependent to a large extent on the "personal relationship" and the ethics of the parties, and thus extremely unstable. The social status of the organization cannot be not formally confirmed, making it difficult for the outside world to place stable expectations on them. All this makes it impossible to accumulate the innovations from informal organizations, resulting in the inability to take up the task to substantially save organization costs and transaction costs.

As of today the reform has not made real progress within formal organizations. There are two characteristics of formal organizations: first, the behaviors of members have to follow uniform and clear norms; second, violations will be penalized by social enforcement. As mentioned before, although China has a strong tradition for having formal organizations, their behavioral norms and restriction system have long been obedient solely to the vertical administrative system. To move away from the administrative power means the system is not formal, and this has almost become the unwritten golden rule in China. The monotony in the form of formal organization is rightly the main obstacle to hinder deepening the reform. It has always been difficult to implement the principle to "separate the government and the enterprise" since the start of the rural reform. The key is because our "enterprises", once separated from the government (such as being contracted by individuals or households), can no longer find space to exist as a formal organization except that they can seek informal protection and recognition by blood ties and "personal relationships" from informal organizations. In the history of China, we have never seen any independent economic organization that is neither attached to any family or clan nor dependent on administrative power. The determination to reform and empower alone cannot make up for the congenital flaw.

Once reaching a critical point in the reform, informal organizations will have the intrinsic requirement for formalization. Because clear and unified behavioral norms and the mandatory compliance are necessary for any organization engaging in large-scale commodity trading. At this point, they have felt the pain of not having the "third space", and they have to go to the original vertical administrative system to complete the formalization. Therefore, for a great deal of farmers creations in the informal category (e.g. independent property rights-based co-operative or joint ventures, partnership companies, "joint stock companies", private finance, and various horizontal alliances) to formalize themselves, the first thing they need to do is to complete the nominal affiliation, namely to find an administrative boss for themselves. The budding new organizations cannot be legalized and formalized unless by compromising their commodity economy nature. That is why we keep on seeing new things arise, but arise without growing up; even some do grow up, the flavor has more or less changed. In the language of economic analysis, whatever the form they adopt, they cannot save substantial transaction costs.

Why is the comprehensive and large-scale application of market mechanism closely related to the beyond-tradition innovations within formal organizations? To answer this question, we need to come back and re-understand how the market economy was born. In reality, the two previously-mentioned pivots for the market's underlying structure, i.e. the independent property rights and the commercial laws and regulations behind the contracts, can indeed support the classical market, but the subsequent in-depth market development will impose time and space limitations on the realization of the Pareto optimal resource allocation through equilibrium prices. It takes time for prices to form and for the supply and demand to respond and make adjustments. Time has a value, and information comes at a cost. This is the origin of the concept of "transaction costs".[10] The larger the market space, the more complex the economic process, and the higher the transaction costs. Hence the classical market becomes a costly structure.[11] This phenomenon is usually referred to as "market failure". In order to overcome this failure, the culturing of various market organizations is placed on the agenda to modernize the commodity economy. Enterprise is the first organization that engages in market activities but does not use market rules but orders, plans, and a hierarchical levels within itself. The most succinct explanation is that the enterprises save transaction costs.[12] After them, "intermediaries" as the

[10]Lepage (1985: 9).

[11]Lepage (1985: 11).

[12]Coase (1937).

organization between a series of enterprises have made lots of progress. The modern market economy has greatly enriched the variety and scopes of "production labor" and "division of labor", and created a series of new organizations ranging from joint-stock companies, modern banking systems, securities exchanges, wholesale and retail markets, futures exchanges, all the way to information service networks. One thing they have in common is that their ground for existence is to save transaction costs without destroying the foundation of the underlying market structure. The most important institutional innovation in this regard is the founding of the corporate legal person system, which enables any large organization that saves internal organization costs to enjoy the same type of protection as the early market institution has provided to personal property rights.

The scattered small private property of the early market grows, through organization and development, into large-scale private property, which drives the world towards market relationship, while causing lots of social inequalities through monopoly, technical stagnation, and infringement upon small private properties, and jeopardizing the market mechanism itself. Then comes the era of "economic interventionism", which leads to another innovation in the taxation, banking, and financial policies. It not only comprehensively updates the rules for market mechanism, but also makes the absolute ownership—mainly large-scale private ownership—not fully exclusive, but still requires the degree of incomplete exclusivity to be regulated by laws and regulations. All this has become the common hallmarks for all modern market economies. However, the game between the market and the organization does not end accordingly. Along with economic interventionism by the government, comes the sharp declines in the desire to investment, the prevalence of welfare disease, the inefficiency of state-owned enterprises, and the acute criticism from neoliberal economists.

China as a developing country, is by no means a bystander of this worldwide game. We can draw from this phenomenon the following conclusions that are useful to ourselves: First, the underlying market structure is not unalterable after its formation; it never stops the evolution from low-level forms to advanced forms. Second, higher-level market organization forms contain the most basic rules from the low-level forms; For instance, joint stock companies abandon the absolute exclusivity of ownership, but still clearly state to maintain the incomplete ownership. Third, business laws and regulations, due to clear and incomplete property rights, become much more sophisticated than earlier systems, but they are still unified binding upon the behaviors of all parties in question through social enforcement; Fourth, the experience of a few organizations in the market economy in different eras and from different social systems contains the common civilization wealth of mankind accumulated from overcoming difficulties in economic life. Even for a backward country, if it is a good learner and directly faces up the tremendous organization norms, it is possible to make an even more optimal choice in establishing the deep structure for its market.

Thinking about the direction of deepening rural reform from this perspective, we cannot be complacent just with the rapid innovations in informal organizations. The focus of reform must be shifted to formal organizations, and the key is to create institutional norms to accommodate new economic organizations that are free from the traditional limitations of informal organizations and administrative affiliation, paving the road for completing the thorough reform to UPMS and achieving large savings in transaction costs.

Based on the existing understanding, the fundamental foundation to support the establishment of new formal economic organizations is still the two major factors of the underlying market structure, namely a modern property rights system and sound commercial laws and regulations. To work on these two aspects goes beyond China's experience and involves some uncertainty risks. Here I will only be able to briefly touch upon some key difficulties.

In terms of property rights system, the first fundamental question is whether or not the legal manifestation of ownership system only has the significance of form. Theoretical economists seem to have developed an academic tendency to throw away the legal manifestation of system of ownership and discuss "the essence". However, the problem for China is, precisely the severe lack of legal manifestation for all forms of ownership. Under this circumstance, updates and changes in ownership cannot get the corresponding affirmation from the law (for instance, the rural contracting economy involves the fundamental interest of several hundred million people, yet there is still no specific solid law on it), and it becomes difficult to punish backpedaling.

The second question is how to deal with the "non-labor income" from the property. Needless to say, for any country, let alone a developing socialist country like China, too high a proportion of "non-labor income" will have a negative impact on its economic and social development. However, how do we define non-labor income? Can business activities and commercial "intermediary" activities be counted as "labor"? Moreover, how to determine the amount of labor of different types. Lots of confused understanding needs to be straightened. In the form of commodity currency, "non-labor income" such as bank interest and dividends constitute an important organizational medium for commodity production. In reality, the rapid development of monetary relations has materialized various forms of "non-labor income", such as dividends and rents (including land rents). How to deal with this question in social concepts and in legislation has become a sensitive aspect in establishing China's property system. The experience of the market economy shows that to impose restriction through legal procedures (e.g. imposing income tax) on "non-labor income" clearly has a low management cost. The question is how to apply this experience in China.

The third question is how to establish rights systems for public property. This is closely related to the independence of the "enterprises" that are currently still affiliated to the administrative system. The validity of detailed legal stipulations and procedures on the establishment, use, income, and transfer of collective public property depends on their ways to recognize the individual interests of each member and the degree of incentive to true co-operation. The incompleteness of the rights of the whole people's public property (such as a state-owned grain enterprise) is a fact as obvious as the incompleteness of private property of a joint stock company. However, it is difficult to use clear legal language to describe the different degree of incompleteness of rights for the whole people's property of different scales and of different industries. It should also be noted that to make legal adjustments to incomplete state-owned property rights, even in the most developed economies, there is no precedent of full success.

In terms of commercial regulations, the first thing to do is to figure out which should go first: straightening out the relations in interests or establishing market rules. The popular view is that if the interests are not straightened out, the rules cannot be established. However, without rules, the interests may never be straightened out. For example, currently governments at provincial to township levels all have the rights to block markets, if we do not pass an "anti-blocking law" first to put preliminary restrictions on such rights, then even the "dual-track" strategy will not work. Among all the rules, to formulate procedures to restrict fiscal overdraft from banks and restrict administrative authorities from arbitrarily exercising super-economic power, is most important for the establishment of market relations. Second, to provide simple and effective legal protection to the increasingly active credit economy is also exceptionally pressing. To go from primary commercial credit to advanced financial transactions, is undoubtedly important for the survival and development of new organizations that aim to save transaction costs. However, the lack of stringent regulations can lead to a chain of breaches and even frequent frauds. The imperative task is to establish procedures for assets verification and guarantee for parties engaged in credit activities so as to prevent the traditional unorganized force from using credit to jeopardize market and public interests. On a broader basis, we must start with the clean-up of the most basic norms for business activities. For example, for buying and selling activities, the obligations to maintain fair competition must be assumed so as to curb the amplification of irregular disturbances to the reform from the tradition of "profiteering". In short, there is a lot to be done, yet there is no tradition or experience from commercial civilizations. The lack of basic support from clear and resolute public opinion and business ethics, the scarcity of professionals, and the almost society-wide contempt for "rules" will inevitably become major obstacles in this regard.

To move from organizational innovation to institutional innovation, it is inevitable to involve the relationship between diversity and standardization. In order to break through the shackles of the old system and its values, diversified reform practices clearly reduce risks and increase the chances of success. At the same time, the vast expanse of China and its unbalanced economic, political, and social development, are also objective basis for diversified reform models. Nevertheless, diversification cannot exceed a reasonable limit, because in the process of substitution of the old system there will always be some common problems at the deep level, which can only be truly resolved through shared policies and organizational norms. If the answer seems to be applicable only to a certain region or a certain time, then the solution cannot be institutionalized, or propagated on a larger scale, and it will delay the progress of the reform. For China as a unified country with very strong central authority, local model also falls into the category of informal organization, and the viewpoints of previous paragraphs are still applicable. If creations and breakthroughs are only allowed in informal organizations, we will never get institutional results. For example, various local models, including the Wenzhou model, have not yet fully resolved the question of a clear property rights system. Therefore, the stability, solidification, and further development of all local models should roll out and face up problems that share the same deep structure essence and thus can only be resolved by the same principles. The inherent and stable commonalities contained in the diversified individualities are what we need to pay special attention to in the deep-level rural reform.

Finally, we would like to particularly stress the importance of reference. Studies on modernization comparison shows that large-scale transformation of modern relations all includes two basic processes for the change: conversion and reference. Conversion refers to modification of some of the existing traits, and reference means to borrow from others and establish a new system and value standard that suit the national conditions. Countries with the main necessary preconditions ready for modernization may mainly rely on conversion. However, for those short of certain necessary conditions, there are fewer opportunities for conversion, and the need for reference increases accordingly. China's lagging behind in the global modernization process has a lot to do with its refusal to reference and learn. Therefore, it is exceptionally important to smartly and independently reference all useful international experiences. Just as Marxism is definitely not the outcome of deviating from the road of human civilization, socialism, in practice, cannot accomplish its self-innovation in isolation. Countries that embarked on modernization after World War II faced an ocean of new knowledge, which could not be digested just by one generation like in Japan in the late nineteenth century. Chinese people should open our eyes to look at the readily available fruits of innovation, and bravely practice borrowing. To maintain the national consistency without disintegrating the society in the process of referencing will be of greater significance for facilitating the absorption of modern knowledge and civilization.[13] The post-HRS stage is a stage of innovation, and it shoulders the heavy mission of deep structural reform. Eight years of successful reform is an encouragement, and the danger of stopping and losing all previous merits serves as a good reminder.

References

Agriculture Statistics Department of National Statistics Bureau. 1984. *Tremendous Changes in Chinese Farmers' Life*, 5–9. China Statistics Press.

Bruse, Virlyn W. 1983. Socialist Economy and Operations. In *Selected Works on Socialist Economic Models*. The People's Press.

Coase, R.H. 1937. The Nature of the Firm. *Economica* 4: 386–405.

China Rural Development Research Task Force. 1987. *New Stage of National Economy Growth and Rural Development*. Zhejiang People's Publishing House.

Cyril E. Black et al. 1984. *Modernization of Japan and Russia*. Commercial Press.

Gao, Xiaomeng. 1986. Memos on Grains. *Development Research Communication*, October, General Issue 21.

Huang, Zongzhi. 1986. *Social Changes of Small Peasant Economy in North China*. China Publishing House.

[13] Black et al. (1984).

Lepage, Henry. 1985. *Neo-Libralist Economics in the United States*, 9–11. Peking University Press.

Liu, Yunzhi. 1985. Agriculture and Rural Areas in Developed Capitalist Countries. *China Society of Agriculture Economics* (Lead Printed Copy), 92.

Song, Guoqing, and Xiaopeng Luo. 1985. Economic Structure and Economic Reform. In *Rural Areas, Economy and Society* Vol. 2 by Rural Development Research Task Force, the Knowledge Publishing House.

Chapter 5
Property Rights of Agricultural Land and Land Requisition System: A Major Reform Faced by Urbanization

This paper studies the transfer rights of agricultural land in the process of urbanization. The focus is the restrictions and options faced by redefining the agricultural land transfer right rather than its right of use.

5.1 Introduction

The decisive role of institutions in economic performance has long attracted the attention of scholars.[1] If they do not properly reflect resource scarcity and corresponding economic opportunities, there will be distortions in economic behaviors.[2] For any society, the foundation of institutions is always a set of legal provisions on property rights that define the scope of the rights to use the ad hoc property by members of society.[3] Property rights generally include the exclusive right to use the resources, the right of income via collecting rents from the resources, and the right to transfer the resources to others through sales or other means.[4] This way they not only provide incentives for economic behaviors that can positively affect economic performance,

[1]Coase (1937, 1960), North(1990).
[2]North (1990).
[3]Barzel (1989), Libecap (1989a, 1989b), Eggertsson (1990), North (1990), Alston et al. (1996).
[4]Cheung (2002).

The paper is based on a working paper completed by the author during his visit to Yale Law School from September to December 2003. The article was presented to a panel discussion at a seminar hosted by the China Law Center at Yale on November 17, 2003. The author is grateful to the panelists, especially Robert C. Ellickson, Carol M. Rose, Paul Gewirtz, CHEN Zhiwu, WEN Guanzhong, CHEN Jie, and other participants for their comments, criticism, and suggestion. In particular, the author would like to thank Jamie Horsley and the Center for their thoughtful arrangements for the visit, as well as Yale University library for facilitating the research. Of course, any error in this article will be the responsibility of the author and not of the above-mentioned institutions or individuals.

Q. Zhou, *Property Rights and Changes in China*,
https://doi.org/10.1007/978-981-15-9885-2_5

but also determine who are the players of economic activities and, therefore, the distribution of social wealth.

Among the various functions of property rights, the right to transfer plays a crucial role. In theory, a clearly defined right to transfer must involve clearly defined right to use the resources and the right to earn income from them. However, conversely, it is not necessarily true. In practice, economic growth often leads to changes in economic structure, which are precisely the result of large-scale transfers of resources. If the right to transfer is restricted, then the potential transfer of resources, along with economic growth, will be hampered.

History must be full of cases where drastic economic changes require existing laws to change the definition of the right to transfer. As economic changes entail accelerated resource transfers, a large number of violations may occur before necessary revisions are made to the existing legal system, which has not clearly defined the right to transfer. If illegal activities are not stopped, the economic order will be compromised. However, if we eliminate chaos by enforcing the old property rights systems, then resource transfer will be hindered. The solution is to change the legal definition of the right to transfer in due course. The question is, however, under what conditions can the needed legal change take place easily?

The accelerated urbanization in China in recent years provides a rare case for studying the above question. Between 1978 and 2000, the number of Chinese cities increased from 193 to 663, and the number of towns increased from 2,173 to 20,312. The urban population increased from 170 million to 456 million. At the same time, tens of millions of migrant workers moved from rural areas to towns, and millions of acres of agricultural land was converted for industrial and commercial development. Based on the cumulative effects of reform and opening up and economic growth, it is generally expected that China's urbanization will continue to accelerate in the next 20 years.[5]

However, in reality, the accelerated urbanization in recent years occurs precisely when the existing law is seriously lagging behind. China's existing Land Administration Law (LAL) is based on the planned economy and public ownership, which main feature is that the transfer of economic resources is achieved by administrative orders rather than market transactions. Although the market-oriented reform for more than two decades has shaken the foundations of the existing land law, the modified land law is still far from meeting the economic requirements. As a result, the accelerated urbanization, compounded with the intensified conflicts of interests, has led to a dilemma: should we continue accelerating urbanization at the cost of conflicts of interests in land transfer, or should we curb urbanization to mitigate the conflicts?

The root of the problem is that accelerated urbanization—an important source of China's long-term economic growth—takes place in the context of ambiguous rights to transfer for agricultural land. The process has bumped into a dilemma pointed out by Barzel: without the clearly defined and well-executed property rights systems, people will compete to seize scarce economic resources and opportunities without

[5]For example, the State Council Development Research Center (SCDRC) predicts that China's urbanization index will reach 60% by 2020.

being restricted by law. Importantly, this snatching usually suggests that chaos and opportunities are often intertwined. Failure to recognize and analyze the act of seizure will make it difficult to re-establish property rights by law.

Based on the above, this article explores the following issues: What kind of actions do people actually take under the existing legal arrangements for land transfer rights? How to understand the economic implications of these behaviors? Then, we will discuss the main options for the Constitution and LAL to be revised. The structure of this paper is as follows: Part Two investigates the legal system of existing transfer rights of agricultural land; Part Three analyzes seizure behaviors in land transfer; part Four studies the practice of redefining the right to transfer; Part Five introduces the economic analysis of controlling the land transfer right; Part six discusses relevant policy recommendations and the options facing the revision of LAL; finally is the conclusion and issues for further study.

5.2 The Transfer Rights of Agricultural Land in Existing Laws

Mainly there are two existing laws to cover the transfer of agricultural land. One is The Law of the People's Republic of China on Land Contract in Rural Areas (LLCRA), and the other is Land Administration Law of the People's Republic of China (LAL).[6] The issue of the right to transfer is so significant that in order to formulate and revise these two laws, it is necessary to amend the relevant provisions of the Constitution. This section briefly reviews these laws with a focus on their inherent conflicts and their impact on economic behavior.

5.2.1 The Laws Recognizing the Right to Transfer

It took almost two decades to fully embody in the law the contracting rights and operation rights of rural land that were de facto established in the late 1970s and early 1980s. On August 29, 2002, LLCRA was adopted by the National People's Congress Standing Committee (NPCSC), which not only confirmed and announced the protection of the land use rights and income rights of farmers, but also the land transfer rights. At this point, the collective ownership of agricultural land has been comprehensively transformed into a land tenure system.

Full recognition and a clear definition of the transfer rights of agricultural land is the main content of LLCRA. The following are some essential excerpts:

[6]The two laws will be abbreviated as LLCRA and LAL from here onwards.

- The land transfer right belongs to the "contractor" (i.e. "the farmer") rather than the "owner" (i.e. "the collective")[7];
- The primary principles for the land transfer are equality, consultation, voluntariness, and compensation, and it shall not be subject to any organization or individual's coercion and obstruction;
- The form of land transfer can include multiple forms such as subcontracting, leasing, and swaps;
- The price of the transfer rights is determined by the parties;
- The proceeds of the transfer rights belong to the contractor.

Since the object of transfer is the land contracting right, it is imperative the LAL take into consideration and sum up all the policies and regulations on land contracting since the reform, and define the full scope of contracting rights of farmers in a clear legal language. The main point is that all the collective agricultural land now adopts a household-based land tenure system. Therefore, the law needs to stipulate the procedures, the term, and the forms of contracting and operation, and the rights and obligations of the parties of the contracts.

It is fair to say that LAL has completely modified the collective ownership of land in China. According to the norms in property rights economics, property rights that include use rights, income rights, and transfer rights are the substantive content of ownership in the legal sense. Therefore, property rights, instead of abstract legal ownership, constitute restrictions on economic behaviors. China's agricultural land is still collectively owned, but the only thing that the collective can do today is to contract the land to rural households according to law. In the 30-year contracting period, only the contractor has the right to use, to operate, to obtain corresponding income, and to transfer the tenure of the land in the market. The collective owner, on the other hand, has no right to terminate, reclaim, or change the contracting rights of farmers; nor does it have the right to intercept the generated income, or interfere with the contractor's right to transfer. It is clear that the HRS-based collective land ownership is no longer the collective land ownership system in the era of people's commune.

An important experience from this reform is that it is easier to establish the right to use through the contracting agreement, but far more difficult to grow the right to use into the right to transfer. More importantly, if the law can clearly define the right to transfer, it must even more clearly define the use rights and income rights. Owing to the limitation in space, this article will not comment on the meaning of these experiences. We simply point out that the land use rights, income rights, and transfer rights of farmers clearly defined and protected by law provide a stable yet flexible institutional basis to effectively utilize agricultural land resources in the context of rapidly changing economic structure.

[7]"Article 34. The contractor shall have the right to make his own decision, according to law, on whether to transfer the rights to land contractual management and on the means of the transfer. "Article 10. The State protects the transfer of the rights to land contractual management, which is effected according to law, on a voluntary basis, and with compensation.".

The LLCRA is still flawed. A significant flaw is that the 30-year term for contracting agricultural land is still too short. Given that the lease period of urban residential land is 50-70 years, is the 30-year term for agricultural land reasonable? Besides, the current law does not cover the principles for renewal of the contract. If the law stipulates that the incumbent contractor is given a certain priority for renewal, then the length of the contract term may not be that important.

Another flaw is already unevadable today. The LLCRA clearly defines that the contracting rights, and transfer rights of the farmers are limited to "agricultural use". For example, LLCRA (2002) stipulates in the General Provisions: "Without approval granted according to law, no contracted land may be used for non-agricultural development." (Article 8). Regarding the rights of the owner, it stipulates, "the contractor is not allowed to damage the contracted land and agricultural resources" (Article 13). Regarding the obligations of the contractor, it stipulates that "keeping or using the land for agricultural purposes and refraining from using it for non-agricultural development" (Article 17). Regarding the principle of land transfer, it further specifies that "no change shall be made in the nature of the land ownership or the purpose of use of the land designed for agriculture" (Article 33). It is clear that once the land is used for non-agricultural purposes, the law will not recognize or protect farmers' contractual rights.

5.2.2 The Laws Negating the Right to Transfer

The conversion of agricultural land into non-agricultural land is regulated by LAL, which was adopted on June 25, 1986, at the 16th Session of Sixth NPCSC, and was enforced on January 1, 1987. However, only two years later, on December 29, 1988, the Fifth Session of the Seventh NPCSC decided to amend it. The amendment, which stretched over almost ten years, was adopted by the Fourth Session of the Ninth NPCSC on August 29, 1998, and was enforced on January 1, 1999. From formulation to the revision of LAL, the Chinese economy was experiencing the deepening period of the market-oriented reform. However, with all the revisions, this law has still not dealt with such an important resource allocation issue as the conversion of agricultural land after the provision on the right of transfer.

In the 1998 LAL, except for an abstract statement in Article 2 ("the right to the use of land may be transferred in accordance with law."), there is no mentioning whatsoever regarding the content, subject, ownership, transfer procedures, enforcement principles, and pricing of "land transfer rights" in all the 86 articles of the total eight chapters. That is to say, although the land tenure can be "transferred according to the law", there is no relevant specific content at all. As an example, Article 16 of this Law states that "the dispute over ownership and use right of land shall be settled by the parties through consultation; if it cannot be settled through consultation, the people's government shall handle it." The question is, how about the transfer of tenure? What procedures should be followed in case of a dispute?

In terms of the conversion of agricultural land to non-agricultural land, the 1998 LAL clearly stipulates: "No right to the use of land owned by farmer collectives may be assigned, transferred or leased for non-agricultural construction" (Article 63).[8] Then, when it is needed to transform part of the agricultural land into non-agricultural land for economic development due to urbanization, how can this need be lawfully met? The only legal way stipulated in the current LAL is to convert the collective ownership to state ownership.

5.2.3 The Origin of the State Ownership of Urban Land

Why does the ownership have to be transformed into state ownership for the collective-owned and farmers-contracted agricultural land once it is to be converted into urban construction land? The answer has something to do with a constitutional principle. The *1982 Constitutional Amendment* declared that "Land in the cities is owned by the state" (Article 10). This is the first time to extend the state ownership to cover all urban land from the previous scope of "minerals resources and waters as well as the forests, and deserted land" according to *Constitution* and its previous amendments. According to the explanation to the constitutional amendment at the time, Article 10 originally regarded the land of towns the same as the rural land and the urban suburb land, i.e. as collective land. In plenary discussion, it was pointed out that the situation across the country was quite different, some towns were big and had great potential for development, and therefore, they were actually small cities. As a result, the wording regarding towns was deleted. That is to say, the land of the larger towns will also be state-owned, and will no longer be collectively owned by the farmers.

However, the origin of "all urban land is state-owned" is not so clear. Article 6 in the 1975 Constitution states as follows: "The state may requisition by purchase, expropriate, or declare nationalization of urban and rural land as well as other means of production under conditions prescribed by law." This clause clearly demonstrates that, not all China's urban land was owned by the state when the Cultural Revolution was about to end. Otherwise, there would be no need to state "the state can purchase, expropriate and declare nationalization of urban and rural land." When the "Cultural Revolution" was over, the 1978 Constitution did not declare the nationalization of all urban land either. Since then, China has entered a new historical period of reform and opening up. Until 1982, there was no historical record of how "the state can purchase, expropriate, and declare nationalization of urban and rural land". For such as major issue as state ownership of all urban land, there have never been specific government actions, wasn't it realized directly just by the announcement in the 1982 Constitution?

Anyway, "urban land is state-owned" constitutes the guiding principle of the current land regulations. This principle, as we will discuss in detail, not only implies

[8]There is an exception to this Article, which will be quoted and analyzed later.

that "all existing urban land is state-owned", but also "all land that will become part of a city is state-owned". The latter includes both the scenario of expansion of existing cities to their suburbs and surrounding countryside and the scenario of new cities growing out of rural areas, small towns, and suburbs. Few people have noticed that after 1982 China has gone through, are going through and will continue to go through massive nationalization of land.

5.2.4 Land Requisition Paradox

The current land law stipulates that all agricultural land used to develop cities must be converted into state ownership, and thus the land requisition has become the only legal way for the conversion. Originally, urban or rural, even private land could be requisitioned by the state legally. For example, the 1954 Constitution (First Edition) declared: "The state may, in the public interest, buy, requisition or nationalize land and other means of production both in cities and countryside according to provisions of law" (Article 13). As we all know, although the general principle to transition to a socialist system was announced at that time, most of the urban and rural land was still private, recognized and protected by the *Constitution*. Therefore, the nationalization of agricultural land is just one form of conversion of agricultural land into construction land. In order to define the boundary between nationalization and private land transfer, the 1954 Constitution imposed an essential restriction on nationalization, i.e. "in the public interest". At least legally it is quite clear: the conversion of agricultural land in the public interest has to go through nationalization; if not in the public interest, the conversion can be realized through the private transfer right which was then recognized by the law.

With the completion of urban and rural land ownership reform, especially after the said 1982 Constitution first stipulates that all urban land is state-owned, the conversion of agricultural land into urban land now must go through nationalization, which means government's requisition has become the only legal way for agricultural land conversion. However, here comes the inharmony: both the 1982 Constitution and the subsequent LAL keep the constraint on land requisition stipulated in the 1954 Constitution—"in the public interest". That begets a problem: What happens with the conversion of agricultural land that is not in the public interest? It is unconstitutional not to nationalize the land and keep it collective-owned because it goes against the constitutional principle of "all city land is state-owned", yet it is also unconstitutional to nationalize it because it does not meet the constitutional constraint of "in the public interest".

5.2.5 *The Profit-Seeking Motivation of the Government to Administer the Land*

A bigger problem is that while the existing land law prohibits farmers from converting land for non-agricultural use, it stipulates a system of compensated use of state-owned land—including land acquired from farmers—(Article 2).[9] It implies that the government can transfer the requisitioned land—whether "in the public interest" or not—to the urban land use rights market for compensation.

It should be noted that the paid state-owned land transfer system stipulated by LAL, after all, is a factual reflection of the reform to introduce market mechanisms into land resource allocation. In fact, since 1987, when Shenzhen and Shanghai municipal governments tried to lease land to the market, China's urban construction land markets have developed rapidly and formed a set of laws and regulations.

The problem is that land marketization is limited to the paid transfer and re-transfer of use rights of only some of the state-owned land. As to the conversion of the aforementioned agricultural land to non-agricultural construction land, and some urban land appropriated by administrative orders, they still have to follow the principle that the administrative authority allocates land resources. Here is the new hybrid model: the government obtains urban construction land based on the administrative monopoly on the conversion of agricultural land and then leases part of the state-owned land to the secondary urban land market, and the rest stays in the hands of the government for appropriation. This special mix of administrative allocation and market allocation cannot but encourage administrative entities to become profit-seeking. If the difference between the cost of expropriated agricultural land and the income generated from the leased land means the dividends for the government, then the difference between the "free-of-charge appropriation" and the market value of the land on secondary urban land markets represents the value of rents of the "appropriation right".

The existing laws even expressly stipulate that the compensation for land requisition can totally be different from the price for the leased land. On the one hand, LAL stipulates that the expropriated agricultural land shall be compensated for based on its original purpose of use (of course, the agricultural use—noted by the author) (Article 47). On the other hand, the law allows the government to lease the acquired land in accordance with the "market value of the urban construction land". This is tantamount to ensuring that the government is legally entitled to enormous dividends from the land. In a seriously under-urbanized and rapid growing economy, the market value for land converted from agricultural use to urban construction purpose is way above ten times. The larger the market value of the land, the higher the rents for

[9] "A construction unit that wishes to use state-owned land shall get it by such means of compensation as assignment" (Article 54). "A construction unit that obtains right to the use of state-owned land by such means of compensation as assignment shall, in accordance with the rates and measures prescribed by the State Council, pay, among other charges, compensation for use of land such as charges for the assignment of land-use right, before it can use the land" (Article 55).

the government power to appropriate land. This, in reality, becomes a new business monopolized by the government for exorbitant profits, and it is also legally guaranteed.

5.2.6 Three Exceptions and Two Ambiguities

Yet there are three exceptions. The existing law stipulates that agricultural land generally needs to be requisitioned and nationalized in order to be converted into non-agricultural construction land. Certain circumstances can be treated as exceptions where the agricultural land can also be converted into construction land without being requisitioned and nationalized.

The guideline sets out in Article 43 of LAL ("All units and individuals that need land for construction purposes shall, in accordance with the law, apply for the use of state-owned land"), the exceptions permitted by law are as follows:

The collective economic organizations and villagers that have lawfully obtained approval of using the land owned by farmer collectives of these organizations to build township enterprises or to build villagers houses, and the units and individuals that have lawfully obtained approval of using the land owned by farmer collectives to build public utilities or public welfare undertakings of the township (town) or village.

That is to say, the land used by farmers for enterprises, houses, public utilities, and public welfare undertakings, although it is also converted into construction land, can remain collective-owned.

Second, "if a rural collective economic organization that works together with other units or individuals to set up enterprises in the form of joint operations or through equity injection in the form of land using right" (Article 60), and the land use complies with the master plan for land utilization and has obtained necessary approvals, such agricultural land can be lawfully converted into non-agricultural construction land.

Third, the right to the use of land owned by farmer collectives may not be assigned, transferred or leased for non-agricultural construction, with the exception of land-use right transfer by enterprises that have lawfully obtained the construction land in conformity with the master plan for land utilization as a result of bankruptcy or merging or other reasons (Article 63). To put it straight, that means the land-use right owned by the collectives complying with the aforementioned requirements can be assigned, transferred or leased.

The laws do not state that the principle that "urban land must be state-owned" also has exceptions. The trouble is that in the rapid urbanization, the rural areas where farmers started their businesses or joint ventures may become part of cities in the future. As we will see, once this happens, the lawful transfer rights as "exceptions" in the existing laws will lead to much confusion. Because at that future point the land is already urban land, yet there is no clear stipulation in the existing laws on whether or not such land must be requisitioned and state-owned.

In addition, of the three exceptions, only the third stipulates the transfer is based on the "collective land use right", which means that the transfer right belongs to the contractor. In the first two exceptions, it is "rural collective economic organizations" that have the legal right to transfer the land for construction purpose. What is unclear is that, in the case that the agricultural land has already been contracted to the farmer, whether or not the "collective" can or must reclaim the land tenure from the farmer in order to benefit from the lawful exceptions for agricultural land conversion, and then establish enterprises, or joint enterprises or other facilities in the name of the collective?

5.2.7 An Overview of Existing Transfer Rights

Let us sum up the legal provisions on the transfer rights of agricultural land in China. After more than two decades of reform, existing land laws clearly define and protect the transfer rights of agricultural land within the scope of agricultural use. As the holder of such transfer rights of agricultural land, the contracting farmer can subcontract, lease and swap the land tenure on the basis of equality, consultation, voluntariness, and compensation, and without being subject to coercion and obstruction by any organization or any individual. The price of the transfer is determined by the parties, and the proceeds of the transfer belongs to the contractor. The above stipulations constitute an important institutional basis for China's agricultural economic activities.

However, once the agricultural land is converted to non-agricultural construction land, the farmer's transfer rights will no longer be acknowledged by the law. Even the rural collectives have no right to convert agricultural land into construction land. With a few exceptions, the law requires that the conversion of agricultural land into urban construction land must be based on the prerequisite of nationalization of land. Thus the national expropriation of agricultural land has become the only legal way for urbanization to use agricultural land.

While the existing law confirms that the government not only has the right to requisition agricultural land but also to sell the right to use of the requisitioned land to the market. On the one hand, the government's compensation for the requisition is determined according to the income of the original use of the land, that is, agricultural use; on the other, when it so sells the land tenure, the price can be market-based, i.e. based on the expected return on the future use of the land, and usually, the highest bidder gets the land tenure. That is to say, the current law not only acknowledges the government's monopoly of land requisition rights but also guarantees that this right can help the government obtain the maximum lawful profits. Such a legal basis constitutes a powerful driver for the government's land operations.

In short, with the conversion of agricultural land into urban construction land, the right to transfer of the converted land goes from the contractor to the government. In order to restrain the government's land requisition and operation rights, the existing laws have repeatedly reiterate the legislative intent of "strictly protecting farmland", continually improved the land approval procedures according to different administrative levels, and always adhered to the constitutional guideline that "agricultural land can only be requisitioned *in the public interest*". Next, we will look at, under the incentives and constraints of the existing laws, the actual government-led behaviors for the transfer of non-agricultural construction land.

5.3 Capture and Conflict

People's behavior is always governed by realistic constraints. As the written law is only part of the constraints, the approach in our survey starts with real cases involving the conversion of agricultural land, and then analyzes the relationship between the observed behaviors and the existing legal constraints. In order to obtain solid facts, the examples selected in this section are generally judicial cases that have been publicly reported, plus our own investigations, if necessary.

5.3.1 *Land Requisition Case of Dengfeng Railway, Henan Province*[10]

At the end of 1998, the Dengfeng Municipal People's Government of Henan Province and Henan Dengfeng Railway Co., Ltd. signed a Land Acquisition and Demolition Agreement for the Malingshan-Baiping Section of Deng Feng Railway. According to the agreement, the Dengfeng Municipal Government (Party A) promises to complete the land acquisition and demolition required for the railway construction of the said section at a package price of 8,500 yuan per *mu*[11] (including land compensation, young crop compensation, and resettlement compensation); the packaged price is agreed upon by both parties based on the existing laws, actualities, and the low limit, and is to be paid in lump sum to Dengfeng Municipal People's Government (Party A) by Dengfeng Railway Co. (Party B) with no right for Party A to claim any additional payment if the packaged price is exceeded. The specific land compensation, and methods for the distribution and the use of the fee are determined by Party A. Party A shall be responsible for paying the amount due to relevant collectives and farmers to each village, villager group, and household.

[10]The public reports used in this section include: "Dengfeng City (Henan Province) Government intercepts compensation of nearly 10 million yuan for land acquisition" by Xinhua News Agency Zhengzhou, July 8, 2003; "Dengfeng, Henan decided to return the intercepted compensation for land acquisition" by *China Youth Daily* and Xinhua News Agency Zhengzhou, July 13, 2003; "Investigation on the land acquisition compensation by Dengfeng Railway" by Journalist CHEN Lei, *Weekend*, July 23, 2003; "The Henan shrinking compensation for land acquisition in Dengfeng" by CCTV Economic Half Hour, July 25, 2003; "Investigation on the farmers' land acquisition compensation by Dengfeng Railway" by Journalists ZHAO Ping and DONG Zhaowu, *China Business News*, September 8, 2003.

[11]1 *mu* = 666.67 m^2.

One year later, on January 27, 2000, the Dengfeng Municipal Government issued the No. 4 Document [2000], setting the compensation standard for land acquisition at 4,300 yuan per *mu* for farmland and 1,000 yuan per *mu* of for non-revenue generating land. The compensation standard caused dissatisfaction and petition by farmers involved in the requisition. Among them, WANG Dongyue, a farmer from Kuzhuang Village, whose high-yielding vegetable greenhouses were acquired at a low price, together with two other farmers from the same village, launched a law suit against Dengfeng Railway at the Chengguan Court of Dengfeng City.

During in-court debate, Dengfeng Railway argued that it should be Dengfeng Municipal Government instead of the railway company to compensate for WANG's vegetable greenhouse. As evidence, the respondent of the railway company presented the land acquisition agreement between the two parties. After WANG and his fellow got a copy of the agreement, they negotiated in private with the responsible officials of the Dengfeng Municipal Government. The final solution was as follows: the government would grant through the township an amount of 200,000 yuan as "land reclamation fund"; the money will be collected by WANG, the Village Party Secretary, and the other two farmers; in return, WANG gives back the copy of the agreement, and promises to work well on and convince other villagers so that there will be no more appeal on the compensation. The time was on October 10, 2000.

Since then WANG withdrew from the appeal and petition activities. However, other farmers of the same village continued to make petitions, meaning WANG's promise was not delivered. In order to quell the petitions, WANG agreed through an official surnamed ZHAO at the city's petition office to pay 6500 yuan. The backfire was this became the reason for villagers to be convinced that WANG had received hush money. The petition got escalated, and this time pointing at private allotment of the 200,000-yuan silence fee. In September 2002, Dengfeng Procuratorate filed public prosecution against the four villagers on the charge of embezzling the "land reclamation fund". In April 2003, the four villagers were sentenced to 18 months to 66 months of imprisonment for the offense of "encroachment leveraging positions" by the Dengfeng People's Court.

Yet, the villagers' petition was getting even more raging. It turned out that WANG kept a copy of the agreement to himself. After WANG was sued, his family distributed the copies far and wide; as a result, more farmers along the rail way became aware of the municipal government's interception of land compensation. The local farmers also obtained the supplementary agreement to the requisition agreement through their relatives working in the railway company. Article 10 of the supplementary agreement clearly states that the Dengfeng Municipal Government will intercept a total of 4.276 million yuan out of the land compensation fee "as investment into Dengfeng Railway by Party A". A number of journalists verified with Dengfeng Railway that Dengfeng Municipal Government invested altogether over 7 million-yuan, accounting for about 1% of the total equity of the railway company; apart from the intercepted money form the land requisition compensation fee mentioned in the supplementary agreement, the city government raised 3 million yuan invested in 1994 to kick off the railway project.

How come the intercepted compensation for the land acquisition got changed to the government's investment and became its equity instead of investment and equity of the farmers whose land had been acquired? The responsible deputy mayor of Dengfeng City replied: "Because of the use of treasury bond requires matching local funds." Some reporter pointed out that "this investment made by the local government didn't belong to the local government, but belonged to the villagers." The deputy mayor responded, "We had fiscal stress at the time." What a nice answer! The fact is: the fiscal pressure of the city was not just the lack of matching local funds, because the total intercepted amount was roughly 10,000,000 yuan, taking away the several million yuan of equity injection, there was another several million yuan missing, and no one knows its whereabouts in spite of repeated questions from reporters.

Continued farmers' petitions, plus the exposure by major national media including Xinhua News Agency and CCTV, finally brought the Dengfeng Railway Land Acquisition Case to its closing. On July 8, 2003, under the direct intervention of the governor of Henan Province, the new Dengfeng City leadership decided to return all the intercepted compensation funds to the farmers. Although WANG and others were still serving their time for "the encroachment", the tens of thousands of farmers from four townships now got their money back.

The focus of this case analysis is: when the right of land requisition "in the public interest" conflicts with the property rights and the tenure rights of the acquired land, how should the existing laws require the former to compensate the latter, and how can the compensation mechanism be enforced in a practical way?

The Dengfeng Railway Project is undoubtedly of great significance to local economic development. So far, there is no evidence to show that the officials of the Dengfeng Municipal Government have committed illegalities for their personal benefits in the case. Therefore, we can regard the case as a typical case of land acquisition "in the public interest". After the railway project is completed, local people and the government, including those whose land was acquired, can all benefit from it. However, equally obviously, farmers whose land was acquired have to pay more cost than other beneficiaries, because it will cost only them the benefits that they could have earned from the land. When the land requisition, enforced by the government for the public interest, occurs, the farmers give up their rights to the land and therefore receive compensation from the government. The question is, how should the compensation be implemented under the current law?

We already know that the original compensation standard of 8,500 yuan per *mu* was determined according to the "low limit" principle. In view of the fact that the new version of the 1998 LAL was not yet reinforced, the compensation stipulated in the agreement between the local government and the railway company must have been based on the 1986 edition, which says the land acquisition compensation is comprised of three parts: land compensation, ground attachment and young crop compensation, and resettlement subsidies. According to the provisions, "Compensation for expropriated farmland shall be 3 to 6 times the average annual output value of such land, calculated on the basis of three years preceding such requisition."; "Rates of compensation for attachments and young crops on expropriated land shall be prescribed by provinces, autonomous regions, and municipalities directly under the Central Government" (Article 27); "the maximum resettlement subsidies for the expropriated cultivated land shall not exceed ten times its average annual output value calculated on the basis of three years preceding such expropriation" (Article 28). Here, there is only one "low limit" prescribed by law, that is, the compensation for the expropriated cultivated land shall be 3 to 6 times the average annual output value of the expropriated land. As for the resettlement subsidies, the law only stipulates the high limit but not the low limit!

Of course, the old edition also stipulates that "should the land compensation and resettlement subsidies be insufficient to enable the re-settled farmers to maintain their original living standards, the resettlement subsidies may be increased upon approval by the people's governments of the province, autonomous region and municipality directly under the Central Government. However, the total land compensation and resettlement subsidies shall not exceed 20 times the average annual output value of the expropriated land calculated on the basis of three years preceding such expropriation" (Article 29). This Article sets another bottom line standard for land compensation. The problem is that this standard is ambiguous. For example, what does it actually mean by "maintaining the original standard of living"? And for how long? According to the highest compensation provided in the 1986 edition, it seems to refer to 20 years—plus we have to assume that other conditions remain unchanged. However, the land acquired is a permanent asset, which serves theoretically as the condition to maintain their original living standards for their lifetime. Now after the compensation is used up, what can the landless farmers count on to maintain their "original living standards"?

If the law expressly confers the "compensation negotiation right" to farmers—that is, if the farmers can participate in determining the compensation amount under the compensation principles stipulated by laws, then the logical conclusion will be: the total amount of land compensation shall be equal to an asset that is of the same value as the requisitioned land, and the annual income from such total amount should permanently satisfy maintaining "the original living standard" for land-expropriated farmers. In the terminology of modern law and economics, it is to ensure that "the interests of the farmers unaffected regardless of the land acquisition".[12] If the law clearly stipulates that the transfer rights of agricultural land to be converted into construction land belong to the contractor, then the "compensation" obtained by the contractor will certainly be equal to the market value of the non-agricultural land from such conversion.

The above analysis attempts to reveal the nature of the current land laws: it clearly prohibits farmers from converting contracted agricultural land into non-agricultural construction land, but at the same time it does not expressly confer to any organization or individual the unexercisable transfer rights of the farmer, i.e. the right to decide at least how much compensation must be paid for the land transfer. Although the existing laws have established the government's exclusive land acquisition rights, they do not clearly state how the government should pay the price (compensation). When exercising the land requisition rights, within the scope of the existing laws,

[12]Ellickson (1993: 6).

at least the following three compensation standards are all legal: equal to the legal minimum; any amount between the legal minimum and the legal maximum; and equal to the legal maximum.

The Dengfeng case tells us that because the land-expropriated farmers have no negotiation rights, they have to resort to petitions and appeals, and even other collective actions beyond the permission by the existing system to exert influence on the final decision on compensation. If based on market mechanisms, the seller, with his transfer rights in hand, only has to weigh whether the offer is good enough or not so as to decide to sell, and he pays the market trading fee if he sells, that's all. However, under the current land acquisition system, the land-expropriated party has no right to transfer and has to resort to "the subsistence right", "fairness", "justice", and increasing the execution cost of the other party (government) to increase the compensation. This shows the cost of land acquisition includes non-productive and non-market-based transaction costs. We will continue the analysis with other cases to demonstrate that it is the precisely the neglecting of such special costs that makes the actually-expensive land acquisition look so cheap.

Even if the 1998 LAL is reinforced, the story is not much different. Although the compensation standard has been raised, the low limit is far less clear than the high limit. The fundamental ambiguity of "maintaining the original living standard" remains in the article, and the government still pays the compensation for land acquisition to the "units" rather than directly to the contractor who suffers the loss. With the land acquisition compensation mechanism unchanged, the possibility of enforcing the newly-added economic democracy provisions is very small.[13]

5.3.2 Land Acquisition Case of Southeast Auto Town, Minhou County, Fujian Province[14]

In 1995, Fujian Automobile Industry Group and Taiwan Yulon Group reached a co-operation agreement to build the Southeast Auto Town at Qingkou Town, Minhou County, Fuzhou City. That was the largest Fujian-Taiwan co-operation project with a total investment of 352 million US dollars. The planned requisitioned area for Phase One is 2400 *mu*.

---

[13]For example, the 1998 LAL stipulates: "After the land requisition compensation and resettlement scheme is determined, the relevant local government shall make a public notice and draw opinions from the land-expropriated rural collective economic organizations and farmers." (Article 48), and "the land-appropriated rural collective economic organization shall disclose the income and expenditure situation of the compensation fee for such expropriated land to its members, and accept surveillance" (Article 49).

[14]The public reports used in this section include: "The Aftermath of Southeast Auto Town Land Acquisition" by Reporter ZHENG Xueqin, *21st Century Business Herald*, June 30, 2003; "What Did the Farmers Gain from the Modernization of Qingkou Town" by Zhao Yan, Jiang Jiansheng, Chen Chunhua, etc., *China Reform*, December 8, 2003.

From July to August, a number of working groups have been dispatched by Minhou County and Qingkou Town to the villages involved in land acquisition to promote and make the policy known: the land-expropriated farmers can get 10,000 yuan compensation each, and each elderly over 50 years of age can get a pension of 60 yuan a month, and each household has at least one job opportunity at the Southeast Auto Town. The villagers were satisfied with the government's offer, so even before actually getting paid the government compensation for the land, about 20,000 land-expropriated farmers had handed over their land.

The Southeast Auto Town project soon entered construction phase. However, one year later, the land-expropriated farmers received only 800 yuan each. They also could not help but worry: their land was taken away, yet the tens of thousands of yuan plus one job per household commitment disappeared in the thin air. The local farmers felt that they were deceived and what is worse, they could not maintain their livelihoods. Then later, they "got together to make public disturbance" as recorded by the government documents of Qingkou Town.

Different from the Dengfeng case, the land-expropriated farmers in Qingkou Town eventually did not know the amount of the actual compensation for land acquisition paid by the project. However, this did not prevent them from finding other references. A clear reference, of course, is the original promise made by the county and town governments. The problem is that what they got was verbal publicity, and there were no written agreements or contracts as evidence. Moreover, the farmers who understand accounting made calculations and concluded that the government did not have the fiscal foundation (strength) to deliver its original commitments. Another reference is the compensation case that took place in the vicinity. They found a report on the compensation for land acquisition of the Fuzhou University Town project in the local newspaper. The university town project requisitioned 12,886 *mu* of land in Shangjie Town of the same county, and paid 13,000 yuan per *mu* as compensation.

The reporters from central government media, at the end, found out the actual land requisition income of the local government. According to the report of *China Reform*, their reporters received a copy of the official documents of the People's Government of Fuzhou City, which clearly stipulates:

> 1200 mu of land is planned for the Southeast Auto Town and 1200 mu for the auto parts supporting base. The auto parts supporting base is allowed to be developed by the Taiwanese investor in land tracts with projects to push forward such development. The land transfer price is 33,000 yuan/mu (including associated taxes and fees), 10,000 yuan/mu of which will be used for compensation to farmers. The rest of the land compensation will be centralized and used by Minhou County to construct infrastructure for the Auto Town. The city and county shall refund the normally-to-be-handed-in associated taxes and fees from land acquisition and transfer to the Qingkou Town Investment Zone in Minhou County for the infrastructure construction of the project…

In other words, Fuzhou City Government decides to transfer the land to the project at 33,000 yuan per mu, of which 10,000 yuan per mu is the compensation to farmers, and the balance is to be "centralized by Minhou County to make overall arrangements of use" for the project construction. The problem is the 10,000 yuan/*mu* stipulated by Fuzhou city ends up arriving at the farmers as 800 yuan per person.

The investigation found out that the Minhou County and Qingkou Town Governments intercepted the land compensation, and, just like Dengfeng Government, they used the intercepted compensation to invest into the Southeast Auto Town project. According to reports, the investment of Phase 1 of Southeast Auto Town was 1.3 billion yuan, with the equity of mainland investors accounting for 50%, among which 10% was for Fuzhou City, 5% for Fuzhou Trust and Investment Company, and 5% for Minhou County. At that time, the Minhou County Government simply did not have the financial resources to invest. To follow the decision by Fuzhou City, namely to invest all the differentials between the land transfer price of 33,000 yuan per *mu* and the farmer's compensation of 10,000 yuan per *mu* for the 2,400 *mu* of land acquired for Phase 1 into the project, the total would be 55 million yuan. To reach 5% (65 million yuan) of the total investment of 1.3 billion yuan, they couldn't help but intercept some of the 10,000 yuan per mu land compensation fee which was stipulated by Fuzhou City.

The explanations of CHEN Huojin, the Party Secretary of Qingkou Town, were all amusing craps. He said to the reporter: "Many farmers are not well-educated. If all the compensation is paid to them all at once, some would have squandered it in a few days." He also made up stories that "most of the money was invested on behalf of the farmers into the county agricultural funds, including production support fund, food ration funds, retention fund, and pension fund" etc. etc. However, when the reporter questioned him, "How much farmers' compensation was deposited in the funds?", "Did the farmers agree?", "What about the yield of the funds?", "Were there any contracts?", and "Who will bear the loss if the fund suffers losses?", then "CHEN and the town mayor turned speechless".

By the end of 1996, the farmers who felt cheated by the government, petitioned to the municipal, provincial, and central departments dozens of times. In March 1997, when the Provincial People's Congress was held, dozens of farmers from Qingkou Town went there to report the problem. Subsequently, Minhou County and Qingkou Town Governments dispatched police to arrest the petitioners. Later, Minhou County decided to allocate 1 million yuan every year to Qingkou Town to compensate the land-expropriated farmers. However, the villagers today are still demanding the compensation for 1997–2002, and asking to share the county government's equity in Southeast Auto Town.

In fact, Southeast Auto Town is commercially very successful. By the end of 2002, the cumulative vehicle sales reaches 100,000 units, with a cumulative sales revenue of 13.1 billion yuan, and a tax and profit of 1.8 billion yuan. For 2002 alone, Minhou County collected from this project a state tax of 72.83 million yuan, a local tax of 36.93 million yuan and received a dividend of 12.31 million yuan. The profits have stimulated the continuous expansion of the Auto Town. The number of auto parts factories has increased from 30 in 1999 to 78; correspondingly, the land area grew from 1,500 *mu* to 3,800 *mu*. The project co-operates with a German auto company in Phase 2, the construction has started, and the plan is to acquire 3,000 *mu* of land.

The increasing demand for land has increased the land transfer price at Minhou. In fact, with the approval of the provincial government in 1996, the transfer cost of the 9.4 hectares of land acquired for the construction of supporting facilities for the Southeast (Fujian) Automobile Industry Co., Ltd., reached an average of 67,000 yuan per *mu*. The approval document from Fujian Provincial Government points out and that this is the just price for the "raw land" with a term of 50 years, the price for the "five connections and one leveling" and ancillary facilities should be agreed separately. That is to say, the agricultural land acquired by the government can receive an income of 67,000 yuan per *mu* without any additional investment. It is said that the farmers also managed to negotiate to increase the compensation to 26,000 yuan per *mu*. However, if the land-expropriated farmers hope to share the appreciation of the land value, they have to confront, in terms of the benefit, with the land-expropriating government, because the net rent for the latter from the land, is the gap between the land transfer fee obtained by the government and the land compensation paid to the farmers.

Southeast Auto Town is a commercial investment project, not a project "for the public interest" that provides "public goods". However, under the current laws, for any commercial projects that involve the conversion of agricultural land into non-agricultural construction land, the land will have to be acquired by the government, which is compulsory. Here the law provides a dual incentive structure: high profits of the commercial projects drive the government to exercise the land acquisition rights, and when enforcing the land acquisition rights, the government pursues more rents.

The investigation of the land acquisition case of Southeast Auto Town tells us that the commercial project-driven land acquisition is carried out in the context of fierce competition for the investment project. An official from the Fuzhou Municipal Planning Commission who knew the inside story pointed out that the location of the Southeast Auto Town was originally not in Minhou County, but the competitive land prices offered by the local government and the relocation commitment made by the county leaders have made Qingkou Town the winner. This is a significant constraint because the competition between different local governments for investment projects will inevitably set restrictions and put a cap on the land transfer fees, and too higher prices may just frighten investors away. Under this constraint, to get more rents from the acquired land, the only way for the local government is to lower the compensation for farmers.

To this end, like what we see in the Dengfeng case, the current land acquisition compensation mechanism gives much leeway because it only clearly sets the high limit but not the low limit. The real thing to set the low limit for the land compensation is the pressure from petition, appeal, and other collective actions of the farmers. In this competition, the "withstanding capability" of the pressure from the dissatisfaction of the land-expropriated farmers is a necessary condition for more commercial investments and greater rents. Clearly, it is not a matter of "good conscience", but a matter of "survival of the fittest".

Commercial competition is a great driving force for industrialization and urbanization. The success of commercial projects brings considerable external economic benefits to the society, and it indirectly increases the public interest as well. The competition of local governments for investment can improve the investment environment and promote overall social and economic progress. No question about that. The question is, what kind of property rights system regulates the "commercial competition"? Different property rights constraints lead to different competition behaviors. We need to focus on the economic implications of the government's participation in land competition in the context of unclearly defined private land transfer rights.

5.3.3 *Land Acquisition Case of Maichen Town, Xuwen County, Guangdong Province*[15]

Commercial behaviors are supposed to be cost-effective because they are profit-seeking, and commercial projects are supposed to improve the efficiency of land use. However, the massive agricultural land expropriation driven by commercial activities has been accompanied by chaos; some expropriated land simply lays waste. According to the preliminary survey of a nationwide land rectification ordered by the State Council in July 2003, there were more than 5,000 development zones in China with a total acquired area of 30,000 square kilometers, which is equivalent to the combined construction land area of all existing cities and designated towns (or *Jianzhizhen* in Chinese, meaning the geographic organizational unit that has the political status or administrative ranking of a town rather than a township). A similar rectification campaign was carried out in 1997. The question is how commercial development and land waste get intertwined. Could it be true, as some speculate, that the greed for profit has led to the waste of land resources?

Let us look at a case of illegal land acquisition without utilization. The story took place in Maichen Town, Xuwen County, Zhanjiang City, Guangdong Province, a well-known fruit and vegetable production and distribution center. At the beginning of 1997, the town government applied to the county for land acquisition to build Maichen East Fruit and Vegetable Market. The application stressed the importance of building such a market:

> Due to lack of a fruit and vegetable market, most fruit and vegetable buyers have to set up their stands along the road, causing traffic congestion and disorder, which in some cases has led to forcing up prices and bullying market by some lawbreakers. The legitimate rights and interests of the producers and business people are compromised, seriously hindering the development of the fruits and vegetable market in our town. Besides, it causes dirty and chaotic conditions in the bazaar, which is detrimental to the appearance of the town and the city. Therefore, to build the Maichen Fruits and Vegetable Market has become an imperative need for the economic development of our town.

The market construction planning made by the Maichen Town Government is as follows: The market will set up 200 simple stands. The investor can obtain a profit of 800,000 yuan upon construction completion, pay 2 million yuan tax to the state

[15] The public reports used in this section include: "The Intensified Dispute over Land Acquisition in Maichen Town, Xuwen County", Jiao Huidong, *Life Times*, December 24, 1998; "The Pain of Losing Land: A Four-Year Review on the Dispute over Land Acquisition at Maichen Town", Zhang Wen and Chen Yong, *South Reviews*, December 10, 2001.

per year, and create 1,000 jobs. In July of that year, Zhanjiang Municipal Bureau of Land and Resources approved 42.3 *mu* of land for the project.[16] However, in the subsequent *Notice of the Demolition and Construction of the Maichen East Fruit and Vegetable Market*, Maichen Town announced a land acquisition area of 90 *mu*. On November 1 of the same year, the town government issued a demolition notice, which ordered that "all to-be-resettled households must finish the demolition procedures and complete the demolition by November 5; otherwise, from November 6 onwards, the town government will execute forced demolition, and all the materials will be confiscated." On November 6, the government of Maichen Town called the town's police, its land resources office and other departments to bulldoze villagers' houses and cash crops, and beat up the villagers who rejected the demolition; many people were injured on that day. "The town was filled with cries and cries that day", the memories of many witnesses are still live and fresh today. The town government also detained and man-hunted those "rock stubborn" villagers defying the land acquisition such that some of them dared not go home for several months. The villagers strongly condemned the town government for illegal administrative measures, while the town officials complained that the villagers' legal awareness was too weak and their quality as people is too low.

What is funny is that years later, most of land acquired with so much violence remained idle. In 2002 when the reporter from *South Reviews* came back to the town, he did not see a single stand in the planned "market", but he saw quite a number of new houses on the land plot, some completed and others under construction. CHEN Quan, the then Party Secretary of the town, and the commander for the forced expropriation, admitted to the reporter that the current situation was not what had been originally planned, but he was transferred in 1998, and it was not his responsibility anymore.[17]

It turns out when the government of Maichen Town applied for land acquisition, the Party and government organs could not even pay their employees, and they had no money at all to build a fruit and vegetable market. So, the town government decided to attract investment. The plan was after the land is sold, and the market begins to

---

[16]On May 5, 1997, the State Land Administration issued a "Notice on Freezing Farmland Occupied by Non-Agricultural Construction Projects", which stipulates to freeze the farmland occupied by non-agricultural projects for one year from April 15, 1997 to April 14, 1998. During this period, only the State Council has the authority to approve farmland for non-agricultural construction projects that have already been included in the annual asset investment plan of the state, or provinces/autonomous regions/municipalities and are in urgent need of construction. It was surprising and incredible that Zhanjiang Municipal Bureau of Land Resources ignored this notice, overstepped their authority and gave approval to the land for construction. The heads of the relevant departments of the bureau excused themselves in an interview in November 1998 by saying: "when we were at the job site, we saw that town government was not occupying any farmland. We didn't know if they occupied the farmland for the project construction or not. But the application from them says it's not farmland, so what we have approved is not farmland.

[17]In fact, as early as October 1997, the Xuwen County Transportation Bureau opened a fruit and vegetable market in the western Maichen Town, which was quite able to serve as a fruit and vegetable distribution center. However, due to the obstruction by certain officials, this market stayed idle. When the reporter came here this time, he only saw cattle grazing at the empty "market". Therefore, many villagers were outraged: "They (the town government) had no intention to build a fruit and vegetable market. Clearly, they only wanted to make money by speculation and selling the land!".

make a profit, the government and the developer would share the profits 30 to 70. The compensation for land acquisition decided at that time was 40,000 yuan per *mu*, and the land acquired was priced according to their locations: 22,000 yuan per meter (15 meters depth) for Grade I, 18,000 yuan per meter for Grade II, and 16,000 yuan for Grade III, translating into an average sales price of 880,000 yuan per *mu*.

Let's do the "break-even" analysis. The total compensation for land acquisition of 90 *mu* is 3.6 million yuan; if the town government and the developer sell 4 mu, they can get 3.92 million yuan; if they can sell 8 mu, their profit from the land requisition would be 100% (if 30% of the profit goes to the town government, the amount is 1 million yuan). That is to say, even if 90% of the land acquired stays idle, the town government and developer have already earned several million yuan in gross profit, which is not a bad deal. Moreover, the idle land can be sold in the future.

The key here is not profit-seeking or "greed" because the profiting motive of normal merchants is restrained by other people's motive to make money. The developer acquiring the land is not only restrained by the interests of the land-transferor but also faces pressure from other developers' bids. However, under the current land acquisition system, the government's compensation for the "forced land acquisition" can be much lower than the opportunity cost of converted agricultural land. The lower the "land acquisition" price for the government, the larger the land area they can afford to stay idle. This explains why land acquisition for commercial use generally occupies more land than necessary and why they often occupy without utilization. What is more, the compensation from the government is paid by public finance. In the absence of necessary surveillance on public finance, the waste of acquired land takes place as the government doesn't care if the investment can be recovered or not. Many people praise China's current land acquisition system for ensuring smooth industrialization and urbanization with "low-cost land". What they did not see is that the "low-cost land" not only results in much waste but also leads to misallocation of huge amounts of capital.

5.4 Practices to Redefine the Right to Transfer[18]

From the perspective of ownership, land acquisition is to change the collective ownership of land to state ownership. Therefore, when the land acquisition takes place, the "collective" rather than the contracting farmer(s) immediately becomes a legitimate party. As mentioned before, the rights of the collective regarding land acquisition are not clearly defined by the law, and in the context of ambiguous definition of the rights, the collective organizations also leverage their advantages to compete for the compensation. From our investigation, we find many cases of collective organizations participating in driving down and intercepting the compensation, and even directly occupying the land. In this respect, the logic behind the collective behaviors

[18]The survey materials used in this section include: "Investigation on Nanhai Land Joint-Stock System", LIU Shouying et al., SCDRC; Bledsoe and Prosterman (2000).

is no different from that of the aforementioned governments. We have also seen other cases where some collective organizations bypass the expropriation as specified by the current laws, and directly supply land to the developer in various forms such as equity investment and leasing.

5.4.1 Nanhai Model

After 1992, the Nanhai local government leveraged the opportunity of considerable local and foreign investment into setting up factories to accept the approach by collective economic organizations, under the premise of not changing the collective land ownership, to perform overall planning for the collective land and lease such land or shop buildings to enterprises, thus breaking the state monopoly of land conversion from agricultural to non-agricultural use. By 2002, the city's industrial land totals 150,000 *mu*, of which 73,000 *mu*, almost half of it, remains collectively owned and not requisitioned. In the Nanhai model, farmers pool their land and inject as shares and all benefit from the soaring value of the land.

The Nanhai model was tried and established from practice by a small number of villages. Let's look at the practice of Xiabai Village at Luocun Town. In 1993, the village planned 1,300 *mu* for agricultural protection area, 60 *mu* for commercial and residential area, and 1,700 *mu* for industrial development area. In the beginning, the industrial area was developed by attracting investment and leasing the land to investors. And then they rolled out the development by providing electricity, water, and obtaining permits, and delivering the land with "three connections and one leveling". The tenancy is generally 50 years, and the rent increases at 2%, 3%, or 5%, per year. By 2002, more than 60 companies had settled in the development zone, and the annual land lease income was over 6 million yuan. The agricultural land was also leased. For example, 200 *mu* of vegetable land was rented to a Macao businessman, and the annual rent was 300–500 yuan per *mu*; an agricultural company paid over 200,000 yuan per year for renting the fish pond, and over 100,000 yuan for a vegetable plot, and the total was over 400,000 yuan. The 60-*mu* commercial and residential area was leased to villagers to build houses at a price of 200 yuan per square meter, water and electricity facilities installations were charged at 10,000 yuan per room, the total income was also more than 1 million yuan.

The land rented to external investors was the land already previously contracted to the farmers in the village. Therefore, the change here is the conversion of farmer's contracting rights into equity. Their specific practice is that the village converted all the collective property and land into shares, and allotted shares to all the households in the administrative village or the village group. The allotment of shares was based on the household registration (Hukou); Different levels of basic shares, contracting rights shares, and labor contribution shares were set for the allotment according to different member situations. The proceeds from the rental of land by the village joint-stock company were distributed to all shareholders according to their shares. The income of the collective equity was invested further into land development and operation, and the dividends of the farmers' shares were distributed to their households.

With increased capital, the village joint-stock companies also began to construct shop buildings for rental so as to increase the added value of the land. For example, Pingnan Village introduced a Taiwanese investor in 1989. They raised more than 2 million yuan and built a 2,400-square-meter factory building and leased it to the Taiwanese company. Later, the village introduced 32 Taiwanese companies, two Hong Kong companies, and 230 plus private enterprises from China's mainland into its industrial zone, and the village joint-stock company thus obtained stable land income.

The Nanhai Municipal Government has summarized and replicated this village-level land system innovation, and formulated the following two points for the land joint-stock system: (1) conducting the zoning to categorize the land by function into agricultural protection area, commercial and residential area, and industrial development area so as to protect farmland and implement urban planning; (2) converting collective property and land and farmers' tenure into stocks, and formulating the articles of association to set the equity structure, dividends distribution, and equity management so as to regulate the business activities of the village joint-stock organization. At the same time, Nanhai also announces that the land-converted equity is lifelong and can be inherited.

According to the survey conducted by SCDRC, the Nanhai Land Joint-stock System has generated tangible results. First, industrialization has been kicked off with collective land, which has lowered the threshold for industrialization. For a start-up, if land is to be obtained through government-led acquisition, not only the schedule will be delayed by the complicated red tape but also it has to pay very costly land transaction fees and transfer fees. Take Nanhai City, for example, the cost involved for conversion of one *mu* agricultural land to non-agricultural construction land includes 4000 yuan for farmland occupation tax; 1500–1800 yuan for land acquisition management fee; 10,000 yuan for reclamation fund; 6000 yuan for agricultural insurance fund; 1,333 yuan for farmland water conservancy fee. For the land transfer fee, the rate is 10,000–25,000 yuan per *mu* for industrial land, 125,000 yuan for commercial land, and previously 80,000–100,000 yuan for residential land. As the market value of land has gone up, the city has calculated the price for enterprises to use requisitioned land to be generally 150,000 yuan, and a high limit of 400,000 yuan per *mu* for industrial land, and 0.4–1.5 million yuan for commercial land. Nanhai City offers the land for rental to drastically lower their upfront costs for enterprises. The rent for agricultural land was, on average, 500 yuan per mu per month; the rent is higher if the land is along the road, or lower if the location is remote and if the land is hilly or deserted land. It is this flexible use of land that has attracted a large number of enterprises to settle in Nanhai, forming a famous industrial belt in the Pearl River Delta, and opening up a new road towards industrialization.

Second, unlike government's land acquisition, after paying all the relevant taxes and fees, the collective organization can collect the land rent as an income, which is shared by all the rural households according to their equity. In Nanhai, the annual rent by an industrial enterprise is generally 6,000 yuan, and the land lease contract usually requires three to five years of rent upfront. This way, the collective organization and the farmers obtain a land rent from 18,000 to 30,000 yuan per *mu* all at once, and besides they will continue to enjoy the benefit of future land rent increases.

Third, the farmers' land tenure is now turned into permanent dividends sharing right, which not only maintains the core of the HRS but also extends the farmers' land income rights into the non-agriculturalization process.

According to the survey and statistics to some villages of Guicheng District, Pingzhou District, Lishui Town, Dali District, and Huangqi District, the per capita dividends for the farmers increased from 1016 yuan to 1951 yuan from 1994 to 2000, and the dividends accounted for 1/4 to 1/3 or even 1/2 of farmers' total net income in most areas. However, a bigger survey by the Nanhai Agriculture Bureau showed that the dividends per share of the rural joint-stock co-operatives across the city only increased from 310.8 yuan in 1997 to 314 yuan in 2000, and the dividends per share of the joint-stock group companies only increased from 97.74 to 99 yuan. The problem is that many land joint-stock organizations actually did not pay dividends to villagers. Among the 191 joint-stock group companies established by the village committees, only 17.8% of them ever paid dividends to villagers during the survey period; and only 52% of the 1678 joint-stock co-operatives formed by the villagers' groups paid dividends.

The Nanhai model danced in some grey areas of the current land laws. As we analyzed in Sect. 5.2, the current laws allow a few exceptions and leave some ambiguities relating to the basic principle of "agricultural land must be requisitioned and nationalized in order to be converted for other purposes". The main circumstances include for farmers (1) to set up their own enterprises; (2) to work with other organizations or individuals and convert the land-use right into investment to set up enterprises in the form of joint operations; or (3) the collective ownership over the non-agricultural land can remain unchanged in case of land tenure transfer caused by bankruptcy or merger or other reasons.

The problem is that the Nanhai Model clearly does not satisfy above item (1) because they are not setting up their own enterprises; it also does not meet the requirement in item (3) because it's impossible for so much land to be the legacy of insolvent collective enterprises. Then, does it satisfy condition (2)? The trouble with Nanhai Model is that they do not directly invest in enterprises with their land tenure, but rather they set up joint-stock land organizations, which then leases the land or shop buildings to independent industrial and commercial entities. As for the term "joint operation", it is a form of economic organization that has no clear definition. If joint operation refers to a consortium, the farmers' land shares are not put together with the investor's industrial and commercial enterprises to form a joint entity; if the meaning is "co-operation", then the lease of land and factory building can be regarded as some sort of "co-operation" in the market. In any case, the practice for the farmers' joint stock land organization to lease land to industrial and commercial enterprises is directly contradicting the clause – "No right to the use of land owned by farmer collectives may be assigned, transferred, or leased for non-agricultural construction."

In real operation, they need to either apply for the land use in the name of setting up enterprises by the rural collective themselves or jointly with other parties, then sign the lease contract with the investor; or simply "use the land without permit". Either way, the transfer rights of collective non-agricultural construction land cannot be protected by the law. Once disputes arises with the lessee, the only court verdict will be to return the tenure to the collective, the land rent to the lessee, and generally, the court will also require that the collective organization return to the lessee the investment on the building.

The significance of the Nanhai Model is that it has officially put up the question of "the transfer rights of collective non-agricultural construction land", or the lawful entry of collective non-agricultural construction land into the land market. In 2003, the People's Government of Guangdong Province issued *the Notice on the Trial Implementation of the Tenure Circulation of Rural Collective Construction Land* in accordance with the principles of the rural work documents issued by the CPCCC and the State Council. The administrative regulations from the local government points out that "the right to use of rural collective construction land may be transferred in accordance with the provisions of this Notice. Such circulation of the rural collective construction land may be made in the form of assignment, transfer, lease, pledge, etc. and shall follow the principles of voluntariness, openness, fairness, compensation for equal value, and purpose control." It means that all collective land that has been approved for certain use or obtained in accordance with the law and that has been registered, obtained the land tenure certificate, complies with the overall master planning, and has clear boundaries with no ownership disputes "can be assigned, transferred, leased or mortgaged, and such land enjoys the same rights of use as the tenure of urban state-owned land".[19] This provides a local empirical basis for national-level revision to the existing land administration regulations.

5.4.2 *Kunshan Model*[20]

Chetang Village, Lujia Town, Kunshan City, Jiangsu Province, is adjacent to Kunshan Economic and Technological Development Zone. Since 1992, investors, especially Taiwanese investors, flocked here to set up factories and start businesses. Home to 448 foreign-invested companies, the 77-square-kilometer county-level city creates 205.3 billion yuan annually. SHEN Weiliang, the Village Party Secretary, said: "Before 1992, Kunshan was basically an agricultural county. There was not much industry, and the land was valueless." He noticed that gradually Kunshan was attracting more and more foreign investment, and the land would be more and more valuable if it

[19]Guangdong Provincial People's Government Document [2003] No. 51.

[20]The public information used in this section include: "'Land Revolution' in Kunshan" by Cai Wei, *the Bund Pictorial,* June 2003; "Fully Leveraging Land Polices is the Most Powerful Secret for Villages in Shanghai with Output of over RMB 100 Million", HE Lidan et al., *the Bund Pictorial,* August 22, 2003.

could be bought to build factories. One *mu* of land could only earn 800 yuan per year by growing rice and rape seeds, but the rent would be over 6,000 yuan if it was requisitioned by the government and leased to foreign investors. If the tenure was sold, then the price would be over 200,000 yuan for one *mu*. "But such money had nothing to do with the farmers." The compensation for national requisition was at most 20,000 yuan per *mu*, and that was for a good location near the national highway.

The turning point came in 1996 when some Taiwanese investors asked SHEN to provide standard shop buildings for rental. SHEN knew that it was a now-or-never opportunity. Some bold nearby villages already sneakily rented land to Taiwanese investors. However, he also knew that, according to LAL, it was legal for the government to transfer the tenure for non-agricultural use, but not the farmers.

SHEN thought hard and finally he concluded that he figured out a way that was both legal and could allow farmers to share the earnings from land appreciation. He organized villagers to buy soil to fill the muddy ponds and ditches at the ends of the village, so as to "reclaim" some farmland. According to the policy, the "reclaimed" land can be used for applying for construction land quota. In 1997, Chetang Village obtained 40 *mu* of land for construction in the alternative way of "reclamation".

However, the village did not have the money to build factory buildings. Originally, they thought about fund raising, but the lessons of fundraising in the 1980s were still vivid in villagers' mind. After thinking back and forth, SHEN decided to let the daring farmers make personal investment and build the shop buildings for rent, with the land supplied by the village through leasing. In 1999, CHEN Zhenqiu joined hands with other four villagers to invest 150,000 yuan to rent one *mu* out of the 40-mu reclaimed land and built a standard factory of 432 square meters. In the first year after the building was rented, they received a 12% return on the investment, which incentivized other villagers. By December 2001, 105 households of the village (nearly one-fifth of the total number) established nine "investment associations" with a total investment of 6.79 million yuan and constructed 15 standard factories, two dormitories, a farmer's market, and 66 shop spaces.

Three years later, more than 1,600 rural households in Kunshan joined various co-operative organizations for the purpose of developing non-agricultural land, with a total investment of more than 60 million yuan. These "investment associations" and "investment co-operatives" have been recognized by leaders of local party committees of Kunshan, Suzhou, and Jiangsu. The CPC Kunshan Municipal Committee even issued a document titled the *28-Point Policy on Enrichment*, which clearly said that the specialized rural joint-stock co-operation system was the main means of enriching the people. Yet, there was still no clear legal status for the farmers' co-operative investment organizations. In case contractual disputes arise between farmers and the village or with the lessee, namely the investor, it would be difficult for them to get legal protection.

Director YANG of Lujia Town Industrial and Commercial Bureau believes that this pioneering practice of farmers is very troublesome from the legal perspective. Because according to existing laws, these organizations cannot be registered as limited liability companies, or joint stock limited companies. If they are registered in other forms, the "shareholders" of the co-operatives must bear unlimited liabilities. The root cause of the problem, he believes, is land property rights. The current laws do not recognize the right of the village to lease the land to farmers for non-agricultural construction, nor do they confirm the farmers' right to lease non-agricultural construction land to investors.

ZHOU Daoming, Director of Lujia Town Bureau of Land and Resources frankly admitted and said that Kunshan's current policy is very loose; and in real practice, the agricultural land is allowed to be transferred, leased, or converted to equity shares within a certain scope, but still such operations are in big conflict with existing laws. It is said that during his inspection to Kunshan, the Party Secretary of the CPC Jiangsu Provincial Committee points out that new ways should be explored to increase farmers' income, and he encourages bold experiments and bold breakthroughs in investment-based enriching policies such as the land income distribution policy. This remarks, according to officials of local authorities, has gone a bit too far according to the current law.

"Frankly, we don't want to see each and every village or even family flock to invest into development." The Director of the Lujia Town General Affairs Office expressed a different view. Lujia Town has jurisdiction of over 35 square kilometers, 20 of which already taken up by three industrial parks. The government cannot attract more investment if it does not have control over the land. "Land and government service efficiency are the most important for investors, so the government must control the land." According to statistics, the fiscal revenue of the town in 2002 was 338 million yuan, 100-fold increase over 13 years ago, while the per capita income was 6,500 yuan for farmers, only three times higher. The director admitted, "and no mistake. We are 'fiscally quite strong but the general public is disadvantaged'. Over the past ten plus years of Kunshan's rapid development, the benefit shared by farmers is rather limited, and that in fact creates some problems between the government and the farmers." Although the Kunshan Municipal Government sets aside part of the land acquisition income as social security funds for farmers, it only solves the subsistence but cannot make the farmers rich. The town government had reservations about the farmers direct entry into the primary land market. "According to current laws, this can cause a lot of trouble."

The thoughts of Lujia Town Government were to leave some land for each village in the planned industrial parks; then the villages could fund the construction of factories for lease or sale, and the proceeds could be distributed according to market rules. "We learned it from the Suzhou Municipal Government. The municipal government has set aside some land in the Kunshan National-Level Development Zone for each town. This way, regardless of the location, all the towns and townships can share the benefits of development."

Kunshan's main experience is that farmers can bid-rent rural non-agricultural construction land, build factories and other industrial and commercial facilities, and then lease them to overseas investors, thus sharing the rising rent from the converted lands. Different from the Nanhai Model, Kunshan does not pool the land tenure from farmers together, but instead they leverage the "reclaimed land", namely the newly-added non-agricultural land. Kunshan also does not equally distribute the income from the development of non-agricultural to all farmers. Instead, it uses a within-the-village bidding method to lease the non-agricultural land to the highest bidders. The investment co-operative organizations are voluntarily founded by farmers willing to fully bear the risks and enjoy the benefits of leasing factories to external investors.

Similar land development is very common in the rural areas near the Shanghai metropolis, except that most of the practices were not publicly reported. For example, Guanglian Village of Xujing Town, Qingpu District has a population of 1,553, a working population of over than 800, and an area of about 2,400 *mu*; its per capita land is one of the highest in the suburbs of Shanghai. However, traditional farming can only generate a per capita net income of less than 600 yuan, which at most could feed themselves. As more and more farmers migrate into the cities for temporary work, the cost of holding the farmland has increased, and their willingness to farm has declined. Therefore, the village offered to exempt all farming duties, plus a subsidy of 600 yuan per person per year, to pool the contracted land from those consent farmers for non-agricultural development and construction.

To this end, Guanglian Village as the collective invested money and established Shanghai Guanglian Industrial Co., Ltd and made it land developer whose responsibility also included investment promotion, standard factory building, and then leasing the factories to investors from outside. In 1993, Guanglian Village introduced two companies. Within three years, all the investment in the standard factories has been recovered. With the major infrastructure projects such as expressways constructed in Shanghai suburbs, these villages have become more and more attractive to investors, and investment promotion has become the key to the rapid development of rural Shanghai. Many have recognized that to have collective organizations (enterprises) build factories, warehouses and shop spaces on their land and then lease them is the most direct, least risky, and most long-lasting model.

Of course, considering the explicit prohibitions and unclear "exceptions" of the existing laws, Guanglian Village claims that what they are doing is "not land lease, but land co-operation". The foreign investors welcome such "land co-operation" because if they have to obtain land from government-requisitioned land, the cost for industrial land will be as high as 250,000 yuan/*mu*, and the commercial and residential project will be as high as 1 million yuan/*mu*. Farmers like the "land co-operation" because if their land is requisitioned, generally, they can only be compensated for 3,500 yuan/*mu*, or 5,000 at best. As of today, Guanglian Village has introduced 40 enterprises, and the collected shop building rent also embodies fast value escalation of the land. The village has thus become a well-known "100 million yuan" village.

5.5 Economics Analysis of Agricultural Land Tenure Transfer

In order to understand the agricultural land transfer behaviors under the current property rights systems, perhaps we need to understand relevant academic traditions, define key concepts, and establish a verifiable theory that can explain the complex economic phenomena. But first, let's review some old works to get ready.[21]

5.5.1 The Cost of Losing Agricultural Land

Once the agricultural land is converted into industrial land or urban land, its market value will increase several times or even 100 times. In the process of industrialization and urbanization, the extent to which the property owners of agricultural land can share the increased value from the conversion is determined by the property rights system governing agricultural land—especially the tenure transfer system.

For more than a century, Georgism, the theory inspired by American utopian socialist Henry George, has been known to many. The theory says the rise in the land market value results from social factors and has nothing to do with the owner, therefore it is not fair if the owner profits from the value addition. Dr. Sun Yat-sen was deeply influenced by this doctrine. As the founding father of the Republic of China, Sun Yat-sen not only proposed "equalization of land ownership" as the guiding principle of his revolution, but also was convinced that it was a must to prohibit or restrict the free transaction of land rights; otherwise, the phenomenon that "the rich owns thousands of acres of land, while the poor have no place to stand" would make its comeback. According to the policy tradition of the Republic of China, "the increased land value belongs to the public" has always been a positive slogan (the implementation is another matter).

However, that "the increased land value belongs to the public" is wrong in economics, because this economics believes that the market value of resources is determined by their cost. The "production cost" of land is zero or basically unchanged, but why does its price suddenly soar? In terms of phenomenon, the value of agricultural land for industrial development or urbanization is not about its fertility, but its "location". The farmland can worth a hundred times more because of its "location", yet the land owner obviously does not contribute to the production of "the location" or pay any cost for it. Then why should they enjoy the benefits of the land price increase?

What traditional theory ignores is an important contributions to land's value addition, that is the owner has to give up the tenure of the land. Otherwise if the owner does not surrender the tenure, how can the "location" selected by industrialists, real estate developers, and urban planning officials, etc. have added value?

Giving up a right involves a price. This is a plain truth. The farmland owner could have earned income by using the land; if he gives up the land, he loses that income. Therefore, the income "from their own use of the land" constitutes an opportunity

[21] The "old works" mainly refer to the author's special column "Farmer's Income is a Series of Events" in the *21st Century Business Herald*, 2001; later the article was included in *Income is a Series of Events*, Arcadia Press, 2003 and China Development Press, 2004.

cost for the giving up. Without a decent offer, the owner will not give up the tenure from which he would otherwise get some income.

The tricky part is that the owner will accept to give up the right to use only when he thinks it is worthy to do so? In the real world, "worth it or not" matters, and it should be made very clear. Let me first point out three points. First, facing the same offer, ZHANG may think it is good, while LI may think it is not. Neither is wrong. That is to say the "value" is up to the individual's personal judgment. Not understanding this point means having not entered into economics, as the important concepts such as marginal returns and comparative advantage are all based on subjective judgments of individuals, too. Second, someone buys a pencil for 50 cents. The buyer thinks the pencil is worth it because he thinks what the pencil brings is worth more than the 50 cents. What about the seller? If the 50 cents is more than what he has paid for the production of this pencil, he will also think it is worth it. The conclusion of a business transaction is reached because both parties think that it is worth it, and that's the beauty of the market economy. Third, resource allocation becomes efficient only when both parties are happy with the transaction. Because for the seller it is worth more to give up the use in exchange for the income, and for the buyer it is worth more to give up the income in exchange for the use. If everything goes this way, all the resources will eventually get in the hands of the more efficient user. The bustling business world, at the end of day, is all about constantly discovering who can use resources more efficiently.

5.5.2 Truncation of Property Rights and Exclusion of Market Functions

Therefore, the simplest and most reliable method to prove that the agricultural land will be more efficiently used for industrial or urban purposes is that the price offered should be higher than the income from farming. Only by follow this simple rule of thumb, can land be efficiently used. Then, will it compromise industrialization and urbanization to raise the "compensation" to a level which the farmland owner regards as worth it? Just look at history. Western Europe, North America, and Japan are leading the world in industrialization and urbanization, their land is all clearly privately owned, and freely traded based on value. Was Britain's 25% population urbanization in 1700 the result of all land owned by the King? The Meiji Restoration brought Japan's industrialization and urbanization into full swing, wasn't it the result of a free trade of land protected by the law?

However, under the current land system in China, once agricultural land is converted into industrial or urban land, the private tenure (HRS-based collective ownership) is immediately changed to "state ownership". In order for industrialization and urbanization to take land from agriculture, China has come up with really its own unique land system, which hybridizes the idea of "prohibition of land sales and price increase belongs to the public" (mandatory expropriation), "nationalized industrialization" (super low compensation), collective ownership by the people's commune (only the "collective unit" is the legitimate representative of farmers) and "Hong Kong experience" (land lease system).

Such a hybridized land system is characterized as follows: it is neither the ownership nor the tenure of the agricultural land that decides the land supply to industrial and urban land use. That is to say, the property right of the farmland is legally not qualified to be a party to land transactions and has no right to participate in bargaining. It is the government that makes a judgment on the needs of industrial and urban land use and uses administrative power (including planning, approval, and land requisition) to determine the supply of land. In this process, the rent from the power rather than the rent from the property right of the land—stimulates the conversion of agricultural land to industrial or urban land. As a result, market price functions are excluded from the allocation of land resources for urbanization.

5.5.3 Why Is Low Price Land Requisition so Easy?

The compensation for farmland expropriation is unreasonably low. In recent years, the amount of land acquired at ultra-low-cost compensation has increased significantly. From the perspective of farmers, this is against the law of demand. From the perspective of the logic for economic behaviors, it should be difficult for anyone who wants to take away resources at an unreasonably low price. So why is the land requisition so easy?

There are many possible explanations, and I think the key point is "the collective". Although the rural reform has been carried out for more than 20 years, and the people's commune system is gone, the land, the most important production resources, is still owned by the collective. The visible difference between "the collective" and the commune system is that under the collective ownership system, the land is contracted by farmers for long-term operations, and no more used for collective farming.

However, in the legal sense, the collective unit is still the owner, and the contract issuing party for the land; as such, the collective unit has the right to decide the contracting period and conditions, and also the right to terminate and take back the contracting right. Now thanks to the central government's policy control, land contracting will be long-term and unchanged. However, the central government cannot stipulate other contracting terms and conditions for hundreds of thousands of collective units across the country. Therefore, although the land contract period cannot be easily changed by the collective, other conditions often change; and the collective can resort to the clause "If the farmer does not accept the changes in conditions, the collective can reclaim the land contracting right." The institutional reason for farmers to bear increasingly heavy burden in recent years lies in the collective system.

To convert the agricultural land for non-agricultural use, is, to a larger degree, the right of the collective. The current land system stipulates that the state can expropriate land from the collective but not from the farmers—and this is the biggest difference from the relocation of urban and rural households. LAL expressly stipulates that "the compensation for land acquisition shall be owned by the collective." As for how the collective compensates farmers who have lost their land tenure, there is no legal provision; and in real practice, the methods vary greatly, making the job easier.

In other words, the termination of the "long-term" land tenure of farmers in the name of land requisition is in full compliance with the current land system. In reality, "land acquisition" by governments at different levels that is not consistent with land planning and blatantly selling land for profits is not uncommon in townships, towns and villages. As far as the farmers are concerned, any level of government—even the autonomous administrative village is equivalent to the "state".

As for why the land acquisition cost is so low, I think it has something to do with the fact that farmers are not involved in compensation negotiations. Only the "collective" has the right to negotiate. In fact, the collective is often no more than a few township or village leaders. They are actually "selling" someone else's land. Permanently giving up the tenure with compensation of several thousand or dozens of thousand yuan per *mu*, isn't this not selling for a song? However, it is very much worth it for the limited few to centralize the control of the meager compensation in their hands. Moreover, whether or not the land acquisition can be completed is often a prerequisite for the rural officials to stay in power.

In further analysis, the "collective system" is not the "co-operative system" that originated from Europe—the latter is an organization based on private property rights of its members. Under the co-operative system, the resources contribution of each individual is clearly defined, with clear provisions on proceeds distribution. The resources are used co-operatively, and all members participate in the decision-making; and one-person-one-vote is the mechanism for traditional co-operatives. This is where the co-operative system differs from the shareholding system. The collective system has "eliminated" the private property of its members. Therefore, the "collective property" becomes an asset that cannot be disintegrated, or to use the buzzword, "quantified" into personal properties. It is always owned by the abstract "working people's collective", its control always falls into the hands of its proxies. When such resources get transferred and priced, the information cost is much higher than the case of using the land for themselves, making it easier for these proxies without principals to steal what rightfully belongs to the members.

According to Alchin, "every question of pricing is a question of property rights."[22] Conversely, all truncation of property rights affects the normal functioning of the price mechanism. One of our important theoretical conclusions is that transfer rights regulation has the same behavioral logic as price regulation. The slight difference is transfer rights regulation is an ex ante price regulation. Through controlling the farmers' tenure transfer, China's current land acquisition system turns the rents from property rights into the rents from administrative power, thus regulating the price of farmland conversion ex ante, and hindering land resources allocation by the market mechanism. This system not only leads to unfair distribution, but also to inefficiency in production and trading.

[22] Alchian (1965: 816–829).

5.6 Policy Discussions and Possible Alternatives

Since the 1990s, there have been two rounds of large scale farmland conversion in China. During this periods, no doubt, the central government's proactive fiscal policy and larger scale infrastructure construction have played a guiding role that should not be underestimated, but the accelerated industrialization and urbanization are the more fundamental economic driver for this agricultural land conversion. The problem is that under the current land system, the behavior of the stakeholders will inevitably be distorted. Therefore, with the acceleration of urbanization, the foundation for China's co-ordinated urban and rural development is greeted with a heavy blow. The conversion of too much cultivated land, the low efficiency of land resource allocation, and the severe deprivation of farmers' land rights have become important obstacles to improving farmers' income. At the same time, land-related social conflicts are on the rise. In particular, crimes and violations to regulations by government agencies and officials become frequent, and land corruption has become a serious problem.

The complexity lies in that urbanization not only meets the needs of national economic development but also is the fundamental way to realize the economic benefits of many parties including the farmers. Our investigation and analysis show that the root of the problem is not urbanization, nor its acceleration stimulated by the deepening of market relationships, but rather the imbalanced development of China's institutional conditions that regulate its industrialization and urbanization. The central problem is that the current laws, while allowing the government to assign, transfer and lease the land at the market price, still adhere to the principle of nationalization for all farmers' land except for self-use, and still maintain government's exclusive land acquisition right, and still restrict and prohibit tenure transfer for converted land by rural collectives and the contracting farmers. The improper control over land transfer rights makes the market price mechanism unable to play its due role in land resource allocation during industrialization and urbanization.

In view of the severity of the problem, the State Council decided in mid-2003 to rectify the national land market and suspended a large number of land acquisition projects. The rectification helps stop the indiscriminate farmland occupying and the infringement upon the interests of farmers, and also helps identify the problems and prepare conditions for choosing the right policy. It is also precisely this rectification that makes people aware that it is necessary to adopt various follow-up policies and legal moves to bring up and solve the problem at the institutional level. Otherwise the old story of the 1997 rectification will repeat itself, that is, after a few years from the large-scale rectification and the tightening of converted agricultural land supply, the outbreak of the problem will be even bigger.

In view of the overall idea of achieving co-ordinated urban and rural development, the task now is put on the agenda to "follow the principle of safeguarding the rights and interests of farmers, control the scale of land requisition, reform the system and improve the procedures for land requisition".[23] LAL, coming into force in 1999, now

[23] *The Decision of the CPCCC on Several Issues Concerning the Improvement of the Socialist Market Economic System*, People's Publishing House (2003: 17).

faces another round of revision. Because just emphasizing strict implementation of existing land regulations obviously cannot adapt to the needs of accelerated urbanization that we are facing today and for many years to come. However, there are still lots of controversy on how to, after all, amend the law and related land policies. In this section, we will start with the specific argument, namely "clear and secured transfer right of agricultural land is the foundation to allocate land resources using the price mechanism in the process of urbanization", and discuss relevant policy recommendations.

5.6.1 On "the Most Stringent Farmland Protection Policy"

We have noticed that *the Decision of the CPCCC on the Improvement of the Socialist Market Economic System* by the Third Plenary Session of the 16th CPC has given special attention to the transfer of land tenure rights:

> Within the term of contracting, farmer households may transfer the land tenure in accordance with the law and on a voluntary and compensatory basis. The regulations of land tenure transfer should be improved so as to gradually develop operations at appropriate scale.

Different from the current land regulations which limit the land transfer rights to "agriculture" and "non-agricultural construction for farmers' self-use", the Decision does not set insurmountable obstacles between agricultural and non-agricultural land when defining the right to transfer of farmers' tenure. True the document mentions "to develop operations at appropriate scale", but appropriate scale applies to all economic activities, agricultural, non-agricultural, industrialization and urbanization. As for "In accordance with the law", it could refer to existing law or a new one as the result of revision in accordance with the principle of the Decision. We believe that this important new policy principle—recognizing and protecting the land transfer rights of farmers without distinguishing agricultural land and non-agricultural construction land—provides a very important legal basis for breaking through agricultural land conversion as the only way for requisition.

This does not mean that the land transfer rights are not subject to any restrictions. In our view, one of the tasks of the land requisition system reform is to relax the "absolute legal prohibition on farmers' right to transfer of non-agricultural land", and at the same time to establish restrictions that meet the needs of economic and social development and are easy to implement. At present, the policy recommendations proposed by all parties are mostly on restrictions of the land transfer rights. Then, what restrictions, and how to interpret and express them, will help maximize the economic functions of the agricultural land transfer rights?

The aforementioned Decision of the Central Committee of the Communist Party of China points out, "the most stringent farmland protection system should be implemented to ensure national food security". This serves as the boundary condition for farmland transfer. That is to say, the degree of freedom in agricultural land transfer should be maintained so as to most strictly protect the farmland and not to threaten the country's food security. On the meaning of this restriction, it necessary to discuss a bit more. First, the most stringent farmland protection system does not mean that no cultivated land can be converted for non-agricultural purposes. If that were the case, there would be no difficulty at all to implement this policy. However, empirically, there is not a single economy yet in the world that has achieved industrialization and urbanization without taking up even a little bit of cultivated land. So, the real question now becomes, how to "attain the greater benefits including such objectives as food security, urbanization, and improved farmers' income through sacrificing the smallest amount of cultivated land"?

The Decision stipulates that the bottom line is to "ensure national food security." However, the difficulty lies in that the objective of "national food security" changes with changes in demand, technology, and trading conditions. In a national economy environment with accelerated industrialization and urbanization, the measure (cost) to achieve the goal is also constantly changing. After all, what kind of land system can roughly correctly reflect the changes in relevant economic conditions?

The current basic approach to regulate the transfer right of farmland is administrative approval. For example, the regulation stipulates that the conversion of agricultural land, occupying of cultivated land, and large-scale occupying of cultivated land should follow different criteria and be approved by different levels of government agencies. The problem is that the administrative examination and approval system cannot promptly reflect the real benefits and opportunity costs of farmland conversion. China's experience has shown that although strict protection of cultivated land has long been a national policy, the economic system has always failed to provide an appropriate mechanism to measure the "cost and benefit of reducing cultivated land". From the economics perspective, doing too much is just as bad as doing too little. Too much too fast loss of cultivated land, or take-up without use, is indeed a scourge; but over-protection, namely to totally ban farmland loss at the cost of abandoning the potential gains from urbanization and industrialization, also does no good to economic growth. To sensitively measure the gains and losses of farmland conversion, we must consider adding the economic constraints on converting the farmland.

5.6.2 On Differentiating for Public Welfare and for Commercial Operation

Currently the already proposed economic constraints include "distinguishing construction land for public welfare and for commercial interest", "significantly increasing compensation for statutory land requisition", and "compensating land requisition in the form of social security". These policy recommendations will be discussed below. First of all, based on many investigations and expert advice, the central government decides to adopt the principle of "draw a clear line between construction land for public welfare and for commercial interest" in response to the rampant practice by local governments of buying low in the name of public interest and selling high to projects for commercial interest.

To apply the above principles to the land acquisition system reform and the revision of LAL, a series of questions, mainly the following, need to be considered:

A. Definition of for public welfare and for commercial interest. The constitutional constraint for land expropriation by the state is "for public interest", but now pops up "for public welfare". What does it mean? In the strictest sense, only the products and services provided to all citizens free of charge are for "public welfare", and such a project is a public welfare project. Except for such limited few fields as national defense, social security, public health and public education, most construction projects, including most national key projects, only serve some citizens and can and should charge users at market prices. So, do all sorts of activities with so-called "externalities", or the "non-profit" arrangements for tax avoidance purposes fall into the category of "public welfare"? There is no easy agreement on this question. A mayor in the New York State converts a pasture with five employees into a golf course that employs 20 people. Hasn't he created jobs? Hasn't he helped with poverty reduction and cutting potential crimes, and thus reducing public security spending paid by tax-payers? Are we sure that this project has no elements of public welfare at all?
B. Even if our society or the legislation body reaches consensus on the differences between for public welfare and for commercial interest, should there be different costs legally of obtaining the land by these two types of projects? If no, why bother to distinguish the two? If certain statutory differences is to be set, say the land transfer cost becomes lower for projects for public welfare versus for commercial interest, then what criteria should be adopted to determine the difference? Should the difference be the amount of compensation, or different compensation mechanism? Per se, for instance, projects for public welfare obtain land through government requisition, and projects for commercial interests, through trading on the land market?
C. From the perspective of the land suppliers, why should they get the compensation at the low limit for-public-welfare projects, while they can get the average market compensation by supplying land to for-commercial-interest projects? The crux of the problem is that the land-supplying farmers are admittedly part of all citizens, as public welfare project benefit all the citizens, they also benefit these supplier farmers. But on the other hand, why just they have to bear the sacrifice that other citizens do not have to? Perhaps we may as well reference the soldier conscription policy. If that "All citizens of suitable age should join the army" is the common rule, then that any one supplying land to public welfare project must pay special taxes is a prejudice against some citizens.
D. The "price difference" in any form between for-public-welfare and for-commercial-interest projects will eventually affect the resource allocation between the two. The economic law is that the greater the difference, the bigger the distortion of resource allocation. Needless to argue, at any given income level, if public welfare projects occupy too much resources due to the too low

statutory cost, the national economy will always suffer some losses, which is certainly not in the interest of the public.

5.6.3 On "Higher Statutory Compensation for Land Requisition"

In view of the low statutory compensation for land acquisition and the tendency of enforcement institutions to always go with the "lower limit", proposals have been put forward to increase the statutory compensation. The question that we need to discuss, is that if the fundamental nature of the exclusive administrative monopoly and unilateral decision-making mechanism remain unchanged, and the compensation is raised by increasing the number of folds (of the annual agricultural output value), will this, after all, be able to reflect the relatively true price of the acquired land? Previous experiences have proved this point: From 1986 to 1998, LAL increased the high limit of land acquisition compensation from 20 times the average annual output to 30 plus times. However, as compared to the faster growth of the national economy, especially the even faster growth of land prices in the secondary urban land market, the new statutory maximum compensation actually didn't go up, but went down a lot.

In order for land acquisition compensation to reflect the relative scarcity of land, the first thing we need to consider is whether it is necessary to change the compensation benchmark. The current benchmark is the "revenue from the original use" of the acquired land. For the converted agricultural land, it refers to the agricultural output of the land. This benchmark means the demand for land acquisition escapes from the constraint from the cost, because the demand is based on the future income of the land for non-agricultural use, yet the cost only represents what farmers give up for agricultural use. Based on this benchmark, the greater the value difference between the agricultural and non-agricultural use of land, the more efficiency loss will happen to resource allocation. From the perspective of distribution, agricultural land owners are excluded from the list of beneficiaries sharing the increased market value of the land they give up for urbanization, ruling out the de facto possibility to increase farmers' income, and worsening the distribution structure of national income.

The compensation amount relates to the term of asset income. Land is a permanent resource. Under the current land system, the land acquired by the government can be leased with different and extendable expiry dates and generate permanent income; however, the compensation to farmers is limited to a maximum of 30 years. This may be consistent with the term of contracting of the collective land, but it neglects the fact that farmers can renew the tenure after the 30-year period. Just like the policy's distortion of the compensation benchmark, the distortion of compensation duration also has a negative impact on efficiency and fairness.

The statutory land acquisition compensation is also not intrinsically responsive. The market value of non-agricultural land is determined by the local economic level and the relative locational scarcity of the land. Owing to many regional complexities, it won't be, in any case, right to the point to formulate a national law and set a unified land acquisition compensation across the different localities. With reference to experience of developed countries, the new principle of "land acquisition compensation should be based on the market price" should be introduced into the land acquisition reform and land law revision. For the moment we will not elaborate on the details and the many good things about the "market price-based compensation", but we have to point out that if we consider introducing this new principle, we must also consider breaking the state's monopoly on the primary land market. The reason is simple: without the openness and competition in the primary land market, there is no way of getting the signal of the land's market price.

5.6.4 On "Including Land-Expropriated Farmers into Social Security System"

In the practice of reforming the existing land acquisition compensation mechanism, Zhejiang, Shanghai and Beijing have proposed or tried the new compensation method of covering the land-expropriated farmers with social security and paying the compensation in installments. These practices have aroused the research interest of some scholars, who then came up with the policy recommendation of "the land requisition related social security model". Let's have some discussions on this model.

First of all, we have to note that this method is also a pricing arrangement. Therefore, the amount of compensation is not substituted because of choosing the social security mode, but rather constitutes the foundation for such social security arrangements. Obviously, the land requisition social security fund comes from the compulsory savings from land acquisition compensation. Therefore, the low compensation for land acquisition can only provide land-expropriated farmers with low-level social security. If the pricing mechanism for land acquisition compensation is not changed, only changing one-time compensation to installments will not increase the interests of the land-expropriated farmers.

Secondly, the land requisition social security is in essence a commitment that land-expropriated farmers will receive their compensation by installments. If the model becomes a unified and compulsory establishment from the government, then it is a kind of national credit, rather than a market credit as a result of choosing the contract by the insured. This means should there be any payment problem with land requisition social security, it will be the responsibility of the state credit. That is to say, at the end of the day, the ultimate responsibility goes to all tax-payers or even all citizens.

However, it is the government that is responsible for managing the land requisition social security and the government changes with its term of office. Under this reality, certain currently-imperceptible moral hazards may occur in the future; that is, the current government receives all the proceeds of land acquisition all at once, but leaves the responsibility for installment payments to the next or the next next term of the government. Even with the latest social security policy arrangements in place to allow for independent operation of the land requisition social security and to add additional "personal account", it will still have to rely on the maturity of financial services and the improvement of financial supervision. At present, put the national credit aside, the reliability and universality is still not clear for the operation of "the land requisition social security model". Local experiments may be continued, but global institutionalization and legislation are premature.

5.6.5 On "Allowing Collective Land to Enter the Market."

The most important significance of the practice for rural collectives to enter the non-agricultural land market in Nanhai, Kunshan, and Shanghai is to break through the state monopoly of the market for agricultural-to-non-agricultural land conversion, and break requisition as the sole lawful way for such conversion, thus creating conditions for a market-oriented agricultural land conversion mechanism to go in parallel with the state land acquisition mechanism. However, from the current practices, there are two major questions that need to be studied.

One is how to clearly define the property rights of the collective and the contracting farmer households. When the collective reclaims the land tenure from the contractor in order to develop non-agricultural land resources, it may compromise the basic institutional achievement of more than two decades of the rural reform. As it is not difficult for farmers in Nanhai to land a job, the cost of continuously holding the agricultural land rises, collective reclamation of the tenure generally does not encounter farmers' resistance as long as the compensation is reasonable. However, if the policy of "the collective's entry into the non-agricultural land market" becomes legalized into a common practice, the "rural collective", defined as "the pure landowner" in the 2002 LLCRA, may turn back into an active force that easily infringes upon the property rights of farmers. If the law fails to clarify that the farmer is the rights holder of the land's conversion for non-agricultural purposes, then as we have already seen, the collective and a handful of village leaders will also snatch the rents, or control and dominate the rents income from such agricultural land conversion, giving the farmers a hat of "shareholders" of the joint stock organizations that actually get no dividends.

If the law recognizes that farmers' land tenure transfer rights can enter the field of agricultural land conversion, then the interests of farmers can be more reliably protected, and the new non-agricultural land system can be better linked up with LLCRA, thus avoiding the land requisition system reform from compromising the HRS foundation. A system based on full land transfer rights for farmers may likely lead to higher transaction costs in the non-agricultural land market. To solve this problem, we emphasize that in theory the farmers' full transfer rights include freedom to enter contracts, and they can save transaction costs by signing all types of market-oriented contracts. In practice, farmer can voluntarily choose to join new collective co-operation organizations, or other contractual organizations, such as the Farmers Investment Co-operative in Kunshan.

Another big question is the selection of the form of contracts for collectives and farmers to enter the non-agricultural land market. At present, in Nanhai, Kunshan, or Shanghai suburbs, we can see that the collectives or farmers are renting land, factories, or facilities to companies from other places. Such rental contracts with annual payments are welcomed by investors and valued by authorities.[24] Because to collect the rents annually provides a much lower entry threshold for investors than the leasehold method (basically selling land).

But to upgrade these experiences into policies, laws and regulations, it is necessary to study the potential risks of the annual rental mechanism. In theory, leasehold and annual lease are but different types of market contracts, representing different business risk profiles, and each has its own applicable scope and objects. The construction time and useful life for factories, dormitories, and apartments are quite long, and the investment is capital-intensive. Therefore, the big risk is whether or not they can be fully used in the long term. If the investors buy the land (as in leasehold) for construction, then the long-term risks and benefits rest with the investors; otherwise, they rest with the land supplier namely the rural collectives or the farmers. In theory, these two approaches are equivalent; but in reality, the choice of the contract form depends on the comparison of the grasping of information on market risks and capital strength.

Therefore, it is not a good idea to use a law or a policy to replace the freedom of contract in the market. Current agricultural land suppliers mainly adopt the annual renting mode because rural collectives and farmers do not have explicit land tenure transfer rights. Otherwise, the story will be different if the law acknowledges the full tenure transfer rights for the collectives and the farmers. In particular, if the investment into long-standing buildings can only be recovered with short-term land lease, the contracts may entail huge future risks which cannot be fully fathomed now. We can only infer in theory that the more interventions and restrictions on the form of contracts from regulations and policies, the higher the cost of implementing the contract. Hereby the policy recommendation is that there should be expressly defined full land tenure transfer rights and full freedom of contract; and that the form of the contract can be leasehold (sale), rent, converting to equities, or other types of contracts. The key here is voluntariness and free negotiations.

5.6.6 Recommended Policy Mix and Procedures

Based on the above discussion, we believe that it is possible to find a policy mix with minimal economic loss to deal with the complex problems involved in the conversion of agricultural land. Our proposed policy mix is as follows:

---

[24]See Chen Xiwen's speech at the press conference on the release of Document No. 1 of 2004.

- Put an end to the policy of unitary state requisition of agricultural land, and develop an agricultural land conversion market.
- The government enjoys the ultimate right to requisition land in accordance with law within the scope of public interest as strictly regulated by law; the government's requisition procedures need to be improved to establish a market-based principle for compensation to contracting farmers.
- The full transfer rights of farmers' contracted land shall be recognized, including for agricultural or non-agricultural use; farmers shall have the freedom to choose the contract form and the development method when transferring land tenure in the non-agricultural land market as long as it is compliant with land planning and land use control regulations.
- As the contract issuing party for land contracting, the collective may accept government's entrustment to assist the land requisition and compensation payment, but it cannot intercept the compensation; the collective can also accept farmers' entrustment to develop the non-agricultural construction land or facilities in a centralized manner, but it shall not violate the voluntary principle or infringe upon the farmers' transfer rights.

Not much additional explanation needs to be made here:

1. The scope of government land requisition shall be strictly limited to projects for public welfare determined in accordance with legal procedures; given the difficulty of defining "public welfare", we recommend to add a new principle of "market price-based compensation" in accordance with international practice. This way, the government's financial strength constitutes the economic constraint on land acquisition, which is equivalent to providing "double insurance" for "the most stringent farmland protection" and "the optimal use of converted agricultural land".
2. In addition to avoiding misallocation between for public welfare land or not, the "market price-based compensation" principle also reduces the price gap between the requisitioned land and the market traded land, which helps to eliminate "rent-seeking by power" from the source. The economic significance of the policy mix of "land requisition" plus "market price-based compensation" is to save the transaction costs for public welfare projects. The land for public welfare is secured by the "requisition" so there is no bargain, but the compensation follows the market price and the market functions still remain. As for emergent needs such as for national defense, anti-terrorism, and disaster relief, such provision can be added that the government can "requisition first and compensate later in case of emergency".
3. Add the wording "ultimate" to "government requisition right" because there may be situations where even under the constraint of government having the final requisition right, the market transaction costs for public welfare projects might be reduced to an acceptable level. In other words, even if it is a public welfare project stipulated by law, the government does not necessarily have to immediately exercise the land requisition right, they can negotiate first, and exercise (or apply to exercise) the ultimate land requisition rights later if no agreement is reached.

This can allow involvement of the private sector in the public welfare project, and also increase the role of the market mechanism in public welfare projects and reduce the costs of enforcing land requisition.

4. Logically, to put an end to the unitary way of state requisition for the conversion of agricultural land, it is necessary to open up the non-agricultural land market. In fact, the government's monopoly on the primary land market has already been broken by practice, only that the existing market is too weak and too small. We propose that the future land market be based on the full land transfer rights of farmer households rather than the collective land ownership. This can be better aligned with the fundamental results of rural reform and LLCRA, while reducing the possibilities for village officials to infringe upon farmers' rights and interests, and also improving the efficiency of land use. The problem of rising transaction costs caused by the entry of thousands of farmers into the non-agricultural land market can be solved by voluntary organizations and contracts, including the method that farmers can entrust and leverage rural collective organizations and their entrepreneur resources, but still, we need to prevent the collective from violating the farmers' interests.

In order to bring the above policy mix into reality, it is necessary not only to revise LAL comprehensively but also to amend the constitutional principle that "urban land belongs to the state". Considering the huge adjustment to interests profile involved in land requisition reform, and the inevitable big differences in people's ideas and knowledge, we do not recommend to rush the legal revision, but rather take a step-by-step gradual approach to realize the fundamental change in the land system by absorbing the experience of market operation of land tenure in urban China. Specifically, the following procedures need to be taken into consideration:

- The NPCSC announces to revise the LAL.
- The State Council is authorized to try out some methods that are inconsistent with the existing land laws before the completion of the revision of LAL, including raising the compensation for land acquisition, opening the primary urban land market, allowing collective land or farmers' contracted land to enter the land market and improving land market development and administration, and so on.
- We shall mobilize all walks of life to care about the land requisition policy reform and the revision of LAL, extensively study domestic and international experience, and complete the revision in 3–4 years on the basis of local experiments and comprehensive research.
- Before completing the revision of LAL, it is also necessary to consider whether or not to compensate the too under-compensated farmers in certain forms. The forms of supplementary compensation include: formulating the policy on supplementary compensation based on extensive survey; focusing on key and severe cases; setting aside certain amounts (or proportion) out of the land sales income of the central and local governments for rural education and health expenses. In order to ensure efficiency, education vouchers, or medical vouchers are suggested.

References

Alchian, Armen. 1965. Some Economics of Property Rights. *Political Economy* 30.
Alston, L.J., G.D. Libecap, and R. Schneider. 1996. The Departments and Impact of Property Rights: Land Titles on the Brazilian Frontier. *Journal of Law, Economics and Organization* 12: 25–61.
Barzel, Y. 1989. *Economic Analysis of Property Rights*. Cambridge University Press.
Bledsoe, David J., and Roy L. Prosterman. 2000. *The Joint Stock Share System in China's Nanhai County*, RDI Report 103.
Coase. R.H. 1937. The Nature of the Firm. *Economica* 4: 386–405.
Coase. R.H. 1960. The Problem of Social Cost. *Journal of Law and Economics* 3: 1–44.
Eggertsson, I. 1990. *Economic Behavior and Institutions*. Cambridge University Press.
Ellickson, Robert C. 1993. "Property in Land". *Yale Law Journal* 102 (April).
Libecap, G.D. 1989a. Distributional Issues in Contracting for Property Rights. *Journal of Institutional and Theoretical Economics* 145: 6–24.
Libecap, G.D. 1989b. *Contracting for Property Rights*. New York: Cambridge University Press.
North. D.C. 1990. Institutions and Credible Commitment. *Journal of Institutional and Theoretical Economics* 149: 11–23.
Steven N.S. Cheung. 2002. *Economic Explanation* (the Three Volumes Edition). Huaqianshu Publishing Co., Ltd (Hong Kong).

Chapter 6
The Firm in the Market: A Special Contract Between Human Capital and Non-human Capital

This article discusses Coase's theory on the firm in the market, which regards the firm as a special contract between human capital and non-human capital. One of the characteristics of the firm as a contract is that it does not or is not able to define ex ante all the rights and obligations of the participating factors and the owners thereof; and it always leaves some to be regulated during the contract execution process. This special feature originates from the fact that organization of the firm involves the use of human capital (workers, managers, and entrepreneurs). Different from other studies, this paper brings the "property rights of human capital" and its characteristics into the thoughts on the firm as a contract, and believes that this is a key neglected element in studying Coase's theory of the firm.

6.1 Characteristics of the Firm as a Contract

Why do firms still exist if the market mechanism works? Coase discovers that the market mechanism in the real world is not cost-free, i.e. the transaction costs is positive, and "firms" exist because they save transaction costs. They save transaction costs because "within the firms market transactions are eliminated", as production factors organized within the firm do not need to sign a series of contracts, the costs of signing and executing such contracts are saved. That is why Coase says: "The distinguishing mark of the firm is that it is the supersession of the price mechanism."[1] Nevertheless, the firm is not replacing the market mechanism with a non-market contract. Because in Coase's view, using internal "instructions" and "allowing some authority (an "entrepreneur") to direct the resources", are nothing more than the result of "a series of contracts being replaced by one". "Through the contract, the production

[1]Coase (1937: 4).

The article was originally published in *Economic Research Journal*, Issue No. 6-1996.

Q. Zhou, *Property Rights and Changes in China*,
https://doi.org/10.1007/978-981-15-9885-2_6

factors agree to follow the entrepreneur's commands within a certain scope in order to get certain remuneration. The essence of the contract is that it defines the limits to the authority of the entrepreneur, who can direct other factors of production only within such limited scope."[2] That is to say, Coase does not see the firm as a non-contractual organization which is a supersession of the market contract; to the contrary, the firm is nothing more than one market contract that replaces a series of market contracts. I will call this one contract hereinafter as "the corporate contract" (or enterprise contract) in the market. It is reached with the "consent" from production factors invested into the firm and their owners, and its essence is to define the limits of the entrepreneur' authority. In other words, the entrepreneur's authority, directions, and plans within the firm and these sorts of seemingly anti-free market stuff, are actually awarded and restrained by another type of market contract, namely the corporate contract. This is where the entrepreneur's authority differs from that of the emperor, the serf-owner, and the central planning authorities. The conclusion is that the firm replaces the price mechanism with the corporate contract.

The question that Coase did not address is that if the firm is no more than anything but to use one type of market contracts to replace another, then what are the differences between the two? Steven N.S. Cheung (Cheung 1983) points out that "this contract" takes place in the factor market while "the series of contracts" are about the transactions at the product market. Therefore, the firm here just replaces the product market contract with the factor market contract. The above elaboration of Cheung is regarded as an important contribution to the theory on modern enterprises.[3] However, Coase's 1937 paper already clearly expresses the idea that a firm is one (or a set of) transaction contract in the factor market. Hasn't the previous quotes from Coase already said that "a series of contracts between production factors (or their owners) are substituted by one?" Doesn't this mean that Coase already sees the firm as a contract in the factors market? In fact, on this point, Cheung's view is no different from Coase's.

The real difference between the two of them is that Cheung thinks that there is no special difference between the factor market contract (i.e. the firm as a contract) and the product market contract; and that the interval, the positive transaction costs, and the risks and uncertainties in the transaction process are equally applicable to both the product market and the factors market. Therefore the extent of difference and arrangement details of the two types of contracts are not enough to differentiate one from the other. The real question raised by Cheung is per se, if you won't be regarded as in the same enterprise as the department store just because you go there and buy a pair of socks, then why you and a worker or an engineer is regarded as in one enterprise when you employ them? Cheung believes the contract to buy the socks and the contract to employ workers or to buy materials are both market contracts, and they are not much different in essence, thus he comes to the conclusion: because of the nature of the firm as a contract, we don't know what the firm is![4]

---

[2]Coase (1937: 4).

[3]Zhang Weiying (1995: 13).

[4]Cheung (1991: 148).

Coase expressly disagrees with this conclusion. He believes that in addition to serving as a contract between production factors and their owners, the firm has other peculiarities. In fact, in his 1937 paper, Coase wrote:

> Owing to the difficulty of forecasting, the longer the period of the contract is for the supply of the commodity or service, the less possible, and indeed, the less desirable it is for the person purchasing to specify what the other contracting party is expected to do. All that is stated in the contract is the limits to what the persons supplying the commodity or service is expected to do. The details of what the supplier is expected to do are not stated in the contract but are decided later by the purchaser. When the direction of resources (within the limits of the contract) becomes dependent on the buyer in this way, that relationship which I term a "firm" may be obtained.[5]

Here, Coase demonstrates: because of the long term of the contract to organize the factors into the firm, and due to the risks and uncertainties in this process, it is not suitable or possible to clearly define each and all the rights and obligations of the buyer and the seller of the factors before the contract is signed. Therefore, in Coase's opinion, the feature of the firm as a contract is that only the scope of supply of factors is stated in the contract, while the details as to how to achieve the supply are regarded as the rights of the purchaser (entrepreneur) which can be exercised after the contract is signed. In other words, the contract is a special contract where the rights and obligations are not fully defined in advance, and the purchaser of the factors can add certain provisions during the execution.

This type of corporate contracts in Coase's definition, is obviously different from the contract in the product market. In the product market, the consumer pays and takes the socks, and the transaction is over. He cannot further require to ask for any production details from his counter party. He can return the goods, but that only means he quits the transaction rather than he has control over the production details. He can place an order to customize his socks, but that only allows him to give in advance the detailed requirements, and check against them upon delivery; it by no means suggests that the consumer has the right to intervene in the production. If a consumer does not make clear in advance the design of the socks, and he wants to satisfy his craving by only giving the general description and directing the production himself until he is satisfied, then he not only has to pay a fortune, but also at the same time pay the workers for the labor, agree with him on the working conditions and salary in advance so that he is in control and gives command to production details. However, when he does this, he is already signing a corporate contract in Coase's sense. Now we have to ask the question: where does the fundamental characteristics of the firm as a contract as captured by Coase come from?

[5]Coase (1937: 40).

6.2 Property Rights of Human Capital

The key for the firm as a contract to differ from ordinary market transactions is, first of all, that the contract includes the use of labor. This point was briefly covered by Coase in his 1937 paper, and he says, in terms of the characteristics of the firm as a contract, "It is obviously of more importance in the case of services or labor than it is in the case of the buying of commodities. In the case of commodities, the main items can be stated in advance, and the details which will be decided later will be of minor significance."[6] Conversely, rightly because the firm needs to buy labor, and it is of great significance for labor transactions to "only gives the rough descriptions beforehand and leave the details to future decisions", and this is what makes the corporate contract different from other market contracts.

However, Coase does not further elaborate on why the use, purchase, and sale of labor require such a special contract. Economists of the 1930s, or around Coase's time, seem also not to have made thorough explanations. This is not surprising because before the emergence of the modern human capital theory in the 1960s, economics research has always been weaker on the labor factor than on land and other non-human capital. In exploring the root cause for the total output of the economy to outpace its input, contemporary human capital theory discovers that health, education, training, and more effective economics accounting capacity have become an increasingly important source for modern income growth. (Schultz 1961). Yet most of the literature on human capital theory does nothing more than extending some of the principles of the (non-human) capital theory to human capital analysis. When human capital economists regard human health, production skills, and knowledge as a kind of capital stock, i.e. as a source of current and future output and income growth, human capital and non-human capital almost have no difference in their form.

However, if one studies human capital from the perspective of market contracts, one must notice the important characteristics of property rights in human capital. As Rosen (Rosen 1985) puts it, "Ownership of human capital *in a free society* is restricted to the person in whom it is embodied". In my opinion, this is a unique ownership. For any other economic resources, including various non-human capital and land, the ownership may belong to the individual, or a family, a community, an organization, or a country, or it may not belong to any one or any group of people. However, the ownership of human health, physical strength, experience, know-how, skills and other spiritual beings can only indivisibly belong to the person, and this person must live and breathe.[7] When he explains that the property rights in human capital could

[6]Coase (1937: 40).

[7]Classical economists such as Marx noted that human ability belongs solely to that person. In his envisioned socialist society, all non-human capital is publicly owned by the whole society, and the market will die, but even in such a case, the society "tacitly recognizes the unequal individual endowment, and thus the work capability of different people, as a natural privilege". Therefore, it is necessary to maintain the "bourgeois legal power" to distribute the means of consumption according to the quantity and quality of labor actually provided by the workers. (Marx 1972: 12).

only belong to the individual, Rosen uses a constraint—"*in a free society*". What he means is that human capital belongs to the person only when the law does not allow slavery. But after reading Barzel's economic analysis to slavery (Barzel 1977), we can argue that even if the "free society" constraint is removed, the proposition still stands. A slave belongs to the slave owner and is part of his wealth only in the sense of legal power. Their masters has the full right to direct their labor and take away all the output. However, the slave is a kind of "full-fledged property",[8] who not only can run away but also controls his supply of labor. Forced labor, even with high costs of "supervision and policing", rarely achieves desired results. In order to save the costs, some slave owners must not only be kind to slaves (as found by Fogel[9]), but also had to implement a quota system, which allowed slaves to "own" private property after they handed in their quota. Under such a system, some skilled slaves were able to accumulate wealth to buy back themselves and become free citizens. Doesn't this suggest that as a natural private property, human capital cannot be fully ignored even by the legal power framework of the slavery system?

Legal power and other institutional arrangements against the principle of free market transactions may certainly result in property rights truncation, as described by Demsetz, for the human capital. Just like for any other assets, certain part of the complete bundle of the right to use, the right to contract, the right of income and the right of transfer, may have been restricted or removed. At this moment, even if human capital clearly belongs to the person in the sense of legal power, its property rights intensity will be impaired. In this regard, human capital is similar to non-human capital and has nothing special. However, with its nature as private property, human capital can respond to the truncation of property rights in a way that is totally different from non-human capital. Human capital, as Barzel puts, is a "full-fledged property", and its owner, namely the person, has full control over its development and utilization. Therefore, when part of the bundle of the property rights of human capital is restricted or deleted, the owner of the property can "shut off" the corresponding human capital such that as if it never existed. More importantly, it is impossible for the restricted or deleted part of the property rights of human capital to get centralized into the hands of other owners and become utilized. A piece of confiscated land can be transferred to a new owner without losing its area or fertility; but when a confiscated person arrives in the hands of a slave owner, he may still disobey the instructions, remain "lazy and stupid", or even would rather die. In short, the truncation of property rights in human capital can immediately and drastically push down the economic value of such assets.

It would be extremely difficult to understand the popular incentives theory without knowing anything about the above-mentioned characteristics of human capital. Why land and other natural resources, workshops, and equipment and bank loans do not need incentives, but human capital does? The reason lies in the property rights of human capital. On the one hand, human capital naturally belongs to the individual; on the other, once the property rights of human capital are impaired, its value will

---

[8]Cheung mentioned his contribution to the concept of "full-fledged property" (Cheung 1984: 181).

[9]Fogel and Engerman (1972).

immediately depreciate or even disappear totally. That is why, even in the slavery society, the slave owner could not merely rely on clubs and whips to get the work done. Needless to say, the use of all these complicated labor and skills in a free market contracts! What we incentivize is people, or the individual, to be exact, because only the individual is the indivisible owner and dominator of human capital. What the incentive (or negative incentive) does, is to transmit a market value signal of human capital's utilization (current or expectant) to the relevant individual, who makes a decisions on the scope and the intensity to use the stock of human capital, and then determines the future direction and intensity of human capital investment. Incentives are widely adopted because human capital is ubiquitous in economic life; and the development and utilization of human capital are increasingly playing a central role in modern economy.[10]

6.3 Human Capital in the Firm

Human capital of the consumer and the producer is already very important in general product market transactions. Even under the assumption that transaction costs is zero, the transactions of products and services between the buyer and the seller already contains more or less some human capital. The price mechanism not only allocates tangible economic resources but also provides both producers and consumers incentives for the use of human capital. Questions like what to buy/sell and how much to buy/sell have everything to do with the health, physical strength, experience, know-how, and judgment of both parties. How to mobilize human capital depends on the incentives from the market signal. For the price mechanism to allocate resources, the indispensable critical step is for the relevant people to make the decision in response to the price signal. The reason is simple. The human capital needed by the market transactions only belongs to the person, who will not decide to "enter (buy/sell)" or "exit (not to buy/sell)" unless there is an incentive such that the relative price change causes a change in the relative benefit. If other methods are used to "allocate the resources", thousands and thousands of participants won't be willing to accept it and it is bound to create a lot of trouble.

However, the role of the property rights of human capital only becomes prominent in the context of corporate contract. This corporate contract singles out the hidden human capital from products and labors of general market transactions and sees it as an independent factor that can be purchased by the firm. We already know that at least one party to the corporate contract is the human factor and the owner thereof. The simplest form, such as "a classic enterprise", is a contract between the owner of the enterprise's physical capital and the owner of the labor, i.e. the worker. Isn't the labor input here the workers' human capital (physical strength, skills, and efforts)?

[10]For the role of knowledge and other human capital in economic development, see "A Brief Review and Reflection on the Theories of Economic Development in Recent Years" by WANG Dingding, published in *Economic Research Journal* (Dingding 1995: 49–91).

The labor naturally belongs to workers themselves, and this golden principle also stands in classic enterprises. The owner of the physical capital of the enterprise—the capitalist—has no methods other than incentives to motivate the workers to do their best.

The significance of "measuring and monitoring" within the enterprise, as emphasized by Alchian and Demsetz (Alchianand and Demsetz 1972), is to identify individual workers' contribution to the production, thus to determine the basis for "incentive compensation arrangement". Measuring and monitoring does not mean to "exploit workers".[11] The effort of workers, like any other form of human capital, can be "incentivized" but cannot be squeezed. The abuse of power by capitalists, just like the abuse of other powers, is not uncommon in history, but it does nothing more than provoking the worker's collective actions (strikes, demonstrations, and workers' movements), and it has never achieved the purpose of the full utilization of their labor capabilities. On the other hand, the workers' spontaneous collective actions are limited to the purpose of only counter-balancing the abuse of power by the capitalists. In most cases, workers accept transactions in a competitive labor market and respond to "incentive contracts".

Measuring and monitoring is another type of human capital, which is often referred to as the managerial knowledge and skills applied in the enterprise. In the same vein, "entrepreneurship" refers to the use of human capital of the entrepreneur who usually deals with market uncertainties and makes business decisions such as "what to do and how to do". Therefore, to be more complete in the expression, any firm as a contract cannot be made possible without the labor of its workers, the capabilities of its managers and decision-making by the entrepreneur. These three types of human capital, like any other economic resources, have the same effect in production but very different market prices due to different relative scarcity. However, the property rights of their human capital are commonly different from those of non-human capital: first, human capital naturally can only belong to the person; second, the use of human capital can only be "incentivized" and cannot be "squeezed". That is why we must measure, monitor and manage the labor contribution from all members in the team production of the firm.[12] Alchian and Demsetz advocate incentivizing managers with residual claims because the information cost for "monitoring the supervisor" is too high. Knight (Knight 1921) emphasizes the rationality of rewarding the entrepreneur with "profits" because entrepreneurs face market uncertainties, and no one at all knows whether they are doing their best to make business decisions.

As we mentioned earlier, a firm is but a contract between human capital and non-human capital. What makes this contract special is that it contains human capital. The nature of the property rights of human capital makes it impossible to clearly prescribe each and everything beforehand when the contract is signed for direct utilization of

[11]Coase notices that when Lenin emphasizes on "strict measuring and monitoring" quite a few times when he proposes that socialism is going to turn the country state into a super factory (Coase 1988).

[12]The necessity for "measuring and monitoring" in team production and how the function should be distributed among the members are two different topics. Due to limited space, this paper will not discuss the latter.

these economic resources. In the case of the workers' labor, even when the labor is so simple that all the details can be clearly specified in advance, the execution of the labor contract may still be problematic because the effort of one worker in the team production will be affected by other workers' efforts. To summon up the enthusiasm of all workers, we have no choice but to measure, monitor, and give them incentives. In the case of managers, even if it is technically possible to clearly explain in advance the full details of the management work, the information cost would be too expensive. What gets truly written in the manager recruitment contract beforehand is his/her responsibilities to deal with unpredictable uncertainties at his/her discretion and the targets that he/she needs to deliver. The supply of the managerial efforts is determined by the incentive arrangement and its implementation. It's not surprising to see "poor management" when incentives are not sufficient. As for the use of entrepreneurship, I am afraid that nothing concrete can be written beforehand because things like "market discovery" and "innovation in all directions" just cannot be planned ex ante. In fact, the effect of entrepreneurship is difficult to be monitored and measured even ex post. There is no way to incentivize the entrepreneur to leverage their competence other than share cropping contracts or similar institutional arrangements, namely to enable the owner of the entrepreneurial human capital to share the enterprise's residual claim. Entrepreneur's competence belongs to the individual, inadequate incentive would result in inadequate entrepreneurship supply as if it is "in innate short supply". If business failure becomes too frequent, it might be better off to split the firm into multiple self-employed to make a living in the market. In short, human capital of different types shares some common features in property rights when they enter the firm as an independent tradable means of production. The firm as a contract is a special contract in the market in that the contract leaves more or less certain unclear things to be motivated by the incentive mechanism; and this peculiarity can be substantiated by the nature of property rights of human capital.

6.4 The Firm as a Contract and Ownership of the Firm

The conclusion reached above, that a firm is a special contract in the market of physical capital and human capital, still involves some discussions on the property rights of the firm. First, the firm, as a special contract in the market, already includes multiple factors and their owners, then is there still independent ownership, namely enterprise ownership? Second, is "capital hires labor" the eternal content of the firm as a contract? Third, does the "managerial revolution" really weaken ownership? This section will briefly discuss these correlated questions.

The idea that a firm is a contract clearly encompasses the meaning that "it is impossible for the firm to have only one ownership". How to have a contract in the market without having two or more ownerships? Two or more ownerships work together to utilize their respective resources through property rights transactions, and this becomes the content of the contract. Therefore, it is quite clear that a contract has multiple ownerships, and in practice the contract always has multiple identical copies. Each copy, in addition to its function as a legal evidence, can also have independent market value, and serve as the instrument for a mortgage. However, the market value of different copies of the same contract differs greatly, depending on the ownership status of the holder. For example, both parties of a land lease contract can, theoretically, pledge the contract for their mortgages; but the lessor can borrow 100 yuan, and the lessee, only 10 yuan. This clearly shows that each contract involves multiple ownerships. A contract is a commitment between the multiples owners to deliver their promise of alienating their respective property rights. No one would ask the question "to whom does this contract belong?" because it is owned neither unilaterally by one single party nor jointly by all the parties.

But in the case of the firm, it seems natural that people will think about such paradoxical questions as "who owns the firm?" Generally, the common answer would be "the firm is owned by the owner of capital". But is there just one capital (and its ownership) in the firm? In a classic enterprise, the owner of the physical capital also serves as the manager of the enterprise and the entrepreneur. The combined owner of non-human capital and human capital has created a general concept of "capital" in economics. The capitalist is the human embodiment of such general capital. The capitalist has multiple roles in the classic enterprise. He, as a financial capitalist, does not need to sign a contract with himself as a manager and an entrepreneur. This constitutes the epistemological origin of the proposition that "the capitalist owns the classic enterprise". The often-mentioned "relative scarcity of capital" during early economic development, now seems to be a fuzzy judgment that does not distinguish between financial capital and entrepreneurial human capital. In fact, as the renowned economic historian Fernand Braudel points out, in any era of the economy, there is always wealth that finds no place to invest.[13] In other words, even in the early days, what's really scarce was entrepreneurial human capital rather than financial capital. It is just not so easy to see this point in the days when the owner of physical capital and the owner of entrepreneurial human capital are the same person.

The consequence for the scarcity of entrepreneurs is inadequate innovation, slow economic growth, and a unitary structure. Such an economy cannot generate sufficient jobs, so human resources are "excessive", and the labor and skills of workers become worthless. In the classical period with a relative scarcity of "capital" and a relative surplus of human resources, it was possible that "capital" not only could "hire" labor (Marx), but also "dominate" labor (Knight). If financial capital, entrepreneurial capital and management function are always consolidated into the same person, then the proposition of "capital hires labor" and "the firm belongs to the capitalist" will always be true. In that case, people have reasons not to think about what "hires" labor. People also have reasons to take it for granted that the human embodiment of the pure physical capital (namely the capitalist) has the right to "dominate" the use of labor, i.e. the use of workers' human capital. From this we can see that the proposition of "capital hires labor" is just the reproduction of the statement that "the firm belongs to the (financial) capitalist".

---

[13]Braudel (1977: 35).

However, with the development of modern enterprises, entrepreneurship and managerial skills become separated from the "integrated capital". The expansion of the market, the complexity of transactions from content to form, and the growth of corporate organizations make the independence of the human capital of entrepreneurs and managers not only imperative but also economically profitable. This is the representation of the division of labor in the economic organization. Now the classical "capitalist" is gradually split into two parts: one is the owner of non-human capital, and the other, the owner of human capital of the entrepreneur (manager). In this process, the pure non-human capital increasingly manifests as "passive currency". In fact, even in the classic enterprise, the non-human capital is already a pile of passive currency, but it is then difficult to perceive that the owner of the passive currency himself is also the holder of "the active currency". For example, even in the movie scene when Charlie Chaplin plays so vividly in a story where workers are directed by the assembly lines, the machine and the equipment doesn't know "what and how much to produce", which is determined by entrepreneur competence, namely the ability to take the risk and predict the market. A wrong decision may lead the factory to be closed and then the shutdown of whatever number of production lines and machines, so how can they still dominate the workers? Therefore, even for a classic enterprise, it is not so much about the owner of the physical capital to hire the labor, but more about the human capitalist with entrepreneurship (i.e. "the adventurist who is able to deal with market uncertainties", as Knight put it) to play a key role in the shadow of non-human capital. This shows that the proposition that "capital hires labor" is supported by the vague concept of "capital".[14]

With the evolution of classic enterprises into modern enterprises, entrepreneurial (managerial) human capital not only comes out of the shadow of non-human capital but also goes straight to the center of large corporations. In the 1930s, Berle and Means observed that among the top 200 non-financial companies in the United States, managers controlled a substantial part of the corporate assets even in the context of scattered equity distribution (Berle and Means 1932), and they called this phenomenon a "managerial revolution" in the history of the American corporate system. This revolution created a "new force that is detached from the ownership" such that "those assets providers are given the position of the 'owner' and the new princes are able to exercise their authority". Berle and Means made marvelous observations but their generalization and understanding were wrong. Their noses were already on the entrepreneurial (managerial) human capital and its ownership but they didn't give its owners the right name. Instead, they not only vaguely called them "economic power" or "new princes", but also saw managers in the central stage of large corporations as the guys usurping the power of their boss (i.e. the assets provider). They have misinterpreted the separation of the ownership of entrepreneurial human capital from the ownership of financial capital, as "the separation of the right of

[14]In 1998 when Coase reviewed his paper on the firm written five decades before, he pointed out that one of the main weaknesses of the paper was the use of the employer-employee relationship as the model of the firm. "As a result of the emphasis on the employer-employee relationship, that the contracts can enable the organizers of the firm to direct the use of capital (equipment and cash) by acquiring, leasing or borrowing it was not examined (Coase 1988: 288–289).

control (right of operation) from ownership." After the 1960s, the "Berle-Means Hypothesis" became quite popular and many people even regarded large corporations with scattered equity structure as economic organizations with weakened ownership.[15]

The theoretical error of the Berle-Means Hypothesis didn't get corrected until the publication of Stigler and Friedland's paper in 1983. Stigler and Friedland pointed out that large corporation shareholders have full property rights of and control over their financial capital, and they exercise their property rights through buying and selling stocks; and managers have full ownership of and control over their managerial expertise, and they buy and sell their knowledge and expertise in the advanced labor market. A joint-stock company is not a "separation of ownership and control", but a complex contract between financial capital and the manager's knowledge and skills capital (management) and ownership thereof (Stigler and Friedland 1983). This argument theoretically introduces human capital and its property rights into the understanding of the modern corporation system.

As this theory becomes popularly adopted, we can see that the real changes in the structure of property rights brought about by modern joint-stock companies are the rise of the status of human capital in modern corporations and the relative decline of pure financial capital. On the one hand, specialization of human capital has reached an unprecedented level in modern companies, and all sorts of ways to leverage various human capital—labor, professional skills, management (measuring and monitoring), and entrepreneurship—can all become independent tradable factors in the corporate contract. Hence the contract between human capital and non-human capital has become highly delicate and complicated. On the other hand, the competition and co-operation between various human capital and ownerships thereof in the contract have led to the birth of a variety of new combinations and new forms beyond "classic enterprises". How to fully mobilize all sorts of human capital in the firm, that is, to develop "incentive contracts" has become the premise for effective utilization of the financial capital, and increasingly a central question to maintain corporate competitiveness and productivity. It is now clear that it is not the "passive currency" i.e. the pure financial capital that "gives the bread" to such human capital owners as workers, managers, and entrepreneurs, but rather it is the holder of the "active currency"—the human capital of the enterprises—that assures the preservation, appreciation, and expansion of the non-human capital. So it is only natural to see the appreciation of human capital and depreciation of non-human capital.[16] But make no mistake.

---

[15]Zhang Jun (1994), Chapter 8.

[16]Cui Zhiyuan (1996) quoted that a total of 29 states in the U.S. have amended the Corporate Law since the 1980s, indicating that the Corporate Law in the U.S. has undergone profound deprivatization. According to Cui, the amendments require managers to serve the company's "stakeholders" rather than just shareholders. However, the concept of "stakeholders" is a bit fuzzy. It seems to include both "shareholders" and "workers, creditors, and communities where the companies are located. If we study the background, it seems that the main reason for the amendment is the opposition against "hostile takeovers" (which only brings benefits to shareholders) from workers, senior managers, and the community where the company is located. So, can we also interpret the above changes in American Corporate Law as the rise of human capital in American companies? The cases

The appreciation of human capital is not achieved by "depriving" the property rights of financial capital, and the depreciation of non-human capital is not the result of "weakened ownership". The relative changes in market prices of different capitals is determined by market competition for all factors to be included into the corporate contract. Without well-oiled markets for labor, managers, entrepreneurs and financial capital and without smooth integration of all these markets, how could it possible to "innovate and create" a modern corporate system? Only from the market (i.e. property rights transactions) can corporate as a contract find the boundary of its economic effectiveness, and this rule is equally applicable to both modern times and "ancient" times. A modern corporation, if we may use this name, is but a more complicated "contract" in the market. Its contractual nature becomes even more salient because human capital, with its unique property rights, plays a more critical role in the modern economy and the modern economic organization than ever before.

6.5 Conclusion

This paper regards the firm in the market as a special contract between human capital and non-human capital. The special characteristics of the contract are that the rights and obligations of each factor and the owners thereof cannot be completely stipulated beforehand and that some must be left to the execution of the contract. This is because the corporate contract involves the participation of human capital (workers, managers, and entrepreneurs). The property rights of human capital are quite special: they only belong to the person, and can only be motivated by proper incentives. These special characteristics make it impossible for the corporate contract in the market to clearly prescribe each and everything beforehand; and something must be left unclear and be regulated by incentives. The "Incentive Contract"—the key to the corporate system—needs to consider not only the pricing mechanism in the market for all factors, but also the within-the-firm interaction between all sorts of human capital as well as the relationship between the firm and the uncertain market demand. Only proper "incentives" can help the firm save transaction costs in the general (product) market to the extent that the savings outweigh the organization cost and achieve the "organizational profits".

Coase's theory of the firm as a contract can work together with the theories on property rights and human capital to provide a new insight into corporate organizations in

---

cited by Cui seem to support the argument of this article. For example, Judge Frank H. Easterbrook's rule in 1989 regarding the new Corporation Law in Wisconsin was in favor of "stakeholders." He determined that "hostile takeovers," although beneficial to shareholders, deprived the human capital of creditors, managers, and workers (Cui 1996: 38). Isn't the human capital mentioned by the judge, part of the ownership in the corporate contract? If the human capital is, as understood in this article, a special capital that can only belong to the individual even if all the physical capital becomes public, how can we look at the amendments to the Corporate Law in 29 states and come up with the logic of de-privatization?.

the market. However, it is difficult to directly apply this new insight to analyze "corporate organizations" under non-market conditions. For example, "socialist enterprises under transformation" were set up under conditions that prohibit or restrict market transactions. These "enterprises", not established with the purpose of "saving transaction costs" and pushed into the "market" in the reform, will have their own unique difficulties, which need to be explored in separate and specific discussions.

References

Alchian, A., and Harold Demsetz. 1972. Production, Information Costs, and Economic Organization. *American Economic Review* 62: 777–795.

Barzel, Yoram. 1977. An Economic Analysis of Slaver. *Journal of Law and Economics* 17: 73–96.

Berle, A., and G. Means. 1932. *The Modern Corporation and Private Property*. New York: Commerce Clearing House.

Braudel, Fernand. 1977. *Afterthoughts on Material Civilization and Capitalism*. The Johns Hopkins University Press.

Cheung, Steven. 1983. The Contractual Nature of the Firm. *Journal of Law and Economics* 26 (1): 1–21.

Cheung, Steven. 1984. Knowledge and Communist Political System. *The Orange Seller's Words. Hong Kong Economic Journal*.

Cheung, Steven. 1991. Coase as I Know. *PingLanJi*. Hong Kong EMIS.

Coase, Ronald. 1937. The Nature of the Firm. In Coase. 1988. *The Firm, the Market, and the Law*, 33–55. University of Chicago Press.

Coase, Ronald. 1988. *The Firm, the Market, and the Law*. University of Chicago Press.

Cui, Zhiyuan. 1996. The Theoretical Background for Amendments to Corporate Law in 29 U.S. States. *Economic Research* 4: 35–40.

Fogel, Robert William, and Stanley L. Engerman. 1972. *Time on the Cross: The Economics of American Negro Slavery*. Boston: Little, Brown.

Knight, Frank. 1921. *Risk, Uncertainty, and Profit, Reprints of Economic Classics*. Augustus M. Keller, 1964.

Karl, Marx. 1972. Critique of the Gotha Program. *Selected Works of Marx and Engels*, Vol. 3. People's Press.

Rosen, S. 1985. The Theory of Equalizing Differences. In *Handbook of Labor Economics*, ed. O. Ashenfelter and R. Layard. Amsterdam: North-Holland.

Schultz, T. 1961. Investment in Human Capital. *American Economic Review* 51 (March): 1–17.

Stigler, G., and C. Friedman. 1983. The Literature of Economics, the Case of Berle and Means. *Journal of Law and Economics* 26: 237–268.

Wang, Dingding. 1995. *Economic Development and Institutional Innovation*. Shanghai People's Press.

Zhang, Jun. 1994. *Modern Property Rights Economics*. Shanghai Joint Publishing Press, Shanghai People's Press.

Zhang, Weiying. 1995. *The Enterprise's Entrepreneur: the Contract Theory*. Shanghai Joint Publishing Press, Shanghai People's Press.

Chapter 7
"Reward of Enterprise Control" and "Entrepreneur-Controlled Enterprise": Entrepreneurial Human Capital in Public-Owned Enterprises

7.1 Introduction

This paper takes Hengdian Group (HG) in Zhejiang province as a case study to look into the property rights of entrepreneurial capital in public-owned enterprises (POE).[1] Our observation is that a POE with good performance has at least one outstanding corporate leader to maintain control over the enterprise for a long period of time. Previous enterprise theories limit themselves to the perspective of property rights of physical capital and cannot understand this phenomenon, hence their horizon of theoretical examinations excludes all sorts of manifestations of property rights of entrepreneurial capital in the POEs. In addition, the vast majority of China's POEs are still, in fact, under the integrated institutional framework that does not distinguish "government and enterprise", and their leaders often have multiple hats such as entrepreneurs and government officials at the same time, which inevitably brings difficulty to examining their entrepreneurial capital. Fortunately, the reform has created a team of POEs that have detached from the government. The case in this paper—HG is one of first POEs to clearly define the relationship between business and government functions. Through this case study we will look for answers to study the following questions: Does the property right of entrepreneurial human capital exist in a POE independent of administrative control? If yes, how? How does it actually work in the existing enterprise system? How can it be incentivized? And further, how will it evolve and affect the institutional arrangements of corporate property rights?

[1]For preliminary discussions on entrepreneurial human capital and its position in the firm as a contract, see Zhou (1996a, b).

This article was originally published in *Economic Research Journal*, Issue No. 5 (1997).

Q. Zhou, *Property Rights and Changes in China*,
https://doi.org/10.1007/978-981-15-9885-2_7

7.2 "Community Ownership" in Name and in Reality

The property right of HG is summarized as "community ownership mode". Then what is "community ownership"? *The Outline of the Community Ownership of HG 1994 (Draft)* defines it as following: "The property right of the assets of the community economy is not owned by the state, or the local government, or the villages, let alone individuals of the community economy leadership or individual enterprise employees, but it is jointly owned by all members of the community (namely it is public-owned)."[2] This definition is no simple because it involves many complex concepts from classical ownership theory to modern property rights economics. However, the first question is to what extent does this definition of "community ownership" reflect the de facto property rights relationship of HG?

Our investigation confirms that HG is neither owned nor controlled by the township government or any government at other levels. In the early days, the enterprise model of HG was not much different from normal collective rural enterprises in China. There were inextricable links between the formation of the enterprise' capital and the community government. In those days, in rural China, only production brigades/teams as the grass-root organizations integrating political functions and the collective economy had the legitimate right to set up enterprises. Therefore, even if it was the entrepreneur who initiated the original fundraising and assumed the debt repayment responsibility, the enterprise was still owned by the collective, namely the community or the production brigade/team. According to the records of *HG Charter*,[3] the predecessor of HG was still a "township collective enterprise" until 1989. However, with the official establishment of HG in 1990, the company became "collective-owned, and was brought under the leadership and management of HG".[4] The corresponding substantial changes include: (A) The general manager of group company is no longer appointed by the town government, but recommended, elected and appointed by the Board of Directors (BOD) without approval by the town government[5]; (B) Investment projects regardless of scale do not need to be approved by the town government; and (C) The model of profit distribution to the town government has changed from ratio-sharing to fixed quota and then to paid

[2]Shen et al. (1994: 128).

[3]*HG Charter* is revised and promulgated once a year to standardize corporate management since the establishment of its predecessor Hengdian Town Industrial Corporation. Before 1994, it was titled *Regulations on the Economic Responsibilities System*. These documents provide important records for studying changes in the company system (hereinafter referred to as the *Charter*).

[4]See the *Charter*, 1991: 1. All previous versions of the *Charter* clearly defines the enterprise as "township collective ownership."

[5]According to people involved, the town government had, in fact, long stopped appointing the management of HG. The last appointment record we found in the archives dated back to December 1984 when Xu Wenrong was appointed by the Hengdian Township People's Government as the Manager of Hengdian Company and concurrently the Director of Dongyang County No.1 Light Textile Factory, and Director of Dongyang County Electronics General Factory (Hengdian Government Document No. (1984)-9). XU's title changed from the Manager of Hengdian Town Industrial Corporation to the General Manager of HG) without appointment by the township government.

services, i.e. the amount paid to the government is determined by the quantity and quality of services provided by the government.[6] In short, the formation of HG marks the completion of the separation between government administration and enterprise operation, which makes HG fundamentally different from most POEs which do not separate government function and business operation.

Second, no member of HG has a personal share of any form in the "public-owned" corporate assets. (A) The fundraising from company members for initial establishment was later repaid and doesn't stay as share capital. (B) The "responsibility deposit" from employees is used to cover job-related responsibilities and risks. It is neither equity nor debt; thus no interest or dividends needs to be paid. (C) Most of the company's profit stays in the company and is not distributed to individuals. Community members do not receive shares, interests, or any other forms of property income except for wages and bonuses (which will be discussed in future sections) from the enterprise. The assets of HG are "jointly owned by all community members", and the community membership is open to all. "You can become a member no matter where you are from", "Anyone that works in the group is a community member, and anyone that leaves loses the membership."[7] The members do not equal to farmers of the community.

The above shows that "the community ownership model" reflects two basic features of HG: first, HG is neither owned by the government nor controlled by the government; second, the corporate assets of HG are not distributed down to employees. This is a very unique POE: the ownership is different from state-ownership (SOEs) because it is not the public ownership practiced throughout the country that is owned and controlled by the central government; it is also different from collective ownership because it is neither owned by "the collective" comprised of just "the locals" from within the community, nor is it controlled and managed by the township government. The fundamental difference between HG's community ownership and all traditional public ownership is that it achieves "complete separation of government administration and enterprise management". At the same time, the community ownership is also different from other variants of public ownership from the reform, such as the joint-stock system or the joint-stock co-operative system, because it does not involve private property rights in the form of equity.

7.3 The Quantitative Down-to-Individual Incentive Mechanism

However, the concept of "community member's public ownership" does not reflect the reality of HG's "highly quantitative down-to-individual incentive mechanism". The institutional arrangements on wages, bonuses and profit distribution over the

---

[6]*Charter* since 1994.

[7]Xu (1994: 74).

years indicate that HG has been making efforts to define the contribution and responsibility of each employee, and on this basis, to explore to establish a distribution system that correlates the income of every employee with their efforts, responsibilities, and contribution to the company. The HG distribution model can be summarized as: each member receives different wages based on their individual contributions and responsibilities, and they follow the same principle in sharing the profit in the form of bonus. Since the actual incentive mechanism manifests de facto property rights,[8] we must pay close attention to the property rights implications in its following incentive mechanisms.

Salary: The salary system consists of approved salary and appraised salary. All the approved salaries are set by the Group as the graded salary standards from apprentice all the way to the general manager (GM). What makes it special is that HG emphasizes "salary-profit linkage", that is, the approved salary level is related to the company's profitability.[9] Approved salary multiplied by the number of people is the total salary approved by the Group; within the total amount of approved salary for member enterprises, the salary is appraised and determined based on the actual enterprise situation for people below the factory director/manager level (while the salary of factory directors/managers and employees of the Group headquarter are determined by the Group headquarter), and such salary is called appraised salary. The actual salary paid is based on the appraised salary for each member enterprise, but the salary of apprentices and other low-pay positions must not be lower than the uniform minimum wage set by the Group. At HG, the highest approved salary is 5–7 times of the lowest approved salary; the appraised salary varies from enterprise to enterprise, and generally with a larger gap; currently within the whole group, the actual highest salary is estimated to be about ten times of the lowest salary.

Bonus: Generally, the total amount of bonus is appropriated from profit and accounts for 25% to 30% of the total profit. Enterprises within the Group appropriates bonuses according to their respective profitability and then distributes them to individual employees based on their individual contributions and responsibilities. HG's bonus distribution has two "iron rules": First, "profit-bonus linkage", which means loss-making enterprises receive no bonus, and only profit-making units and their employees can share a part of the profit through bonuses; Second, profit sharing are by no means evenly distributed but based on different contributions and responsibilities of different members. Generally speaking, the bonus is determined by referencing to the salary for workers, by their professional contribution for technical people, and by enterprise profit for enterprise managers.

Collective Fringe Benefit: Out of expectations, such a financially strong POE as HG does not spend much money to buy many collective fringe benefits and distribute them to its "community members". For example, except for providing apartments to external technical experts at market prices, the housing for all members of HG, from the president to ordinary employees are invested and built by themselves rather

[8]The author have already discussed concluded: the concept of "human capital naturally belongs to the person" is the foundation for understanding the Incentive Theory (Zhou 1996b).

[9]All versions of the *Charter* since 1991 clearly defined the principle of "salary-profit linkage".

than the Group. The Group invests heavily on the infrastructure of the small town, but its "community members" share these infrastructure in the same way as non-community members without any membership privilege. As for the public cultural and entertainment facilities invested by the Group, the community members also have to pay for use. This shows that HG offers very few benefits to its members. Most of the company's distributable profits are quantitatively distributed to individuals based on their amount of work, merits, and contributions, and leave the spending to their own decisions.

From the above overview of HG's incentive mechanism, we can see that its feature is that it tries its best to quantify the remuneration to individuals according to their contributions to enterprise output. Here two questions need to be further studied. First, how on earth HG accurately measures the contribution of each member to total team output; second, who will effectively perform the quantification "assessment". According to Alchian and Demsetz (1972), the correlation of these two questions is that if "the measurement" is not difficult, whoever performs "the measurement" doesn't matter for the incentive mechanism, and if the measurement is difficult, then who does the job matters. Then how does HG solve these two interrelated problems?

The distribution system of HG has long clearly set the principle of "contribution-based reward". However, for it to work, it is essential to accurately identify the individual's labor or contribution to the team performance. Furthermore, the identification should be made not only during the production process for later distribution of bonuses, but also made and paid in advance (such as the salary). The challenge is, can an "objective" criterion be followed to identify, ex ante and ex post, the contribution from individual members of the team?

Let us revisit and carefully examine HG's experience. First, the approved salary is obviously not fully equivalent to the real contribution of each position to the Group's total output. For example, the difference between the approved president's salary and the average worker's does not reflect the difference in their contributions. Therefore, the approved salary is only the artificially-determined total salary that the Group plans (or is ready) to invest into the production. Second, in implementation, the approved salary is only partially paid first, and the balance is determined "later": profitable enterprises get full make-up payment to arrive at the approved salary, and the loss-making ones can only get partial make-up salary. Third, with the pre-determined or approved total salary and its ex post final implementation, the appraised salary is used to quantitatively distribute the total amount of salary to every individual. The appraised salary is not based on the real share of contribution, but a "subjective estimate" of the contribution. Fourth, the total amount of bonuses is a subjectively-determined share of the actual profit. Fifth, bonuses for individuals are quantified based on their "as assessed" contributions. In short, for both salaries and bonuses, HG first determines the total amount at the Group level, and then breaks it down level by level to enterprises, factories, shift teams and individuals.

This "level by level breaking down" is quite tricky. The distribution system at HG is not jointly decided by all its members just because "its assets are jointly owned by them". In fact, the total amount of salary and bonus is determined by the joint meeting chaired by the Group President between managers of its headquarters and enterprises, not by "the majority approval" or "the unanimous approval" by the all-members conference.[10] The basis for the decision is the market competition situation and corporate strategies, rather than the willingness of all members of the community. The so-determined total salary and bonus is split down step by step. First, the total amount of distribution is determined for enterprises, then the enterprise manager chairs the further splitting to individuals in the form of salary and bonus through "assessment". Obviously, whether or not the salaries and bonuses subjectively "assessed and determined" by different levels of managers is consistent as much as possible with the "objective" (or acceptable) contribution of individual members, or whether or not mistakes at any step can be corrected by an effective "correction mechanism", will have a decisive impact on HG's incentive mechanism. Therefore, we need to find out how HG incentivizes its managers at all levels such that they are adequately motivated to act in the interest of the enterprise when implementing the down-to-individual incentive mechanism.

7.4 "Pricing" the Contribution of Managers and Entrepreneurs

First we confirm that HG has always been working hard to "price" managers and entrepreneurs according to their contribution. This unique pricing mechanism also includes two aspects: the determination of the amount of salary, bonus, and other remunerations for managers and its payment in implementation. What's special about the mechanism is that it is even more difficult to measure the manager's contribution to the enterprise, their remuneration is even more "subjective", and thus the implementation is even more "top-down".

As explained before, managers' (including factory directors) salary at HG is assessed and determined by the Group headquarter, and their bonus is linked to the enterprise profit. Over the years, all versions of the Group's *Charter* only lay down the principles for determining the amount of the salary and bonus for the management without setting specific numbers. Our survey confirms that the compensation of the heads of sector groups and direct affiliated enterprises is directly decided by the Group president. The bonus of a subsidiary company manager is a certain percentage of the total profits generated by the company, and the absolute amount is quite competitive and motivating in the local managers market. Along with handsome rewards, there are also heavy penalties. The *Charter* stipulates that all enterprise managers must pay risk collateral (property or cash) to the Group: the amount is ten times the annual salary of the manager of the contracted enterprises, and 10% of the total leased assets for leased enterprises. The risk collateral from managers at HG is mainly used to compensate for enterprise losses. The *Charter* stipulates that if a factory loses money, its director shall compensate 10%; if a subsidiary company

---

[10]This fact distinguishes the HG model from the "ownership by workers' society in Yugoslavia".

loses money, the manager shall compensate 5%; if the group company loses money, the group GM shall compensate 3%.

Since the compensation of average employees at HG is appraised and determined by the management, and the compensation of the management, by the headquarters and the president, therefore the Group President is actually the final decision-maker of the entire incentive chain. Then, how does HG motivate its president? Let's first look at the president's compensation. First, the president's approved salary is the highest in the whole group for each and every year. Second, the president's bonus is the highest among the managers. The *Charter* from 1991 to 1993 stipulates: "If the group generates target profit, the Group President shall be awarded 1.2% of the after-tax profit as the bonus."[11] Our impression is that the president of HG—the final decision-maker for all manager's contributions—enjoys the highest remuneration in the Group not just according to the system, but also maintains a sufficient gap with the pay for other members of the Group.[12]

In short, the measurement problem at HG is solved this way: the Group president evaluates senior managers, senior managers evaluate junior managers, and junior managers evaluate workers. Since the final assessor of the enterprise group enjoys the biggest share of the profit according to the system, profit targets thus enter the stratified principal-proxy relations within the system and become the foundation for the correction mechanism for all layers of "the subjective evaluation". At the first glance, the effectiveness of HG's incentive mechanism is precisely established on the Alchian- Demsetz effect, namely to use residual claims to incentivize enterprise managers, examine all sorts of input instead of the contribution of various human capital to the total team output, and thus effectively save the measurement cost for team production.[13] However, we must not ignore this "little difference": the final assessor of HG—the president—is legally not the asset owner of the group, and he can only share 1.2% of the group's profits at most. Property rights economists cannot help asking how can such small "residual claims" be commensurate with the enormous responsibility of overcoming the moral hazards from the whole group's management system?

---

[11]Before 1987, the *Charter* stipulates that the bonus for the Group President shall be the highest bonus for subsidiary managers; since 1987, the *Charter* says that the bonus for the GM (namely President) of the Group shall equal 140% of the highest bonus for subsidiary managers.

[12]Take 1993 for example, HG total after-tax profit was 61.15 million yuan. According to the company policy, the total amount of annual bonus for the president can be 733,800 yuan (The director of the corporate finance center told us that Xu Wenrong usually would not withdraw his bonus. But our focus of study here is the incentive mechanism, so that is another story). For the same year, the bonus of the workers of loss-making enterprises was zero, and that of the manager was negative (meaning the manager had to compensate 5–10% of the loss).

[13]Measuring the actual contribution of team members can be costly; therefore, examining the inputs to instead of the output can save the measurement cost (Barzel 1982).

7.5 Enterprise Control

One right, namely enterprise control is usually easily overlooked in the study of POEs. This paper defines enterprise control as the exclusive use of corporate assets, especially for investment and market operations.[14] Enterprise control is highly concentrated at HG. First of all, the right of investment and asset disposal of the group and all the subsidiaries is highly centralized at the Group headquarter and the president. The total assets of HG grows at a breathtaking speed. Between 1993 and 1995, the total assets of the Group including 140 core subsidiaries grew from 590 million yuan to 1.63 billion yuan; increasing by over 1 billion yuan in two years, and with an average growth rate of 66%.[15] The investment model is also highly centralized within HG. Till 1995, "all new project development, investment, establishment of new enterprises (including non-independent legal entities) and suspension, shutdown, merger and transforming of existing enterprises" are all specified in the system as Group headquarters functions. In actual implementation, all investments proposed by affiliated enterprises are submitted to the headquarters for evaluation by a special team, and then the final decision will be taken by the president. The foundation for the highly centralized investment decision includes: (A). The Group headquarters and the president directly control a considerable amount of investment capital.[16] (B). Loans are obtained by putting the total assets of the Group rather than of the subsidiary as collateral; the Group takes the risk for the loan, thus the right to use it is centralized at the Group. (C). The Group headquarter and the president have a good track record of investment, and the so-derived credit, goodwill, and other intangible assets. Therefore, in HG's practice, the investment decision and its implementation are neither a joint decision by all community members nor the autonomy of affiliated enterprises, but the highly centralized power of the Group headquarter and the president.

---

[14]Grossman and Hart (1986) are the first scholars to use "residual rights of control" rather than "residual claims" to define "enterprise ownership". Hart and Moore (1990) "give a more definitive meaning to the definition of residual rights of control", and define it as "the right to determine how the assets can be used for purposes beyond its special purpose specified in the initial contract". However, this shall not become the reason to interpret "residual rights of control" as a right to move away from the "contract". Because although how to distribute the income is a right that is not clearly specified in the contract, but it is still part of the content of the contract, especially of the company as a contract. Therefore, whether we go with "residual claims" or "residual rights of control" to define ownership, it does not change the fact that the "residual rights" are contract-based property rights. In reality, POEs are not formed based on contracts. Without the initial contract, there are no "residual rights" to be defined. This is why it is difficult to find clearly defined "residual rights" in POEs. However, the decision-making process and the decision power regarding how to use corporate resources still cannot be skipped by POEs. Therefore, this paper directly defines the decision-making power of the exclusive use of corporate resources as enterprise control.

[15]HG's Balance Sheet (Chen 1995, Tables 2–4).

[16]HG's asset-liability ratio is not high (generally 50–60%, see Chen 1995). The main source of group investment is its own capital. Since over 50% of the retained after-tax profits of HG's affiliates are handed to the Group headquarter, the headquarters and the president directly control a considerable amount of capital.

Relatively speaking, HG's operations decisions are "decentralized". The managers (factory directors) of affiliated enterprises at all levels have clear responsibilities and the corresponding management authorities. The responsibilities and rights of managers and factory directors regarding day-to-day operations have become increasingly clear with years of evolution of the enterprise management system within HG.[17] However, these managers at HG are neither "democratically elected by all group members" nor appointed by the township government, but appointed by the group headquarter and the president. The top-down appointment hierarchy is as follows: Group BOD → Group Economic Bureau → Group President → GM of Subsidiary → Factory Director; each level appoints the next lower level, and the appointed report to the appointer. The group headquarters and the president are at the top of the management appointment chain. It is fair to say that they have control over the day to day operations of the decentralized enterprises within the Group through the centralized right for the appointment of managers.

The direct investment and assets disposal right and the indirect enterprise operations right obtained via appointing managers owned by HG headquarters and its president, are clearly not the "residual claims" as defined by Alchian and Demsetz (1972), because the president, as mentioned before, only controls 1–2% of "the residual" from such activities as investment, asset restructuring and appointment of people. However, from the HG property rights model, what we have seen in parallel to the very limited residual claims, is the direct or indirect control over enterprise investment and business activities by the group head office and the president. The amount of resources under this type of control is enormous. The investment alone is 60–70% of the Group's annual after-tax profits, plus the banks loans using the Group asset as collateral and other credits. Other members of the group also share residual claims but do not participate in activities such as corporate-controlled investments, assets disposal, and manager appointment. That "enterprise control is disproportionate with the residual claims" is the real picture of the HG's "joint ownership and private operation" model.

[17]This trend can be seen from the changes in the corporate management system defined by the *Charter* over the years: in 1986, it was a collective contract responsibility system with factory directors or managers as the main contractors; in 1989, the collective contracting was changed to just one person's namely the director's contracting; in 1990, it was changed to director (one person) contracting or leasing system; in 1992, it became director/manager risk-based contracting responsibility system"; in 1994, it stipulated that "the general managers and the factory directors are the legal representatives of the enterprise". At present, as the legal representatives of HG affiliates, the managers have the autonomy in personnel organization, production management, operation, labor management as well as reward and punishment and income distribution within the prescribed scope" to ensure various enterprise targets are met (see the *Charter 1996*, Page 5).

7.6 "The Reward of Enterprise Control"

How come an entrepreneur does not have sufficient residual claims yet enjoys sufficient control over the enterprise? In the "public economy" where the government and the enterprise are not well separated, enterprise control is directly a part of the administrative power or is given to the "appointed manager" through administrative order. However, in the HG model, the entrepreneur obtains sufficient enterprise control through his entrepreneurial capabilities, which need to be tested by the market. HG's starting capital in 1975 came from private loans and bank loans, and the founder Xu Wenrong's personal ability, credibility, and track record attracted the "passive money" from creditors and turned it into investment for which the entrepreneur took the risk.[18] Then in the corporate asset expansion featured by the cycle of "converting credit into investment, investment into assets, assets plus the entrepreneur's credit into greater credit', the entrepreneur's capacity, vision, judgement on the potential profiting opportunities and decision-making played a decisive role.[19] In short, the entrepreneur controls the results of his previous investment and operational decisions.[20] In this case, the enterprise control is not fully an "investment trust" of other people's wealth, but, in the first place, the result of the entrepreneur's competence tested by the market.

The enterprise control is not automatically obtained. The HG model "where the entrepreneur controls the enterprise" is the result of institutional reform and innovation. In 1984, XU integrated 17 PBEs derived from the same parent company in Hengdian Township into "Hengdian Industrial Corporation" and decided to use the company to exercise the functions of the "decision-making center and investment center". This meant that the township Party and government authorities, and the

[18]Hengdian Silk Factory, founded in 1975, is the starting point of HG. The initial total investment of the factory was 295,800 yuan, 50,000 yuan of which was borrowed by Xu Wenrong from 39 production brigade members (promised to repay in 3 years), and the rest was bank loans. Here, the entrepreneur's fundraising played a decisive role. First, the 50,000 yuan Xu raised became the credit basis for bank loans. Second, bank loans became the basis for further larger scale fundraising, which accounted for the majority of the total investment. When I asked for the reasons why the villagers were willing to hand over "the money they saved song long and so hard" to Xu to set up the factory, they mentioned Xu's "credibility", "ability", and "track record". I would interpret this as the Hengdian townfellows were using their own words to summarize the "trust" as proposed by Casson (1982), namely "how can the fund contributors trust that the entrepreneur will use the funds in their interest?" The fact that XU can earn the trust of the village creditors is due to his personal reputation, which later was translated into corporate credit. Ever since then, Xu's personal reputation has become an inseparable part of HG's intangible assets.

[19]This is the unanimous conclusion of the scholars who have researched HG's experience. For example, *Study on HG by Renowned Experts and Scholars* (1994) edited by He Wei, Wei Jie, and Shen Weiguang collected 14 articles and reports on the study of the HG model. Almost every expert and scholar elaborated on XU's outstanding contribution to HG. Among them, the paper of Lin Zili and Zhang Xiaodi's thesis is directly titled "HG Model: XU Wenrong Model".

[20]The resources retained by the group also include the "residual" contribution from other human capitals. Even under the private property system where various factors are invested in the firm according to an initial contract, there is still the "public domain" proposed by Barzel (1989) (see Wang [1996]), which poses particular difficulties to POEs and will be discussed later.

former factory directors should hand over their enterprise control to the manager of the company. This, of course, created frictional struggle and bargaining on the redistribution of enterprise control right. As per records, in order to free the enterprise control from the traditional administrative control and achieve enterprise autonomy, XU successively "drove away" five township leaders in charge of industry development who refused to stop interfering with enterprise operations. Finally, he won the consent from a "liberal Town Party Secretary" and the support from the County and achieved thorough separation of government and enterprise, and made Hengdian Industrial Corporation a veritable "decision-making center and investment center".[21] In hindsight, this was a key step in the formation of the HG model of "entrepreneur-controlled enterprise". One of the questions we kept on digging and digging at HG was, where did Xu get the bargaining chips to lead this unusual "institutional change". My conclusion is that Xu's source of strength comes from two abilities: the usual entrepreneur's ability namely the ability for successful investment and business decisions, and the institutional entrepreneur's ability namely the ability to achieve "institutional and organizational innovations". As Umbeck (1977) proposed "might makes right" when studying the Gold Rush of West America, we may say that at HG, "the ability of the entrepreneur and the institutional entrepreneur makes control.[22]

Enterprise control constitutes a reward for the entrepreneur's efforts and contributions. The basic mechanism here is that the entrepreneur's responsibility and contribution have a positive correlation with his amount of control over the enterprise. As an incentive to the entrepreneur, the effectiveness and intensity of "the reward of control" depend on the degree of symmetry between the contribution of the entrepreneur and his control of the enterprise. This seems to be the same as using "residual claims" to reward the entrepreneur; but the difference lies in that "residual claims" means to enjoy the residual created by the enterprise, while "enterprise control" means that the entrepreneur has the right to control corporate resources and engage himself in decisive work. When "enterprise control" does not bring the corresponding "residual claims" (this is what happens at HG), doesn't the so-called "enterprise control reward" just mean that the entrepreneur enjoys the right to continue his work as the reward to his hard work? Then, we have to ask, under what circumstances can this "right to work to reward work" be seen as an incentive?

In order to answer this question, we need to further understand the entrepreneurs. According to Casson (1982), the entrepreneur is the person to provide "decisive judgement" and the "implementer of a certain undertaking". The decisive judgement is not just the marginal calculation using some the public information provided by the pricing system, but an activity "governed not only by objective information but also by subjective belief". Therefore, today's entrepreneurial spirit, including ambition, self-confidence, will power for competition, professionalism, religious belief, outlook of life, sensitivity and intuition to potential profit opportunities, etc. is an indispensable part of the entrepreneur. Although "entrepreneurial spirit and talent" are subjective

---

[21] Xu (1994: 103).

[22] "The ability of entrepreneur and institution entrepreneur defines enterprise control" can be fully understood in the framework of "game of property rights" elaborated by Wang (1996).

and difficult to observe and measure, the results of "judgement and decision" by entrepreneurs—the competitiveness of enterprises can be observed as they must pass the "survival test" in an uncertain market environment (Alchian 1950). The problem is, potential entrepreneurs with great "entrepreneurship" must first be given an opportunity to control an enterprise in order to allocate corporate resources in accordance with his or her judgment. Here, enterprise control can be understood as having the opportunity to sell the "entrepreneurship and talent" through competitive bidding in the market. It is in this sense that enterprise control constitutes an incentive for entrepreneurs.[23]

The effectiveness of the HG model to motivate the entrepreneur lies in that although the enterprise does not pay the entrepreneur the "residual claims" commensurate with his contribution, the "difference" between his contribution and his share of the profit, is still controlled and dominated by the entrepreneur himself, not by anyone else. That is to say, the asymmetry between the entrepreneur's contribution and his "profit sharing right" is compensated by another asymmetry, namely the asymmetry between his profit sharing right and his right of enterprise control. Putting the profit sharing right and the enterprise control together, we can find the consistence in the HG model between the contribution of the entrepreneur and the total result he could enjoy from the contribution. This is what I see as incentive compatibility. It must be pointed out that not all "public ownership economies" have such an incentive mechanism as in the HG model. For example, under the "public ownership by worker's society in Yugoslavia", the "difference" between entrepreneur's contribution and his share of the income is distributed equally to all workers; and in the "public economy" where the line between the government and the enterprise is blurred, this "difference" is controlled and distributed by the administrative power. With this we can understand why entrepreneurship can enjoy such a full play in the HG model.[24]

7.7 Capitalization of Entrepreneurial Human Capital: A Surmountable Logic?

The "reward from enterprise control" contains a very important feature: this mechanism requires that the person to be motivated must be "in power". Unlike the "residual claims", the enterprise control right requires that the entrepreneur must be "in power" in order to "enjoy" this right. One can only make decisions if he is in office, and

[23]Enterprise control only works as a reward to entrepreneurs and would-be entrepreneurs. For others, it is probably a burden.

[24]And we understand further why Xu Wenrong himself was against the HG Joint-Stock System Restructuring Plan from higher government in 1993. "According to instructions from the higher level, Xu Wenrong can get rightly at least 10% of shares and remain to be the boss" (Sun 1995: 96), but his total control of the enterprise may shrink as the Group asset gets quantified down to individuals (as a result of the joint stock system restructuring), or he may need to make even greater efforts to obtain the same level of control in another property rights structure.

it is the very right to make decisive judgement that constitutes the incentive to the entrepreneur to attain certain undertakings. This is to say, the ownership defined as "enterprise control" cannot become de facto owner's rights if the person in question is not in office. Furthermore, the "enterprise control incentive" also requires the entrepreneur to "remain in office" or stay "perpetually in office". Just imagine! The entrepreneur's current efforts is rewarded by "enjoying" the right of control over the outcome of his or her work, and when he or she "enjoys (exercises)" the control, he or she is contributing to the next phase of enterprise development. Therefore, if the enterprise forever pays the entrepreneur with enterprise control as the main approach and with residual claims as the supplement, then the entrepreneur must be forever in power, namely forever control the "difference" between the contribution and the residual claims, such that the reward will be commensurate with the efforts.

However, as I have pointed out elsewhere, one of the characteristics of the property right of human capital is that it naturally only belongs to the person.[25] Therefore, the enforcement of property right of entrepreneurial human capital will have to be affected by various conditions of its "carrier". Even if the entrepreneurs' attempt, ambition, and sense of responsibility to attain something remain unchanged, we will find that their capability to realize their aspiration may change during their tenure; what's more, they will inevitably age and die. Therefore, we have to examine whether or not the "enterprise control reward" mechanism will work for a longer period of time.

The change in capabilities of "in office" entrepreneurs may have different possibilities. Those who become more and more capable will continue to contribute to the company, because, under the "enterprise control incentive" arrangement, greater capabilities brings more enterprise control, and more control provides the entrepreneur with further opportunities to make the best out of their talent. Obviously, strengthened entrepreneurial capabilities will strengthen the "enterprise control reward" incentive mechanism. The trouble is that the abilities of the entrepreneur may also weaken during the tenure. One situation is that as the enterprise grows bigger and the activity becomes more complex the entrepreneur's judgement and decision-making capability falls increasingly short, or he becomes dwarfed by potential competitors, just as the old saying goes: "there are mountains beyond mountains and skies beyond skies". This is the case of relative weakening of the entrepreneur's capabilities. Another situation is absolute, namely the decision capability of the "in office" entrepreneur will absolutely decline due to health, age, or other reasons. Either way, the weakening of capabilities of the "in office" entrepreneur poses a severe challenge to the "enterprise control incentive" mechanism. Hence the paradox: on the one hand, it's natural that in the "enterprise control incentive" mechanism the entrepreneur must be "in power" or stay forever "in power", any arrangement to abdicate him who has made contributions will impair the supply of his efforts; on the other hand, if the weakened entrepreneur continues to stay in office, the eventual result would be that it will hurt the enterprise and then the entrepreneur himself.

[25]Zhou (1996b).

From the logic perspective we might be able to find the answer to the above question. For example, "enterprise control" can be separated from the entrepreneur's reward, and the entrepreneur can be paid for his contribution with a reward that is independent of the right of control such that he does not necessarily have to "enjoy" the enterprise control in person. This approach will not spoil the incentive mechanism of matching the entrepreneur's contribution with his reward, and save the enterprise from the risk of being controlled by an entrepreneur with weakened decision capabilities or with the tendency of short-term behaviors due to bad expectations. When the "residual claims" are paid to the entrepreneur in the form of property ownership rather than cash, we say that the entrepreneur's human asset investment into the enterprise is "capitalized". This way, the entrepreneur's human capital—the contribution from judgement and decision-centered entrepreneurship—is partly rewarded in the form of cash (salary, bonus, and so-called on-the-job consumption), and partly converted into capitalized assets. As long as the market value is the same for the "capitalized" entrepreneurial human capital and the "in office enterprise control", the problem will get solved: because the human capital of the shareholding entrepreneurs is "materialized" into enterprise asset structure, they can quit the controlling position or even exit the enterprise when their abilities get weakened, but still have the right to enjoy the residual that they have contributed to the enterprise.[26] Here again, we see the difference between "residual claims" and "enterprise control": the holder of the former does not have to directly control the enterprise, while the latter can be regarded as holding the right only when it controls the enterprise. We cannot talk about the pros and cons of the two without considering the condition of entrepreneurial human capital. However, if the decision capability of the entrepreneur is weakened and may even disappear, the "residual claims" arrangement must be superior to "enterprise control", because to reward the entrepreneur with "residual claims" for his yesterday's contribution will not compromise the today and tomorrow of the enterprise.

However, under the "enterprise control" model it is difficult to translate all the "difference" between the entrepreneur's contribution and his reward into "residual claims". First, entrepreneurs themselves may not accept the arrangement to use shares to replace the control, because "the enterprise control" is the right to hold active currency, while the capitalized equity is passive currency. Whether the two have equal market value can only be found out afterwards. From an ex-ante perspective, the two

[26]In fact it is a very common arrangement in the history of enterprise institution for pure "salary taking managers" (let alone the founder) to get some shares of the enterprise as they make more contributions. This kind of arrangement is nothing unusual in the "modern enterprise institution" in the West. But the tradition of Chinese enterprises also offer give shares to its pure managers as a reward. For example, there are two arrangements in the famous "Piaohao" (early form of banks) in Shanxi Province: the founding shares and the "identity shares" (management shares). The founding shares are the investors' shares, and the identity shares are shares awarded to managers and senior managers for many years of contribution (the identity shares can still get dividend after the holder dies, and the name changes to "posthumous shares"). For Piaohao with longer history, the identity shares accounted for a bigger share in the total capital. For instance, 57% of Xiechengqian Piaohao's shares were identity shares in 1906, and 54.5.5% of Dadetong's shares were identity shares (cited from Huang 1992: 57–59).

are in no way equal, because the value of the equity when detached from the right of control relies on the competence and even luck of other in-office entrepreneurs, while enterprise control may create greater residual in the future. More importantly, under the "entrepreneur-controlled enterprise" model, the entrepreneur has the right to reject any alternative arrangement. Secondly, the "residual claims" is a concept linked to the concept of the firm as a contract. If the firm is formed by a contract i.e. an ex ante contract, then it is possible to leverage the "residual claims" as per the contract to distribute the "public domain" left in the enterprise by the property rights of human capital. However, in a POE where there is no such contract, and thus no ex-ante specified "residual claims", it is extremely difficult, even if not impossible, to determine the share of human capital in the "public domain" via ex post tracking.

Finally, under the "enterprise control incentive" model, although the entrepreneur actually controls the residual, in appearance, he can only exercise enterprise control by "working" and "continuing working". The capitalization of entrepreneurial human capital will lead to the separation of "reward" and "effort", turning the seemingly "voluntary labor" into the right of income that can be made known to the public, enjoyed directly and no more related to "labor". Then the veil for the "public ownership economy" would eventually be taken away, would this be accepted?

We cannot predict how much the potential benefit from the above-mentioned institutional change has to be to cover the cost for such institutional change. Therefore, we cannot assert the future direction of enterprises under the "enterprise control" mechanism. What can be observed at present is that in HG, the endogenous contradictions of the "enterprise control reward" mechanism have appeared in practice as the company expands and as the founder becomes aged. First, the scale of HG has been too big for effective decisions to be made by the centralized president's authority. Second, the succession of the founder and final arbitrator is gradually put on the agenda. In fact, HG once considered the shareholding restructuring plan but had to drop it because the "quantification problem" was so severe that it might threaten the company's current operation.[27] Nevertheless, HG has never stopped exploring new challenges faced by its property rights model. For example, XU Wenrong has recently proposed the following ideas: (1) To establish a group foundation to pool together the capital of the whole Group, conduct capital operation and ask subsidiaries using the Group capital to "pay rent" to the foundation. (2) He himself to gradually withdraw from day-to-day business decisions. (3) To select one subsidiary as a pilot for the "shareholding system reform". These ideas and their implementation are worthy of follow-up observation and research. And the central clue is: whether or not at the end of the day the logic for capitalization of the entrepreneurial human assets can be superseded such

[27]In 1989, the *Outline* proposed to improve the bonus responsibility system and create conditions for transitioning to the shareholding system. However, HG found that to quantify the stock of assets formed in the past few decades will inevitably cause problems. It is not just HG who finds it difficult. According to the author's investigation in 1994, another major township enterprise in Zhejiang, Wanxiangjie Group, under the leadership of the famous entrepreneur Lu Guanqiu, also stayed away from shareholding restructuring, because it also found that it was not only difficult but also troublesome and it was likely to disrupt the normal operation of the business.

that the effective operation of "the entrepreneur-controlled enterprise" will outlive the "natural life" of one generation of prominent entrepreneurs.

7.8 Conclusion

Previous theories on enterprises failed to understand the ability of the "real-world enterprise" because they only considered the ownership or property rights arrangements of physical capital. However, no enterprise, including POEs that are not formed by initial contracts, can do without human capital which "naturally belongs to the person. Furthermore, enterprises operating in the market cannot avoid decision-making to deal with uncertainties, which means they need "entrepreneurial human capital" as an indispensable element. However, the concept of POE does not answer the question on the position of entrepreneurial human capital plays in the enterprise. Only in the real world, we see that the positions of POEs vary greatly from one another as the entrepreneurial capital plays a different role in them. This is the basic clue for us to understand their differences in efficiency. We must observe how the "public" resources and the "private" entrepreneurial human capital are combined within the POE, and what kind of incentive mechanism (that is the actual property rights arrangements) is implemented. Without such observation and analysis, we cannot understand POEs, because, regardless of business performance, POEs cannot be explained only from the perspective of the "public ownership" of their physical capital.

In this research the method for POE to recognize the property rights of entrepreneurial human capital is: to reward the entrepreneur for his contribution in providing judgmental decisions with some profit-sharing plus total enterprise control rights, so as to motivate the entrepreneur to assume the ultimate responsibilities for corporate investment and development and enterprise management. Here, the entrepreneur's effort and contribution are commensurate with the total reward which mainly focus on enterprise control. The foundation for enterprise control is entrepreneurial human capital rather than physical capital. The enterprise is an "entrepreneur-controlled enterprise". The entrepreneur decides on corporate development strategies and controls the management, through which the down-to-individual quantified incentive mechanism is implemented. The precondition for the incentive mechanism in "the entrepreneur-controlled POE" to work, is that the entrepreneur himself must stay in power, and be able to maintain a competitive edge in his human capital in both absolute and relative terms. If these conditions are not met, the effectiveness of the "enterprise control incentive" will be compromised. Based on the above findings, this paper makes the following inference for further testing: the "enterprise control incentive" mechanism can be effective in one generation of outstanding entrepreneurs. However, without "capitalization of entrepreneurial capital" or other institutional changes with the same efficacy, it might be, in the long run, difficult for "entrepreneur-controlled enterprises" to compete with and outlive joint stock companies which seem to have a permanent life.

References

Alchian, A. 1950. Uncertainty, Evolution and Economic Theory. *Journal of Political Economy* 58 (3) (June): 211–221.

Alchian, A., and H. Demsetz. 1972. Production, Information Costs, and Economic Organization. *American Economic Review* 62 (50): 777–795.

Barzel, Y. 1982. The Costs of Measurement and Market Organization. *Journal of Law and Economics* 25 (April): 27–48.

Barzel, Y. 1989. *Economic Analysis of Property Rights*. Cambridge University Press.

Casson, M. C. (1982). *The Entrepreneur: An Economic Theory*. Oxford: Martin Robertson.

Chen, Jianbo. 1995. Securing Technologies and Rapid Expansion of Township Enterprises: Basic Clue for Expansion at Hengdian Group, Dongyang, Zhejiang (Unpublished research report).

Grossman, S., and O. Hart. 1986. The Costs and Benefits of Ownership: A Theory of Vertical and Lateral Integration. *Journal of Political Economy* 94 (4): 691–719.

Hart, O., and J. Moore. 1990. Property Rights and the Nature of the Firm. *Journal of Political Economy* 98 (6): 1119–1158.

He, Wei, Jie Wei, and Weiguang Shen (eds.). 1994. *Study on HG by Renowned Experts and Scholars*. People's Press.

HG. *HG Charter*. HG Archive, 1984–1996.

HG. *The Outline of the Community Ownership of HG 1994 (Draft)*. Shen, Weiguang et al., 1994: Appendix, pp. 128–131.

Huang, Jianhui. 1992. *The History of Piaohao in Shanxi Province*. Shanxi People's Press.

Shen, Weiguang, Lijun Xu, Shiyan Sun, and Cansong Lu. 1994. *Study on Community Economy Model of HG*. The People's Press.

Sun, Shiyan. 1995. *The Power of Culture: Enlightenment from Hengdian*. Central Party School Press.

Umbeck, J. (1977). The California Gold Rush: A Study of Emerging Property Rights. *Explorations in Economic History, 14*(2), 197–206.

Wang, Dingding. 1996. Gaming on Property Rights. *Economic Research* (10).

Xu, Wenrong. 1994. *The Road of Hengdian*. The People's Press.

Zhou, Qiren. 1996a. "The Property Rights of Human Capital". *The Finance* (3).

Zhou, Qiren. 1996b. The Firm in the Market: A Special Contract Between Human Capital and Non-Human Capital. *Economic Research* (6).

Chapter 8
The Nature of the Public-Owned Enterprise

This paper studies the nature of two types of public-owned enterprises (POEs): state-owned enterprises (SOEs) and collective-owned enterprises (COEs). Generally speaking, a POE is either as "an enterprise distinctly belonged to the state or the collective", or an "ownerless property" and an organization with absent owners. This article focuses on the actual property rights of POEs. The main question is: for an enterprise distinctly owned by the state or the collective, is there any other property rights owner besides the state and the collective? In the case of the so-called "absence of the owner", will the original rights and responsibilities due to the owner really disappear completely?

Let's start with the public passage in an apartment building. To ensure entry and exit and access for all residents, the passage is collectively owned; and it cannot be sold or rented to any individual household. However, in reality, we often see private sundries piled up on the public passages. It is an interesting empirical research topic to analyze how the de facto "rights" are formed and distributed for storing stuff on the passage. But one thing for sure, it is never legal for any household to take up the public passage. Even the worst-managed apartment will publish the document on the removal of private dumps from the public passage. The problem is that these regulations will not be followed automatically. In an environment where the laws and regulations are not enforced, households occupying the public passage becomes a common phenomenon. It is so common that people no longer think about the question: is the public passage partially occupied by individuals still the passage distinctly "owned by the public", or can this property (space) also be called "ownerless property" or "passage with absence of owners"?

The economic nature of the POE is already embodied in the above-mentioned public passage. However, in order to make the question more clearly, some analysis is needed. After the Introduction of this paper, Part 1 explains the concepts used in this paper and related theories; Part 2 analyzes the property rights of POEs from the legal power perspective; Part 3 discusses the contractual nature of enterprises in the

---

This paper was originally published in *Economic Review*, Issue No. 11 (2000).

Q. Zhou, *Property Rights and Changes in China*,
https://doi.org/10.1007/978-981-15-9885-2_8

market and non-contract-based POEs; Part 4 discusses the de facto private property rights of human capital that cannot be eradicated by any POE; Part 5 explains how POEs motivate internal human resources through national rent defined in this paper; and the last part is a brief summary.

8.1 Concepts and Questions

SOEs and COEs are regarded as POEs, because the ownership of their assets belongs to the state or the collective rather than any private individual, and this ownership is also not any form of ensemble of private ownership. However, the de jure ownership and de facto ownership of economic resources are not always the same. In order to clarify this difference, we need to bring in some new concepts.

Since Coase (1937), economists have generally recognized that it takes resources to define property rights. Barzel (1989) particularly emphasizes that it takes less resources to define the de jure property rights than the de facto property rights. Because it is no easy job to define property rights in reality, even if all resources are clearly defined as private-owned by the law, in the real economic life there is always the "public domain", namely the nominal private assets of which the exclusive rights cannot be maintained due to the too high actual enforcement costs.[1]

However, what Bazel does not specifically point out is, the resources in the "public domain" are not clearly defined by law, and they are also not "ownerless property". Individuals will not automatically step back outside the boundary of the "public domain" unless these resources have no value. There are always people attempting to capture the value of public resources and establish de facto exclusive rights. The public space occupied by households as we see in the public passage has established de facto exclusive private rights. Bazel refers to the de facto right of individuals over "public domain resources" as "welfare capture". Here, as the wording "capture" suggests "to snatch" or "to plunder", therefore it is not a righteous "claim". Economically, the capturer has spent private costs on the capture, but there is always a portion of what he gets as the proceeds that comes from other people's contributions to public resources and their corresponding rights. For example, he who occupies the public passage, although, has to take care and spend the nursing cost to increase the available space for himself, has actually forced his neighbors to share such costs as the rents, lighting, inconvenience of access, higher probability of fire, potential escape difficulties and the eyesore. In short, the public passage was partially snatched by a private person. Here, the income from the resources has its "owner", so does its cost. In terms of cost and benefit, the occupied public passage is never in the state of "owner's absence" despite the fact that the owner of the cost and benefit is not the same as the nominally distinct legitimate owner. The real situation is, the de jure ownership of the resources is detached from its de facto ownership, leading to the

[1]See the introductory part of Barzel (1989), and also the Preface by Wang (1998), for the Chinese version of *A Collection of Barzel's Papers* (1989).

decoupling between the rights of benefit and the responsibility of cost of resources. That is to say, due to the "capture" behavior, the owner of the partial value of the public domain is not the de jure owner, but the de facto capturer.

The main reason for the public passage capture is that the de jure property right of the resource is inconsistent with its de facto property right. If there is no de facto property right that differs from the ownership of the public passage, and if the exclusivity of the benefits snatched by the household from the public passage is not protected, there would even be no motivation from any individual to occupy the public passage. In this sense, it is practically meaningless to use the rational person hypothesis to infer that the public passage is bound to be captured. The focuses of the study should be: why can't the legally (or morally) clear-cut public ownership eliminate the de facto private property right? What are the behavioral characteristics and efficiency of utilizing nominal public resources under the actual constraint of de facto private property rights?

Capture will result in "capture loss" or "rent dissipation". That is primarily because part of the costs for the captured benefits is borne by others, the capturer usually does not well treat the value of the resources in the public domain. Second, in order to cover up the illegality of their capture, the capturer is forced to adopt some inefficient methods. Finally, the welfare capture will motivate more people to participate in the capture, thus increasing the cost for capturing or monopolizing the capture and leading to rent dissipation by non-productive uses. However, we are not presuming that any public passage that still has a little use value will surely trigger the motives and behavior of capture until all the possible rents are dissipated. Steven N. S. Cheung (1984) has an explanation for this: "The survival of the fittest means that certain arrangements must be adopted to reduce the rent dissipation." This means that the opportunities for the individual to capture public resources, on the one hand, stimulate the capture and cause capture loss; on the other hand, capture loss as the reality also motivates the vested interests to adopt certain arrangements to "defend" their rent from being dissipated. It is the latter aspect that provides the foundation for understanding the existence and operation of institutions and organizations, including the diverse systems for "atypical private property rights and pricing mechanisms". This suggests that the rights of capture are defined in the game between all current and potential capturers and between capturers and public ownership defenders of the public passage. Therefore, the "property rights gaming" framework proposed by Wang (1996) may be equally applicable to the analysis of captured ownership, but we just need to distinguish the de jure and the de facto captured ownership and property rights. This paper focuses on how the nominal public resources are captured in the real world and attempts to understand the nature of POEs by comparing the efficiency of alternative institutional arrangements.

8.2 The Foundation of Property Right of POEs

As the opposite of the "capital hires labor" system, POEs choose to "eliminate all private ownership of production materials" and make all physical capital and financial capital "public-owned". In order to fully eliminate any possibility for production materials to be private-owned, the legal power system for the public ownership system stipulates that all production materials shall belong to the state and the collective, and announces that individuals are not allowed to have the legitimate rights to own any productive resources. Here, the public entity can only exist in its entirety as an indivisible property owner, and it is not allowed to decompose the public property rights in any form into private property rights.[2] Therefore, the state-ownership or collective-ownership based public ownership system is completely different from the co-operative or joint-stock system that is based on the assemble of individual's private properties. According to the traditional theory of political economics on public ownership, individuals under the socialist public ownership system only have the right to possess non-productive livelihood resources.

If lawful private property rights are recognized, any assembled organization can be traced back to the individuals who formed the assemble, because, in the final analysis, it is the individuals that choose the forms of assemble, the method of managements and thus bear the corresponding financial outcome. At this time the entity of the assemble can be seen as the result of choice by individuals, who pool together their property rights, entrust them to the collective organization, and formulate the conditions and execution procedures for the assemble. However, when the lawful right of individuals to own productive resources is denied by law, it is impossible for individuals to choose the economic organization, and thus to assume corresponding financial responsibilities. In this case, the POE becomes an abstraction that cannot be decomposed into any specific individuals and it is no longer possible to trace back further to individual members of the organization. In the bulky system of the POE, all the performers are just all sorts of proxies (agents), and it is impossible to trace to the final principal. Therefore, it would be difficult to use the "principal-agent theory" to discuss about and analyze the POE. The feature of the POE is that it is an "agency without final principal". None of the agents themselves has the lawful private property rights over the means of production, or is responsible to any individual who owns the property rights of the means of production.

---

[2]The Theory of Rent Dissipation by Cheung (1970) argues that if public resources do not go against being used by free competition, it will definitely cause rent dissipation. However, here the foundation for anyone to use public resources through competition is not the private right as defined by law over the assembled property, but rather the "de facto right" as discussed in later sections. Fan and Zhang (1990: 25) propose that "the labor is not the owner of public property"; Rong (1996: 18) points out that public property "has a unique internal exclusivity", namely the exclusive right of the collective will to go against the will of the individual, who is required by the public ownership not to steal, damage, abuse, or waste public property. Their common focus is on the provision of rights of public ownership in the sense of legal power.

Individuals are not even legally allowed to own their own human capital. Therefore, it is not possible for any individual to reach a contract with others for the productive use of their human capital.[3] The most compelling evidence that POEs prohibit individuals from enjoying the right of productive use of their human capital, especially the right of contracts, is that market transactions of human capital are prohibited by the law in the public ownership system. The system of following administrative plans to dispatch labor resources replaces various types of labor markets: the labor market is replaced by the planned assignment from the state (or the collective); the technology market, by the state's or the collective's planning and control of scientific research and technology development activities; and the enterprise manager market, by the administrative appointment system. Under the traditional public ownership system, the mechanism for individuals to realize the value of their human capital through legitimate market transactions, disappears.

The POE that eliminates private property rights has logically achieved public ownership over all resources. The individual cannot act as the final principle of financial capital and other physical capital of the POE, nor can he leverage his own human capital and become a factor owner in the corporate contract by choosing to enter into a market-oriented contract with the POE. The POE is no longer a "firm" by the definition of Coase because it is not based on a contract or a set of contract(s). The POE still needs to use various input factors, yet the foundation for the POE to utilize these factors is not the alienation by these factors' owner as per a contract, but administrative scheduling and dispatching after all resources become public-owned. Therefore we can see the fundamental feature of the POE is that it is not based on a market contract.

8.3 The Contractual Nature of the Firm and the Non-Contract-Based Firm

The non-contract-based nature of POEs fundamentally eliminates a mechanism for ensuring enterprise efficiency: the market correction mechanism. To illustrate this point, it is necessary to use a market contract-based firm as a reference. According to the theory proposed by Coase (1937), Alchian and Demsetz (1972), Cheung (1983), and Barzel (1989), the firm in the market can be understood as one/a series of market contract(s) by input owners.[4] Here the resource owner's freedom to choose among different market contracts is the foundation for all forms of production exchanges

---

[3]The property rights include the right to trade, that is, the right to enter into a market contract. The exclusivity of property rights is important, but it is mainly for trade, not just for exclusive self-use.

[4]The idea that a firm is a series of market contracts makes the statement of "the ownership of the firm" a paradox because it takes the ownership of at least two or more resources to form a firm, so "the corporate contract", just like "a tenancy contract", cannot only belong to either one of the contracting parties; and the market value of the same contract is different for different parties (Zhou 1996: 76). The non-contract-based POE that announces elimination of private ownership of the means of production seems to have only one ownership because all resources are owned by the

and organizations. The resource owner can utilize the resource himself to produce the products and sell them to the market, or sell his resource once for all for income, or follow the conditions set in a contract and transfer the right to use his resources to an agent in exchange for an income. When this last option is chosen, namely when the entrepreneur or the agent leverages the limited right of resource use conferred by contract and directly coaches production activities, rather than follows the instantaneous price change to organize the production and sell the products to the market, an enterprise is born.[5]

Why would the owner surrender the right to use the resources to an entrepreneur rather than directly organize the production according to market price mechanism and sell the products? If the right of use can be surrendered for income, then can't the income equally be earned by directly selling products or selling the resource once for all? Coase's theory on the firm reminds us that there may be a gap between the two incomes: the income from the firm as a contract in the market (namely surrendering the use of his input to the entrepreneur) is greater than that from producing and selling the products (or the input) by himself. Coase further finds that "an important reason to make profits through establishing a firm is that there is a cost to use the price mechanism"[6] whereas the firm can directly organize production without price discovery, thus saving the most overt transaction costs. Coase's above analysis is simplified to a proposition: "The firm is an organization that saves transaction costs in the market." However, this proposition is easily misinterpreted as any enterprise will save transaction costs. If the firm will surely save transaction costs just because it directly commands the factors and avoids the use of price mechanism, then the larger the firm, the more inputs can be directly commanded, and the more transaction costs can be saved? If the whole society is turned into one big firm, then all market transactions are eliminated, and the transaction costs of the whole economic system are saved and become zero?

This certainly is not what Coase meant. He points out that the firm has to pay organization costs to save transaction costs. If the organization costs are too high and offset the savings in transaction costs, the firm will lose more than it gains. "At the margin, the costs of organizing within the firm will be equal either to the costs of organizing in another firm or to the costs involved in leaving the transaction to be 'organized' by the price mechanism."[7] However, what Coase is trying to say, is not to have a center to measure the transaction costs and organization costs for all. On the contrary, the comparison doer here is the owners of all the inputs entering the market and all the entrepreneurs competing with each other. What this comparison does is that it finds out the better option among all the possibilities for the input owner to produce the products by himself versus all the possibilities of surrendering the resources, and among all the possibilities of surrendering the resources to one

public, so there is no second ownership. However, the main purpose of this paper is to show that this is only true in the sense of legal power.

[5]Cheung (1983: 3).

[6]Coase (1937: 6).

[7]Coase (1937: 5).

entrepreneur versus all the possibilities of surrendering them to other entrepreneurs. In any case, the resource owner's choice of a contract is based on their scattered respective transaction costs and enterprise organization costs. Without the freedom of choice of market contracts by the input owner, there is nothing to guarantee that the firm's transaction costs can be saved (or at the margin, be equal to the organization cost so arising).

The reason is that firms and entrepreneurs are prone to errors. The firm is prone to errors because it needs to organize various inputs into the firm ex ante through contracts, and go through its process (that is, under the command of the entrepreneur and other agents) to produce the products and services, and then sell them to the market. In this process, the "uncertainties" defined by Knight (1921) often defeat the preset strategic plans of the firm and the entrepreneur along with their adaptive efforts. In order to deal with the uncertainties of the market, the entrepreneur's talent is important; what is more important is a system to effectively and fully incentivize the entrepreneur, namely to enable him to share the residual claims and the right of enterprise control.[8] But even if he can take all the residual claims, even the wisest entrepreneur cannot guarantee that he will stay unbeatable each and every time in the wake of market uncertainties.[9] A contract previously committed by the firm and the entrepreneur may become unperformable in the process of the market; or the input owner who has entered into the firm finds that the offer of another firm is more appealing. Similarly, when the comparison is made between producing the products, selling the input outright, and surrendering its use to the enterprise, the previous expectations of the resource owner may also often be disrupted by uncertainties. Only the market can correct errors made by the firm and the entrepreneur. Or, in a broader sense, the market process corrects errors that all resource owners may make.

---

[8]The role of entrepreneurship is difficult to monitor and measure even afterwards. Except such institutional arrangements as a sharecropping contract, where the entrepreneur is allowed to share the residual claims, probably nothing else could "incentivize" entrepreneurs. (Zhou 1996: 76).

[9]The selection of qualified entrepreneurs or company managers is important, but the effectiveness of such selection is inseparable from the overall market environment. As for the theory of Zhang (1995) that the financial capital owner of the firm should have the priority to choose the manager, this priority can only be correctly interpreted when it is placed in the market environment, especially in the markets of various factors. The shareholders and BOD usually select the GM once a year, but workers, technicians, and other input owners who enter into the firm can select their managers every day, and they can even select the "company boss" who chooses managers. They can withdraw from the firm at a certain exit cost, or stay in the firm to create trouble for their boss. Whether the financial capital owner will choose managers from the "leftovers" from other inputs owners depends on whether these "bosses" meet economists' assumption that they are always rational. In the real empirical world, there are stories and stories of "bosses" destroying their financial capital to zero with their stubbornness, capriciousness, arrogance and dictatorship. We only assume that all "bosses surviving bosses are rational" when the competitive market will eventually oust all bosses who fail the survival test. In theory, I think Cui Zhiyuan's "stakeholders" concept (1996) is meaningful for understanding Coase's concept of "the firm as a set of market contracts". But I just disagree with Cui on his argument that to acknowledge that company manager is responsible to all stakeholders is to "transcend the logic of private property rights", because the foundation for stakeholders to enter the company as a contract is that they have the property rights over their respective resources (including human capital).

The basic mechanism for the market to correct the entrepreneur's and the resource owner's mistake is a free and competitive choice of contracts. When a contract appears to be uneconomical or relatively uneconomical in the market competition, the resources can flow to other contracts. Economical or not here is based on the subjective judgment by the individual input owner. It does not matter whether such judgment is "rational" or not. For example, an input owner might make a bigger error when he withdraws from one contract and enters into another. What matters is, provided that the input owner takes responsibility for his choice, all market contracts will eventually go through the "survival test" as defined by Alchian (1950).

After all, having the freedom to select contracts means that the resource owner has the right to make and correct mistakes. This is the most important economic function of the property rights, and also the most basic mechanism to ensure effective allocation of resources in the market economy, because only the right to freely choose contracts can guarantee that the "survived" contracts or forms of resource organization will have the competitive edge. In theory, the liquidity of resources between different market contracts is the foundation for the existence and innovation of various contracts. More interestingly, when resources flow between different contracts, the supply and demand dynamics in each market changes accordingly. For example, when the owner of a shoe-making workshop gives up his status as the "boss" to work in a shoe-making factory, or vice versa, the market supply and demand for the shoe workshop and the company will change; and then the supply and demand of the shoe-making labor market and related factor markets will also change. In this sense, the relative price system is actually a record of contracts chosen by input owners. Without the relative price system, transaction costs and organization costs cannot be measured. In general, that "the price mechanism allocates resources" is built on the freedom to choose market contracts by property owners.

No central authoritative agency or person can judge which direction of the resources flow is "correct", or which forms or scales of organization are "correct". Although, according to empirical observations, as the economy grows, more and more resources are organized into firms, and the firms seem to get larger and larger, the reliable foundation supporting this phenomenon is still the free choice of market contracts. Economists have long predicted that small firms will be wiped out by big ones; but till today, we still see in the era of each generation of technology, the co-existence of large, medium, and small companies, as well as innovations and innovations in the forms of market contracts. The foundation of the efficiency of large firms is absolutely not just their scientific internal management and the market competition between large firms, but rather the market system that allows the resource owners to make free choices between all forms and sizes of firms as well as between firms and non-firms. Employees of large firms have the right to select different contracts, such as quitting the firm to join SMEs, mon-and-pop operations, start their own business, or sell their inputs once for all. That is the criteria to test large firms and force them to prove that their organization has a competitive edge in the market. In the final analysis, the real foundation for the firm's profitability is the freedom to choose different market contracts, including non-firm contracts. Therefore, just as Steven N. S. Cheung emphasizes, the main point of Coase's theory of the firm is the choice of contracts.[10] In this sense, property rights, markets, and firms are addressing the same thing. There is no point in distinguishing which is more fundamental as this will lead the discussion to vague directions.

The POE have eradicated the foundation for market contracts, and at the same time, the mechanism for the market to correct the enterprise's and entrepreneur's mistakes. This is not to say that the initial error of the non-contract-based "enterprise" must be more serious, but that if that the market-based contract is restricted, there is no way for the enterprise's mistakes to be corrected in time. A bigger problem is that if the right to choose contracts is fully prohibited, the POE may not even know the occurrence of "errors", because once the market relationship is restricted, the criterion to judge the effective or ineffective use of inputs in the sense of opportunity cost—the market price system and its formation mechanism—will be distorted. In practice, the POE system often closely follow the technical and economic parameters provided by the "capitalist market system", such as the elasticity coefficient between standard energy consumption and national income growth. However, even if the POE grasps the signal from the macro perspective and gets to know that its energy efficiency is extremely low, there is nothing it can do at the micro-level to improve the energy performance. Because the mechanism for the factor owners to make decisions among all directions of economic activities and all forms of resource utilization, is eliminated in the POE system. From the perspective of information cost, even if the POE uses robots with preset maximizing programs to do all the economics job, it is still impossible to achieve the optimal solution by the so-called rational calculation. What's more, the POE still has to use a special resource, that is, people.

8.4 The Ineliminable de Facto Private Property Rights

That human itself has economic value is a long-discovered truth. Distinguishing the quantity from quality of human resources in the economic process and regarding the quality of human knowledge and skills as the key to economic growth is a major advance in economics in recent decades.[11] Since the 1960s, lots of empirical research by economists on modern economic growth discovers that human capital, especially

[10]However, Cheung's interpretation of Coase's theory of the firm is often summarized in much of the literature as "the firm is organization that replaces the products market by the factors market". The reason for the firm to exist is to use input contracts to get the right to use the resources through the owner's alienation, while the owner could otherwise use the resources to produce products and sell them. However, the firm, as a profit-making organization as described by Coase, cannot replace any market, including the product market. If the product market is truly completely replaced, then the resource owner can no longer choose to be an entrepreneur to make the product in the market, he has no choice but to transfer the right to use the resource to other entrepreneurs, and then how to guarantee that this enterprise (of other entrepreneurs) will have a real competitive edge?

[11]For the evolution of economics thoughts about the role of knowledge and other forms of human capital in economic growth, see Wang (1995). The author would like to thank Wang Dingding for his comments on the draft of this article, especially for his insight that "learning" is the most important component of human capital.

the knowledge and skills grasped by people, contributes tremendously to economic growth, and these human resources with certain knowledge and skills as well fit into the definition of capital as the "source of future income". Therefore, some economists see human resources as a kind of capital, and the "human capital" that makes even greater contribution to long-term economic growth. In short, human resources with knowledge and skills are productive and capitalized in nature.

However, what is derived from the human capital theory, is not just limited to the significance of education and training for economic growth. The more fundamental question is the conditions for human capital to effective play its role in economy, because these conditions not only affect the effect of human capital on economic growth, but also the formation of human capital itself. Then we cannot but to touch upon the property rights of human capital. According to the research by Barzel (1977), Rosen (1985), and Cheung (1984), human capital can be understood as an asset that naturally belongs to the person.[12] All human resources with market value, such as labor, skills, knowledge, learning capabilities, responsibility, innovation, risk-taking and sensitivity to potential market opportunities, are not only attached to the person, but also can only be evoked and transferred by the person. Therefore, in the case where private property rights are not recognized and protected by the society's legal system, individuals can use their de facto control to "close" the channel for effective use of their human resources, increasing the cost of use by others and lowering the value of human resources. Understanding this feature is the foundation for understanding the incentive theory in economics, and also for understanding the firm as a special contract between human capital and non-human capital.[13]

The POE system legally denies individual's lawful private ownership of the productive human capital. However, it cannot deny that "the individual is the natural de facto owner and controller of human capital". Thus the POE has an inherent tension. The POE can follow the plan or the command and put human capital and non-human capital together, thus getting rid of all the trouble from the private property rights-based market transaction mechanism. However, human capital legally owned by the state or the collective cannot play its role just by directly following the dispatching and commanding of the POE. All sorts of humble private interests and

[12]Zhou (1996: 73–74).

[13]Zhang (1996) believes that the feature that "human capital is indivisible from the person" puts human capital at a disadvantage as compared with non-human capital: first, human capital cannot be mortgaged; second, human capital owners can get benefits by "slacking off" and "abusing" non-human capital. Therefore, he believes that the correct logical inference is "capital hires labor", and he believes that "(non-human) capital owners should be given the precedence to be entrepreneurs" (Zhang 1996: 9–10). I believe if "reputation" is regarded as an intangible part of the human asset, then the statement "human capital cannot be mortgaged" is not necessarily true, because it would be rather too difficult to interpret modern companies if we throw away the market mechanism to price the reputation and only rely on the mortgageable financial capital. As for the tendency of "slacking off" and "abusing", it seems to me that the problem cannot be solved by giving the non-human capital the priority to be the entrepreneur, for the same reason as Barzel (1977) points out the slave owner with the absolute priority cannot solve the problem of "slacking off" and "abusing" by slaves. The effective way to solve the problem is the market contract with incentives, rather than establishing the precedence of "capital" over "labor."

motives not only still exist in the POE but also actually determine the real delivery of human assets, i.e. the actual supply of labor, knowledge, skills, responsibility, and creativity is still be determined by the person who carries these assets. Unless the de facto owner of the human resources, namely the person, is happy to accept the objective of the state or the collective, the POE just cannot automatically mobilize the human capital that has been "allocated within the enterprise" and legally made public-owned.

Just like enterprises under any other system, the POE cannot avoid the question of incentives. In fact, because the resource scarcity won't disappear, and due to the transmission of the pressure of competition between countries in the overall political, military and economic strength, the POE actually never gives up its efforts to encourage individuals to increase their human capital supply. But the POE that does not recognize private ownership of productive resources in the legal power will meet some special obstacles with its incentives. We have pointed out that underlying difficulty for the POE is that it has no traceable final principal, and the prohibition of market contracts has made it impossible to generate the market price signal to measure the efficiency of resource utilization. Now let us move on further to discuss how the POE, in practice, seeks institutional alternatives to enable the exertion and utilization of the private human capital under public ownership.

The first thing to see, is that the state rent has taken place of profit and become the target of the POE. The existing research points out that the POE does not chase profit as the target of its behavior, which is, instead, to fulfil the national planning task. However, few people have noticed that the POE is unable to chase profit in the economics (not the financial) sense.[14] Because strictly speaking, when private property rights of productive resources are eradicated, especially when the right to choose market contracts is gone, concepts like market prices, production costs and transaction costs no longer exist, and therefore, the concept of profit does not exist either. Then, what is the "national planning task"? Historically, the public economy sets the economic goals of its own country according to the overall strength competition with other countries. However, the national economic goals cannot be automatically determined by following "objective laws of economics". The competition landscape between countries and the competition strategies depends first and foremost on the perception of the national agents. At the same time, there is no ready-to-use and easy technical function that can calculate how much output can be generated from the resources centralized in the hands of the state, or forecast what kind of economic

[14]Many economists advocating the POE reform propose that the introduction of the "profit" into the POE system can help the POE to increase productivity. In 1962, the famous "Liberman's proposal" of the Soviet Union advocated highly simplifying the state plan for business indicators, and using the "profit" (uniformly approved sectoral profit level) as the main indicator for assessing enterprises. In the 1960s, Sun Yefang of China also made a similar proposal (see Wu 1994: 122–129). However, "profit" is the product of enterprise contract in the market transactions. When the POE system abolishes the market transaction, the so-called "profit" that is "uniformly approved" and directed by the central planning is not the "profit" in its original sense. In contrast, Gu Zhun's proposal is not so compromised. He believes that "the mandatory plan and mandatory pricing system must be abolished to liberalize prices" in order to guide enterprises towards making profits" (see Wu 1994: 127).

structure should be formed. Empirically, the national economic goals under the public ownership system are often determined as a result of the political balance between the subjective judgments and the different will of the state agents.[15] Of course, whether the national economic targets subjectively set by the state agents is achieved or not, the resources concentrated in the hands of the state will always generate real economic benefits, and to increase the economic benefits controlled and distributed by the state agents, namely the state rent, can itself become the economic target of the public economy.

What is important to our analysis is that all national agents are natural persons. Therefore, in determining the national economic goals, the first logical step to run the public economy, there is no way to fully rule out the role and influence of the individual natural person. The extent to which national agents will work to maximize the national interest, rather than their own interest, depends on the incentives and constraints. What needs to be examined is: after the legal right of individuals to own property rights of productive resources is abolished, what impacts will be generated on the behavior of the state agents themselves, the social supervision, and the driving mechanism for the counter-balance for state agents and its effectiveness? We would like just to point out here: the state rent's replacement of the profit under the market mechanism cannot fully expel from the system of public economy the fact that the person with noble or humble motives still actually controls his own intelligence and capabilities.

8.5 The State Rent Incentive: An Alternative Institutional Arrangement

The extent to which the POE will engage in productive activities to maximize the state rent is a day-to-day unsolved problem. Because it involves many individuals who are nominally owned by the public but actually control their own human assets. Experience has shown that people do not automatically provide labor, invention, learning, measurement, supervision, and management efforts to maximize the state rent simply because they are owned by the public. Since its establishment, the POE management system has never stopped trying to improve itself from all dimensions fundamentally because it still needs to motivate the human resources to increase the supply. The POE has been constantly looking for institutional arrangements that can replace the recognition of private property rights and motivate human resources. From mobilizing workers to directly participate in decision-making to establishing a strict administrative management system; from establishing the rationing system to maintain the revolutionary passion and political loyalty to introducing all sorts of "material incentives"; from large-scale ideological education and mass movements to the formulation of regulations by imitating the capitalist Taylorism and emphasizing

[15]This is the fundamental reason why the decisions on the growth targets, speed, priority sectors, and even key projects under the planned economy are often full of political struggle.

labor discipline; from measuring output by direct labor time to respecting the law of value, and establishing a price, cost, and profit accounting system under the public ownership. To name just a few.

In the process of finding alternative institutional arrangements, which seem to be unstable and inconsistent, the POEs gradually converge to motivate the human resources supply by establishing a positive relationship between the efforts to produce (or manage) the state rent and the sharing of the state rent. For example, the administrative hierarchy for management and the remuneration system based on "the material incentives" have become the common basic systems for the POE. This is not accidental. Because the institutionalization of the administrative ranking-based sharing of the state rent enables the POE to leverage the right to share the state rent to incentivize individuals to increase their management and labor efforts. Under what is called the "state rent incentive" system in this paper, it is precisely the de facto rights of human capital that enables individuals to choose to either increase their labor and management efforts so as to get a higher share of the national rent, or to decrease their labor and management efforts and share less of the national rent. The "state rent incentive" has established vested interest that can be obtained by natural persons within the public ownership system although the ownership does not nominally belong to any individual; the foundation for this mechanism is exactly the recognition of the property rights still owned de facto by individuals.

At the first glance, the state rent incentive is not very different from the incentive principle in market-oriented enterprise system, because the core of the enterprise as a contract is nothing more than establishing a positive correlation between the efforts to produce profits and the sharing of profits. While the enterprise system in the market economy gives the right to share profits to those who contribute to the profit generation, the POE distributes the right to share the state rent to those who contribute to the creation of state rent, too. Individuals compete for profit in the former case, and for state rent in the latter case. So, if the concept of state rent is called "profit", and if the incentive intensity of two is similar, these two systems will have no real differences, will they?

The fundamental difference is the formation process for the profits and the state rent. Profits are formed under decentralized power in the process of voluntary market contracts, while the state rent is the result of economic resources centralized by administrative power and centralized economic decisions. The firm's profit is an "organizational profit" generated by the contract-based firm. It is the result of the competition between various types of firms in the market and the competition between firms and non-firms. The state rent system eliminates all market competition and produces the state rent under the enterprise organization model with centralized decision-making. To examine the question from the perspective of the individual's rights to choose and the scope of choices, it is easy to see the differences between the two systems. The profit system recognizes the rights of individuals to enter, exit, or organize firms themselves based on the property rights of their resources, and protects the income from the right of contracts in the market. The state rent system denies private property rights in the legal system, thus denying the individuals' freedom to choose the market contract; individuals can only compete within the framework of the given POE; they cannot exit from enterprises which they find ineffective, let alone create a production organization to compete with the public ownership model selected by the central authority. Therefore, the profit system is far more competitive than the state rent system in making full use of "every individual's unique information advantage over others" and in "exploring productive innovation in all directions" as emphasized by Hayek (1945).[16]

The state rent system of the POE and the profit system of firms in the market are also substantially different in terms of incentive intensity. First, since individuals can only legally own "living materials" under the POE system, so the amount of state rent that individuals can legally own is rather limited, and it cannot be comparable to the un-capped profit sharing incentive. Second, in order to maintain the distributability attributes of "living materials", much of the state rent is distributed per the hierarchy in the form of physical benefits; it is allowed to be occupied, consumed, and enjoyed by individuals, but not allowed to be traded and invested, which indeed seems to be more equal and fair, but at the same time weakens its incentive effect. Third, the rent claims available to individuals under the state rent system are very small, but the rent control right that may be obtained is huge. Here, "the state rent control right" refers to the decision-making and command authority controlled by POE agents for the production and distribution of the state rent. This asymmetrical combination between the rent claims and control rights is, in reality, to use the control right to compensate for the inadequate incentive from the rent claims; but such institutional arrangements may lead to abuse of the control power, and thus may not be regarded as positive incentives. Fourth, the state rent claims, especially the control right, are always distributed to those in power, which intensifies the competition for the incentives to incumbent positions, but does not encourage people to think about the long-term effects of their behaviors. The principle of emphasizing the incumbent in the state rent distribution often lead to disastrous consequences resulting from the behaviors that may produce far-reaching influence on the enterprise.

On the other hand, the profit system has never limited the profits distribution to individual's "living consumption", nor does it restricts the use of the shared profit to consumption or to investment. Since the profit incentive system is based on private property rights, even those who have nothing more than their human capital can obtain market opportunities by using their human capital, realize the market value, and possibly get a share of the profits, and then own non-human assets through reinvestment. In other words, the tangible and intangible human assets owned by individuals can be converted into the property right on non-human assets. This point is important for understanding the effectiveness of the profit incentive system. After all, the owners of human capital all have their natural life cycle, not only the fluctuation in output is inevitable, but also eventually they will all face loss of production capabilities, aging and death. If income from the property of the owners of human capital is limited to only the consumption of "living materials" and they can only take it as they consume, then when the individual's human capital productivity decreases or disappears, the only source for their consumption of "living materials" has to

[16]See Wang Dingding's systematic interpretation of Hayek's thought (1995, 1999).

simply rely on pensions and subsidies provided by the POE.[17] Therefore, the individual's property rights to his human capital must include all the right to trade, invest, and convert to non-human capital; if any aspect is limited, the incentive intensity will decline.

The only thing in common between the state rent incentive and the profit incentive is that neither can change the fact that human capital naturally can only be controlled and mobilized by the owner namely the individual himself. The difference lies in the degree of productive use of human capital. When property rights of human capital are legally recognized, the ineffective or insufficient incentive from an enterprise contract can be corrected by the flow of the human capital factor to other firms or non-firm organizations. Therefore human capital is more productive because individuals have greater freedom of choice. On the other hand, when property rights of human capital are denied, individuals have no right to freely withdraw from an ineffective or inefficient organization, or to enter into a contract with what they believe to be a more efficient organization. The only thing that they can "choose" to do is either to reduce the supply of labor and management efforts, or to use de facto control and leverage inadequate supervision to snatch the public resources for their illegal personal benefits. In both options, the human capital is either idled or used for a non-productive purpose. Since the state rent comes from the administrative monopoly of resources, the competition for the state rent makes some human capital become dedicated to rent setting and rent seeking within the POE system, leading to "counter-productive" development of the human capital.

We are not asserting from the analysis that the POE along with the state rent incentive system won't be able to survive though. In fact, this enterprise system can exist for a long time. Because the POE system only eliminates the de jure nominal ownership of human capital, and in reality it still faces the fact that the human capital is controlled by the individual, and motivates the human resources within itself with the state rent incentive. Our analysis only demonstrates that the state rent incentive is at a competitive disadvantage against the profit incentive. This helps to explain why the POE can still operate "normally" when isolated from the market competition, but it will only get worse and worse when competing with the profit incentive system on the same platform. Economists forecasting that the POE only needs to introduce market competition without reforming the property rights, fail to see that the introduction of market competition will first stimulate the human capital that has not been fully motivated under the state rent incentive system, and lead some high quality human resources to "exit" the POE and join competing non-public enterprises. Therefore, when the overall political, military, and economic competition between countries

[17] In theory, the value of pensions and other funds appropriated from POEs can achieve value addition through investment into productive assets such that the individuals no longer need to worry about themselves in case of loss of productivity. However, the pooled funds are like another type of public passage. There must be incentives to ensure that these funds are well managed. Otherwise, they could as well be drained and depleted due to mismanagement. Empirically, if POEs cannot fulfill their welfare commitments, it will cause serious social unrest, and it may lead to the so-called "59-year-old phenomenon" (The phenomenon refers to graft and corruption of officials bordering retirement—Translator's note).

changes its gear and turns to opening the market, namely when the POEs compete with non-public enterprises in the same product market, the destiny of the POEs will just be either to be eliminated in the market competition or to carry out the market-oriented property rights reform.

Finally, let's briefly cover what is the POE's market-oriented property rights reform. When Coase pointed out that "market transactions are nothing more than property rights transactions", he actually already mentioned that establishing private property rights is the foundation for market-oriented reform. However, the traditional POE system that legally denies private property rights will not accept this view easily. As a result, a new theory on "public ownership-based market economy" has emerged, and it seems that market transactions can be limited within some of the POE's products. However, all products and production factors are the input and output mutually between each other, this nature of the market will determine that any artificial efforts to pick out only some products (services) for free market transactions will be futile. The market economy of some products (services) will eventually expand into all products (services), and then into all factors of production. When the human capital finally becomes legally tradable in the market, the POE's market-oriented reform has touched its fundamental root. Because the person is the carrier for any kind of human capital, and it is only the individual natural person rather than the abstract "entire people", "the state" or "the collective" that can go to the labor market, the technical expert market, the manager and the entrepreneur market. In the end, the POE reform must answer the following questions: to acknowledge or deny private property rights of human capital, and to acknowledge or deny that the private property rights of human capital can be transformed into property rights of non-human capital. Based on the above reasons, this paper defines the POE's market-oriented property rights reform as the reform that eventually points to clearly-defined private property rights, and uses them to interpret the logic of the POE's market-oriented reform.

8.6 Summary

This paper discusses the nature of POEs that have not undergone market-oriented reforms. In the context of legally denied private property rights of productive resources, the POEs become non-contract-based organizations; but in order to fully motivate the human capital that still belongs to individuals in reality, the POEs use the state rent incentive mechanism to replace the market transaction and profit incentive mechanism. The POE is like an apartment without even any private rooms because all the space is recognized as public property by law. Therefore, all resources here are public passages, and the state rent system is followed to define the de facto right of individuals to occupy and benefit from these passages. The implementation of the state rent system determines the visage and the efficiency of utilization of the public passages. This paper does not believe that the popular "principal-agent" theory or the framework of "separated ownership and operation" is suitable for analyzing the economic nature of the public passages. Instead, it attempts to analyze the POEs from the perspective of the inconsistency between the de jure property rights and the de facto property rights. We will continue to study the logic for the POE's market-oriented reform within the framework provided in this paper. The central clue is how the POEs will be transformed into market-based contractual organizations that recognize the legal position of the private property rights in the context of the individuals' de facto ownership of their human capital.

References

Alchian, A. (1950). Uncertainty, Evolution, and Economic Theory. *Journal of Political Economy, 58*(3), 211–221.

Alchian, A., and Harold Demsetz. 1972. Production, Information Costs, and Economic Organization. *American Economic Review* 62: 777–795.

Barzel, Yoram. 1977. An Economic Analysis of Slavery. *Journal of Law and Economics* 17 (I): 73–96.

Barzel, Yoram. 1989. *Economic Analysis of Property Rights*. Cambridge University Press.

Barzel, Yoram. 1992. The Property Rights of Public Property. In *The New Palgrave Dictionary of Economics*. Economic Science Press.

Cheung, Steven. 1983. The Contractual Nature of the Firm. *Journal of Law and Economics,* 26 (1), 1–21.

Cheung, Steven, N.S. 1970. The Structure of a Contract and the Theory of a Non-Exclusive Resource. *The Journal of Law and Economics* 13 (1): 47–70.

Cheung, Steven, N.S. 1984. The Orange Seller's Words. *Hong Kong Economic Journal*.

Coase, Ronald. 1937. The Nature of the Firm. In *The Firm, the Market, and the Law*, ed. Coase, 1988. Chicago: The University of Chicago Press.

Cui, Zhiyuan. 1996. The Theoretical Background for Amendments to Corporate Law in 29 States of the United States. *Economic Research* (4): 35–40.

Fan, Gang, Shuguang Zhang, et al. 1990. *The Outline of Macroeconomic Theory of Public Ownership*. Shanghai Joint Publishing Press.

Hayek, F.A. 1945. The Use of Knowledge in Society. *American Economic Review* (September).

Knight, Frank. 1921. *Risk, Uncertainty, and Profit*. Reprints of Economic Classics. Angustus M. Kelley, 1964.

Rong, Zhaozhi. 1996. On Inherent Conflicts in Public Property Rights. *Economic Research* (9): 16–23.

Rosen, S. 1985. The Theory of Equalizing Differences. In *Handbook of Labour Economics*, ed. O. Ashenfelter and R. Layard. Amsterdam: North-Holland.

Wang, Dingding. 1995. *Economic Development and Institutional Innovation*. Shanghai People's Press.

Wang, Dingding. 1996. The Gaming of Property Rights. *Economic Research* (10): 70–80.

Wang, Dingding. 1998. Foreword to Chinese Translation. In *Property Rights Economics Analysis*. Shanghai Joint Publishing Press and Shanghai People's Press.

Wang, Dingding. 1999. Study on Hayek's 'Extended Order'. In *Towards a Clearing in the Forest (WANG Dingding's Anthology)*. Shandong Education Press.

Wu, Jinglian. 1994. *Modern Companies and Enterprise Reform*. Tianjin People's Press.

Zhang, Weiying. 1995. *The Entrepreneur's Enterprise: The Contract Theory*. Shanghai Joint Publishing Press.

Zhang, Weiying. 1996. Ownership, Governance Structure and Principal-Agent Relationship. *Economic Research* (9): 3–15.

Zhou, Qiren. 1996. The Enterprise in the Market: A Special Contract Between Human Capital and Non-Human Capital. *Economic Research* (6): 71–80.

Chapter 9
The Theory of the Firm and China's Reform

9.1 Start with Coase: Firms Are Islands in the Sea of the Market

The origin of the concept of the planned economy is the theory of the firm. Karl Marx reasoned: big companies have internal plans, while the society has no plans; it is this conflict that will push capitalism towards annihilation. At that time the viewpoint was that as the productivity becomes more and more socialized, companies will grow larger and larger until they cover the whole economy and turn the big company's internal plan into the whole society's plan. From this perspective, the theory on planned economy was, in its earliest days, a theory of the firm. Lenin made it more clearly and said that socialism under the leadership of the proletariat will convert all members of the society into employees of the state-firm, and the entire economy will be a super state-firm.

When Coase reviews his theory of the firm, he explicitly admits that he was influenced by the above thoughts from Lenin believing that a country can also be regarded as a large firm. Indeed, Coase has provided economic analysis for the firm. He first asks: "If the allocation of all resources in a "fully competitive" market can be achieved through the price mechanism, why do firms not relying on the price mechanism for their internal operation still exist?" His answer is that the price mechanism of the market has a cost. This "cost" is not the production costs that we are familiar with, but the transaction costs incurred to complete the exchange of goods in addition to production costs. As the market expands, the transaction costs a lot of resources. Under certain circumstances, lots of cost can be saved for the transaction if the price mechanism-based "market co-ordination method" is replaced by the "enterprise internal co-ordination method" through commanding and without

This article is based the author's speech at Symposium on the 30th Anniversary of Reform and Opening up organized by UIE and the Guangdong Humanities Society. The text was revised by myself.

Q. Zhou, *Property Rights and Changes in China*,
https://doi.org/10.1007/978-981-15-9885-2_9

bargaining prices. According to this theorem of Coase, the firm is nothing more than an organization that saves transaction costs.

Interestingly, Coase starts from the "perfect market", finds out that the transaction is not cost free, and then arrives at the firm as an organization in the market. Nevertheless, he does not go very far to the super-state-firm, because he takes into account in his analysis another kind of costs: "organization costs"—If the firm internalizes activities that used to take place in the market, its organization costs (including the cost of decision making, supervision, and management) will rise.

Viewed as whole, Coase's theory of the firm considers two types of cost simultaneously: the firm can save transaction costs, but it has to pay the organization costs arising therefrom; when the saved transaction costs, at the margin, equals such incremental organization costs, the boundary between the firm and the market is determined. Coase cites an analogy once used by his teacher: the real market economy is like the sea, and the firms are islands of various sizes in the sea. In Coase's view, with the co-existence of transaction costs and organization costs in the real world, the sea water cannot cover everything, still less can the islands cover the whole sea.

9.2 The Starting Point of the Reform: The Dysfunctional Super-State Firm

The reform of the socialist country happens to stand at the other end of Coase's journey. Coase starts from the "perfect market" assumption in modern economics and discovers and the reason for the existence of enterprises or firms, while China's institutional reform starts from the in-practice planned economy, i.e. the reality of a super-state firm. This super-state-firm holds all the economic resources in its own hands and relies on the authority, coercive power, and overall planning of the state machine to organize the national economy. Although Lenin implemented the "new economic policy" after he came to power, that is, the country only controlled the economic lifelines, and left large numbers of small industries, small businesses, and small farms to the private sector and the market, but that period was very brief. Stalin nationalized the whole country, organized the Soviet economy into a super-state-firm envisioned by Lenin before the revolution, organized the planned economy with administrative orders, and granted no legal status for private property rights and market activities.

The main framework was borrowed from the Soviet Union when it was China's turn to build socialism from a more backward and agricultural country. But Chairman Mao was not quite satisfied with the high degree of centralization of the Soviet Union, and he tried a couple of times to decentralize and delegate. Looking back, however, it was only the decentralization from the central government to local governments, i.e. adding many local government firms to the super state-firm. Of course, such a model did not constitute the foundation for the market economy, because Chairman Mao would not budge on such important questions as the "large size and high degree of public ownership for the peoples' commune". If any local government decided to hand over the economic decision-making power to the private sector, this respected leader would immediately call it off. For instance, in 1962, he put a halt to the practice of "private land plot, free market and letting enterprises be responsible for their own profits and losses" and stopped the household responsibility system (HRS). Therefore, on the whole, China somewhat decentralized the power before the reform, but it never accepted the private property rights, nor did it allow any legal leeway for private parties to conclude any market-based voluntary contracts. The overall economic structure is still a super state-firm, except that internally the degree of the planned economy was not as high as in the Soviet Union.

Therefore, what prompted the socialist reform was not the high transaction costs which should be brought down by expanding enterprise organizations. What crippled the socialist economic construction for years was the too high organization costs of the super state-firm, leading to the failure of the planned economy and too low efficiency of resource allocation. Just imagine the tremendous number of supply and demand variables and co-ordinations involved to meet the needs of improving the livelihood for hundreds of millions of people in peacetime! To make do with and rely on the mandatory planning and the centralized decisions by the super state-firm, the information cost is too high, plus there is not enough incentive to work harder. On the eve of China's reform in 1977, the State Council convened a meeting to discuss why the economic and technological gap between China and major western countries was widened. The main conclusion was that the planned economy over-centralized by the central government was becoming increasingly dysfunctional.

9.3 Initiating the Reform: Delegation of Authority and the Household Responsibility System (HRS)

The problem is, that it is an unprecedented task as to which path to take to lower the cost for the economic operation after the super state-firm is established and then finds itself troubled by too high organization costs. Coase's theory finds that the too high transaction costs in the market can be brought down by expanding the firm. However, what the socialist reform faces is a problem with the unique style of its own: the super state-firm is too large, and the organization costs are too high, how to effectively bring them down?

The direction seems easy, that is, to go from the super state-firm that covers the entire national economy to the broader sea of the market and allow the invisible hand of the prices to play its role in resource allocation. This is perhaps how the term "the market-oriented reform" strategy was originated. However, under the rock-hard public ownership system, there is no ready-made experience or theory to draw on as to how to re-build the market.

Coase mentions in a 1959 paper that the clear definition of property rights is the key condition for market transactions. This proposition contains a simple truth: if something is not mine, then how can I have the right to sell it to you? Therefore, transactions must have the recognition of rights as the precondition. Since the market economy is based on the transactions, then the prerequisite for the market is clearly-defined rights.

China's reform, in practice, starts with redefining property rights. I reviewed this process in the article "The Unfolding of DENG's Drama – What DENG Xiaoping did Right". The original public planned economy is actually a set of definitions of rights, namely a set of institutional norms to regulate what people can and cannot do. Under the pressure from the reform, the rights were redefined, especially private property rights, including rights to transfer, regained recognition, and the market relations got re-developed in China.

The reform deployed by the Third Plenary Session of the 11th CPCCC in 1978 was to expand the autonomy of state owned enterprises (SOEs). The reform was based on the local reform experiment in Sichuan province, which delegated the decision-making power from the state economic organs to enterprises. This was also a reaction to external shocks, because foreign companies began to invest in China, and they were able to make quick decisions while the SOEs were not. The SOEs must apply for approval for everything, even when a very large SOE builds a toilet; you cannot use the money for soy sauce, so to speak, to buy vinegar. A state-owned factory director from Fujian said that it was not that the factory was uncompetitive, but that our hands and feet were tied up; the country must first untie us. The story about the investigation by a Xinhua News Agency reporter to Chongqing Iron and Steel Company was very well-known. A set of equipment in the factory was a legacy from the Westernization Movement in the late 19th century and the energy consumption was huge. If some modifications were made to the power unit, the investment could be recovered by the energy saved in two years. However, the application was submitted for many years without getting approval. Therefore, the motto of reform at that time was to delegate and to untie.

Interestingly, the practice of giving more autonomy to enterprises was yet to be rolled out globally when the household responsibility system reform was already put on the agenda for rural China. DU Ruizhi, who was then in charge of rural work in Guangdong Province, made marvelous remarks at a meeting to commemorate the 30th anniversary of rural reform: the first driver for the rural reform was the farmer's belly! When farmers didn't have enough to eat, and they were so hungry that the situation forced the government to practice the HRS. But that was not the first time to implement the HRS. The earliest HRS practice took place in Yongjia County, Wenzhou City, in the second half of 1956 when the advanced co-operative was introduced there. By 1961, 40% of the production brigades in Anhui Province already adopted HRS. The problem was that once the situation improved, the makeshift measure was taken back.

9.4 China's Path: Bottom-Level Innovation and Upper-Level Acknowledgement

If we follow the post-1978 rural reform closely, we will find that just as in the past, it was the farmers and production brigades' cadres who first initiated the reform from the bottom and spontaneously adopted the HRS. So, what is different this time? The difference lies in the fundamental change in political thoughts and routes at the upper level: the ruling party reflected upon the pains from past and proposed to seek truth from facts as opposed to sticking to bookism, dogmatism and ossification. Under this ideology, some places dared to be the first to recognize the grass-root reform practices, or at least not to punish the reformers but to allow them to try. After seeing the results from places to places, the central government acknowledged the reform with policy documents, and finally legislated it to complete the legalization process to redefine the rights.

This "China path" is very valuable. Because the definition and redefinition of rights involve behaviors and expectations. If the expectations are not stable, people won't have long-term behaviors. China's approach is to recognize the bottom-level reform at the local level, constantly reiterate that "the policy will not change", and "the policy will remain unchanged long term", and then eventually push forward the legislation when at last the time is mature such that the rights redefined by the reform are confirmed by law.

DU Runsheng mentions in his memoirs that DENG Xiaoping said this as early as in 1962, "As to which form of production relations is the best, we need to see and decide whichever form in which places can restore and develop agricultural production more easily and more rapidly, and whichever form is more welcomed by the masses. If the form is illegal, we will make it legal." Fortunately, such political attitude has become the mainstream at the Third Plenary Session of the 11th CPCCC. That has changed China's fate because the frontline grass-root level is always forced to find ways to solve practical problems. The question is whether or not they can be legally recognized by the "superstructure". If yes, they become institutional results in redefining the rights. If not, the grass-root experience will just be isolated cases, or at best, an expedient that cannot last long.

"Superstructure" is not simple. Thoughts and ideas are intractable, not to mention the conflicts of interest between different stakeholders, and plus people look at the question from different angles. At the 1980 central meeting on rural reform, some such high ranking officials as Provincial Party Secretaries even ended up quarreling and breaking up with displeasure at the end of the meeting. The story about "you go your sunny road, I will take my single-log bridge" reflects that it was not easy for the bottom-level spontaneous reform to get recognition from the upper level. Therefore, although "practice is the criteria to test truth", it's not easy to walk the talk.

The rights can be redefined in a radical or gradualist approach. Generally speaking, China's reform was historically performed step by step. Even today, rural land is still collectively owned, and it seems to be the same as a few decades ago, except that the inclusions of the ownership have changed. The contracting agreement now has defined and conferred to farmers, item by item, the right to use, the right of operation, the right of income, and even the right to transfer within the contractual period. The collective ownership of the farmland is still there, but in the box of the collective ownership, there is no more than one thing to do: to contract the land periodically to farmers. Hence the "collective" becomes a passive owner. It is the farmers who are active in the production and economic activities.

Some friends criticized the HRS for not being thorough, arguing that the collective is still maintained in the sense of ownership, leaves some institutional foundation for grass-root officials to violate the interests of farmers. The criticism is justified. However, had it not been the HRS, there would be no way out for rural China. Wouldn't it be better that we first take this current step, and follow the right path, and continue to further define the property rights? For example, the HRS is still a form of operating collective resources, but the income generated from the farmer's contracting is clearly legitimate private property. This means the "unthorough" contracting system can also serve as a feasible bridge to re-build the "thorough" private property system. The logic for the reform is true not only in agriculture contracting, but also valid in rural non-agricultural activities, and the SOE contracting reforms in small towns and large cities alike. This is another topic to be discussed later.

The contracting system is a Chinese way of redefining rights, and it is also a realistic channel for super state-firms to step out of the high organization costs. The contracting system under public ownership, and the formation of multiple property rights systems, including private property, have finally laid the foundation for China's market economy.

9.5 Suspicion of Exploitation and Recognizing the Legitimacy of Labor Hiring

Property rights do not serve empty talk, but are used especially to protect the cooperation with others and help with specialization through exchange. Yet here comes the troublesome question of labor hiring. Along with the ending of the "big pot rice", came large amounts of "surplus labor", who could not be absorbed by agriculture and needed to enter commercial and industrial sectors, thus labor hiring started to appear. And this touched the sensitive point of the traditional socialism. One of the purposes of the original super state-firm was to eliminate capitalist exploitation. Back then, an individual hiring more than seven people was regarded by the policy as an exploitative capitalist.

This is the second major issue that the reform encountered after the HRS introduction. The issue was successfully handled. The primary method was to hold and not to rush to the decision; suppressing and knocking down was not even an option on the table.

Let's look at several typical cases. One case is about CHEN Zhixiong of Gaoyao County, Guangdong Province. CHEN contracted over than 300 *mu* of fish pond. His family and several helpers could not provide enough labor, so he employed more than seven people. Was this capitalism? Many people started to discuss this question. Later, the question attracted the attention from the then General Secretary HU Yaobang, who attended to the matter in person and asked the situation to be clarified and allowed to debate on different opinions but not to put a simple ban on it. He also decided that the matter be publicly discussed on the *People's Daily*. Such issues were not allowed to be discussed before; now it turned out that open discussion was not as terrifying as imagined.

The second case is about NIAN Guangjiu, the owner of "Shazi Sunflower Seeds" in Wuhu, Anhui Province, who employed more than 60 people. The salaries of NIAN's workers were even higher than that of local SOE workers except that they had no benefits, but these people hired by NIAN originally did not have the "iron rice bowl" from SOEs anyway. The most important finding of the investigation was that because of the success of NIAN, many people followed him to the same business, as employers they all needed to hire people to help them dry fry the seeds, and the increased competition was good for the workers. Mr. DU Runsheng personally organized the investigation and left no stone unturned: all details like the number of people hired, their salaries, whether the owners paid taxes or not, and how much they made, and the reasoning for arguments from different opinions were put together in the investigation report and submitted to DENG Xiaoping. The instruction from DENG was: "Don't touch him for now". The wording "touch" is very particular because previously capitalism was not just criticized, but also "criticized with weapons", meaning "attacked" or "dealt with dictatorship". So when DENG said "Don't touch him", that means that NIAN should not be dealt with the same old method. As for the word "for now", our take is to have some buffer for people in the Party to express different opinions, to at least hold, or wait and see before drawing the final conclusion.

It seemed that there was no real risk for the socialism to recognize private enterprises. And this is a very important step in China's economic development. In fact, shortly after DENG Xiaoping regained power, he re-appointed RONG Yiren, a representative of previous national bourgeoisie. The approach was that the government contributed the capital to set up China International Investment and Trust Corporation (CITIC), Mr. RONG himself also contributed some capital but was given the full right of management. The method actually combined state-owned capital and entrepreneur's capabilities, which was unimaginable before. In addition, after the HRS was introduced in rural China, farmers spontaneously came up with some enterprises with new forms of organization. DENG always said that we should wait and see and make no move first. Such a policy orientation probably lasted for two to three years. Then the No. 5 Central Document for 1986 declared that private enterprises could be included in the socialist framework. Correspondingly, China's industrial and commercial registration began to include the category of "private enterprises". Initially only a few people dared to register because most people felt that it would be safer to wear a red hat, meaning being affiliated to POEs. Only Wenzhou was an exception. It is said that on the same day as the regulation was promulgated, there were about 100 private enterprises registered in Wenzhou. Some of them shed tears when they received the license and felt that they finally had a legitimate status. This is the second leap in China's reform. It not only recognizes the property rights of the fruit of the workers' own labor, but also allows, within the framework of laws and regulations, to use market contracts, including labor hiring contracts to leverage the capabilities of entrepreneurs to deal with market uncertainties.

9.6 The Perilous Pricing Reform

What's most remarkable about DENG's reform is the timely launch of pricing reform after the formation of various forms of economic organizations. The logic is: when the super state-firm is split into many independent firms, plus the newly formed private companies, the economy can no longer be commanded by plans and orders, thus the market regulating function of the pricing mechanism must be fully utilized. In the spring of 1988, DENG Xiaoping started to push for pricing reform. China called this price reform "price breakthrough" for very good reasons, as it was the core and the key to economic restructuring. The reforms of the former Soviet Union and Eastern European countries, such as Poland, encountered big problems when they reached prices. Pricing is a big gate, without firm political support, the reform could not make it.

DENG Xiaoping resolutely pushed forward the price reform, which is truly commendable. Generally speaking, it is easy for economists to understand and believe in the pricing mechanism, but not so much for powerful politicians. Because the "invisible hand" inadvertently would replace the visible hand of planning. When the price mechanism played its role, those hands with the power of signing for approval would lose their jobs. As the General Secretary of CPC Central Committee and the chairman of the Military Committee to command millions of troops, DENG obviously had a very powerful "visible hand". To earn unswerving support from politicians like him and his colleagues was the most difficult part of the reform. The price reform could not be a success without strong political endorsement, but it was no easy job for politicians to support the pricing reform.

Nevertheless, the first round of efforts didn't bring the pricing reform to success in 1988. The announcement of Central Political Bureau's decision on the price and salary reform immediately triggered shopping rush and bank run. The main lesson is that when there is too much currency, liberalizing prices will make the implicit inflation into explicit inflation, which is unacceptable to the public. However, DENG did not consequently regard the pricing reform as off-limit and no more touchable because of this failure. He waited patiently for a few years and did not relaunch the reform until the excess liquidity was taken back in 1992. The big step for the price reform was completed in 1993, when even the toughest piece, the grain prices, was liberalized. The reform laid a foundation for China's socialist market economy.

To sum up, China's reform led by DENG Xiaoping has fundamentally changed the traditional socialist super state-firm model through three main aspects: redefining property rights, activating market contracts, and establishing the price-based market regulating system. Throughout the process, there was no major unrest in the society; economic activities were not disrupted and high growth was maintained. It is the reform and opening up that has made China a large developing country with global influence.

9.7 Restricting Power Through the Rule of Law

Let's come back to Coase's theory of the firm. His starting point moves away from the "perfect market" of the then mainstream economics, and he does not believe in the perfect market because he discovered transaction costs. Firms and contracts of various forms thrive in the real world for the very purpose of saving transaction costs. As Coase sees it, firms save transaction costs through internal instructions, planning and strategies, and the commanding by the visible hands of bosses and managers. However, he does not believe that the bigger the company, the better, because he also discovered the "organization costs" that big companies must face. As for the super state-company, which organizes the whole national economy into the centrally planned economy that completely disables the market price mechanism and fully relies on orders and commands, it indeed saves all the transaction costs, but this kind of saving has a price to pay because the organization costs of the super state-firm is unprecedentedly high. From this perspective, Coase's theory is to analyze the market, the enterprise, and the government in the real world from the constraints of cost. "Cost" is a real constraint and requires lots of efforts on investigation. Without the cost constraint, the "ideal model" ranging from the perfect market to the super state-company is nothing more than imaginations.

The starting point for China's reform is not a perfect market, but a super state firm, or in other words, a perfect planned economy. The system was there for so many years, and the reform faces the intrinsic problems of the planned system: high information costs and low incentives. Therefore, the base tone of the reform is to go from the super state-firm i.e. the planned economy towards a more market oriented price mechanism. Then, are we moving towards the "perfect market"? Thankfully, because of Coase's work, we know that there is no such thing at all. The realistic solution for the problem is somewhere in between the two extremes of the super state-firm and the perfect market.

What are the difficulties for the reform? Between the perfect market and the super state-firm, there is lots of space to move around. It was the redefinition of rights that China counted on to step out of the framework of the super state-firm. The problem is that it takes time to redefine the rights; and this process involves one key question, which DENG raised but did not resolve. That is, to define and restrain the state administrative power. Because the super state-firm was an integration of the government and the enterprise, and of the government and the economy. The reform was about empowerment, namely to delegate the administrative and economic power to lower levels. Then comes the problem of how to restrict the delegated power? Without effective restrictions, the administrative power would enter the market and create corruption, which is not just an ethical issue for the limited number of officials, but an institutional problem. The market transactions often became entangled by the administrative power, how to solve this problem?

DENG Xiaoping explored quite a lot. As early as in 1980, he talked about the restructuring of the Party and the state. In 1986, he revisited this topic and made it very clear: first, if the political system is not restructured, the results of the economic reform cannot be safeguarded; second, if the political system is not restructured, the economic reform cannot be continued. That means after some time into the economic reform, the political system restructuring must be launched in time and follow. The key is to restrain the administrative power previously belonging to the super state-firm. In 1987, the 13th CPC National Congress adopted the outline for political system restructuring. However, the failed pricing reform in 1988 and the followed political turmoil in Beijing kicked away the opportunity to implement the outline of the political reform. In 1992, DENG Xiaoping's remarks during his Southern China inspection tour was mainly about economic reform, marketization and accelerating development. The political restructuring was an unfulfilled aspiration for DENG Xiaoping.

A super state-firm is not just a company; it is also a "power" system, which is not as simple as the property rights relations. "Power" is a legitimate coercion force not restricted by the competitive market. Therefore, redefining power is much tougher than redefining property rights. In my opinion, it is not suitable to adopt the theoretical framework on contracts to look at the super state-firm decentralizing into a market oriented system. By habits, some economists tend to use the market-oriented contract theory, the principal-agent model, and local government competition etc. to deal with this transformation; I think they may have missed a key constraint, that is, the lawful coercion is not subject to market contracts. In reality, although the central government departments or local governments, resemble companies in many ways, there is one thing in their behavior, namely, the power of legal coercion that cannot be addressed by market contracts. Take for example the unfair income distribution which the general public feels strongly about. The issue of income is not just about the income gap, but more fundamentally about the cause for the gap. It's alright for YAO Ming to have a high income; but the high income of the corrupt director of Wuhan Railway Station is another story. The illegal income from scalping tickets comes from the power i.e. legal coercion, which cannot be restricted by market competition.

"Unfair distribution" is to make money by legitimate coercion. It must be made clear that this problem cannot be solved just by economic reform, let alone by disguising the activity as market competition. We must commend China's reform for stepping out of one extreme, i.e. the super state-company and delivering the tremendous success. The HRS, the private enterprises, the SOE reform, and the foundation for market economy to allocate the resources by the price mechanism, all of these have greatly emancipated productivity. However, we must also see that the reform has not yet been completed. The biggest challenge is that, for the political-business integrated super state-firm, after the decentralization, the property rights can be restrained through market competition, but the administrative power can only be effectively contained by the rule of law. And this is a more difficult reform.

9.8 Three Difficulties: Land, SOE Monopoly, and Pricing Reform

Some believe that China takes a gradualist approach to the reform, or in some scholars' words, China's reform is an "incremental reform" to distinguish it from Russia's "big bang" approach. However, it is not easy to keep the gradualist reform progressing. The most daunting challenge is that once the aforementioned delegated administrative power enters the market and takes huge economic benefits, it will not be easy to change it. The difficulties are no longer epistemic or purely ideological problems, but very real vested interests. According to our observation, all the difficult reforms have something to do with vested interests.

For example, the land property rights reform got started first, yet as of today there are still some crucial problems left unresolved. The agricultural use of agricultural land has been straightened out: The household contracting responsibility system (HRS), the policy of keeping it long term, and the confirmation of the transfer right can adapt to productivity requirements. However, once the agricultural land is to be converted for non-agricultural use, it has to be brought under the sole umbrella of mandatory state requisition. Why must the land of farmers, once converted for non-agricultural use, be requisitioned and then leased to the market by the state and the government? This is the most obvious example of administrative power entering the market. Nowadays a large number of social conflicts take place in this area. Why can't the rural collective construction land directly enter the land market? After years of discussion, with experience from many local trials, and a number of underground or semi-underground practices, why can't it be legalized nationwide? I believe that there is no reason other than the too high benefit for the power to force its way into the market, and the parties with vested interests simply won't automatically give up.

The farmer's "housing with small property rights" in the suburbs of big cities cannot be seen elsewhere in the world: the house is private property, yet the house site underneath is not. With hundreds of millions of farmers migrating to cities, the urban land demand will, of course, increase. However, farmers have no right to transfer or trade their countryside homesteads which have been distributed to them as a welfare. The allocation of those land plots is, therefore, not regulated by market prices. The net result is that China's rapid urbanization has not led to more but less intensive land utilization. On the one hand, urban land prices are soaring, yet on the other, there is a large amount of unutilized construction land in rural areas. Such a "land crisis" is the inevitable result of inadequate reform. The recent redefinition of forest land property rights pushed forward by the state is an important reform.

Moreover, much more can be done to the redefinition of similar resources such as water rights and mining rights.

Another example. Private enterprises have developed rapidly in China. In recent years, we have also adopted *the 36 Guidelines for non-public sectors of the economy.* However, there are still too many and too big monopolistic SOEs. After all, with 30 years of reform, any state-run sector losing money must have already been reformed. The problem is, for the exorbitant profit of the remaining highly profitable sectors through banned or restricted market access, what is the significance on the national economy as a whole? This type of questions remain untouched today. The profit is an astronomical number all the same, and it is rising, the only task remaining seems to continue to grow it bigger.

Has the price reform completed? It's true that most prices are determined by the market, but some key prices are still set by administrative directions. Exchange rates, interest rates, energy resources such as oil, coal and electricity, not to mention medicine, to name but a few. It is fair to say all the items severely troubling the national economy in recent years have something to do with the disabling of the price mechanism. Experience has proved that price control affects not only the quantity of resource allocation, but also the quality of goods and services. Without further price reforms, it will be difficult to eliminate the chaos.

In short, China's reform has achieved a lot and it still has a long way to go. Only by looking back at the experiences can we move forward better. The reality and problems are complicated. This article leverages the simple framework of theory of the firm to review the past and face the future. I welcome comments and suggestions.

Chapter 10
Competition, Monopoly, and Regulation: A Background Report on Anti-Monopoly Policy

10.1 Introduction

This report was commissioned by the Industry Department of the State Council System Restructuring Office to provide an academic background report to the government for the formulation of an "anti-monopoly policy for the infrastructure industry". Obviously, the theoretical opinions and recommendations presented in this report are the personal views of the author and do not reflect those of the institution for which the author works or any other institutions. According to the provisions of the contract, this report is only for the client's reference for policy-making.

This report includes the following parts: First, the basic principles of the "anti-monopoly" policy, which can be seen as a policy overview of this report. The second part provides the definitions of and theories on competition, monopoly, and anti-monopoly and introduces the focuses of academic debates, providing relevant theoretical background. The third part is about regulations and regulatory reform; it outlines relevant international experience and distinguishes the three main forms of government intervention in developed countries, namely "macro control", "anti-monopoly" and "regulation", focusing on the formation and evolution of regulation in the market competition and then leading the discussion to the experiences and problems with "the regulatory reform". The fourth part focuses on China's own experiences and lessons, mainly from the deregulation of the civil aviation and telecommunication, and discusses issues worth of attention in China's "anti-monopoly" reform. The fifth part proposes anti-monopoly policy options and constraints in the coming years, based on the above-discussed theories as well as domestic and international experience.

For the ease of reading by the client, this report is written by giving an overview of related academic works, and will not make detailed literature citations unless absolutely necessary.

This article was written in July 1999, and not published.

Q. Zhou, *Property Rights and Changes in China*,
https://doi.org/10.1007/978-981-15-9885-2_10

10.2 Basic Principles of "Anti-monopoly"

10.2.1 Opening Up Market Access and Reforming Administrative Monopolized Sectors

In order to develop the socialist market economy and maintain a healthy growth of the national economy, it is necessary to gradually open the market wider in all sectors of the infrastructure industry. The main objective of "opening the market wider" is to significantly increase the investment and operational efficiency of the infrastructure industry, and increase the overall competitiveness of the national economy through introducing and enhancing the market competition mechanism.

The current system of China's infrastructure industry is characterized by the administrative monopoly, which prohibits market access in the name of the government. It is different from other types of monopoly in the market economy, such as those formed through innovation or competitive strength, and the so-called "natural monopoly" formed by cost characteristics. Since administrative monopoly can exclude all current and potential competitors in favor of the incumbent monopoly enterprise, it often goes against the original intention of government monopoly over the infrastructure, leads to distorted economic behaviors and poor economic efficiency, and suppresses the supply and demand of the industry. The more serious problem is that special vested interests formed by long-term administrative monopoly hinders this important sector from responding promptly and effectively to changes in technology and market demand.

The infrastructure sector has experienced rapid growth during the recent couple of five-year plans with the following main driving factors: first, the strong market demand; second, the mobilization and investment of fiscal resources; third, the implementation of some market-oriented reforms. However, on the whole, the growth of China's infrastructure industry was mainly achieved through government's mobilization of fiscal resources so as to cope with the market demand. As a result, it has masked the system setback of the administrative monopolized industry and market. At present, the high tariff and poor service of the administratively monopolized sectors have become serious hindrance to the development of the national economy. In order to facilitate rapid recovery of consumer demand and investment demand for the short term, and to develop an infrastructure industry and competitive companies to support sustained growth of the national economy, it is necessary to implement comprehensive and fundamental reform to China's administratively monopolized industries.

10.2.2 Long-Term Goals and Special Tasks

According to international and domestic experience, it is a must to have clear and unwavering long-term goals to resolve administrative monopoly. Our goals here are to permanently remove the ban on market access to infrastructure industry and achieve efficient resource allocation, division of labor, and economic growth through various forms of market competition.

In order to achieve the above long-term goals, it is necessary to understand that China faces two special constraints. First, the infrastructure industry has long been under the monopoly of the state owned system, which means it is directly operated by the government. Second, the market-oriented corporatization reform has not been long, and the reform is shallow. Therefore, unlike developed countries, China cannot simply announce the opening up of the market, and expect an immediate emergence of competitors that are on a par with the incumbent monopoly companies to form a competitive infrastructure industry very soon.

Instead, China first needs its government to implement a drastic restructuring to the administratively monopolized sectors to obtain an operable competitive framework, and then achieve its long-term goals through market restructuring. Without the government's initiative to act as the "first propulsion", it will take an extremely long time to break the vested interests and form a competitive market.

The tricky part is that when restructuring the administratively monopolized industries with special administrative measures, the government should prevent itself from being trapped into the cycle of being pulled away from its long-term targets by the administrative re-organization efforts aimed at removing the prohibited market access because of the inherent clumsiness of administrative measures or improper use of administrative power. To avoid the backfire, the following issues must be brought up and addressed properly.

10.2.3 Consistency of Opening Up to Domestic and International Market

China's accession to WTO signifies a new stage of reform and opening up. Opening up China's infrastructure sector to market competition will be a major event of this new stage. In general, WTO requires gradual opening-up of the lifeline sectors of the national economy, so there is no need to formulate a separate policy framework to demonopolize the infrastructure industry. However, further opening up will lead to major adjustments in the vested interests, and will also have some impact on people's mindset, which may stimulate narrow-minded populism and even lead to certain complicated situations. For this reason, China needs to appropriately emphasize opening up to domestic players for some time before and after joining the WTO. It means to open up, to domestic non-state owned economy, the industrial sectors and markets that have long been monopolized by the government in the form of state owned economy. The degree of this opening-up should be equal to, or higher than, the level committed in the WTO Agreement.

To grant easier market access to the inside, we can draw on the valuable experiences accumulated from the process of joining the WTO as describe below: (A). It is essential to set a basic principle as the "pre-agreed rule", which is, to learn from the 20-year experience of China's opening-up and reform and international experience, give up the government monopoly over all sectors and open up the markets to all forms of ownership that make up the socialist market economy; (B). to identify the scope, main steps and key details for each major industry according to specific situations; (C). to comprehensively sort out and amend existing laws and regulations, especially those drafted by the industrial department for the purpose of industrial protection, and reformulate *the Telecommunications Market Act, the Electricity Market Act, the Railway Market Act,* and *the Civil Aviation Market Act*; (D). to come up with a package of timetable for opening up the market and revising the laws and regulations.

Like other major decisions such as reform and opening up and joining WTO, opening the market wider to domestic non-state ownership economy is, first and foremost, a strategic judgement about the general trend of China and the world as a whole, and it requires strong political leadership. It should be made clear that tactical details should be guided by strategic judgement, not the other way around. We need to be particularly mindful of getting lost in the entanglement of local vested interests and contradicting "experts' opinions", thus missing the mega trend and losing the opportunities.

10.2.4 Government to Withdraw Orderly from the Market

The steps for government to exit market monopoly should be different from industry to industry, but according to the existing international and domestic experience, the exit must be orderly. First of all, the government should take the initiative to act as the first driving force to open up the market, separate the government and the enterprise, and set up several competing companies in the originally monopolized industry; and firmly and steadily transform the pricing setting from by administrative control to by market competition, allowing the market price mechanism to allocate resources and guide enterprise behaviors. Secondly, the government needs to further remove barriers, expand the market access in all manners, and especially drop the ownership discrimination in relation to market access and widen the spectrum for domestic non-state-owned economies to enter into the market of all sectors. During the above process, the government needs to gradually shift to qualification management, license management and behavior supervision and treat all the competing operational companies the same way, and foster multiple non-government supervision mechanisms, such as peer supervision, industry self-discipline, supervision by consumers and consumer organizations, and supervision by public opinions so as to gradually reduce the administrative load from market regulation and meanwhile strengthening the awareness of rule of law and legal system development for market management.

The government's regulatory agencies need to gradually expand the scope and narrow the focus of oversight. Because substitutional competition is common between many products and services, the government regulators must gradually jump out of the production management box of the planned economy, perform overall administration over the broader transportation, energy, and communication markets, pay attention to relations between products and services, and eliminate the factors that hinder substitutional competition. It must be made clear that to expand the scope of regulation can only be truly achieved when the focus of regulation is narrowed down. The government must shift from direct approval of market access and price control to regulation of the players' qualifications and competition behaviors.

Once a competitive infrastructure market is formed, the government should take advantage of the momentum, guide and let the market mechanism play a greater role in re-organizing the market structure. It must be clarified that once a competitive market with several players has taken shape, especially once the companies have entered the capital market, further spin-off or merger shall be decided by the market rather than led by the government so as to avoid too much decision load on the government and too high risks. The government may make a good start, but that does not necessarily mean it can take the companies to a happy ending. It is more sensible to let the market mechanism play its role in the re-organization of the infrastructure industry in accordance with the Company Law and other market regulations. Take civil aviation and telecommunications for example, because market access in those sectors opened earlier, the existing market structure and company positioning, including business segmentation, must constantly change with market conditions; and certainly it is impossible to fully count on government administrative orders for the fulfillment of all restructuring.

10.2.5 Expand Involvement from Court in Market Regulation

In order to handle more effectively and properly various conflicts of interest in the infrastructure market and prevent the difficult-to-avoid corruption in the process of "enhanced supervision", the unitary top-down vertical relationship currently between the administrative agencies and the corresponding enterprise should be gradually reshaped into a hybrid system composed of multiple forms, such as administrative regulation, court ruling, self-organized market arbitration, and out-of-court settlement. This will have strategic significance for improving the quality of market management information exchange and processing, counter-balancing the regulatory power, and increasing the authoritativeness of the procedures for mediation of interests. In particular, it is necessary to expand the court's involvement in market regulation. To this end, in revising and re-establishing relevant laws and regulations, it is necessary to establish specialized market management courts to specifically deal with the conflicts that may occur between the regulators, companies, and consumers. The court cannot only restrain the administrative power, prevent abuse of power, but also reduce the burden and pressure of administrative regulation, and create conditions for demise of regulation.

10.2.6 Taking into Account the Interests of Investors, Companies and Consumers

Opening up the market and breaking the monopoly is aimed at better developing China's infrastructure industry and laying solid foundations for the sustainable and healthy growth of the national economy. To this end, it is necessary to co-ordinate the interests between investors, companies, and consumers, and to pay special attention to avoiding serious conflicts of interest during the transformation period.

Given the "capital-intensive" nature of the infrastructure industry, it is important to keep attracting capital to the construction and technological revamp of the infrastructure industry. To this end, we need to treat investors well, be them domestic or foreign, from SOEs or private sector. It must be clearly understood that high monopolistic profitability is an important incentive for capital investment into these sectors. With the opening up of the market, the monopoly profits will be brought down; then, how to create new incentives to attract investment is a new challenge. Based on international and domestic experience, artificial incentives created by the government is never sustainable, and may even bring some serious side effects. However, the government can play a major role in reducing policy and institutional risks, reducing market transaction costs, improving government services, and maintaining equitability and transparency in market competition. These should become the focus of the government's work in the new era.

Investors at different stages face different institutional risks in the process of breaking the monopoly and opening up the market. The earlier movers may encounter higher risks of policy and institutional changes and thus have expectation confusions. Hence, it is necessary to refer to international experience and, in the case of accelerated market opening, provide appropriate compensation to investors who originally expected to a longer period of monopoly profits. At the same time, it is necessary to announce publicly the timetable for market opening as early as possible to help potential investors to evaluate and prepare.

Large state monopoly companies in the infrastructure industry, together with their accumulated managerial and technical know-how, upstream and downstream connection and integration capabilities, are important resources for the development of national economy. Some problems and bad habits of the staff in these industries are, first and foremost, the result of the monopoly system because whoever does the job, the result would not be much different. Therefore, in the process of opening up and breaking the monopoly, we should not make it personal. Make no mistakes, anti-monopoly is not equivalent to "anti-big companies", and introducing competition is by no means egalitarianism. We need to understand that if competition grows the market, China need to have and will certainly produce larger and stronger modern companies. It should be noted that the objection, criticism and dissatisfaction from the public and media are an important force to break the monopoly and open up the market, but we must also be wary of getting emotional, which may equally prevent the orderliness of market competition.

The purchasing power of consumers is the driving force for industrial development. Breaking monopoly, opening up the market, and forming competition can, in theory, expand consumer choices, stimulate market demand, and increase people's real income. These are our expected policy outcomes. However, we must also understand that it takes time to improve products and services with guaranteed quality. To effectively protect the interests of consumers, that is, the purchasing power of the market, during the process, we must identify new problems and come up with new measures. China's awareness of consumer's rights is recently emerging and increasing, and we need to make sure that the consumer's rights will also be incorporated into the framework of market competition so as to avoid major deviations. It is wrong for the government to favor the company, and equally wrong to be biased towards consumer's requirement that goes against economic laws. The government should act as an independent and impartial conflict mediator and take into account the interests of all parties.

10.3 Definitions and Theories

10.3.1 Definition of Monopoly

The verbal meaning of "monopoly" is "exclusive control" or "exclusive possession". Therefore, monopoly in the economic sense generally means the exclusive control of economic resources, products, technology, or market by individuals, organizations, or groups. Hence in lexicology, "monopoly" is a neutral word. Admittedly, "exclusive control" behaviors may produce many negative effects on economic growth and economic efficiency, but "exclusive control" is also the pivot for economic order. For example, the basic feature of property rights is exclusive possession, and the administrative power is monopolized by one government in all civilized countries. If two or more entities all claim the title to the same house, or if two or more governments all claim the administrative power over the same jurisdiction, then there will be chaos and no economic growth or efficiency.

The economic concept of "monopoly" is much more complicated than its semantic meaning. Although we can simply say that monopoly means there is only one buyer or one seller in the product market. However, the reasons for the market being monopolized are diverse, and more importantly, the impact on economic efficiency from monopoly due to different reasons is different. The disagreements between different economic theories and policies usually originate from different understandings of the causal relationship for monopoly behaviors.

10.3.2 Different Causes for Monopoly

There are roughly five main causes for market monopoly:

First, monopoly due to unique natural endowments of products (services). For example, Longjing Tea, Laiyang Pear, and the songs of Teresa Teng. Such products are unique in the market, and consumers are willing to pay, so the resource owners have developed the exclusive right of possession.

Second, patents or copyrights, or trade secrets like the Coca-Cola formula. These resources are not naturally unique but are unique in imagination and the commercial applications of technologies. If the government does not protect patents and trade secrets by law, the supply of inventions and innovations will be undermined to hurt economic growth. Sharing the invented technology by the society can indeed speed up the popularization of new technologies, so patent protection usually has a term; when the term expires, the patent will be available to the society free of charge.

Third, the winner's monopoly. The winner of the market may rely on its strength and strategy and momentarily drive all competitors out. The typical cases are IBM and Microsoft. They simply have no competitors that can do just as good in the field of computer hardware and software for a while.

Fourth, monopoly by cost characteristics. Some industries require huge one-off investment to develop the supply capacity. These investments once spent, will become as "sinking costs" (meaning there is no other use). For these industries, new competitors will face a high "entry barrier", because they cannot compete with current manufacturers unless they invest huge amounts of money. This is commonly referred to as "natural monopoly".

Fifth, mandatory monopoly. This kind of monopoly uses non-economic coercive forces to eliminate competitors and maintain the exclusivity in the market. Such coercive forces can be non-institutionalized, such as bullying and extortion, or highly institutionalized, such as government-controlled licenses or administrative monopoly through eliminating competition by legislation. It should be noted that although the motive of mandatory monopoly is totally different, in terms of behavior, the status of the monopolist is caused by non-economic forces.

In the real world, the monopoly may have multiple causes. Take AT&T for example, in the early years, the monopoly came from innovation (the invention of the telephone), then it became a natural monopoly (by building a national telephone network), and after 1926, it enjoyed mandatory monopoly (a telephone market monopoly established by legislation). As for the hilarious anti-monopoly case against Microsoft, the focus of the debate between the plaintiff and the defendant is whether or not Microsoft's monopoly by innovation comes along with improper ways to prevent competition. In order to get a concise analysis of the consequences of monopoly, we need to further distinguish the two major types of different monopolies.

10.3.3 *Differentiating Monopoly from the Perspective of Property Rights*

If we move into the details of the aforementioned causes for monopoly, the question will become very complicated. For the sake of clarity and accuracy as required by policy formulation, it is necessary to simplify the complexity. This article makes a further distinction of the monopolies from the perspective of property rights.

We must be clear that in many cases, "monopoly" is synonymous with property rights. The above-mentioned monopolies built on resource uniqueness, invention and innovation, competitive advantage, and cost advantage all derive from "exclusive property rights". The protection of property rights is consistent with the protection of these monopolies. Property rights are exclusive rights and the foundation for market economy. Property rights, like all other rights, depend on the social consensus on "righteousness and justice" but are inseparable from formal and informal social coercion. Among them, the government's protection of property rights in accordance with law, is the most important factor in the modern economic order. The government's protection of the property rights, of course, is to protect the exclusive rights. In this sense, the protection of property rights will inevitably generate some derivatives, such as monopoly or exclusive control.

We must also clarify that the principle of government protection of property rights is to protect the exclusive right of choices of the property owners over their own resources, but only to the extent that such exclusive rights do not prevent others from exercising their property rights. For example, the government protects the house owners' exclusive right to live in the house. However, the owner will face restrictions or legal punishments if his behavior in the house harms the interest of others, such as making noises or harboring drugs.

In the market, the question of property rights becomes complicated. Because there are many buyers and many sellers on the market, each having their own property rights, and they affect each other. For example, both A and B sell goods, and competition has caused prices to fall. In this sense, both A and B are "hurt" by the other party. Can we drive B out of the market in order to protect A? No, because it infringes upon B's property rights (transaction rights). Can we protect both A and B by ordering to raise the market price? No, because it infringe upon the buyer's rights. Therefore, in the market, the government can only follow one principle: to protect the rights of all parties to trade on an equal footing, but not to protect the market value of resources of either party. Otherwise, it goes against the principle of universal protection of property rights.

The fifth monopoly mentioned above—mandatory monopoly—is to protect the property rights of one party while restricting or even prohibiting the property rights of other parties. Unlike the first four market monopolies, mandatory monopoly is not the result of universal protection of property rights, but the result of an infringement of property rights.

10.3.4 What Hinders Technological Advancement and Economic Growth

Traditional economic theories do not clearly differentiate different monopolies, nor do they clearly distinguish their different impacts on economic behaviors and efficiency. Popular textbook says, "market power" brought by monopoly—only one supplier in the market—enables the monopolist to control the output to increase prices and make monopoly profits. In addition, exclusive monopoly will weaken the motivation for technological innovation, and the quality of products and services is often dis-satisfactory.

However, the above "laws" have neglected that in the real market, the monopoly generated by the protection of property rights and the monopoly generated by infringement of property rights have different behaviors and effects.

Is it possible to rely just on unique resources to continually control prices and obtain monopoly profits? Experience has proved the answer is no. This is because most products and services deriving from the unique resources have potential substitutes. The substitutes for Longjing Tea include Huangshan Maofeng Tea, Fujian Oolong Tea, and Nestle Coffee. The substitutes for Coca-Cola could be Pepsi. How about the pop song of Teresa Deng? The substitutes could be the "Four Pop Kings", Mao Amin, and Anita Mui Yim-fong. It is natural that scarcity drives up prices, but too high a price invites substitutes. What is technological progress? Its job is to constantly discover and invent substitutes.

The monopoly by innovation cannot last long either. The market, like the battlefield, is filled with competition for life and death. The government protects patents, but as long as it does not deprive the rights of others to innovate, the monopoly by innovation usually does not last long. Can innovation be relied on for monopoly profits? The nice profits will invite competitors to create substitutions, and the competition is always very intense.

It is possible for the winner to reduce the output and raise the price after establishing advantages in the market. However, just as Friedman points out, this equals for the monopolist to subsidize all potential competitors. As long as the potential competition remains, the monopoly described in classical textbooks will eventually disappear.

Lastly, about the "natural monopoly". Previous analysis suggests that the huge sunk cost increases the barrier to potential entrants and thus constitutes the monopoly advantage for the incumbent player. However, as long as entry barrier is formed "naturally", the competition pressure of invention or technology substitution is always there to prevent the incumbent player from going too far under the pressure from potential competitions.

Among all the types of monopoly, only the mandatory restrictions on market access will truly hinder technological progress and economic efficiency. Because only mandatory prohibitions and restrictions on market opportunities can fully or partially eliminate substitutions, namely potential competitions.

10.3.5 Two Wrong Reasonings on Monopoly

Because of the absence of a clear theory on property rights, for more than a century, the theory of monopoly economics has been ambiguous, leading to fallacies spreading. The serious and common mistakes are the following two reasonings:

The first misbelief is that in order to protect unique resources, innovation, commercial success, and natural monopoly, the government should impose administrative restrictions on access to these special markets so as to reduce the waste of resources.

This reasoning mixes up the protection of property rights with the protection of market value. The government should protect property rights, but it should not and cannot protect the market value of specific resources. The government's responsibility for protection of all property rights should not be changed to the protection of some property rights through restricting or eliminating the protection of other property rights. What is more dangerous is that as long as the government can find the reason to infringe upon the trading rights of some in order to protect the property right of others, it eventually will find reasons to infringe upon any kind of property rights.

From the perspective of economic outcome, we question if it truly "reduces the waste of resources" to protect Longjing Tea by banning Oolong Tea, or to protect Coca-Cola by banning Pepsi. Waste or not should be judged by buyers in the market, rather than by the subjective conclusion of the government or experts. If the buyer is willing to pay for the product or service, then where does the waste come from? The attempt to eliminate this "waste" is tantamount to eliminating the economy.

A more common mistake holds that the government should restrict market access to industries under "natural monopoly" so as to "reduce repetitive construction and vicious competition". It seems to them, that natural monopoly is not enough, and has to be compounded with a monopoly by coercion to make it "more optimal". However, with the administrative monopoly, the natural monopoly is no longer "natural". We can no longer tell: is it the economies of scale that has led to a better technical supplier, or is it the administrative monopoly that has eliminated all potential competitors? Is it a cost advantage that keeps potential competitors behind, or does government power suppress technological advances and substitutions?

The monopoly rent created by administrative power will continuously induce people to spare no resources to snatch the rent. As days go by, the loss in monopoly rent will offset the savings from avoidance of repetitive construction. The final conclusion should be made only after watching for a long term on whether or not the government monopolized industries can save resources.

In another scenario, even if the government controls the market access to natural monopoly industries, it is still difficult to completely eliminate substitutions, but the cost would be dearer. For example, if tap water had long been opened to market competition, would there still be such a huge demand for bottled mineral water on the streets? Wouldn't it save much total investment into potable water? Therefore, the arbitrary judgement saying that the government's control over the market access to natural monopoly industries will definitely "reduce waste", is nothing more than the result of neglecting even more wastes.

The second fallacy goes to another extreme. This view believes that since the competition is the foundation for economic growth and technological progress, the government must use its administrative power to oppose any form of market monopoly.

The mistake here is to mix up the monopoly created by the protection of property rights with the monopoly formed by infringement of property rights. Competition is, indeed, the basic driving force for technological and economic progress, but it has to be constrained by clearly defined property rights and effective protection thereof. Competition without effective property rights protection will cost the society a huge price in the economic order.

Despite the government protection of all property rights, there will still be monopoly of various forms in the market. However, the monopoly doesn't do much harm to the economy as long as it does not infringe upon the property rights of others. Unique resources and unique ways of using resources can lead to monopoly; winners with market power can lead to monopoly; patents within the validity period can lead to government-protected monopoly; let alone trade secrets. We shall not rashly oppose all these monopolies, because some of them are synonymous with exclusive property rights, and some are the means, goals, and results of market competition. To vote for property rights and market competition, these monopolies should not be opposed.

To generalize and oppose all monopolies and go against all big companies, all market winners, all oligopoly and monopoly under any circumstances, and even innovation and leading positions is to vote against property rights, market competition, technological progress and economic growth.

The first of the above wrong reasonings on monopoly emphasizes that the economy is backward, and the private economy is immature, so it is a must for the government to restrict property rights, especially trading rights so as to accelerate economic growth. The second wrong reasoning emphasizes that large companies have too much power in developed economies and the government needs to strike a balance through its legal and administrative moves. The essence of these two mistakes are the same: they fail to understand the core relations between competition, property rights, government, and monopoly.

At present, China is in a transition from a low-income economy to a middle-income economy, and from a planned system to a market system. It is necessary to study the lessons from practice and prevent the two mistakes from misleading China's Anti-Monopoly Law and policy framework. What's more, we need to be mindful that the two mistakes may become hybridized under China's special national conditions.

10.3.6 Summary: The Key to Anti-Monopoly Is to Open Up Market Access

To sum up, we believe that what really hurts technological progress and economic efficiency is the mandatory prohibition or restriction of free access to the market. Other issues such as control over unique resources, leading by innovation, large scale, technical strength, already paid sunk cost, large market share, and the "probable desire for monopoly" are not the real problem.

Only clear concepts can lead to clear policies, and only with clear policies can the key to problems be targeted. Therefore, this report recommends that the slogan of the government's policy should be "open up administratively monopolized markets" with the focus on "removing prohibition on market access". The report believes that it is necessary to weigh the pros and cons, take into account both current and long-term interests, and avoid too general "anti-monopoly" in guiding public opinion and publicity. In particular, "anti-monopoly" should not be mixed up and equated to opposing big companies, market success, innovation and even any exclusive rights.

The form of market monopoly in the reality is complicated. The monopoly through protection of property rights may expand the protection and turns out to infringe upon the property rights of others. The monopoly obtained through unique resources, innovation, market success, and cost advantage may also give birth to a variety of forms of exclusivity requirements. We admit the complexity of the reality, but it is the very complexity of reality that requires us to have a simple and clear concepts as the policy foundations. In the formulation and implementation of anti-monopoly policies, the government should adhere to the following principles: universal protection of property rights and removal of the ban on market access. The key to dealing with the "composite" market monopoly is to completely remove the mandatory barriers to market access without any over-stepping.

10.4 Regulation and Regulatory Reform

After formulating and implementing the policy to eliminate monopoly and open up to competition, how should the government regulate the infrastructure industry? Currently the main idea is to give equal importance to opening up the market and strengthening regulation (or supervision). This report will focus the discussions on regulation and regulatory issues in the subsequent sections. The central point is to demonstrate that "regulation" is a special form of managing market economy by governments of developed countries. Along with the development of market economy and the practice of regulation, the experience of developed countries to go from "regulation establishment" to "deregulation" and then to "regulatory reform" is worth our learning. The debate on "re-regulation" and "the demise of regulation" in the countries that first implemented regulatory reforms also deserves our attention.

10.4.1 The Concept of Regulation

"Regulation" is not a traditional or an everyday Chinese term, its verbal meaning includes "control, provisions, and rules". As a borrowed word, regulation reflects a relationship between governments and enterprises where the government uses legally binding rules to modulate enterprises.

There are many definitions of regulation in economics and in law. However, according to Daniel Spulber in *Regulation and Markets (Chinese version, Page 28)*, a universally applicable definition of regulation has not yet appeared. Some economists point out that regulation is the government's public policy on enterprises. Some stress that the essence of regulation is the explicit substitution of government orders for competition; or, in addition to the formal implementation of the general law, the use of government coercive power to cater for certain special purposes. Some simply say that regulation is what regulators do.

However, all definitions include a common behavioral characteristic, namely the government imposes direct administrative intervention in enterprises' market access, pricing, product quality, and service conditions in accordance with the laws and rules. Putting aside the debate on the origin, effects, and value judgement, the differences in the evolution of the methods and focus of regulation and the differences between countries, regulation is always about direct government intervention in the market activities. This is the basic feature of "regulation", and the essence will not change even if another word is used in the Chinese translation.

10.4.2 Main Forms of Regulation

The above-defined "regulation" takes place in developed Western market economies. It has very important, but easily overlooked, background restrictions. This report emphasizes the following three points: (A). The rule of law, especially the tradition of performing administrative functions in accordance with the law, has been established; (B). The boundary between the government and the enterprise is clear, generally without mixing of the two; (C). Unless otherwise restricted by law, private property rights include the rights to use, to earn income from and to trade the resources shall not be infringed upon, plus the law is legislated (revised) in an open and participatory manner. This report particularly emphasizes that this background shall not be neglected when drawing "regulatory" experience from developed countries.

In order to clearly understand the above background, it is necessary to point out that "regulation" is only one of the many forms that the government of developed Western countries adopts to manage its economy. There are very important links and differences between regulation and other forms of government intervention in the economy.

In short, there are mainly five basic instruments that the government of Western countries uses to administer the economy, as described below:

A. Common law (mainly property law, contract law, and civil law) to govern private economic behaviors. The core is to ensure the effective definition and non-infringement of property rights. Since property rights interact with and influence each other during their exercising, a set of code of conduct is needed to regulate the use of property rights. Nonetheless, lots of disputes may occur in the exercise of property rights, which require equitable judgement, ruling, and mediation. Therefore, apart from legislation, "the role of the state is limited to providing a system of courts." As the old Chinese saying goes, "the official will not investigate the case if there is no prosecution from civilians". The "official" here is not the administrative "parent officer", but the judge responsible for judicial functions. Historically, the common law is the basis for administrating market economy in western countries, which have built their market economy civilization on the foundation of the common law over the past few centuries.
B. Anti-trust law. This is a new tradition for the government to administer the economy established first in the United States after 1890. In view of the expansion of the market power of large companies, the US Congress passed this special bill. Since then, not only private citizens are able to file antitrust litigations, but also the Department of Justice has been given special power to examine and approve business mergers, and to investigate, collect evidence and prosecute companies that violate the Anti-trust Law. It should be noted that originally the activity of the US government was limited to the public law domain and could only prosecute criminal cases. Now, the government could prosecute companies on special civil cases too (i.e. relating to the Antitrust Law). Therefore, the Antitrust Law is also seen as a mix of public and private law. However, the government's anti-monopoly administrative power is checked and balanced by the independent judicial system, because the verdict on the anti-monopoly prosecution by the Department of Justice will eventually be decided by independent courts and judges. For many cases, the government spent huge administrative fund on investigation and evidence collection, but still lost.
C. Macro-Control. After the Great Depression of the 1930s, the government gradually adopted the practice of regulating the economy through monetary and fiscal policies based on Keynesianism. It must be emphasized that macro-control is an indirect intervention by the government in economic activities. That is to say, the government only changes the parameters for economic decisions by enterprises or individuals, but does not interfere with or restrict, not to mention to replace them in economic decisions and behaviors. At present, many people regard all government interventions, even the government's direct control of price and market access restrictions, as macro-control. This is the result of misunderstanding Keynesianism.
D. Regulation. The government directly imposes in accordance with law administrative intervention in the economic activities of enterprises and individuals. The origin and development of regulation are different from country to country, and from time to time (see the next section for details), but one thing in common, is that regulation comes into play when the constraints in the common law, and

the implementation of the Antitrust Law and even the macro-control are considered inadequate to satisfy the need for market order. It should be made clear that regulation differs from the antitrust approach in that it is direct intervention by government agencies in accordance with the law, rather than merely acting as a public prosecutor. And it also differs from macro-control in that regulation is not about trying to change the decision-making parameters, but exerting direct control over decisions and behaviors. In addition, we must also point out that the regulation in developed countries is still rooted in the deep soil of the common law, specifically because: (a). The regulation requires a legal basis; (b). The department exercising regulation must obtain special authorization from the Congress; (c). Enterprises and individuals being regulated can file legal proceedings against the government's regulatory actions in accordance with Common Law and Administrative Law.

E. Nationalization. In accordance with laws and regulations, the government may use financial resources to establish an SOE or to acquire all or part of the company's shares. Since the government is the owner of the SOE, it can directly achieve the government's policy objectives through internal control of the company without resorting to external management forms such as antitrust and regulation. However, SOEs in Western countries are subject to the supervision by legislators, voters, as well as public opinion, and have to compete with non-SOEs. In addition, after the Second World War, the proportion of SOEs was higher in Western Europe than in the United States. The United States also has a lot of state-owned resources, but in general, the government does not use state-owned resources to participate in market competition with private companies, so it rarely organizes SOEs to participate in market operations.

Of the above five categories, nationalization is the government's direct control and intervention in the enterprise internal system; regulation is a direct administrative intervention exerted from outside; macro-control is an indirect intervention in economic parameters; antitrust is an indirect judicial intervention; and the common law is general legal restrictions on private property rights.

10.4.3 Origin and Development of Regulation

According to the above, regulation is a series of actions with which the government directly intervenes in the enterprise by administrative means. Why does regulation take place in the developed market economy?

Many people simply believe it is impossible to achieve full alignment between the individual interests of businesses, and the interests of consumers and the society. Because spontaneously formed prices do not reflect and cannot fully reflect the social cost of commercial activities, solely relying on the price mechanism cannot completely eliminate the negative "externalities" brought about by corporate and private behaviors; they believe common law, macro-control and antitrust law are still inadequate, and direct government intervention in corporate activities is necessary. The theory of "market failure" in the mainstream western economics has strengthened this point of view, thus providing systematical theoretical basis for government regulation.

According to the above understanding, regulation is an administrative measure proposed and implemented by the government in response to the needs of consumers so as to protect mainly the consumers and the whole society from possible damages caused by profit-seeking activities of enterprises.

However, experience has shown that the "demand" for regulation comes not only from consumers but also from companies and government agencies themselves. Although the purpose of regulation is often claimed to benefit the society, in reality the beneficiaries are not only the consumers, but also manufacturers, stakeholders, and government regulatory agencies themselves. It is the complicated interaction between these stakeholders, driven by international and domestic politics, ideologies, and incidental events, that has led to regulation and its evolution.

Take the United States for example. The earliest regulation that still works today is direct government intervention in the production and sale of alcoholic beverages. After the failure of the famous "Prohibition", the governments of all the states directly regulated the entrants to the alcohol market, the age of consumers, and the lawful places and time for selling alcohol through granting licenses. Yes, the regulation of alcoholic beverages has always treated "welfare" of minors, the public, and the families of alcoholics as public requirements. However, this system severely limits the degree of competition in the liquor market, and thereby protects the interest of the incumbents, and noticeably increases the power and interest of relevant government approval agencies, licensing agencies, and officials thereof. Therefore, those who push for and maintain the alcohol regulation system are not only parents and alcoholics families who may be harmed by "free trading of alcoholic beverages", but also the incumbent sellers protected by the regulation system, government agencies and officials.

What needs to be explored is why the government's antitrust is not enough to meet the society's requirements on the government to manage market transactions. The popular explanation is that regulation may save more law enforcement costs (and time) than antitrust lawsuits and may lead to more efficient resource allocation. This is because: first, the regulatory agency has a professional team and more specialized knowledge than the government's antitrust department and courts; second, the regulatory agency as authorized by law has the authority to make a decision, so there is no need to wait for a lengthy judicial process to deal with the problem. James McCauley Landis, known as the "Prophet of Regulation" in the New Deal Era in the United States, Dean of the Harvard Law School, and Member of Securities and Exchange Commission appointed by President Roosevelt, once wrote: "to meet the requirements of specialization, it is necessary to create more regulatory agencies to expand the influence of the government at all stages of economic development, creating more, not fewer, regulatory agencies will help improve the efficiency of the government's regulatory process." He advocated that various independent regulatory committees should be the government's fourth branch, and they need to be "semi-legislative, semi-administrative, and semi-judicial".

Yes, with the expansion of the market, further division of labor, and increasing complexity of trading activities, the government is required to have more and more economic management knowledge. The specialization of regulatory knowledge, and the large numbers of "regulatory experts", are both the results of the division of labor and the cause of a more complex regulatory structure. Like any specialized division of labor in the market, regulation experts tend to recommend a regulatory regime that adds value to their expertise. However, the government is the only "buyer" of the "experts and their regulatory knowledge and expertise", so there is a lack of screening and elimination by market competition. Therefore, if there is no proper restraint, regulation—as an administrative behavior of direct government intervention in the enterprise—will continuously and automatically enhance itself until the overall economic growth loses vitality and efficiency due to excessive regulation in the name of "social interest".

10.4.4 The Logic and Consequences of Regulation Extension

The United States was once a paradigm of "regulated capitalism". The US government, like many other countries, also directly owns some important institutions (such as the Tennessee Valley Authority, local public utilities, postal systems, airports, terminals, and transportation companies), but relatively, the degree of nationalization in the United States is very low. The US government also owns lots of resources, such as state-owned land and national parks, which, under constitutional principles, cannot be engaged in commercial activities. Perhaps it is for this reason that the US government's intervention in the economy is more focused on the market behaviors of the private sector.

In fact, long before the "Antitrust Law", the Interstate Commerce Commission (ICC), established in 1887, had the power to regulate the railway. The function of this federal agency, which marks the beginning of economic regulation, is to ensure "fair and reasonable" tariff for rail transport, "fair treatment" for carriers and the public, and to restrict the business manipulation by railway giants. Initially the US courts also restricted the power of ICC, but then the pressure from "progressionism" (the thoughts and social movement that aims to expose scandals, evils, and degenerations in business activities) substantially increased the ICC's power to regulate market price and market access.

In 1913, the United States established the Federal Reserve System (Central Bank) and the Federal Trade Commission (FTC), followed by the establishment of the Canning and Livestock Fencing Authority (1916), the Food and Drug Administration (1931), the Federal Communications Commission. (1934), the Federal Securities and Exchange Commission (1934), the Federal Maritime Commission (1936), the Civil Aviation Commission (1938), and the Federal Highway Administration

(1966). In the 1970s, the Federal Railroad Administration (1970), Environmental Protection Agency (1970), Federal Postage Commission (1970), National Highway Traffic Safety Administration (1970), Consumer Product Safety Commission (1972), Federal Energy Regulatory Commission (1974), and Nuclear Regulatory Commission (1974) were established. Together with state-level regulatory agencies, more than a hundred regulatory agencies were established in the United States by 1975, and the output of regulated sectors accounted for a quarter of the total GDP.

If we go to extreme things will turn around. Excessive government regulation and direct intervention in market entry and pricing will hinder the market mechanism from its normal resource allocation functions, dampen entrepreneurship, encourage bureaucracy, and all kinds of moral hazards of shifting the bad consequences of behaviors to others. In the 1960s, even Landis, who made a major contribution to the creation of the American-style regulatory system during the Roosevelt New Deal Era, began to blame the regulation system for its ossification and incompetence. He concluded that "sluggishness has become the symbol of federal regulation". For example, it would take 13 years to complete the pending natural gas pricing applications, even if the headcounts increased by three times, processing new applications accumulated during the 13 years would not be completed until 2043.

10.4.5 Regulatory Reform: The U.S. Experience

"Regulatory reform" originated in the United States in the mid-1970s. Like all institutional changes, ideological emancipation has played an avant garde role. Empirical research-oriented economics, law, and other social sciences, which try to test the correctness of economic institutions and policies with actual outcome rather than with the claimed great aspirations, have gathered lots of information from the U.S. practice from 1930s to the prime time of 1970s, and proved that the negative impact on economic efficiency from "regulation failure" is even more severe than from the so-called "market failure". The well-known discovery by Professor Stigler at the University of Chicago saying that "the regulator is the captive of the regulated industry and enterprise" has made him the winner of Nobel Prize in Economics. However, not until he was joined by the centrism-advocating Brookings Institution and renowned scholars from Yale and Harvard, had the thoughts and theories challenging regulation become an irreversible trend.

At the operational level, the first politician to perform surgery on the New Deal tradition was not a Republican, but Democrat Edward Kennedy, the then the Chairman of the Administrative Practices and Procedures Committee. In 1974, Kennedy asked Professor Breyer at Harvard Law School to prepare a list for investigation; and the first batch of investigatees decided by the Senate includes the regulation of civil aviation. Of course, the political glory of deregulation should still go to President Reagan because it was this often-underestimated Republican president who made up his mind to appoint Mr. Alfred Edward Kahn, Chairman of the New York State Public Service Commission and a former professor of economics at Cornell

University, to be the Chairman of the Civil Aeronautics Board (CAB). Kahn's policy agenda was unique: he introduced competition to the civil aviation, an industry that required everything must be administratively approved, and left economic decision to the market instead of the five committees under CAB, and eventually dissolved CAB.

Kahn's reform was recorded in the history of the U.S. regulatory reform for "opening up the skies". The main practice was for the government to stop using administrative approval (including hearing procedures) to intervene in flight fares and market access of the civil aviation industry. Carriers can freely and competitively determine their prices, and they can also decide whether to enter or exit certain markets or certain routes. All other companies and new investors may decide for themselves whether or not to set up new airlines. Subsequently, airline fares dropped sharply, and civil aviation demand shot up. Some established carriers went bankrupt, while successful newcomers were thriving as they adapted to the market. Perhaps the most important point is that thanks to competition, the American aviation industry created a hub-and-spoke system (which uses regional jets to carry passengers from all locations to some central hub airports and then fly to all parts of the country and the world).

The success earned wide acclaim for the Reagan Administration, and set a precedent for deregulation in the U.S.. Subsequently, railway and truck transportation, telecommunications, finance, and power sectors all begun to remove the "regulatory monopoly" system, a legacy of the Roosevelt New Deal, and introduced market competition in accordance with their technical characteristics. "Deregulation" even permeated in businesses which traditionally could only be operated by the government. Emerging courier companies challenged the government postal service, and turned the American courier industry into a global leader. In addition, competing security companies partially replaced the "exclusively operated" police department, providing the society with security services that operate in accordance with market rules. Environmental protection became a "business" because some localities have accepted the advice of economists: the state legislature to determine the annual "pollution quota" and put it on tender. New emerging things even included "private prisons", which operated like a company and "took purchase orders" from the government judicial department through bidding and provided market-oriented prison management (By 1996, there were 170 U.S. prisons and detention houses run by the private sector). Of course, there was also the American-style "privatization": the federal and state governments sell government-owned corporate equities through the securities market, including state railway companies, ports, airports, and the army's commercial service resources, and urban water supply systems.

Deregulation does not mean that the government does not manage anything at all, but rather it "quits" from the most unsuitable areas and steps, and focuses its time and financial resources to strengthen government administering the aspects that need government management. For example, after the CAB was dissolved as Kahn and Reagan planned, the Federal Aviation Administration (FAA) was established. However, FAA no longer engages in the regulation of fare, route allocation, and market access, but instead supervises and regulates the flight safety of airlines in accordance with the law. Deregulation and re-regulation take place alternatively in transportation, telecommunications, electricity, and finance. However, based on the essence rather than the name, the so-called "re-regulation" is just for the government to explore new experience in administrative management after it has liberalized all these sensitive and "strategic commanding heights" and opened up the market.

10.4.6 U.K.: Directly Drawing Strength from "Regulatory Reform"

The central slogan of the market revolution led by Mrs. Thatcher in the late 1970s was "privatization" rather than "deregulation". This is due to the UK's national conditions and shows that each country must always solve its pressing problems in its specific economic, political, and social environment.

As an established capitalist country, Britain's gradual decline in national strength stems from the loss of its competitiveness. By the 1970s, Britain was deadly ill and almost reduced to an "impoverished country in Europe". The key issue, as Mrs. Thatcher pointed out before she took office, was that monopolizing SOEs and monopolizing unions stagnated Britain's productivity, while the country's welfare and subsidy expenditures went crazy like an unbridled bronco. "If people consume more than produce", even an established capitalist country like the UK becomes feeble. Mrs. Thatcher's Conservative Party government took the right approach and chose to "privatize" and reduce the welfare demands of British unions that was detached from productivity.

It is worth attention that the British government did not simply copy the traditional model of "regulating the market", but directly absorbed the experience of "regulatory reform" from the United States, and explored to establish a more efficient regulatory system. Originally, as explained previously, "nationalization" means that the government directly controls from the inside the lifeline of national economy by directly using its control over SOEs. Therefore, under the nationalization model, the government and large companies act together, plus large SOEs are not for profit, so they generally do not need to "be regulated" from the outside. With the privatization, private equity participation became a reality, or even the majority shareholder for the SOEs; now the company is motivated to seek profit, will it use its existing "market power" to convert the state's monopoly into a private market monopoly?

The answer is positive. Therefore, while the United States was deregulating, it was necessary for the United Kingdom to "re-regulate". In fact, Thatcher's administration paid great attention to the market regulation experience of the US government while implementing privatization. However, Thatcher and her Conservative Party's think tank had made profound reflection on the British disease and were intuitively vigilant about the resurgence of "government supremacy through re-regulation". Coupled with Reagan's "unfolding deregulation," the United Kingdom was able to directly draw experience from the "regulatory reform" without falling into the quagmire of traditional government regulation.

Specifically, the following four aspects from the British experience deserve special attention from China.

First, selling state-owned assets ("privatization") went hand in hand with opening up the government-monopolized market. It must be pointed out that this was not an easy job, because, from the perspective of financial operations, the government can usually sell the equities of large SOEs at higher prices if the monopoly status remains intact. Therefore, if the reform is only driven by higher short-term fiscal revenue, the "administrative monopoly" can be sold for a higher price in the short term, but the competitive market will not be formed, and the industry's productivity won't be much improved, and the company will not be competitive, and thus won't have long term sustainable financing capabilities.

Second, the government initiated the formation of a competitive structure. Due to the suffocation of entrepreneurial spirit by the wide range of nationalization, the UK, unlike the US, could not form a competitive market structure immediately after it announced to open up the market. Under this specific constraint, the British government passed legislation to set up a new company to enter the market that was originally monopolized by the government, forming a "duopoly" situation first, and then gradually issued more licenses and increased the number of players until market access became fully open. The shortcoming of this approach is that the government could make mistakes in "choosing" the first entrant; and with limited market opening, if the government picks the wrong "candidate", there is no cure. For example, Mercury, set up by a special government decree in the British telecommunications market with the same operating rights as British Telecom, still only had less than 10% market share after seven years, way below the "duopoly competition" design. However, the government's timetable for opening up can help investors, operators, and consumers to have a general expectation for future institutional changes, and it is conducive to coordinating conflicting interests of all parties during the transition period.

Third, non-administrative regulatory bodies. Because the government's regulation of an market that is being opened up involves huge interests of diverse parties, establishing pure administrative organs to regulate the market, may not only lead to information monopoly, excessively centralized power, and thus failure to look after every aspect, but also administrative corruption, and even political corruption such as rent-seeking and rent-setting. Therefore, UK has established many regulatory agencies made up of members from industries, consumers, independent experts, and government officials, with special laws and regulations to govern their procedures for information exchange and operations of power. That is to say, the UK paid special attention, from the very beginning to the issue of "regulating regulators".

Fourth, gradually expanding market-based supervision and reduce administrative supervision. In fact, all the purposes for the government to establish regulators, such as lower prices, quality assurance, non-discrimination, and market order, can be achieved in many ways. Take for example *the Telecommunication Market Management Plan for 1999/2000* released in May 1999 by Office of Telecommunications (Oftel), we can see that UK has divided the "supervision" into four categories, i.e.

supervision by the specialized regulator, self-discipline supervision by the industry, "behavioral restrictions on each other from competitors" (namely when consumers have the right to choose, competitors compete with each to please consumers so as to maintain market share) and supervision by other government agencies. In the early stages of privatization and market opening-up, the specialized regulator's supervision is the main way, but with the gradual increase in market competition, industry self-discipline supervision plays more role, and supervision by competitors is becoming more and more important.

This way, the regulator must gradually "disable" itself, which seems to confront the "rational behavior" of the regulator that is usually expected to continuously strengthen its power. How did the British resolve the problem? Their approach was to "commit" to gradually cut the regulation budget within a time-frame. Let's again take Oftel for example, as the regulator of the British telecommunications industry, not only has it decided to reduce its budget year by year from 12.79 million pounds for 1998/1999 to 12.63 million for 1999/2000, to 12.1 million for 2000/2001 and 11.97 million for 2001/2002, but also made it public to the society.

10.4.7 New Regulatory Economics

However, many scholars emphasize that regulation should not be abolished. In order to solve problems with the old-style regulation, "new regulatory economics" has developed as a speciality in recent years. The background of this new learning is the mechanism design theory, which aims to use the advanced modern economics theory to provide "guidance" to regulation and improve the traditional regulation model.

For example, new regulatory economics comes up with the concept of "incentive-based regulation". The traditional price regulation principle is "cost plus", which means that the regulator determines the price based on the cost of the enterprise plus a reasonable profit. However, in this way, regulated companies do not have enough incentive to reduce costs. Of course, regulators can check the "real" costs of the business. However, costs are not so easy to verify because companies "will always find ways to cover up their actual low costs". Moreover, even if the regulator can magically get the true cost of a monopolizing company, it is still questionable whether the real cost is truly a "low cost" since the company is not motivated to reduce costs. As a result, the cost of regulated companies is always "terrible" and "unsatisfactory" no matter how sophisticated cost verification procedures are introduced. This provides a place to use new regulatory economics, which comes up with a "high-performance incentive scheme", also called "price cap regulation".

According to the design, the price cap regulation is sort of a fixed-price contract, and every dollar saved in cost is a dollar earned in net income, which encourages enterprises to save costs. In addition, the price cap can rectify the "irrational price structure" of the "cost-plus pricing model"; and under the new mode, as long as the overall (average) price does not exceed the cap, the company can charge different customers with different rates. This way, the price cap model is theoretically consistent with the Ramsey pricing principle, that is, under the condition that the profit is ensured not to be negative, the pricing of the regulated company shall maximize social welfare.

In fact, from Smith (1776) to Coase (1945), the "classical views" of economics have pointed out that if industries, with high fixed investment costs and average costs higher than marginal costs, will definitely incur losses if their price is based on marginal costs. However, how can we protect social welfare if the price is above marginal costs? The answer is "appropriate price differentiation"; that is, we "must identify, from the company's positive benefit generating prices, various prices of services that are welcomed by consumers". The key word here is "various", which means differentiated prices.

However, do not cheer over the victory of rationality too early because at least one problem remains unresolved. How can the regulator set a price cap so exactly that it guarantees that the company will not lose money and the social welfare will be maximized? Here, the subtlety of the theory relies once again on the premise that the regulator needs to have full information on the cost of the regulated company. Otherwise, there will already be some "rent" in the price that guarantees the company will not lose money, and the company can still earn a profit unrelated to its cost cutting efforts if the cost is overestimated under the price cap model. This shows that the price cap scheme of the new regulatory economics using more complex theoretical tools though is not necessarily bound to be "better" than the cost-plus pricing; the traditional model, on the other hand, can effectively squeeze potential rent-seeking despite the lack of incentives to reduce costs.

In other words, if the market access is prohibited or restricted, no matter how smart the regulator is, it can only choose one out of the two regulation models that cannot completely eliminated waste: the cost-plus to squeeze out rent or the price cap to motivate regulated companies to save costs. This shows that there are no such theories yet that can "guide" the optimization of price regulation. On the contrary, there is simply no one-size-fits-all model that is suitable for all operators.

What the new regulatory economics fails to point out is that under the constraints of prohibited market access, due to the lack of competition, it is impossible to rely on accurately articulated theory to fully remove the "social welfare loss" (namely the "rent") in price regulation. Various well-designed regulation mechanisms can at best change the distribution of monopoly rent, thus guide the parties in question change their rent-seeking methods. A more general conclusion is that market competition has never been the result of a rational design. The practice of the regulatory reform have shown that the prohibited market access for all industries can be lifted. Only by breaking the monopoly can the price mechanism come back. After all, the competitive pricing system has a comparative advantage over the "mechanism design" of new regulatory economics in dealing with divergent information streams.

10.4.8 The Demise of Regulation: Theory and Practice

In fact, some theorists discussed "the demise of regulation" long ago. The groundbreaking classic ideas in this regard can be traced back to Coase's study on Federal Communication Commission (FCC) in 1959. In chasing down the origin of the power of this regulator, he found that the allocation of a special resource, i.e. radio waves, laid the foundation for the FCC's dazzling power. In the early days, occupying radio channels was related to maritime safety as ocean-going vessels depended on radio positioning to make emergency calls. Because there was never a market for the invisible channel resources at the time, the government had to be relied on to assign (regulate) channels. However, from Day One of the scarce economic resource allocation by the government through the use of administrative means, economic and administrative efficiency has become a lingering question. Unlike the economists who stuck to the dogma of "externalities," Coase asked a question: why can't the government excuse itself from direct distribution of channels and organize an auction?

Coase's question is straightforward. By organizing the auction and setting the simple rule that "the highest bidder wins", the government can change the allocation of the originally "ownerless" public channel resources through the price mechanism. Since the price mechanism comes back and works, regulation (direct control of prices and access by administrative means) becomes, of course, unwarranted. Inspired by Coase, economists expanded their research horizons. Only one railway? Why can't the "exclusive operating right" be put on auction in the market? Should the city limit the number of taxis? Why not use auctions? Further, why can't "pollution" be auctioned as a right?

To be clear, none of these economists are anarchists, and the "demise of regulation" does not equal to the "demise of government". The point of Coase and his followers is that government regulation—direct administrative control over prices and market access—can be replaced through the establishment of new rights and the launch of market mechanisms, and even return to the basics of "using the civil law to co-ordinate property rights transactions". The government is indispensable in providing rights establishment and court decisions and enforcement. Their belief is: for such complicated industrial regulation issues as co-ordination of interests, it would be better for the government to act as a middleman between the prosecution and the defense than to directly use the "visible hand" to allocate scarce economic resources; the former can generate better results in terms of efficiency, equity and order.

The idea of "demise of regulation" has already permeated in practice. A typical example is that the United States has to date adhered to the "non-regulation" policy on the Internet, although the petitions for regulating the Internet takes place from time to time. The author has consulted an FCC official in person, and his explanation was that it was not that the Internet did not require management, but it did not require special regulation. "Credit card theft is illegal under any circumstances, and online transactions are no exception in the same vein as it is illegal to spread pornography to minors no matter where you are." In the time of rapid technological progress, if new legislation and special regulation need to be designed for every technology, the society will be unable to inch forward because of the heavy regulatory burden.

In New Zealand, the telecommunications regulator has been formally dissolved. New Zealand introduced competition in the telecommunications market in 1989, and the original monopoly operator Telecom was subsequently privatized. The company was brought under the ownership of a consortium by two regional U.S. telecommunications companies—Thatcherite and Bell Atlantic Corp. and faced two main competitors: Clear in long distance calls and Southern Bell New Zealand in mobile communications. All telecommunications industry questions are co-ordinated by the Commerce Act 1986, and market conflicts between the plaintiff and the defendant are resolved in the court. New Zealand's experiment will test whether the telecommunications market can work or not without a special regulator whose power usually has no counter-balance.

10.4.9 Summary: Avoid the Regulationism Quagmire

The market inevitably makes mistakes, but it is often able to correct the wrong expectations, decisions, and behaviors of all parties by spontaneous transactions. In fact, it is in the constant process of making and correcting errors that the market exchanges and processes massive information caused by specialization, and drives all parties to learn and benefit. However, the market as a process is not cost-free as it takes time and other resources to both make and correct mistakes, and someone has to pay. Therefore, people always hope - those wrong theories and doctrines often grow the hope stronger- the cost of the market process can be reduced, or be paid by others rather than themselves.

Regulation takes place against such a backdrop. The strict definition of regulation is that the government uses administrative power to directly intervene in prices and set barriers for market access. Even in western capitalist countries featured by "private property + democracy", regulation is easily misunderstood as being able to replace market errors and corrections, leading to the conclusion that government is able to directly prevent mistakes. As for the price of government market regulation, it is usually paid by the whole society and all market players, so it is less noticeable than the market cost and even seems acceptable.

Regulations can easily form large vested interest groups, including market players who accept regulation in exchange for blocking the market competition, and professional regulatory bureaucrats as "government branches". The latter relies on their highly specialized regulatory knowledge to seize regulation power that overrides market competition and is often difficult to check and balance. Under various political constraints, this kind of power has become the source of corruption of different degrees. Another major impact of over-regulation is that the cumbersome approval system increases market transaction costs, suppresses entrepreneurship, and hinders innovation. The historical experience of major western capitalist countries shows that even "mature market economies" cannot automatically be immune from the "self-expanding regulation" logic.

However, the inefficiency and stagnation of economic growth caused by "regulation" are observable. In any political framework, government direct intervention in prices and market access through administrative measures causes economic losses with no exception. The larger and more complete the regulatory system, the longer it lasts, the greater the loss of efficiency in resources allocation. A basic economic conclusion here is that there is no administrative mechanism that can be, in terms of economic efficiency, equivalent to competitive pricing mechanism in an open market. To regulate market access is to announce that the government has the ability to "select" the most capable entrepreneurs and the best companies in the regulated industry; and to regulate prices is to claim that the government has the ability to "reasonably price" products using models such as cost-plus pricing. Regrettably, based on empirical facts, the government, as an essential watchman for market economy, has never been able to deliver the above two points.

The huge amounts of conflicts of interest, inharmony, and stagnation accumulated through continuous and large-scale regulation require a comprehensive reform to regulatory policies, laws, and the corresponding economic system. "The regulatory reform" does not come without reasons. It needs certain political conditions, and also generate tremendous rewards to political groups advocating the reform by releasing the huge economic potential.

10.5 Emphasizing China's Own Experience

In the historical process of state-owned economy reform, separation of government and enterprises, and transformation of government functions, China has long encountered the uphill battle of reforming the "lifeline sectors of its national economy".

At the end of the 1980s, China began to open up the civil aviation, the industry under semi-military management, implemented corporate operation with independent accounting, established multiple competing companies and introduced the market mechanism. In the 1990s, the reform of the telecommunications and postal systems was launched, and the new tasks were proposed for the reform of the investment and operation systems of power, highway, and railway sectors. This section is based on existing reform practices and outlines China's basic experience and lessons in the reform and opening up of these sectors.

10.5.1 Basic Experience and Lesson One

Adhere to the basic policy of opening up the market, introducing competition and breaking the monopoly. Civil aviation, telecommunications, railway, and power sectors have always been regarded as the lifelines of the national economy. From a technical economics point of view, these sectors are the infrastructure for the operation of the national economy and are responsible for providing basic services to all other sectors. In addition, these sectors have important implications for national defense and national security in a broad sense, and their strategic value often cannot be measured in monetary terms. To establish a nationwide service capacity in these sectors requires huge amounts of investment and a long investment and construction cycle. Mainly for these reasons, people have long believed that the infrastructure industry can and can only be operated under monopoly. If we say these sectors are long monopolized by regulated private companies in the U.S., then for socialist countries like ours, they must be brought under public-ownership monopoly, or in other words, state monopoly or government monopoly.

However, the use of administrative power to implement monopoly operations and exclude market entry creates similar economic behaviors and effects in any of the political systems. That is, because of excessive government protection, the monopoly sector stops improving themselves, provides poor yet expensive services, and lacks innovation and progress. The result for the infrastructure sectors to pass inefficiency onto the whole society is a big drop in the overall efficiency of the national economy, and worsened unfair income distributions.

China's basic experience is that the state monopoly of the lifeline sectors can be and should be broken gradually, by introducing competition and opening up the market through pilots first and then exploratory efforts. If we jump out of the old box of thinking, it is not difficult to find that market competition can be introduced at different links and at different levels to every infrastructure sector according to its own technical and economic characteristics. Take the telecommunications sector for example, the oldest perception was that value-added services can be opened up to competition, but the basic telecom services cannot. However, the good results from opening up the value-added business encouraged China to introduce competition to the basic services too, and then to the basic communication networks. This shows that correct principles will generate a progressive force. Otherwise, we would not be able to see the pattern of 6 to 7 interconnected and yet independent and competing telecom operators in one single country. By the same token, the aviation, railway, and power markets were also opened up by different layers and different scopes. The basic experience is that the policy of opening up the market must be steadfast and unswerving, and a gradualist approach can be adopted at the operation level.

10.5.2 Basic Experience and Lesson Two

The government and the enterprise must be separated. The essence of a state monopoly is that the government is directly engaged in business activities. In this regard, we must draw the experience from not only the US regulatory reform, but also the nationalization of Western European countries. More importantly, we must be aware, that the omnipotence of the administrative power under the traditional planning system simply means that economic activities, especially those in the lifeline sectors, have become highly administrative even militarized. In this context, simply setting up a few companies affiliated to government agencies definitely cannot solve the problem. There must be a clear institutional separation line between companies participating in market competition and government agencies responsible for market regulation. In 1993, the Chinese government decided to establish China Unicom to compete with China Telecom. The policy was correct, and the action taken seemed to be world-leading (at the time, there were no similar moves in Singapore or Hong Kong), but the competition in China's telecommunications market was still far from satisfactory till 1998. China's reform of the former Ministry of Posts and Telecommunications in 1999 and the telecom restructuring in 2000 attracted worldwide attention, demonstrating that the separation of the government and the enterprises is essential to break the existing vested interest structure. More importantly, the separation laid an institutional foundation for future market order and prevented the administrative power from being mixed up with market interests.

10.5.3 Basic Experience and Lesson 3

Pricing mechanism is the key. The traditional concept excludes the infrastructure sector from the market competition because it was believed that the allocation of economic resources of the lifeline sectors should not be based on the pricing mechanism. Infrastructure supply and demand was mainly adjusted through planned allocation prices and quantities rather than following the basic bidding principle of the market, namely the higher bidder gets the first opportunity to buy and the lower bidder gets the first opportunity to sell. Consequently, China's infrastructure sector has long been dominated by two kinds of deviations, causing an enormous waste of resources. First, the planned pricing of the products and services is too low, resulting in severe short supply. Second, to compensate for the long-term insufficient investment in the infrastructure sector, the planned charging is set too high and artificially increases the production costs of other sectors of the national economy and the living costs of residents. Generally speaking, before the reform, the first deviation was the main problem; the under-development of infrastructure sector became a drag to the national economy. When reform was just initiated, with the monopoly yet to be broken, the second deviation quickly took over, and prices of the infrastructure sector rose too fast, stimulating repetitive construction and curbing economic demand.

This actually shows that the clumsy administrative pricing cannot effectively connect the infrastructure sectors with their diverse "customers" in the context of accelerated technological changes and increasingly complex division of labor. The infrastructure sectors are undoubtedly special, but not so special as to disable the pricing mechanism. The multi-party bidding system looks messy, but it is the only way to adjust supply and demand, and adapt to the ever-changing needs from the technology and the markets in a responsive manner.

However, till today, the perception has not fully moved away from the belief that infrastructure sectors are special. This is not surprising, as we have, so far, no experience with the large-scale practice in market pricing for these sectors. However, we can still summarize some local experiences and lessons; such as the airfare discount race between airliners, the controversy of the ban on discounts and recent attempts to loosen it up again, the “illegal competition” between telecommunications and cable TV in some regions, the price competition between the two major mobile operators and its effect in stimulating demand and expanding the market, the relationship between the prices of the emerging IP phones and market demand, the relationship between railway fares and scalpers activities, the debate on the railway fares during the Spring Festival, and the “price hearing system” that has been legislated and has put in place in some localities and departments, etc. All these cases are partially related to the pricing mechanism and are worthy of summary and discussion so as to provide conditions for larger-scale application of the pricing mechanism in infrastructure sectors.

10.5.4 Basic Experience and Lesson 4

Opening up the market should go in parallel with the reform of player’s property rights. It was believed that socialist reforms like ours should not go too far and should only draw half of the British experience in opening up the lifeline industries by selling the control right of SOEs to the market–often referred to as “privatization”. Their point is, as long as the market competition between SOEs is organized in a planned way, it is feasible and even strategically significant to maintain the monopoly and control over those sectors through SOEs.

However, China’s experience has shown that the “designed” market competition between SOEs, regardless how lofty the idea is, cannot respond to the following three grave challenges:

First, the opening of infrastructure sectors is an important part of the opening up of the national economy, and it requires, during the opening up, large-scale technological revamping to enhance future international competitiveness. For this reason, it is imperative to use the international and domestic capital markets to raise funds. This will inevitably involve selling part of the control of large SOEs to the market and change the traditional operations structure with solely state-owned capital.

Second, if the government is to be the only shareholder of operating companies in the lifeline sectors and at the same time the regulator for the competitive market, such a structure will inevitably lead to conflicting roles of the government as the market administrator. On the one hand, enterprises will do everything possible to require the government—its sole shareholder and boss—to provide administrative protection and reduce the intensity of market competition; on the other, the government will administratively intervene more naturally in corporate business. In a word, fake it does not mean to make it.

Third, although SOEs are responsible for their operations, the ultimate responsibility for companies' assets is still in the hands of the government. Such a property right restriction mechanism inevitably results in a tendency of short-termism: the company may enhance its short-term performance and obtain more distributed income from it at the expense of its assets.

The first two challenges mentioned above have attracted some attention from government decision-makers and research institutions; but for the third challenge, because infrastructure market pricing has yet to be put into wide practice, we can only start with local and short-term experience, plus some reasoning of economic behaviors to get some clue about it. Take civil aviation for example, we can already see that first, the market competition between multiple companies will eventually lead to a price competition (manifested as discounts); second, once the administrative control over air ticket pricing is loosened, state-owned airlines will jump into the price war until losing money; third, when large-scale losses or industry-wide losses occur, the competent government department will have to re-strengthen its administrative control over prices (i.e. prohibiting discounts), and the "excessive" capacity will re-appear.

In comparison, competition between private companies in any industry can also lead to a price war to win over customers. However, when the bid of a market player is marginally equal to its operating costs, the company will theoretically have to withdraw from the competition, because it will suffer a "loss" if it further cuts the price. In market practice, companies with competitive edges will acquire assets of those that don't have a cost advantage, and merger or acquisition takes place, or the latter will change their business and find another way out. This shows that the company's property rights matters in market activities and can restrict competitive behaviors. Effective property rights restrictions not only lead to effective market competition, but also control the "degree" of competition, and "adjust the structure" under the principle of economic rationality.

The operations right of SOEs is at the company's management, and the company's performance is directly related to the interests of the management and the workers (the degree depends on the progress of the reform). From this point of view, SOEs competing in the market are similar to any private company, i.e. they are motivated to compete. However, the "boss" of the SOE is the government (and the control is scattered across different government departments in accordance with the principle of hierarchy), who is not a market player, does not grasp the ever changing market, and makes decisions through complicated procedures; plus government workers have very indirect relationship in terms of interests with the government-owned assets. Once the market landscape change is related with the value and security of the assets, it will be impossible for the government to make agile, prompt and reasonable responses. Under such constraints, it is only natural that SOEs would rather join the price war and suffer a loss. The government could not help but swing between the two extremes of "ossification of administrative pricing" and "liberalizing prices and losing big money from the state-owned capital".

Therefore, opening markets must go hand in hand with the reform of property rights. The property rights reform is to turn the SOEs into joint stock companies, which means it is necessary for the state to transfer or sell part of the state-owned equities, but also the state can consider selling the controlling shares, or even all of the equities, thus becoming a minority shareholder or even withdrawing completely. Otherwise, it is impossible to resolve the above-mentioned conflicts from an institutional perspective. As for whether or not to call this "privatization", it is a matter of wording that has some political, cultural, and ideological considerations, which has nothing to do with our discussion - the logic of economic behaviors.

10.5.5 Basic Experience and Lesson 5

Take into account the interests of investors, enterprises, and consumers in the reform at the same time. It is of strategic significance to take into account the interests of investors, the operating company, and consumers to ensure co-ordinated development throughout the process of opening up the infrastructure sector for market competition. Investors include state and non-state capital owners from home and abroad. China's experience is that the government must aim to improve the overall investment environment, rather than simply to guarantee the maximum return on government investment. Only by protecting the interest of all investors can the government protect the interest of itself as a partial capital investor. In addition, the governments of all strong countries in today's world live on taxes instead of return on capital from their investment. If the government relies on investment return, or puts profit target of the government capital first, competes with the people for the benefit, spoils the market order, and hurts private investors' confidence, it will lose more than it gains from the perspective of long-term growth.

Domestic and overseas private capital investment into originally government monopolized industrial sectors comes with complex motivations and expectations. China's experience is that the mainstream capital markets such as Hong Kong, and even Europe and the United States, may take the market monopoly right of SOEs as an investment target for a period of time and look forward to sharing the high administrative monopoly rents. However, once the government adjusts the policy, opens the market wider, and changes the pricing policy, the originally expected high monopoly profits may vanish in the competition. That is to say, in addition to general risks, such investors also have to bear the special risk of wrecking on a reef, so to speak. It goes like this. When making investment decisions, they expect that a large amount of monopoly profit will flow, like the water, into their pockets, but when their investment is in place, the water subsides, and the reef stands out, making their investment strike "on the rocks".

In a period of drastic changes in the market environment, it is difficult to avoid the "wrecking on the reef" risk, and how to deal with it is worthy of our study. The tricky part is that to emphasize the "investing at your own risk" principle will not only easily lead to volatility in the secondary market, but also increase investors' doubts about the future; but to cater to investors' expectations of monopoly profits by the government and slow down the infrastructure opening up will be bound to curb market demand growth and undermine consumers' interests. An important case of dealing with the so-called reef risk is the turbulence of the Hong Kong stock market caused by the mainland's abolishing "two-way charge" policy in the mobile phone market and the subsequent "packaged deal" to balance the interests between companies, investors, and consumers. The most important lesson here is that the interests of all parties shall be balanced under the general precondition of an open market. In order to rectify the deviated expectations, the government should have a master plan for opening up infrastructure sectors, like the practice in WTO accession. By announcing in advance the main steps and a rough timetable, the government can guide all parties to establish the reasonable expectation that the market will gradually open up and thus evaluate their benefits and strategies. If the timetable needs to be adjusted during the process, such as opening at a faster pace or with greater intensity, we should consider giving the companies, and their investors appropriate financial subsidies as Singapore and Hong Kong SAR did, so as to reduce their loss from "wrecking on the reef".

10.5.6 Basic Experience and Lesson 6

Gradually shift the focus of government work. The role of the government is different at every stage of opening up the infrastructure sectors. China's main experience in this regard is that the government reviews and evaluates the situation, identifies different priorities for different stages, and makes every effort to eliminate the adverse effects of administrative inertia and interest inertia; at the same time, it must constantly adapt to changing requirements from the situation and re-distribute the power between relevant government departments, re-adjust the organization setup, staffing, and requirements for the quality of government officials.

Since the traditional practice in the planned economy is for the government to manage the investment and operations of the lifeline sectors, it is imperative that the government act as the "primary driving force" for opening up these key sectors. The reforms in China's civil aviation and telecom sectors and the upcoming reforms to the railway and power industries are all started by the government with no exception. Experience shows that a central government championing reform and opening up can greatly reduce the cost of emancipating the mind, improving consensus, and taking practical actions (rather than empty talk) by virtue of its authority. The strong political will of the central government to open up the market is the foundation for mobilizing the strengths of all parties.

After the monopoly of a certain sector by one SOE is broken, the government should take the initiative to give up administrative pricing. It must be clear that price competition is the foundation for all market competitions. If the government allows free competition among companies but still imposes an administrative approval and regulation on the pricing mechanism, we will not see reasonable resource allocation in accordance with economic principles as we had wished. As for possible corporate loss or even sectoral loss caused by deregulation, we need to conduct a cool-headed analysis and solve the problem by further strengthening the property rights constraints for the enterprises and market restructuring rather than backpedal to the old road of government controlled pricing.

With the transfer of operation functions to competing companies, the focus of government departments needs to be shifted to the supervision and regulation of corporate behaviors. Either for ex-ante company qualification control or ex-post supervision, it is important that the government gradually reduce the scope of administrative approval.

Experience also shows that to have the central government's strategic determination alone is far from enough. Without the concrete deployment, implementation details of relevant departments and their efforts to solve numerous specific problems during the transformation, the mega-policy of opening up the market cannot be automatically implemented. However, the administrative inertia of the competent authorities and the tendency of "monetizing" or even "capitalizing" regulatory power under market conditions are likely to be roadblocks along the way. For this reason, in the process of opening up major sectors, it is imperative for the government to emphasize political discipline and emphasize the execution of both orders and prohibitions. At the same time, in accordance with the general policy of "separating the government and the enterprise", we must resolutely require that all regulators be completely decoupled from their regulated enterprise with respect to people, finance and facilities. The exit of the government from all direct market activities is the hallmark of a modernized government and is also essential to eliminate corruption during the transition period.

The set-up of government departments and the qualifications of civil servants must change accordingly with the opening up of the lifeline sectors. The general trend is that government departments directly setting the specific business goals and controlling operational behaviors should be gradually downsized until their complete demise, and the agencies overseeing the compliance with abstract legally defined rules by industrial sectors and corporate activities should be gradually strengthened. To this end, the skillset and knowledge structure of relevant officials must be adjusted in a timely manner. The general trend is that officials familiar with technical economics for the industry and with "hands-on skills" should be transferred to enterprises, and more officials with supervision capabilities and relevant knowledge on abstract rules are needed by the regulators. It must be understood that the fact that a large number of officials with engineering backgrounds in government departments is the legacy of the planned economy era. Under the new historical conditions of deregulation and changing government functions, more experts with legal training are needed to work in government departments.

10.6 Policy Choices and Constraints

10.6.1 General Framework and Political Leadership for Market Open-Up

In the negotiations and agreement on China's accession to WTO, the issue of opening up the infrastructure sectors for market competition has already been decided. Therefore, it is not necessary to reinvent the wheel and set up a separate "antitrust" program. However, during the process of opening up, it is necessary to pay heed to possible narrow populist sentiments triggered by the major adjustment of vested interests and to avoid complicated situations. To this end, this report recommends that the near-term emphasis be placed on opening up to the inside, which means to open up the long government monopolized sectors and markets in the form of state-owned economy to non-state-owned economy in China. The degree of such opening up intends to be equal to or higher than what is committed in the WTO agreement.

In the process of opening up wider to the domestic market, we should draw on and even copy China's experience in joining the WTO. First, based on China's experience of the two-decade of reform and opening up as well as international experience, we need to put forward a crystal-clear basic principle, which is to give up government monopoly in all sectors and open up the market to players of all ownerships that make up the socialist market economy; second, it is necessary to identify the scope, main steps and key details for opening up the market for each specific sector; third, it is critical to comprehensively sort out and amend existing laws and regulations, especially those old laws drafted by the industrial department with the purpose of protecting the sectoral authority and interests, and re-formulate the *Telecommunications Market Act, the Power Market Act, the Railway Market Act*, and *the Civil Aviation Market Act*; fourth, a timetable for opening up and revising the laws and regulations needs to be developed.

To do so in the context of China's situation requires strong political leadership. Just like such other major decisions as reform and opening up and WTO accession, opening wider to the inside world, first and foremost, involves the strategic judgment about the general trend in China and the world at large. The tactic details should be guided by the strategic judgement, not the other way around. We need to be particularly mindful of getting lost in the entangled local vested interests and contradicting "experts' opinions" thus missing the mega trend and losing the opportunities.

10.6.2 Setting the Steps for Government's Exiting the Market

The government can adopt different exiting steps from sector to sector, but based on existing international and domestic experience, the following steps can generally be taken: (1). as the primary driver for market open-up, separate government with enterprises, and establish a number of competing companies; (2). shift from administrative pricing to market pricing; (3). further open market access with particular emphasis on eliminating ownership discrimination; (4). the government to shift to management of qualifications and licensing and supervision of behaviors of companies without ownership discrimination; (5). cultivate a variety of non-government supervision mechanisms, including peer supervision, industry self-discipline, supervision by consumers and consumer organizations, and by public opinions, etc. so as to gradually reduce the administrative load of the government; (6). strengthen the awareness and practice of the rule of law; and build on China's tradition of "civilians reporting and official's corrections" on the track of the modern civil law and commercial law.

10.6.3 Considering Multiple Forms of Market Access

A number of competing companies can be set up for civil aviation, and several parallel basic networks can be formed for the telecommunications. However, the question of how to have several competing companies in airports, railways and marshaling stations as well as the power transmission networks, has not been fully resolved. Based on the current experience, China can consider multiple forms of market access, including:

First, substitutional competition. For example, all transportation tools can substitute each other to a certain extent. Therefore, although there is only one railway network, in fact, it has to compete with highways, aviation, and water transportation. Eliminating restrictions on "substitutional services" and connecting various means of transportation can eliminate or mitigate monopolistic behaviors.

Second, competitive bidding. For industries virtually with no substitutions, such as power transmission, we may consider introducing multiple players through competitive bidding. That is to say there is still only one power grid, the operation right can be opened for competitive bidding by several participants. In that case, the sole incumbent operator will behave differently due to the pressure from potential competitors versus if it has the permanent monopoly right. Of course, the design of the bidding, the criterion of selection, and the term must be carefully crafted and justified.

Third, open up the access from the legal perspective. This mode means the law does not prevent multiple player to enter the sector, the market has no second company to compete (with the current one) only because expected income cannot offset the cost as newcomers needs to pay huge sunk costs. In contrast to the scenario where the law only allows one company to monopolize the market, this mode differs in that there is potential competitive pressure on the incumbent player. Once it reaches a certain threshold where the price is so high, and the quality is so poor, that the expected income of potential entry will rise, and the potential competition will be materialized.

10.6.4 Expanding the Spectrum and Narrowing the Focus of Regulation

In order to give full play to the role of substitutional competition, the setting of government regulatory agencies should gradually go beyond the boundaries drawn for the era of managing the production through government planning. For example, the respective regulation of air, railway, highway, and water transportation should be gradually replaced by a comprehensive regulation of the entire transportation sector. The comprehensive regulation not only has to deal with each transport segmentation, but also regulates the behaviors that hinder substitutional competition between them. Another example is that substitutional competition also exists between telecommunications and television broadcasting, and between various energy markets. It is necessary to set up cross-department regulatory agencies for comprehensive management and utilization. However, the government's regulation over the broader transportation market, communication market, and energy markets has to focus more and more on the key aspects. Such regulation should shift from direct market access approval and price control to the management of qualifications and supervision of behaviors in accordance with law.

10.6.5 Gradually Expanding the Role of Courts in Regulation

In order to properly and more effectively handle conflicts of interest in the infrastructure market, it is essential to gradually change the unitary "top-down vertical relationship" currently between the regulators and the corresponding regulated markets and enterprises to a diversified mechanism to resolve conflicts of interests for the industry. A hybrid system composed of such multiple forms as administrative regulation, court ruling, self-organized arbitration, and out-of-court settlement should be established so as to improve the quality of information exchange and processing, prevent escalation of conflicts and procrastination, counter-balance the power, and enhance the authoritativeness of interest co-ordination procedures. To this end, in revising and re-formulating relevant laws and regulations, it is necessary to establish special market courts, such as for the communication, the energy and the transportation, to deal with the conflicts that may occur during market regulation between the regulators, companies, and consumers. The courts cannot only restrict the power of administrative regulation, prevent abuse of the regulation power, but also reduce the load and pressure of administrative regulation, and create conditions for the demise of regulation.

10.6.6 Leaving Room for Market Restructuring

Once competition kicks in, we must leverage the momentum and facilitate the market mechanism to play a greater role in the infrastructure industry. It is necessary to make it clear that in order to form a competitive market, the government can set up a number of competing companies as the aforementioned "first driver". However, once a number of competing companies are set up, especially after they have successively entered the capital market, further re-organization (including spin-offs and mergers) may become the new normal and must follow the dynamics of the market. If the further restructuring is entirely dependent on government decision, it may overburden the government's decision-making function and easily lead to excessive risks. Therefore, the government can kick off the game but doesn't have to finish it. Instead it can and should often leave the re-organization to the market in accordance with the company law and other regulations. Take civil aviation and telecommunications for example, as these sectors opened up earlier, their existing market structure, company positioning, and business segmentations have to cope continuously with the changing market conditions, and it is impossible to fully count on the government administrative instructions for all restructurings.

10.6.7 Compensating "Wrecking on the Reef" Loss by Adjusting the Stock of State-Owned Assets

To formulate a timetable for opening up the market to the inside and the outside will help investors, companies, and consumers establish reasonable expectations and facilitate sustainable financing. However, changes in future economic landscape involve many variables, some of which are not fully within the government control. Once the situation changes, there will be a significant impact on the expected interests of all parties. To this end, according to international experience, necessary financial compensation mechanisms must be prepared. Since opening up the market is beneficial to the whole society, the costs so incurred should generally be borne by the government's finance. However, when the government does not have sufficient financial resources or the compensation becomes unaffordable to the government, it may fail to deliver the commitment.

Taking into account the special circumstances of China, that is, all large companies in lifeline sectors are owned or controlled by the government. Therefore, China has the conditions to consider adjusting the stock of state-owned asset and guaranteeing the delivery of its commitment to provide some compensation to the stakeholders and reduce their "wrecking on the reef" loss. Take China's mobile telecom industry as an example, the move from two-way to one-way charge policy caused stock dumping by foreign investors. In hindsight, when the policy was introduced, an announcement could have been made that the company was to de-register some state-owned shares in favor of non-state owned investors as a compensation for the "running onto the rock" risk on existing investors from new policy. By nature, this mechanism is no different from cash compensation. However, for both new and existing investors, the de-registering of state-owned shares could be an even more positive news, as it represents another form of exit of government capital.

Chapter 11
Health for All?—Debate on the New Round of Healthcare Reform in China

This article discusses the new round of healthcare reform in China. As usual, the analysis and interpretation are based on empirical facts. With agreement or disagreement, the judgments, opinions, arguments, and evidence in the debate on healthcare reform are often the direct "stimuli" for the author's discourses. However, thanks to the empiricist methodology, I am never used to simply challenging arguments with arguments, or refuting opinions with opinions, and what I would always like to do is to "verify the phenomenon and test the judgment".

11.1 Is China's Healthcare Marketized?

Many experts argue that the myriad of pressing problems of China's healthcare sector are caused by "marketization". According to them, the particularity of healthcare will inevitably lead the market-oriented reform to failure, and the general direction of the new round of healthcare reform should logically be "government-led" rather than marketized.[1] In order to get to the crux of the problem, this article will first analyze

[1] The following are the representative arguments I have read:

In 2003, professor WANG Shaoguang, at the Chinese University of Hong Kong, wrote that the deterioration of China's public health is "probably related mainly to the two blind faiths that are looming in our overall reform thinking". One is the blind faith in economic growth, and the other, in the market. According to WANG, "In the 1990s, the market economy was established as the target of reform; medical and healthcare services were gradually pushed to the market." The end result is that "China's healthcare field is probably one of the most market-oriented in the world" (see Crises and Opportunities in China's Public Health. Comparison, Issue No. 7 [2003])

In 2005, an SCDRC research task force led by GE Yanfeng published a special report. After eulogizing "the outstanding achievements in China's medical and health service during the planned economy", the report points out that "the basic direction of the medical and health system since the reform is commercialization and marketization", its negative consequences

Q. Zhou, *Property Rights and Changes in China*,
https://doi.org/10.1007/978-981-15-9885-2_11

the status quo and try to answer the question "whether China's healthcare system has been marketized". In my opinion, judgement on the status quo is less interfered by the subjective values of the opinion than such questions as: Is the market-based healthcare reform good or bad? Should we do this? Should the future medical care reform be government-led or not? More importantly, the judgement on the status quo is the basis for policy recommendations. Just imagine how can the doctor give the best cure if his diagnosis is wrong?

Many people believe that China's healthcare has taken the path of marketization and the evidence is just apparent. Nowadays Chinese people have to pay for medical treatments (whether out of their own pocket or first by the social security or taxes); hospitals, public or private, will not take the sick unless paid, and they even leverage their information and technology advantage to induce patients to spend more. Aren't these frequent buying and selling of healthcare services the evidence of marketization?

Data also seems to provide evidence. According to statistics, the total national healthcare expenditure in 2005 increased 77 times than that in 1978, of which, the residents' cash expenditure increased by 196 times, much higher than the GDP growth and per capita income growth over the same period.[2] People tend to point figures at "marketization" for the exponential growth of their healthcare spendings.

Yes, Chinese people are spending more and more on medical services. However, let me ask when lots of buying power is concentrated on medical and healthcare services, what is the response from the supply side? The question is not difficult to answer. The first result is of course that hospitals and people in healthcare services will be rich, with money coming and coming to them above the board or under the table. Then let's further ask, what phenomena will follow if medical institutions and their employees make lots of money in the context of rapid demand growth?

If healthcare is truly market-based, as many experts are so certain about, and once people learn about the good market and big money, it will attract swarms of determined investors to build more hospitals and clinics, more talents will practice medicine, and more medical and healthcare services will be added until the "excess profit" is averaged out. That is to say, if China's healthcare is truly marketized, the immediate response is that lots of people make a fortune, the second response

are "the decline in the fairness of medical services and the low efficiency of health investment", and that "The root of the problem is that commercialization and marketization go against the basic rules for healthcare development" (see Evaluation of and Suggestions for China's Healthcare Reform (Summary and Key Points). *China Development Review*, Supplementary Issue No. 1 [2005]).

In the same year, Professor LI Ling at Peking University also published an article, repeating WANG and GE's opinions without citation. LI's explanations were exactly the same: "The main reasons are government negligence and market failure. The government had no clear direction or goal for healthcare development, but irresponsibly left the healthcare to the market (see China Should Adopt a Government-Led Medical System. *China and World Affairs*, Issue No. 1 [2005]).

[2]For data and source, see Table 11.1.

Table 11.1 Demand, supply, and potential supply of China's medical services (1978–2005)

	1978	1990	1995	2000	2005	1978–2005 (%)
GDP (RMB 100 million)	3,645	18,718	59,811	98,001	184,739	5,068
Healthcare expenses (RMB 100 million)	110	747	2,155	4,587	8,668	7,865
• Government Budget	35	187	387	710	1561	4,404
• Social Security Expenses	52	293	768	1,172	2,586	4,950
• Out-of-pocket Expenses	23	267	1,000	2,705	4,521	20,075
Per Capita Healthcare Expenses	11.5	65.4	177.9	361.9	662.3	5,759
Population (10,000)	96,259	113,368	121,121	126,743	130,756	136
Number of Medical Institutions	169,732	208,734	190,057	324,771	298,997	176
• Hospitals	9,293	14,377	15,663	16,318	18,703	201
• Outpatient Clinics	94,395	129,332	104,406	240,934	207,457	220
• Disease Control Centers	2,989	3,618	3,729	3,741	3,585	120
Number of Beds	1,847,300	2,624,100	2,836,100	2,947,900	3,134,930	170
Number of Beds per 1000 People	1.92	2.31	2.34	2.33	2.40	106
Health Workers	3,105,572	4,906,201	5,373,378	5,591,026	5,426,851	175
• Doctors	1,033,018	1,763,086	1,917,772	2,075,834	1,938,272	188
• Physicians	609,608	1,302,997	1,454,926	1,603,266	1,555,658	255
• Nurses	406.649	974,541	1,125,661	1,266,838	1,349,589	332
University/College Enrollment	402,000	608,850	925,940	2,206,072	5,409,412	1,346
• Medical Enrollment	46,772	65,695	149,928	386,905	386,905	827

Source China Health Statistics Yearbook (2007: 3, 19, 57, 83, 327, 333)

will be that more resources will be mobilized into the sector. Clearly, the former is the income distribution change triggered by demand growth, and the latter is about resource re-allocation by the price mechanism.

Following this logic, I checked the following questions: with the drastic increase in the total healthcare expenses, especially from personal spending, what is the amount of increase in the number of hospitals, clinics, and medical staff? The result is astounding: between 1978 and 2005, the number of hospitals across the country only doubled (increasing by 101.3%), the number of clinics increased by 119.8%, and the number of beds in hospitals and health centers only increased by 69.7% (during the same period, the number of beds per 1,000 people only increased by 24.9%), the number of doctors increased by 87.6%, physicians by 155.2% and a little more for nurses, still only by 231.9%. In other words, in contrast to the 77 folds increase in total healthcare expense and the 196 folds increase in personal healthcare spending, the net increase was the highest at more than two times for the number of nurses, one and half times for the number of physicians, and less than 100% for all other items, including the number of hospitals, clinics, beds and doctors. So, could it be due to improved "productivity" of doctors and nurses? The answer is no. During the same period, the number of patient visits nationwide increased by only 40%.[3]

These sets of data have several meanings: (1) the growth of national health costs and personal expenditures outpace the growth of patient visits by dozens of times, indicating medical care has become extremely expensive; (2) the average income of medical institutions and their workers has increased by dozens of or even more than one hundred times; (3) the growth of the number of health workers is faster than the growth of patient visits, meaning on the whole the productivity of China's healthcare has not increased although the situation may vary from hospital to hospital; (4) Most importantly, the heavy spending on medical services for quite some time has been unable to stimulate corresponding growth from the resource supply side!

What sort of "marketization" is this? Since the reform and opening up, the livelihood of Chinese people have changed a lot. Generally speaking, the time of shortfall and scarcity has turned into abundant market supply with lower prices and good quality. In this process, the basic trajectory is like this: once the market demand is identified and the sellers make a fortune, many investors will follow to build factories or open shops, mobilize human resources, and dig deep into technology and management; so the capacity will soon be built up. Then all the companies use different strategies in the competition, such as cutting the prices or innovation until the products and services become affordable to average people.

It is the very lateral comparison of experience that enables me to see the fracture of the conclusion that China's healthcare is marketized. Let me reiterate, the question to be analyzed here is not whether marketization is good or not, or should it be implemented or not, but rather the Chinese healthcare has been marketized or not. WANG Shaoguang sees the drop in the ratio of government funding to total health expenditure as the basis for his conclusion of marketization. I believe he has neglected whether or not the government has opened up the market access to medical services

[3]For data and source, see Table 11.1.

while decreasing the ratio of funding for healthcare? GE Yanfeng and his research group state: "All kinds of capital are allowed to enter the medical service market, basically without entry or exit restrictions; the layout of new medical institutions and the positioning of their services mainly depend on market demand conditions." If this is the case, why haven't so fast-growing demand, and the dozens of even over one hundred folds of increase in the average price of medical service stimulated the corresponding increase in the number of medical institutions and health workers? Some people argue that since market competition has pushed the TV industry into the era of meager profit, the price of healthcare can also be brought down through market competition. LI Ling criticizes this argument and concludes that "the healthcare market is unable to effectively allocate medical and healthcare resources, and to introduce market mechanism into the system we shouldn't do simple copy and paste from the practices of other sectors." I believe she has shied away from a factual question: has the market mechanism introduced into China's healthcare system or not?

Indeed, every opinion holder can have their own definition for marketization to justify their theory. But I think the real question we need to follow is: why the ability of China's healthcare system to mobilize sufficient resources to increase the supply is so poor in response to the high demand? I am convinced that if this basic question is not figured out, whatever opinion different people may have, the policy objective of improving China's medical services will be very difficult, if not impossible, to be realized.

If there is no demand for medical services, it is normal that little resources is mobilized. For example, fewer and fewer people send letters, so it is not surprising that there are no more additional resources flowing into traditional postal services. Related to this, the service of writing letters on the street is also diminishing. This is natural shrinking, and there is no need to make a fuss or to blame anyone.

However, the situation is different if the demand grows strongly, with insurmountable obstacles for supply, and the market price soars up. Take oil for example. China's crude oil supply in 2005 only doubled compared to 1978. That was not because there was no demand, but because the proven reserves were too small to meet the market demand, so we had to import more and more, the high demand stimulated global resource mobilization. What if the supply falls short? The price will go up.

Another scenario is quite common for the manufacturing industry. Strong demand will continuously stimulate more intense resource mobilization until there is overcapacity, then increasing market competition leads to merger and acquisition to force up the productivity, the number of survived companies will decrease, and, in the end, the entire industry uses only a little human resources to produce massive products unimaginable in the past.

A careful examination tells that what happens in China's healthcare is a different story from the above three cases. First, there is absolutely no lack of demand. In fact, even the total health expenses and personal health expenditures are not the whole picture for demand growth for medical and healthcare services. Even so, the 77-fold and 198-fold growth in 27 years shows that the demand growth is extremely robust. Second, there are no insurmountable supply barriers, because the factors that make up medical services are nothing more than professionals, sites, buildings, and equipment, all of which can be supplied continuously. Third, healthcare is about service, or the caregiving from doctors and nurses, so it is impossible to increase productivity in the same way as we do with the "assembly line". Human input is essential. Given these differences, we can conclude that it is rather abnormal that the healthcare in China is doing such a bad job in mobilizing resources.

What's so strange is that it turns out that China's medical and healthcare system has so poor capabilities to mobilize human resources. A close look at the data tells us that the total number of China's health workers in 2005 was even lower than the previously achieved historic high: a total of 1.938 million doctors and 1.556 million physicians, representing only 92.3% and 95% respectively of the historical high in 2001. The number of nurses was increasing for the same period, but due to the fast decrease in doctors and physicians, China's total healthcare work force in 2005 was only 97% of the highest level in history.

What is even more incredible is that the number of doctors in 2005 was not only lower than the historical high, but also the absolute number was lower by 46,595 people than in 1997. Again, this was not due to any decrease in demand: during the same period, the total national health expenditure increased by 1.7 times (i.e. increased by RMB 539.98 billion), and personal healthcare expenditure increased by 1.6 times (i.e. increased by RMB 277.5 billion). In other words, despite the growing demand for medical services, the number of doctors, the backbone of the services, was decreasing!

It is very difficult to find a similar phenomenon. Certainly not the labor-intensive manufacturing industry: it takes many inconspicuous industry champions only several years or a dozen of years to become the largest global producer. They achieve so inadvertently just by demand stimulating, resources mobilizing, learning and doing. Back in 1997, there were very few talents in China who understood network technology. What about now? Finance, foreign languages, music, sports, and fine arts, and any other discipline that has a market demand, have attracted swarms and adequate number of talents. Even education sector is doing better than medical service; putting other things aside, at least the number of professors is going straight up, isn't it?

Thinking it over, maybe catering can serve as a suitable comparison for healthcare. Both are service industries, related to health (although to different degrees), and both suffer from the so-called "information asymmetry", "externalities", and "supply-induced consumption". More importantly, no one can deny that China's catering industry is a market-based business, which is fully consistent with the characterization of medical service proposed by some experts. So, when facing rapidly rising demand, is the catering industry behaving the same way as the marketized medical services and suffering from shrinking resources?

The answer is negative. According to statistics, from 1978 to 2003 (the 2005 statistics is not available yet), the total sales of the catering industry in the country increased by 112 times, the number of catering outlets increased by 33 times, and the number of employees increased by 17 times. That is to say, the demand growth was only several folds higher than the growth in the number of outlets and the work force.

What's more interesting is that since 1997, the national catering sales increased by 1.5 times, and the number of outlets and employees increased by 43% and 1.25 times. Now it's clear: the strong demand growth in the catering industry has stimulated the supply growth. Over time, the intensity of resources mobilization can almost catch up with the demand growth rate.

Admittedly, it is generally more demanding to be a doctor than to be a chef. But it is after verifying the figures for reserve talents for doctors that I feel almost hopeless about the resource mobilization capabilities of the existing medical and healthcare system in China. In 2005, how many medical students were enrolled by universities and colleges? 338,000. This figure will be 580,000 if adult higher education is included. This large figures are partly due to enrollment expansion, and a large proportion of adult education students themselves are already health workers. Putting this aside, we can arrive at a total number of 854,000 to only count the enrollment by the medical school or colleges from 1997 to 2005, during which period China's number of doctors, as described before, decreased by 47,000. What is the matter after all?

As we all know, medical students need to study longer than students of other majors, and either they themselves or their families need to pay more for their study. Yet over the past eight years, a total of 850,000 medical graduates were facing a job market where the absolute number of doctors is shrinking? Was it because about 200,000 doctors retired during the same period? I couldn't find the statistics, but even so, there were still 700,000 well trained medical graduates who couldn't make their career into medical care. Was it because of the brain drain? Perhaps, after all, doctors in the United States make much more money. But the income of American chefs, engineers, etc. is also much higher than that in China. Why with outflow of people, the domestic work force is still growing and growing for these sectors in sharp contrast to the embarrassing medical and healthcare system? Let's get to the bottom of the issue: what mechanism on earth is hindering the resources mobilization in China's medical and health services?

11.2 "Government-Led" Is Exactly the Key

The ability of medical and healthcare service to mobilize resources is closely related to the system. The reason is simple, there is no choice other than going through a specific system in order to mobilizing resources to increase the supply and meet the demand. So, what kind of system characteristics are decisively influencing the resource mobilization capabilities of China's medical system?

According to statistics from the Ministry of Health (MOH), in 2005, 82.8% of hospitals, 95.1% of beds, and 90.4% of health workers (including 88% of medical practitioners) belonged to state-owned or collective medical institutions; while 52.8% of hospitals, 80.1% of beds and 77% of health workers (including 74.2% of medical practitioners) were directly affiliated to government-run medical institutions. In terms of organizational characteristics of the medical institutions, it is not accurate to claim that the government is responsible for each and everything, let alone to say it is led by the private sector, only the word "government-led" hits the nail on the head.

No matter state-owned hospitals or government-run hospitals, the power to appoint the presidents of most hospitals in China is in the hands of administrative agencies without exception. Below the president, the management personnel is either decided by the president or by the "leadership group" of the hospital, and this in essence is an indirect "government-led" system. Because the positions of the president or the "leadership group" are determined by the government, the behavior of people at the positions will surely be controlled and influenced. Such a personnel system is definitely under government administrative control. Just because the coverage is not 100%, it is fair to use "government-led" to describe the system.

If hospitals and other medical institutions fall short, any new establishment needs to be approved by the health administrative authorities. Unlike the simple procedures of opening restaurants or shoe stores—where the owners just need to register with the department of industry and commerce after they believe it is technically and economically viable, to open-up a hospital must be at any time subject to administrative approval, and it is the same for state-owned hospitals, government-run hospitals, non-state-owned collective hospitals as well as other medical institutions. Not just new hospitals, but new departments and new specialties to existing hospitals must also be approved. In this sense, "government-led" might not be able to reflect the real story, may be "administratively arranged" is a more reasonable term.

Doctors and nurses are hired mostly on an appointment system. However, eligibility for practice is reviewed and approved by the health administrative authorities. The number of medical personnel in public hospitals (including state-owned and government-run hospitals) is also subject to the government staffing quota. This means that even if health workers have the technical qualifications, they cannot work in a public hospital if the staffing quota is running out. In short, how much human resources can be mobilized to lawfully enter the healthcare sector depends on the government and its administrative approval mechanism.

The prices of thousands of medical services, medicines, and supplies are, according to the institutional arrangement, regulated by the government. This is specified by the *Price Law*, as this is something related to life, health, national economy and people's livelihood, how can it be without price regulation? I put the qualifier of "according to the institutional arrangement" because institution is institution, reality is reality, and whether or not the reality can evade the institution is a long-lasting game, which is a separate discussion. But here is just to confirm that, institutionally, legitimate medical pricing is based government price regulation.

Up to this point, I have to express a little bit of admiration for WANG Shaoguang, GE Yanfeng, and LI Ling for insisting that the existing healthcare is "marketized" or even "over-marketized" despite its so obvious and ubiquitous "government-led" hallmarks.

Every year people complain about the inaccessibility of medical treatment, why can't the government run more hospitals? No, because there is not enough budget. Can more doctors be hired through appointment? Also no, because there is not enough quota for staffing and headcount. So strange! The fiscal revenue and taxation are increasing year after year, and the improvement in government office facilities and officials' actual income is remarkable, but there is just no money for medical investment. No wonder there is so much social grievance. When people feel strongly about the situation, some people come out and explain that "that's all the fault of marketization". I wonder, do they have the slightest spirit of seeking truth from facts?!

Even if the government budget is not enough, why not open up the medical service market to private investment? Looking around at the scarcity of food, clothing, and housing, and the difficulty in traveling and communication, none of these are solved by fully relying on government budget. China's own experience has already proven that many then nerve-racking problems can all be alleviated or even resolved by employing appropriate systems and policies to fully mobilize non-governmental, private, and international resources.

How is the government-led medical system performing in mobilizing non-governmental resources? I did some research, and it turns out there is no legal restriction or prohibition on private sector entering medical services. Policy-wise, all resources of the society have been encouraged again and again by government documents and competent authorities to invest into the healthcare sector. But look at the results, the absolute number of non-governmental and non-public medical institutions is small, the growth rate is low, and the share is minimal. That is to say, despite that there is legally no ban and there is encouragement from the policy, the actual results are limited.

An important institutional arrangement worth mentioning is the "non-profit organization". It turns out that China has two categories of medical establishments: "non-profit" and "for-profit". The former have inherited the legacy of all government-run public hospitals, and the government does not levy tax on them because they do not practice medical care "for a profit"; the latter, treated in the same way as other industrial and commercial enterprises, have to pay taxes since they seek profit.

Now here comes the question: which one would you choose to open a hospital, for-profit or not-for-profit? Look at the taxation: the turnover tax, the value-added tax, and the income tax—these three items alone are already a huge chunk. Moreover, government hospitals don't pay taxes by upholding not-for-profit, while private ones, if they are for-profit, have to pay heavy taxes, how can they compete on equal footing? The statistics shows that by 2005, 96% of the beds in China are registered by non-profit institutions. Although for-profit institutions are allowed by law, their actual number is very few.

However, once wearing the "non-profit" hat, it is legally difficult to distribute investment return. Yes, it is still possible to play some tricks, go around, bypass some barriers and use other methods to provide indirect return to the investor. However, these practices have a fatal drawback: too high transaction costs. If the music and tone is very abstract and difficult, very few people would join the chorus, so very few people responded. Plus the on-the-go marketization of other sectors in the national economy pushes the opportunity costs very high for medical investment. The result is very logical: the actual non-government investment mobilized into healthcare is asymmetrical with the strength of the private economy.

11.3 Embarrassing "Public Hospitals"

The government pays a little but administers a lot. This is the basic feature of the "government-led" healthcare system in China. Paying only a little means it cannot be claimed that medical and health care is run as a public welfare; administering a lot, especially with tight regulation on access and pricing, means that there is no way to mobilize market resources into the sector. The combination of these two factors has turned medical service into a closed system and a place where these "not-for-profit organizations" can make big money. Among these, the majority, namely "public hospitals" are faced with multiple dimensions of embarrassment, and this is the sole and only case across the world.

Not just China has "public hospitals". Essentially all countries and regions, the United Kingdom, the United States, India, Russia, Cuba, Brazil, Mexico, Hong Kong and Taiwan… have national, municipal, county, and community public hospitals. But to the author's limited knowledge, almost only here in our country public hospitals are both expensive and inaccessible.

The British public hospitals (NHS), established after WWII, are known for their long queues. In "Questions and Answers about the NHS", I mentioned that in the UK where the government pays for all medical services, there are still people willing to go and pay for private medical services, because the waiting time for public hospitals is simply too long.[4] The story is the same for government hospitals in Hong Kong—long queues and too crowded. Public hospitals in the United States seem to be less crowded, but it is an illusion. The low-income people without medicare (it is said the total is about 40 million people) must first queue up elsewhere to apply for medical subsidies from the government before going to the hospital. There is one thing in common: to go to public hospitals in any country, queuing is more or less a must. The degree of difficulty in getting medical service is generally inversely proportional to the national strength and the financial strength.

However, it is not common for public hospitals that require queuing to be also expensive. This is not to say that all public or government hospitals will always place public welfare first and they will not make any profit. The problem is that it is illogical to be both inaccessible and expensive. Experience tells us that when the queues are very long, usually it is because the prices of goods or services are extremely low; on the other hand, we don't hear people complaining it is difficult to buy a Ferrari. If it is difficult to queue, the item won't be expensive, if the item is expensive, you don't need to stand in the long line. This is common sense.

Yet our public hospitals are both inaccessible and expensive all the same. Queuing is common in China, but after decades of reform and opening up, it is indeed very rare to desperately queue up several times for things other than going to the hospitals. It is not strange at all in China to get up at midnight and line up for popular specialists. And this is for urban people, for those from small towns or rural areas, it takes even more trouble!

---

[4]Zhou (2008: 179–190).

And it is expensive! The average outpatient expenses and hospitalization costs are detached from the income and become unaffordable for the patients, not to mention the "sky high medical bill" cases. According to the survey of a health insurance company, in a metropolitan in mainland China, the average expenses is RMB 440 per outpatient, and RMB 19,000 per hospitalization, which is more expensive than that in Taipei, and even than Los Angeles! These indeed are the charges by top hospitals. Generally, Ordinary hospitals are not expensive like this, but still the average expenses for an outpatient gets easily above RMB 100. In 2005, the per capita healthcare expenses in rural areas was RMB 168.09, accounting for 7.87% of the cash spendings on their consumption, which is a little higher than the proportion of clothing and daily supplies. That is to say, if the average peasant is to spend more than his clothing budget on healthcare, he still cannot afford two hospital visits a year.

It is both difficult and expensive to get medical service from public hospitals in China. This is an elusive phenomenon. Over the years, the prevailing criticism seems to have turned "Seeing a doctor is difficult and expensive" into a buzz word. The first time I heard this catchy phrase, I instantly questioned its logic: if the "inaccessible" is caused by too much demand, and "expensive" is a measure of the monetary price, doesn't this demonstrate that the demand is not restricted by the price? If this is true, then the foundation for behavior explanation in economics will collapse.

Some constraint must be missing. I conducted research for several years, visited a dozen hospitals, and talked with hospital presidents, doctors, and patients, and searched the available documents. When examining a case in 2006, I suddenly came to realize that there is another important phenomenon co-existing with the "inaccessible and expensive healthcare", which is, for some people, medical service is too cheap. After this point is accounted for, the paradox of the co-existence of "inaccessible" and "expensive" can be logically untied.

Readers may ask, is there such a thing as "super cheap" medical service in China? The answer is yes, and it is also within the "public healthcare" system. It is true that the population coverage of China's "public medical care" has noticeably decreased since the reform. Quite a few public units (government agencies, state-owned enterprises and institutions) with financial stresses find it difficult to reimburse medical expenses, even if the "policy" is still in place. On the other hand, for those government agencies and state-owned enterprises and institutions entities with strong and ever improving financial strength, the "public medical care" spending has always been increased. The number of people covered by the public system is decreasing, but the average amount of medical care for the benefiting population has increased dramatically.

The consequences? First, as the high-end portion of the public medical care system very seldom requires patients to pay any out-of-pocket expenses (quite the same as in the commercial insurance), the medical demand from this group of people is usually much higher than their actual needs. Putting other things aside, the peculiarity of medical service (we have to mention this point) has determined that the spending on public medical care is not restricted only by personal appetites. The general observation is that the waste in this piece is even larger than public-funded wining and dining. As a result, "public hospitals" have to face the biggest embarrassment in the system: as a statutory, non-profit organization, they cannot get fully reimbursed for their investment and operating expenses, yet they have to "serve" the runaway high-end medical needs which are constrained neither by out-of-pocket personal spending nor by the purchasing power of those people.

11.4 The Burden of Price Regulation

Unfortunately, in addition to severe imbalances in supply and demand, price regulation is imposed on medical services and drugs, which has further weakened the mobilization of medical resources. The problem is: the strong demand and yet the short supply should bring a high overall income to the healthcare sector. However, there are many factors involved in the medical supply, doctors, nurses, managers, the brand and reputation of institutions, equipment and devices, sites, drugs, and supplies, etc., and all are essential. Now comes the trouble of how to distribute the income among these factors? In theory, it can be allocated by the administrative means, or by the market price mechanism, or a combination of the two. No matter which approach is adopted, one law will always rule: once the price cannot accurately and promptly reflect the relative scarcity of factors, distortions of behaviors will follow, and "chaos" will be unavoidable.

This is exactly what is happening in China's medical and drug industry. Not to mention previous efforts, the National Development and Reform Commission (NDRC) has been up to its neck in issuing notices and notices on reducing the price of certain drugs in the past two years. Does it work? Not really. The only change is that the prices have been shifted from being inflated too much to being suppressed to too low, then no one would manufacture such drugs anymore and they become unavailable in the market. So, which one do you think is the lesser of the two evils?

A closer look will find that "the strange things" have long happened. I have a speech outline of Professor KE Yang, Vice President of Peking University, and head of the medical school. The figures he cited when describing the changes in medical prices are very illustrative. For old medical technologies, compared with 15–20 years ago, the current charge has not increased much after considering the price index. High-cost items, without exception, are all new technologies.

Take the diagnosis of gastric cancer for example. "Upper gastrointestinal angiography" currently costs RMB 380 against RMB 80 of 20 years ago. Routine biopsy and pathological diagnosis costs RMB 100 against RMB 30 of 20 years ago. The number of folds in price increase is about the same as CPI growth (which is slightly below 3 folds). However, the new diagnosis and treatment for gastric cancer is another story: RMB 1,500 for MRI; RMB 8,000–10,000 for PET; RMB 10,000 for laparoscopy; RMB 5,000 for endoscopic stent placement; and RMB 10,000 for endoscopic photodynamic therapy.

Doesn't this seem strange? The ultra-low prices of the old technologies and drugs and the extremely high prices of the new technologies and drugs co-exist in the same regulation system for medical care. Could it be that the regulatory authorities have become the captive of the regulated, as Stigler points out, because the regulator does not have the information advantage? Maybe. But why not simply capture more to beef up the prices for also old technologies and medicines? Wouldn't the profits be greater for medical institutions?

The answer needs to be dug out from the existing price regulation system for medical services and medicines. Looking over relevant policies and regulations since 1996, I found two points: (1) The regulation was based on the "cost-plus pricing", but the cost of investigation is time-consuming and laborious; when the calculation is finally done, the situation may have already changed; (2) Price regulation is not only responsible for determining the competitive price, but also for the stability of the overall CPI. If these two points are taken into consideration, the phenomenon is no longer strange.

First, let's look at the first point. The number of medical service items is beyond imagination. Promulgated by the state in 2001, the "National Price of Medical Services Specification (Trial)" standardizes the original 30,000 items into right below 4,000 kinds for the purpose of regulation. Even based on 4000 kinds, the full-cost pricing activity ranging from surveying, parameter setting, sharing, categorization, totalization, and averaging, and to price setting is, by all means, a mega project.

In other words, the "cost" to grasp the cost of practicing medicine is already very costly in itself. Not to mention, the number of items and the myriad of errors in the cost survey, and the deliberately concealed information. What's more, the averaging could be really troublesome in a country as large as China, with all the differences across localities. Even if all the above-mentioned work is resolved with zero cost, the "cost" obtained from the price regulation survey is wrong. The cost that restricts human behavior in the real world is always the "opportunity cost", namely the highest cost that the person is willing to give up among an ensemble of alternatives. China has two million practicing doctors. Each of them faces different sets of alternative opportunities, and has different criteria for their judgement their own alternatives, different aspirations, different action competences, and different marginal changes. Can a centralized government agency collect all the relevant information and determine "the cost of practicing medicine"? And can it be accurate, timely, and error-free?

As far as I know, it was already 2005 when some hospitals received the specification. So some people from within the sector said the price has been adjusted once in 10 years because the previous version was 1996. But how much China's economy has changed in this decade! If you read the specification, you will find that underpaid health workers is still the same old long-standing problem. Look, as the specification, "a registration fee should be paid for each one of such items as outpatient visit and injection, dressing change, acupuncture and moxibustion, physiotherapy, medical message and plasma osmolality." The standard rate for registration is only "RMB 1 for provincial and municipal hospitals and RMB 0.8 for county hospitals". Has the situation been improved much as compared to several years ago when people joked "to get an injection is cheaper than get the bike tire inflated".

Next, emergency diagnosis and examination fee, defined as "first aid or emergency treatment provided by health workers 24 h a day. What is the guidance price? RMB 10 for provincial hospitals, 8 for municipal, and 5 for county hospitals. Unwilling to believe this, I looked back and forth and finally found that the "renowned experts consultation fee" is a bit more expensive: RMB 30 for provincial hospitals, 25 for municipal and 20 for county hospitals. The most expensive one is the "remote joint consultation fee" at RMB 200 per hour, which is lower than the hourly rate of lawyers, accountants, and faculty. Needless to say, this is the institution-to-institution rate, the doctors' take-home payment is yet to be found.

The most astonishing is the guidance price for nursing: RMB 5 per day for class 2 nursing; RMB 8 per day for class 1 nursing; and only RMB 30 per day for "special disease nursing" including for AIDS and other special infectious diseases. Let me give one last example, for "sputum aspiration nursing", defined as "including percussion on the back and sputum sucking, and excluding atomization inhalation and the cost of the disposable suction tube", the guidance price is RMB 2 per time! My dear friends, how many people will be willing to do this job? Apparently no one, so the hospital has to find money from high-priced items to subsidize it.

No one knows when the next version of "specification" will be issued. Until then, regardless of changes in CPI and other economic parameters, hospitals and doctors can only charge according to the current specification. To survive, hospitals have to "support medicine with drugs" or speed up the upgrading to new medical technologies and devices. So, all these widely criticized practice of supporting medicine with drug and over treatment do have the factual need for financial survival.

The question is, under the same price regulation system, why the prices are too high for some items, and too low for others, why to favor some more than others? Since public hospitals are allowed to generate income, why to force hospitals to increase their income through drug distribution and device upgrade? Wouldn't it be much better to just go straight ahead and deregulate the price control and enable the medical care to support itself?

This involves the second point of the price regulation system. It turns out that the "labor cost" of medical workers is continuously tracked. The figure for last year, the year before last, and even 10 years ago, and the amount of increase can be checked and displayed. However, the prices of drugs, devices, instruments, and equipment, especially new drugs and new inspection instruments, were not recorded in the past, so no matter how expensive they are, they will not affect the price index. As mentioned earlier, China's price regulator is not only responsible for setting prices, but also for maintaining the overall stability of prices. Therefore when suddenly greeted by price index pressure, and the price is like high voltage electricity, regulatory authorities are afraid of approving price increases.

The hybridization of the above two points has lowered the labor costs for health workers but easily raised the prices for new drugs, equipment, and devices. This distorted pricing system for healthcare is formed this way, and it will be bound to distort the behaviors of medical services and undermine the effective supply of medical services in a systematic way.

11.5 The Crux: Integration of Regulation and Operation

When we dive deep into medical service market access and price regulation, it is hard not to come down to the fundamental feature of the current medical service system, namely the integration of regulation and operation", meaning the health administrative authorities (from MOH to local health departments and bureaus) both run and oversee hospitals. Such system has experienced some changes though, its most criticized feature has not changed much—the administrative department plays the integrated roles of the referee, the team leader, and the coach, but does not assume corresponding responsibilities.

The integrated supervision and development dates back to a very important history. The theoretical concept comes from the originality of Lenin in his exposition on planning the future Soviet economy in 1917: "All citizens become staff and workers of a single countrywide state 'syndicate', and "The whole society will become a management office and a factory with equal labor and equal pay" (See *State and Revolution*). In practice, Lenin, after taking control of the Soviet regime, did not immediately implement this original idea, but adopted the new economic policy that recognized multiple types of economic ownerships; however, his idea that the state should act as a super company to organize the entire economic, cultural, and social undertakings has been written in history as the classic institutional design for socialism.

The traditional planned mechanism is to turn the entire society into a super company, which is at the same time a super post office, a super school, and a super hospital. Everything is administratively guided: planning, layout, investment, personnel, staffing, technical specifications, and rates, if any at all. Under this system, there is no difference between social management and internal management of the company, because "the whole society" has become a super company.

In layman's terms, this highly integrated management system is a system that manages "its own people". Because everything is invested, constructed, appointed and controlled by the state, apart from the "country's own people", this society has "nobody else"! Manage "your own people" is the most straightforward management model: just use commands and instructions for transmission of targets, mobilization of resources and division of responsibilities. Because everyone is our own people—for the company, the public and the state—we can and we only need to give orders to command.

In wars and other emergencies, the effectiveness of the command system may be unquestionable. However, such a system has not been proven to be "superior" in meeting the growing and diverse economic and cultural needs of millions of people in peacetime. The experience from last century proves that the information cost of the command system is extremely high. To organize the entire national economic and social life through commands from the central planning authority leads to lots of errors and poor capabilities to correct errors. Those being commanded have no clear responsibilities, no stable benefit expectations, no sufficient incentives to provide products and services. The lack of information and motivation seems to form a lean-oxygen environment and any hope just cannot be placed on the vigor of this system.

The reason that the old system is difficult to change is simply because it creates huge vested interest. It is very difficult to find a system that sets the power and the responsibility so apart: the agencies and officials that give orders are so high above, yet those performing concrete tasks are always the "inferior units": factories, mines, schools, hospitals and all the way down to sanitation stations which responsibility is to sweep garbage. As a by-product of the highly centralized system, the evaluation system of the command system is also top-down, so unless the "top above the top" becomes vigilant, or aware of something, or blames someone, those commanding agencies and officials often do not have to be responsible for their orders; it is always the "inferior" that takes the blame for all problems.

Why can the system separate power and responsibilities so neatly? The answer is that because "the whole society" is integrated. In a market economy, don't the chief executives of multinationals also hold dominating power, from day to day don't they also give orders and expect their subordinates to execute and take responsibilities, don't they also follow the rules of survival in "corporate politics", and don't they do everything possible to cover up mistakes and take the merits?

Yes, the CEOs of big companies look very similar to the bureaucrats of government agencies. The difference is that no matter how big the company is in the market, there is always someone bigger or more powerful. To make the wrong decisions or to misuse power is the very best opportunity given to their apparent and potential competitors. So, admittedly the "big bosses" can always be headstrong, but when they exceed a certain limit and lose all that money, they are out of the game. Also because there are competitors in the market, all resources to form a company, from investing shareholders to employees, can always join the enemy, the CEO simply cannot do whatever as he pleases.

Yet, when the whole of society becomes a single management office, such setbacks no longer exist. With just one entity and no competitors, there is no external pressure on management decisions. When state agents invest and operate using resources of the whole society, different performance may end up having different use value, but the value is not measured. Perhaps only "a sound democracy" can determine the sequence or priority of different use values, but from a logic perspective, it is still a question mark for a society to build democracy when it is composed of "citizens" who have no legal right to own the means of production. Empirically, the Soviet-style central planning system has neither a sound democracy nor a mature market. As a result, the decision-making power of the super office is moving increasingly away from the constraints of being responsible for the consequences of decisions. In all honesty, with sweet power like this, who would vote for a reform?

The reform will only take place when the system totally fails. That is, the crisis is the real driver for change.

So this is the origin for the system with integrated government and enterprise, and the integrated regulation and governance. The medical service system is nothing more than a subsystem of the super office. It doesn't make much difference to say MOH (Departments/Bureaus of Health) is the host or the governor of the hospitals, because here the host is the governor. In any case, all the hospitals and medical institutions are planned, laid out, established, appointed (in terms of leaders), instructed, and inspected by MOH (Departments/Bureaus of Health). This is only one can run hospitals, nobody else is allowed. Therefore, the detachment between power and responsibilities is just innate.

The first strength to tear open the system is the serious shortfall in the government spending on medical and health care. As we have made a brief retrospective, even in the planned era, which is believed to be ideal by some unreliable experts, there was a serious shortage of medical and health resources, and China could only take care of either its cities or its rural areas, only one out of the two. In those days no one complained that medical care is "expensive and inaccessible", mainly because people were so poor that they placed healthcare after the more pressing needs of subsistence.

What really put the traditional system in trouble is the expanding demand for medical services brought about by the income growth of urban and rural residents. Fiscal spending can no longer satisfy the growing demand for medical services. Hence the medical reform was put on the agenda. However, as of today the government is still in control of China's medical and health care system except that at it has entered into a new stage: the administrative agency does not have enough money to run hospitals, but still sticks to the integrated functions. As a result, it allows more out-of-pocket payment from patients, and allows hospitals to continue the practice of "supporting medicare with drugs" and "market-based pricing", but meanwhile it still tightly holds the administrative power to control the entry into medical services, and does not welcome social capital to run hospitals to compete with "its own people". Therefore, the traditional "integration of regulation and governance" has evolved into "control of everything, without responsibilities", and this becomes the institutional root cause of the myriad of problems in China's current medical and healthcare system.

11.6 The Hospital-Oriented Theory

The title of this section is borrowed from JIANG Yiwei, author of "The Enterprise-Oriented Theory" and former director of the Institute of Industrial Economics at the Chinese Academy of Social Sciences. His paper was published 27 years ago in 1980.[5]

At that time, the reform and opening-up just kicked off and people had different opinions on how to reform the clumsy SOEs. JIANG's view is clear-cut: the fundamental problem that SOEs need to solve is "how to give play to the initiative of enterprises that grasp productivity and of workers". For this reason, the reform must not be limited to re-distributing power of administering SOEs between the central and

[5]Jiang Yiwei (1980).

local governments. It has to directly hit the nail on the head—changing the relationship between the state and enterprise, separating the government and the enterprise, recognizing the independent economic status and interest of enterprises, and thus making them the most basic cells of economic activities. JIANG summarized his ideas as "the Enterprise-Oriented Theory" to differentiate from "the State-Oriented Theory" (which advocates strengthening the vertical lines from the control by central authorities) and the "Local-Oriented Theory" (which emphasizes on blocks, namely expanding power of local authorities).

The traditional central-planning and state-owned system treats the entire country as a super company, so it is only natural that the government and the enterprise are intertwined. Since the government and the enterprise is not separated, it is difficult to determine if the "self" of the SOE is the state or the enterprise. However in form, the "government organ" and the "state-owned enterprise" are separated in the traditional institution: the former is the brain and nervous control system, and the latter is the execution system, namely just factories to reactively execute the plans and directions. From this perspective, JIANG's suggestions on the reform strategy is truly remarkable. He treats the limbs as the "self" which strives not only to take autonomy from the "brain", but also to breed its own brains and nerve system at the enterprise level!

Details put aside, the SOE reform truly moved towards the "enterprise sectionalism". Today people who have no idea of the controversy in the early 1980s may not be impressed by the theory. On the whole, the SOE sectionalism has roughly been turned into reality, and the reform has been pushed deeper, and the property rights of all factors constituting the enterprise have been defined and re-defined, contractualized and re-contractualized, organized and re-organized. To our disappointment, once the theorist hits something right, his "influence" will immediately be gone.

If we take the reform of SOEs as a reference, it is not difficult to find out whether the medical system, which many people believe is over-marketized, has really been reformed or not. A simple test would be: If the "Hospital-Oriented Theory" is laid out as a basic proposal, what would be the reaction from the public opinion, and what will be the reaction from decision-making authorities responsible for China's healthcare reform?

Perhaps there will be lots of suspicion: industry is industry, medical care is medical care, how can healthcare reform be compared to industrial reform? Admittedly, medical service has its inherent uniqueness, but what on earth makes it so special that it cannot, should not, and must not draw experience from the reform to SOEs and other service sectors? Or specifically, which features of the medical service can be used as the reasons to reject the "Hospital-Oriented Theory"?

The argument—"the medical service is related to life and health"—cannot stand close scrutiny. Don't industrial products have anything to do with life and health? Not to mention that "drugs", "medical devices," and "medical supplies" are all industrial products. For non-medical industrial products, such as glasses, cigarettes, lighters, clothing, footwear, motorcycles, cars, and houses, which one of them really has nothing to do with life and health? Let me put it this way, all products for human use, are more or less relevant to life and health.

The real question to debate on is, why can't the system on products and services related to life and health be "enterprise-oriented (hospital oriented)", and why it has to be "government-oriented"? My answer is that the system doesn't have to be government-oriented unless these products and services are "public goods" and unless the private sector is unwilling or unable to provide. Only when both of these two "unless" conditions are met, the "government-oriented" system is needed. For all other circumstances, the "enterprise-oriented", or to be more accurate, the "market contract-oriented" practice can play a major role; be it industry, agriculture, commerce, catering, healthcare, education, or culture.

That the government is not directly engaged in production does not mean that the government does nothing. In all economic activities, fraud, malicious or inadvertent damage to others' life or property all needs to be addressed and prevented by the government with coercion through providing appropriate legal, judicial, and regulatory systems. The "Enterprise-Oriented (Hospital-Oriented) Theory" recognizes and protects the interests of enterprises (hospitals) with the premise that they do not infringe upon the interests of others, including shareholders, creditors, workers, suppliers, and customers. In addition to resorting to ethics and corporate self-discipline, it must also resort to the rule of law and government enforcement to bring this point into reality. Therefore, the "Enterprise-Oriented (Hospital-Oriented) Theory" does not reject government's law enforcement, but it also requires improved rule of law and effective law enforcement.

Experience shows that it is precisely the integration of the government and the hospital and the integration of regulation and operation that prevent the government from effectively enforcing the law in medical services. The key is that the system of "managing its own people" easily becomes the breeding ground for officials to protect each other, cover up problems, and shirk responsibilities. Only when the government resolutely exits from the den of "government running hospitals", and no longer plays the dual role of the athlete and the referee, will it be conducive to re-building the legislation for healthcare.

The "asymmetric information in medical services" is even less the reason to reject the "Hospital-Oriented Theory". Generally speaking, information asymmetry is a common phenomenon in division of labor. A patient's knowledge and information about medicines, treatment methods, and effects are, of course, far less than doctors and hospitals. However, such information asymmetry, in nature, is no different from the asymmetry of information or knowledge when he or she as a customer faces milk powder, beverages, leather shoes, clothing, electronic products, automobiles, and other products. Only the degree is different. The question to be analyzed is why information asymmetry means the system cannot be "enterprise (hospital)-oriented" and must be "government-oriented"?

We agree that there is relatively higher level of information asymmetry between the doctors and the patients in medical services. This is perhaps because medical science is more complicated and more specialized and it is not easy for the patient as the person in question to objectively use the medical knowledge. We may even be ready to accept the information asymmetry in medical service as the worst of all. But still, even with the worst information asymmetry, do we have to rule out the "hospital oriented" approach?

The answer is no. The severe information asymmetry cannot be addressed merely by taking the words too literally and shrinking the asymmetry, which means nothing more than going against specialization and making every patient a doctor. To reduce the severe asymmetry, what we really need to do is to rely highly not only on the rule of law, but also on the quality competition of the expert system which enjoys the information advantage. This is also why the ethics of doctors and the reputation of hospitals have always been the most important assets of medical services, and they always have very high market values. "Reputation" takes a long time to build, and it needs a stable entity as its vehicle for good traditions. In this sense, the hospital-oriented approach is even more pressing and more important than the SOE reform.

11.7 The Great Urgency for Hospital Reform

The "Decision of the CPCCC and the State Council on Healthcare Reform and Development" issued in 1997 has made some arrangements for the reform of the operating mechanism of health institutions. The document states: "Through reform and strict management, health institutions shall establish a competitive and vigorous operating mechanism with responsibilities, incentives and restrictions in place. The institutions shall adopt and improve the president/director responsibility system. The autonomy on operations and management of health institutions shall be further expanded. The reform of the personnel system and the distribution system shall be continually deepened, and the egalitarian system shall be broken through proper policy guidance, ideological education, and economic means so as to incentivize health workers." Clearly this is a "hospital-oriented" reform, aimed at totally changing the integration of government and hospital and the integration of regulation and operation functions in the old system.

However, the above guidelines have not been fully implemented. The reason is simple, because the "hospital sectionalism", including the whole set of president's responsibility system, hospital autonomy, personnel and distribution system, etc. is in conflict with the "administrative power sectionalism". Suqian is a telling example: in its old "public hospitals", redundant people who do not grasp any medical technology account for up to 40%. The so-called "public" hospital is often the "private" territory of some officials. The patients suffer the loss, but the all sorts of people with power in the competent authorities benefit a lot. If the old "administrative power-oriented" system is changed, they will lose all the convenience from the old system. This shows that the medical reform cannot be a "Pareto Improvement", which increases the interest of other parties and the society without touching the interest of any party. The problem is, the medical reform means to touch the administrative power of competent authorities under their own leadership. It would be as difficult as asking the tiger to give up its skin.

Some subsequent incidents and changes in mindsets reversed the thinking of medical reform. The most significant event was the SARS outbreak in 2003. The prevention and control of SARS, an infectious disease, is a typical "public goods", which requires the government to assume the full responsibility, conduct the overall commanding, and go all out to use its legal coercive force to fight the epidemic. The sudden outbreak of SARS may technically be accidental, but sort of inevitable from the economic and social perspective. The main reason is that after the reform and opening up, along with other economic factors, the flow of people has shifted from immobility or low mobility under the planned system to large-scale high mobility. This, of course, has a huge impact on public health, and make it vulnerable. In our previously understanding, the medical reform focused more on the organization, efficiency, and restructuring of general medical services, and we didn't clearly distinguish public health, the government responsibility that must be supported by government fiscal income, from general medical service, which can be improved by giving hospitals more autonomy and adopting the "hospital-oriented" reform. The SARS has reminded people to be aware of this deviation, to reflect on the strategies for the medical reform so as to avoid partiality.

However, another extreme also occurred during the reflection, which expanded the public health responsibility of the government to the entire medical and healthcare sector. The correct proposition that public health is a public welfare is expanded to the wrong proposition claiming that "all medical and health care is a public welfare". The policy of increasing government fiscal investment into public health has been "upgraded" to the unrealistic proposal that the fiscal spending should fully cover all medical expenses. Therefore the "integration of government and hospitals, and of regulation and governance" seems to be politically correct again, while concepts such as hospital autonomy, president's accountability system, correcting distortions in medical services and drug pricing mechanisms, parallel efforts on for-profit and not-for-profit hospitals, and mobilizing private capital into medical care, etc., seem to become the forbidden zone again for the healthcare reform. Different comments from the general public, including different analysis and policy proposals from the academia is very normal. Since the reform is a kind of exploratory practice, it is impossible not to have different opinions. But the position and comments of competent government agencies and officials are another story because they are related to policy directions and administrative responsibilities. In May 2005, the Director-General of the Department of Policy and Regulations of MOH published announced on the front page of the *Health News* that "Marketization is not the Direction for the Medical Reform." In July, a newspaper published that diagnosis of a research institute under the State Council saying that "the market-oriented medical reform has failed."[6]

In response to this, the national medical reform was called to halt, but it didn't really stop. It has been a long time that the government gives only policy but no real money to public hospitals. As of 2005, most of the salaries, bonuses, social security, opex, equipment, and training of China's public hospitals were financed

[6]Cao Haidong and Fu Jianfeng (2005).

by their own income. Take the five large public hospitals I visited in the past six months for example, government fiscal funding only accounts for a 1% of their total revenue. In the best case, the proportion is only 5% after the hospital exerts its best and successfully secure special government funding. The president of a hospital in Shanghai once aptly remarked, "Public hospitals do not live on public funding, but they have to hand in some revenue"—China's "public hospitals" are absolutely not the same type of government hospitals elsewhere in the world, they bear the same name but are actually different, and they are just themselves.

Public hospitals, at the front of medical service, must be open every day and cannot be shutdown. Now they are directed to provide public welfare instead of adopt marketization, but where are the financial foundations? There has to be a feasible arrangement, whether the government will provide everything or the charitable organizations will give them the money. To be honest, such an empty yet inaccurate topic as to be "market-based or government-led" might be a good material for verbal battles, but it is never the good clue for solving the problem.

The medical reform actually cannot be stopped; and the so-called "to stop" is actually to "delay". However, the longer it drags out, the more losses would incur to the halfway reformed public hospitals. Because when the reform is in a standstill, responsibilities become more obscure. Take the recent bidding practice for example. It is now the Department of Health rather than hospitals that takes the responsibilities of the bidding for medicines. But who will be responsible for the prices and quality of the medicines, the Department of Health or hospitals? Many localities are busy with building "affordable hospitals", community hospitals, and medical service centers. The one-time financial appropriation is no problem; buildings and equipment are also not that difficult. But do they really have enough budget for future day-to-day operations? Who will be responsible for the operations of these newly developed hospitals, the president, or the healthcare official? If the hospital is in red, how to judge if it is due to "public welfare" or simply poor management? Furthermore, out of goodwill, the government orders that no patients should be denied for medical treatment because they have no money. However, the expenses so incurred still have to be "digested by the hospital", which is the same old practice of the government—"giving policy but not money". All this seems to move further and further away from "the responsible, competitive and vigorous operating mechanisms with incentives and restrictions". The old problem of "no-one-is-accountable" for the public system seems to become even worse.

Relatively speaking, the simple proposal of going back to the "integration of regulation and operation" system comes with a clear logic. For example, one proposal is "to establish a hospital administration agency under the health department, to perform the functions of the investor and owner of public hospitals on behalf of the state, take back the over-delegated management right, and manage the overall personnel, operation and assets". Clearly, the proposal is a master piece to re-define the reforms as "take back the power" to go back to the old system, where the administrative department acts as the brain and hospitals as limbs for the medical service system. No wonder "relevant departments" speak highly of it.

The only imperfection of this proposal is that it misses "funding". Interestingly, the agency is not responsible for public food (funding) but insists on managing personnel, operation and assets. If they can really pull it off, then why the medical reform? Nowadays some experts simply jump out from nowhere with certain proposals, but they never know that the reform, along with hospital autonomy was put on the agenda of the government because it did not have enough fiscal budget, or "food" for public hospitals. The situation has changed with time. Perhaps today the government has a deeper pocket, the operations mechanism does not need to be changed, and it will work to go back to the old system. Let's wait and see! I don't believe this will be the curse of the fate. Next year happens to be the 30th anniversary of China's reform and opening up!

11.8 Constraints on Healthcare Goals

"Health for All by 2000" (HFA 2000) is a global goal set by the World Health Assembly (WHA) in 1977. Thirty years has passed, how much has been achieved? What lessons can be learned by China to plan for its medical reform? These are the topics of this section. The author will discuss the goal at the end of this article, not because it is unimportant, but because the author believes that without grasping the constraints from reality, to set a beautiful goal will not automatically solve the problem.

In fact, "Health for All" is more like a vision. The formal description at the 30th WHA is actually "By 2000, all the people of the world should reach the level of health to lead a socially and economically productive life." This description was too general, so the following year, WHO adopted the Declaration of Alma-Ata and proposed that "primary health care" (PHC) is the key measure and basic approach to achieve the goal of HFA 2000.[7]

The Chinese government soon made a formal commitment related to the above global objective, the then Minister of Health specifically stated that "China should take the lead in achieving the strategic goal of HFA 2000." In the 1980s, "HFA 2000" was mentioned a couple of times in the Chinese government report and long-term development plan. In 1990, MOH and other four ministries jointly issued the "Planning and Objectives for Achieving Health for All in Rural China by the Year 2000". The document defines PHC in China's context and sets the indicators (PHC is the most basic healthcare services that are equally accessible to all and affordable to the people and the government), and states that "the basic way to achieve HFA in rural China is to provide PHC to all rural residents". In 1997, China's "Decision on Healthcare Reform and Development" reiterated that "PHC will be essentially accessible to all by 2000".

[7] See the official website of WHO, http://www.who.int/topics/primary_health_care/alma_ata_declaration/zh/.

The new millennium has come. Has HFA 2000 been achieved globally? Or at least, is PHC accessible to all? WHO does not so claim, nor does China. However, in 2002 the Chinese government issued "the Decision on Further Strengthening Rural Health Work", stating again "to enable all the farmers to enjoy PHC by 2010". Apparently, PHC for all was not achieved in 2000, otherwise there is no need to mention 2010. The question is, 2010 is approaching, can we achieve it by then?

We need to analyze why the government failed to deliver. We can't just pretend that the commitment was never made merely for the reason that it was not achieved. Because we can always draw some lessons from the failure to realize the goal. To evade the reality, even if the embarrassing reality is also to evade the experience and lessons, and it will serves no good to the future. In my view, the reason China failed to deliver the HFA 2000 is not only that the committed goal was over-ambitious, but also that there was a lack of clear understanding of the constraints on practicing medical assurance in current China.

Let's first look at the over-ambitious and improper goal. The financial foundation for rural China's practice of barefoot doctors and co-operative medical care was for the farmers to raise their own funds within a small collective and enjoy a certain degrees of mutual aid. All farmers and educated youths who ever lived in rural areas know that there is no small income and welfare gaps from region to region, and even between different collective units (production teams and brigades) in the same region. It might be possible to build a heath-for-all medical care system on this sort of financial foundation, but to expect the uniform welfare standard is but a beautiful misunderstanding. In fact, even "for each and everyone" is not fully true. Objectively speaking, it is a *relatively* universally implemented low-level health system with considerable differences between different farmers small collectives.

However, when "HFA 2000" was imported, translated and included in the Chinese government report, it becomes a serious matter. If this government commitment cannot be delivered, who should be held accountable? The Chinese government is not a UN agency, which simply writes down beautiful and exciting visions and goals, it does not matter that much if they don't come true, and they just continue hosting conferences, developing documents and spending lots of UN funding. However, the Chinese government has to assume the administrative responsibility for its open commitment. If the commitment is not delivered, it becomes a joke.

To be honest, "health care for all by 2010" is fundamentally a difficult-to-achieve target. This is not just because of China's huge population and extremely uneven regional social-economic development, but also because China is undergoing an unprecedented transformation. The following three major constraints will affect government commitments, including commitments on healthcare, for a long time.

The first constraint is the long-suppressed but accelerated urbanization with the reform and opening up. Large numbers of people from the countryside migrate and integrate themselves into cities. It will take a long time to form a new social structure. This is something unseen during the "barefoot doctors" era under the people's commune system. Forget about everything else, have you ever seen in the history of any other country one hundred million people take trains and another several hundred million take buses during the Spring Festival Rush? This has an important impact on medical insurance: how can a medical security system designed under the territorial jurisdiction principle cope with the massive scale of population migration? If the medical insurance for migrant workers is in Guizhou, Sichuan and Anhui, but they live in Beijing, Guangzhou, and Shenzhen, when they get sick, should they go back to the hometown to go to hospital or be treated locally with the receipts taken home for reimbursement later? These problems were never encountered by Germany or UK, as in these developed countries, the welfare systems were established after the majority of people entered the new urban-rural social structure and had "formal jobs", which took place long after the massive migration and urbanization. This was even less of a problem for the former Soviet Union because free population migration was simply not allowed.

Some experts say that's why China should use taxes to pay for the medical assurance and adopt a "public healthcare model", which means free medical care for everyone wherever they are. Of course, it would be nice if this arrangement is viable and sustainable, I will rest my case. The problem is that it is not. Here comes the second constraint: fiscal conditions. In recent years, China's fiscal revenue has grown much faster than GDP growth, which may make people dream big. In fact, despite the fast-growing fiscal revenue, China still has deficits, and the government still borrows a lot domestically and internationally, which means that our fiscal spending grows even faster and there are many more places to spend money. Take education for example, the government committed that education funding will be 4% of GDP, but is still yet to deliver this promise so far.

I have no objection to increasing the absolute sum and proportion of health expenditures—especially public health expenditures—out of the current total government expenditure. But there is one precondition: this increase has to be accompanied with a decrease for other items. In other words, doing the addition must be based on doing the subtraction. However, what happens now is that everybody does the addition, and no one does the subtraction, resulting in a higher and higher share of the government fiscal income in the GDP. If this trend is not reversed, the "domestic demand-driven growth" will be like water without a source. For this point, maybe it is necessary for experts from all departments to sit together in the same room and debate until the conclusion becomes clear. No one would disagree with significance and the great meaning of health, education, environment, public security; and of course, national defense is even more important. The problem is, everything is important, but where is the money? Continuously increasing the total tax burden to increase government income will inevitably lead to a huge problem.

This brings out the third constraint, the supervision of the public fiscal system and the administrative efficiency of government. I will not talk about corruption, because talking about it does not improve the situation. As for the use of the remaining public funds, I think whoever has read the Report of the State Auditor General will be impressed. As far as I am concerned, I haven't read about any similar scale of misuse of public funds in the UK in Beveridge's report, or in any other welfare state. As for other government extravagance, like fancy buildings, vehicle fleets, and the size of all open expenditures, people can get a feel from the everyday life even without looking at the statistics.

This is important. Because no matter which mode is adopted, the money needs to be put together and be managed by government agencies. If the government efficiency is poor, and corruption is common, then no matter how ambitious the goal is, the practice would be a totally different story, and a bigger portion of the public resources concentrated in the great name of "Health for All" may end up in the pockets of a handful of people with a vested interest. Therefore, we should never equate establishing a medical assurance account with the realization of HFA.

The actual conditions put a constraint on the reachable target for China's medical reform, and also on the selection of modes and timetable for realizing the target. It is easy to duplicate all sorts social welfare schemes from around the world, but not so easy to duplicate their constraints. There is more than one country and more than one government on this planet. Only by starting with its own constraints can China's healthcare reform avoid arousing a big public appetite and making undeliverable commitments.

11.9 The Only Key to the Medical Reform

In the end, it all comes down to reform to change the system, because only by sticking to reform can the success be attained for the medical reform. In fact, all my 40 published commentaries center on this theme. Here I would like make the conclusive highlights so that those who agree or disagree can see my point more clearly.

Some readers may ask, isn't it important to set a goal for the medical reform? After all, the goal is the general principle that guides the implementation of all measures in medical reform, why don't you treat the goal as the key to the reform? In my view, it is indeed important to set a goal for China's medical reform, but any well-intentioned goal must rely on a set of medical service system for the mobilization of resources and for its realization. No matter how good the goal is, without an effective reform, will it make any sense to just make empty talks without delivering the promises?

Take the HFA 2000 for example, a goal proposed by WHA 30 years ago. The Chinese government adopted this goal and has written it in several government reports. Now it is seven years beyond 2000, China still has not achieved the target; so the goal was rephrased to "primary health care for all by 2010". Of course, there is nothing wrong with it, and the tenacity is commendable. But what to do if this still is not delivered by that time? Why not just drop the deadline, just cry out the slogan and without realization forever? Then what benefit can this bring to the country and to the people?

In fact, WHO was not the first inventor. The "Tentative Charter of the Chayashan People's Commune (Draft)" published in September 1958, announces in black and white that "public medical care will be implemented in the commune". A charter is a mini-constitution, and the practice was popularized according to the written instructions from the great supreme leader. The purpose of the Charter was, of course, of great significance. "Public medical care" means "you don't have to pay anything to see a doctor", the highest degree of HFA. Yet, half a century has passed, you can go for yourself to the commune to check if that is true?

We do have some experience to refer to. DENG Xiaoping proposed in 1980 that "the per capita national income of China should be quadrupled by the end of this century". And by 2000, this goal was realized. Why is this goal achievable? Two experiences are essential. First, the goal is realistic rather than some wild goose chase. Second, the economic reform was initiated on full scale to cover agriculture, industry, commerce, foreign trade, and services sectors so as to stimulate the people's creativity and enthusiasm, and move towards a new system of allocating resources through the market mechanism. Looking back, it is clear that without the economic system reform, the goal of quadrupling cannot be achieved at all.

Why is the healthcare goal proposed several times and yet missed? The key is that the reform was not well carried out. In the early days, the government took care of each and everything, then with economic development, the system became for the government to administer everything but contribute no investment for hospital development, and then "allow hospitals to generate some revenue" within the framework of public medical care. This is a "reform" that does not open up market entry and makes money through administrative monopoly. It was already in 1997, only three years away from 2000, when the CPCCC and the State Council started to comprehensively deploy the reform of the healthcare system. How much of the 1997 target has the medical reform achieved? Opinions vary from person to person, and my view is that the reform has failed to advance in full swing till today. For instance, how much has been implemented in opening up to the domestic private and foreign investors, separation of supervision and management, restructuring of public hospitals, development of private hospitals, and loosening price regulation on medical services? According to the author's survey, to date China's medical reform is essentially a halfway project. Although the healthcare is accused of being over-marketized, in fact, except for a few regions and links, the comprehensive deep reform has not even started at all.

Therefore, I disagree that the future medical reform is all about "increasing fiscal funding", and that with the increased government budget we should return to the same old path for the "government to be responsible for each and every thing in healthcare" and cover it up with the "government-guided" principle. Some people think that the reform did not succeed in the past because the government did not have sufficient financial resources. Now and in the future, with improved national strength, the system for the "government to take care of everything" will surely be a success. My opinion is the opposite. No matter how strong the country's financial capacity is, such a medical system cannot effectively mobilize resources and will be unable to satisfy people's increasingly diverse and higher demands for medical services.

Actually, divorced from a comprehensive medical reform, even the single one target of "reasonably increasing fiscal appropriation for health care" cannot be achieved. First of all, the "public finance" system reform lays the foundation for the tax-payers rights to know, to make decisions via proxy, and to supervise and to participate in decision-making for the spending destination, structure and growth of the state financial resources. Without this reform, it would be difficult for the government to deliver its commitments on education, health, and people's well-being. What's more important is that all the expenditures need to be taken into overall consideration under the context of restricting the proportion of taxes out of the economy. Substantial increase in public medical care and other benefits without cutting other government spending, will generate long-term negative impacts on the national economy and the livelihood of the people. Anyway, the wool comes from the sheep. Excessive taxes, fiscal deficits, or oversupply of currency will eventually have catastrophic consequences for economic development, employment growth, and people's morale.

The importance of adhering to the reform, is also that any "free or low-cost medical service" resources centralized in the name of the people or the low-income crowd, cannot automatically become their fringe benefits. Without relevant mechanisms for information disclosure, supervision, and checks and balances, many "sounds good" systems will go sour after some time and become a "paradise" for a handful few to seek rent. For instance, the still-alive "public medical care" severely distorts behavior and leads to sever overtreatment; not only is it inefficient, but also not fair at all. Whether the future healthcare reform will take this problem seriously, let's wait and see.

Different from the popular thoughts on the healthcare reform, this article insists to deal with different sets of medical service demand and supply separately. The existing popular view has mistakenly expanded public health as a public welfare to all medical services, and universally excluded all public welfare services from the system which allocates the resources through market mechanism. My view is exactly the opposite: in the strict sense only public health is public welfare service and the explicit responsibility of the government, which implementation is guaranteed through its legal coercive force and tax resources. That being said, the government can also act according to the actual situation and buy public health welfare services from the market; only when the market is incapable of supplying, must the government provide such service by itself.

As for general medical services as "non-public goods", they can certainly be supplied through the market mechanism. There are many services in the market related to life and health, and indeed they need more rigorous supervision, but no experience and theory can prove that the market mechanism must be ruled out once the service is related to life and health. In concept, I disagree that life and health related services and for-profit market activities are against each other. Because the general experience, including many experiences from production and service sectors since the reform and opening up, has proved that for-profit market activities will significantly improve people's well-being more noticeably and more generally as long as we adhere to opening up the market, constraint by competition and universal property rights protection. For-profit activities under constraints care more about customer's needs, cost saving, service quality and branding, all of which helps with mobilizing rare resources to increase medical services.

I see no reason to exclude general medical services and pharmaceutical production from the market mechanism. The human, material, and financial factors for additional medical services are all scarce and all determined and mobilized in a competitive environment. Take human resources for example. A young man may or may not study medicine. He may study hard or not. After he graduates, he may work hard or not. It is the same way for a medical institution: it can work hard to build a brand, or it can get by with the red tape. All these branch-offs depend on the system, especially the incentives determined by the specific system. If the system and mechanism are not right, shouting slogans every day is useless. Chinese people had such experience and the memories are still so fresh; there is no reason to repeat the "experiment".

The biggest problem for China's medical services today is insufficient resource mobilization. In order to prevent the medical reform from turning from a "halfway project" into an "unfinished building", we need to seize the timing to open up the industry, separate regulation and governance, reform public hospitals, grant access to private institutions, and lift price regulation. The market economy momentum in China is irresistible, and resource allocation of any sector cannot be isolated from this big picture.

References

Haidong, Cao and Fu Jianfeng. 2005. Twenty Years of China's Medical Reform. *South Weekend*, August 4.

Qiren, Zhou. 2008. *Essays of Medical Care Reforms in China*. Beijing: Peking University Press.

Yiwei, Jiang. 1980. The Enterprise-Oriented Theory. *China Social Sciences* (1).

Chapter 12
Monetary System and Economic Growth

The new round of consumer price index (CPI) surge in China coincides with the first anniversary of the decease of Milton Friedman. Perhaps this indicates that the seemingly fading theory of monetarism does not disappear so easily, and it certainly reminds us that some important issues still deserve continued attention and research.

12.1 The Implication of Price Index?

China's CPI seems to have risen suddenly. The index growth rate stood at 2.2% at the beginning of 2007, rose to 6.5% in August, fell a little bit to 6.2% in September, came back to 6.5% in October, and reached 6.9% in November.[1] What do all these figures mean? The popular interpretation is that it is a "structural price rise", namely a price hike for some commodities accompanied by flat or even dropping prices for others, rather than an across-the-board price rise.

In my view, it sounds fair to call this phenomenon "structural price rise" because we do see the parallel existence of rising, flat and falling prices. The problem is that to do a weighted average of all the different pieces, one will find that the overall prices in China since August 2007 have not been unchanged, or let alone dropped, but continuously risen. In other words, China has inflation. What's important is that once the general trend of overall price rise is formed, it will affect people's expectation

[1] China's CPI growth in December 2007 was 6.5% (the annual reached 4.8%), 7.1% in January, and 8.7% in February of 2008. See NBS website (http://www.stats.gov.cn/tjsj/jdsj).

This article was based on the author's keynote speech at the 2007 Chinese Economics Annual Conference and was revised on April 29, 2008. The author would like to thank Professor HAI Wen and the host, the School of Economics of Shenzhen University for the invitation. He also would like to thank XUE Zhaofeng, LU Feng, YU Yongding, SONG Guoqing, WANG Dingding, and LIANG Hong for their discussion and input for the revision. Of course, the author's command principle still rules.

Q. Zhou, *Property Rights and Changes in China*,
https://doi.org/10.1007/978-981-15-9885-2_12

and change their behavior. For example, if many people believe that price is going to rise further, they will buy more, while sellers, with the same expectation of higher prices, will become reluctant and grudge selling their products and services. These two factors come together to make the short supply even worse, and the upward trend in overall prices may be self-enhancing.

From the price structure perspective, the attention may easily be drawn to the question why the prices of some commodities rise more than others? To dig on, one will find that international oil prices is a source. Soaring oil prices do have driven up not only the prices of downstream products but also the prices of substitutes, such as bio-energy, including corn ethanol, which then pushes up global food prices. The oil price hike also gives more direct rise to freight rates, and the consequence is that it is now more expensive to ship the grains that are bought at high prices. Everything in the economy is connected together, and the changes in the price of any commodity or service will bring about chain effect.

However, from the price rise of one individual commodity to the rise of overall prices, there is a key link, without which the rise in the price of one individual commodity will be offset by the decline in other commodities prices and an overall price rise will not be triggered. This "key link" is the amount of money circulating in the market. Only when there is too much money in the market, will the changes in price of one individual commodity not only change the price ratio for commodities, but also trigger constant overall price rise, namely inflation. For example, both Japan and South Korea are major oil importers, but the price level observed there is much flatter than China. Russia exports crude oil, but its inflation index is even higher than China's. These phenomena can all be explained by different monetary situations in different countries.

12.2 Inflation from the Monetary Perspective

Examining the changes in the price level from the monetary perspective is a tradition of classical economics. Of all the contemporary economists, Friedman is the staunchest supporter of this tradition. Incidentally, all his three visits to China (in 1980, 1988, and 1993) were made in the years of peak inflation for China.[2] We have no way of knowing whether the monetarist master was invited to China because the inflation rate was so high, or he came to China of his own accord because he thought that monetarism would be of great help to China. Anyway, the objective result is that in those years China was troubled by inflation, and thus more open to monetary thinking.

We can go back and check the script of Friedman's speeches in Beijing and Shanghai and the Q and A sessions. That was the first time when monetarism was introduced to Chinese audiences. This tradition does not discuss prices in terms of

[2]China's CPI increase in 1980 was 7.5% (only 0.7% in 1978), 18.8% in 1988, and 14.7% in 1993 (even up to 24.1% in 1994), see Table 9.1, *China Statistical Yearbook 2007*.

prices but considers the continuous price hike as a monetary phenomenon. According to this tradition, inflation is not about any specific commodity, be it oil, grains, pork, or milk; it is about money. Friedman reminds people to find the reason from the money supply when the overall price goes up. This line of thinking was quite inspirational to Chinese people. Because the traditional "price management" can neither fully understand nor effectively address inflation, we came to realize that only when we get rid of the way of thinking of seeking the reason for inflation from price changes of certain commodities can we divert people's attention towards currency, and then it will be easy for people to find that the sole reason for inflation is that there is too much money.

So, how does the amount of currency increase? This has something to do with monetary policy. Historically, since the end of the gold standard, currency issuance worldwide is controlled by national governments. By the gold standard, the issuance of currency is spontaneously determined by market forces, but the issuance of fiat money is determined by the central monetary authority. Monetarists believe that such a centralized currency issuance right is an institutional threat to the stability of currency and prices because the administrative authority is likely to misuse or even abuse the right for some short-term benefits. Regardless of the motive, once the currency issuance goes wrong, it will inevitably lead to distortion and disorder of countless economic behaviors. Individuals, families, businesses, and local governments cannot do anything about it. The result of abusing currency issuance right will definitely be hyperinflation, which happened in many countries throughout history. In this regard, Friedman inherited the legacy of his teacher Henry Simons and insisted that "rules should supercede authority", which means currency issuance rules need to be set to restrict the power of monetary authorities. Friedman himself also proposed a simple rule, that is, the amount of incremental money issued each year must not exceed the economic growth, for instance, 4%. He even proposed that a central bank is not needed at all and that a central computer system could control the currency issuance according to the set value to ensure the stability of the overall price level.

The trend was reversed not merely by the powerful logic of Monetarism, but more decisively by the damage caused by the raging inflation to many countries. The so-called "activism" theory and policy orientation got used to seeing "currency" as a policy instrument that serves such multiple goals as stimulating economic growth, creating jobs, and attaining internal and external balance of payments, and can be manipulated by the central monetary authority. However, the continued inflationary pressure and actual stagnation in developed countries created opportunities for the rise of monetarism. Friedman demonstrates that there is no long-term trade-off between inflation and unemployment, and he even discovers that even if the expansionary monetary policy comes with the temporary benefits of low unemployment, the resulting high inflationary costs are usually permanent. That is to say, the "monetary policy action" leaves too much freedom for opportunism, and thus will produce long-term "currency scourge".[3]

[3]Friedman (2007).

In retrospect, Friedman's most important contribution is to constantly warn people of the danger of such abuse of power in the era when the government takes control of currency issuance. As far as Friedman is concerned, inflation is not the product of market failure, but rather a gift with devastating impacts on economic freedom after the spontaneous strength of the market gets replaced by centralized administrative power. Monetarism insists that only zero inflation is the foundation for long-term economic growth and prosperity.[4] This idea can find evidence from historical experience. From the perspective of rights, inflation is a covert robbing of the property of everyone; from the perspective of transaction, it increases transaction costs, and leads to disordered economic behaviors and irrational resource allocation.

We have every reason to ridicule that the idea of having a computer to automatically determine the money supply is inoperable, as to date, no country has adopted the computer mechanism. Even the central computer takes place of the central bank in the imaginary world, it is nothing more than that the authority of the governor of the central bank is now converted to authority of the engineer for the central computer. In addition, as to how on earth to control the money supply, the theoretical principles of monetarism are by far not an operable reality.[5]

However, we cannot dismiss the constructive idea of monetarism. It insists on asking how to prevent the power of currency issuance from falling into the less reliable "visible hand", and can we set up an "impersonal" currency issuance mechanism for the modern credit and currency system? This question is not something conceived out of thin air; because historically in the gold standard system, it was the diffused precious metal distribution and decentralized mining power that "determined" the currency supply of various countries. Since so, while modern currency saves the cost of precious metal mining, can we find an "impersonal" mechanism for the credit system to anchor the currency?

12.3 The Currency Anchoring Challenge

Now we must mention the Austrian school, which is more retro in the monetary framework. These economists, like the Chicago school of monetarism, believe that a free and prosperous economy must be built on a stable currency. However, they believe that a spontaneous market can provide such a stable currency, such as the gold standard in human history, because if the precious metal itself acts as the currency anchor, it will not provide any "visible hand" with the opportunity to manipulate the currency. To get out of the quagmire of frequent inflations created by modern

[4]Skousen (2006), Chapters 3 and 5.

[5]Friedman's proposal to directly control money supply rather than interest rates was practiced by the governor of the central bank of the US (the Federal Reserve) for one term in the 1970s, but the result was very bad, and the interest rate once rose to 21%, which was completely unacceptable. Therefore, since then, all Fed chairmen has returned to interest rate regulation, of which Friedman did not approve, and conducted open market operations against bank interest rates and market interest rates so as to adjust the money supply.

currency, many economists of the Austrian school advocate going back to the gold standard or commodity-based currency system to restore the free banking system, which allows free access, full competition, and survival of the fittest in the market, and eventually all parties using the currency shall choose at their own volition a trustworthy bank.[6]

Hayek later acknowledged that restoring the gold standard under modern conditions is not possible, and "even if possible, it is likely to be undesirable."[7] However, it is precisely because the monetary power seems to be unavoidably centralized in the hands of the government that Hayek has found the root cause of continued inflation after the demise of the gold standard -short-term pressure makes it extremely difficult for the government, private enterprises, and the public to resist inflation.[8] Hayek was apprehensive about this and repeatedly explored the possible path to constrain the central monetary authority when it is not an option to go back to the gold standard. From Simmons's "appropriate rule" to "a commodity reserve standard", and then to sliding-scale contract, which is a contract linked to an inflation index, Hayek analyzed them one by one and found that the contemporary monetary system cannot do without discretionary monetary power, and so each of the above "solutions" have its share of problems. So, what is the solution to the monetary framework? Hayek concluded, "we have little choice but to limit monetary policy by prescribing its goals rather than its specific actions"[9]—as understand, this is the theoretical precursor of Inflation Targeting that originated in New Zealand a few decades later and swept across many countries.[10]

The above review tells us that from a monetary perspective, there are a series of problems regarding inflation that have not yet been fully resolved. In comparison, the term structural price rise simply draws the attention to certain commodities with big price increases. The point is that if it is indeed the total amount of money that has caused the rise in the overall price level, then controlling only the prices of certain commodities will not help. On the contrary, the practice to regulate the prices by the prices will only make rising prices spread to other commodities. See if we control the oil price, the food price will go up; if we control the food price, the pork price will

[6]These arguments show that the Austrian school is even more "disconnected from reality" than monetarism. As Mark Skousen said unless the public and politicians fully trust the spontaneous market-which is not likely-the gold standard plus the free banking system can bring no less trouble than the central computer of monetarism (Skousen 2006). From a purely interpretive perspective, there is always certain reasons for the demise of the gold standard. For example, can't the sudden outflow of precious metals cause serious damage to a country's economy? Perhaps we can say that it is the inherent defects of the gold standard that provide the nation-state's political machine with the opportunity to control the currency.

[7]His reasoning is that once modern business organizations rely heavily on credit institutions, "it is a must that we exercise a sort of deliberate control over the interaction between the monetary and the credit system" (Hayek 1997: 96).

[8](Hayek 1997: 105).

[9]Specifically, "financial institutions must control prices within a certain well-known limit so that they do not exceed this limit-or even make it impossible for them to approach such a level; otherwise, they must make major corrections to their policies". (Hayek 1997: 111).

[10]For international experience on inflation targeting, see Bernanke et al. (2006).

go up; and if we control the pork price, the milk price will go up. This piecemeal fix seems to be targeted, but in the end, it brings two results: first, it misses the window of opportunity to pull the plug, namely tighten the money supply; second, it strengthens the public's inflation expectations since the price goes up for one commodity after another. The combination is likely to exacerbate inflation.

Another specious theory is the "cost-driven inflation" theory. Admittedly, higher price of food and other consumer goods makes workers demand higher wages; higher purchase price causes stores to raise the selling price, and higher costs of inputs causes the company to ask for higher prices of its outputs—these reasonings are all reasonable. The question is, under what conditions can all these reasonable requirements be satisfied? We still have to find the answer in the total amount of money supplied. If there is not too much money supply, at most the higher cost will push up the prices of only some commodities, while other cost claims will not be accepted. Everyone facing higher costs wants a higher price, but the total amount of money is fixed at such a level, how could it be possible to have a cost increase across the board that drives up the overall price level?

This way, the core proposition of monetarism that "inflation is a monetary phenomenon" really makes sense. Just as some critics point out, this proposition is the same as "saying that to fire is merely a phenomenon of shooting, it is nothing but tautology".[11] Even though it is a tautology, it is the correct one, because it directly points to the root of inflation—monetary. Compared to other confusing propositions, for example, to claim that inflation is a price phenomenon, a cost phenomenon, or even a conscience phenomenon (businessmen forcing up the prices, hoarding, etc.), etc., the monetarist proposition helps us to find the cause of inflation from the money supply.

12.4 Different Causes of Excessive Currency Issuance

As mentioned above, it is the government that decides the currency issuance after the end of the gold standard. In this context, to say that inflation is a monetary phenomenon is equivalent to saying that "inflation is a phenomenon for the government to issue excessive money". Next, we need to study why the government does so. Historically, most inflations, especially hyperinflations, are with no exception, the result of maintaining fiscal spending through cash printer by the government, be it for war, for the luxury needs of monarchs, or for the fulfillment of huge social welfare commitments. Generally speaking, inflation caused by war is often the most outrageous, because the authority will surely drive the machine of inflation to its maximum limit. In the late 1940s, the inflation rate in China was as high as 50% per month. Mr. JI Xianlin was a professor at the Kuomintang controlled region, and

[11] "Inflation is a monetary phenomenon in the same way that shooting someone is a ballistic phenomenon" (Henry Wallich), (Quoted from Roger Bootle 2004: 181).

he said that in those days he had to rush out to buy rice the minute he received his salary; otherwise, the price would be skyrocketing.

In peacetime, inflations are often the result of printing money for construction. China in the past practiced a concept of "supra-economic issuance", meaning the government prints more money to support the scale of capital construction beyond the national strength. Because a full price regulation was implemented at that time, the excessive money would not immediately be manifested in the rise in the general price level, but rather in the form of "hidden inflation", which means that nothing can be bought on the market, i.e. an era of general shortage. Different forms lead to the same result: in explicit inflation money is worthless, in hidden inflation you have money but you cannot buy anything; in both cases money is not so useful. In the Soviet era, every housewife went into the street with a big bag, and they would join any queue they saw without asking any questions. That's not the cultural tradition of Russia!

Each of China's three inflation peaks since the reform and opening up has a different reason. The 7.5% CPI in 1980 was unthinkable in the previous "low-price" era. Actually at that time, the coupon system was still there to suppress the general demand, but to facilitate agriculture growth, the state raised the purchase price of grains and edible oil from 1979 and provided financial subsidies to urban residents. The financial strength was weak, and the subsidies for agricultural product price adjustments became the new impetus for fiscal deficits and excessive supply of money. China's CPI in 1988 was as high as 18.9%. On the surface, it was caused by the price reform. The root cause from behind was printing money for construction plus printing money for the price reform. China's inflation hit the historical high in 1994 since the founding of PRC, mainly due to the lack of local financial resources and the eagerness to build projects, and the loosened bank loans under "soft constraints" forced the central bank to issue excessive money. Viewed this way, the three inflation peaks has one thing in common: excessive currency issuance under the pressure of fiscal expenditures.

The direct cause of the most recent inflation is, indeed again too much money; however, as the country's financial strength have been unprecedentedly improved in the past ten years, and the institution no longer allows to use supra-economic issuance to make up for the fiscal deficit, plus commercial banks have been restructured to establish restrictions on loans. In other words, the previous mechanism for excessive currency issuance is gone, but there is still too much money out there, why?

In May 2003, Professor SONG Guoqing led a macroeconomic study, and the summary of the report was printed as a draft for internal discussion by China Center for Economic Research (CCER) at Peking University in September of the same year.[12] This study analyzes China's macroeconomic policies of stimulating the aggregate demand since 1998. It argues that due to the sharp reduction in deposit and loan interest rates, improved enterprise profitability, the policy to attract foreign investment and rapid FDI growth, enterprise capital increased substantially, causing

[12]See the CCER research group (2003). For public reports, see "Does the Macroeconomic Policy Need a Turnaround?".

drastic increase in bank loans. Moreover, because of the stable exchange rate, the rapid growth of China's exports has pushed up the aggregate demand. Based on the above, SONG believes that the Chinese economy which has stepped out of deflation is facing a turning point, and he predicts with certainty that "there is now a possibility to go to a high inflation."

The "stable exchange rate" mentioned above has become a key to understanding the overall situation. The background is that after China successfully corrected the over-valuated Renminbi (RMB) with the market exchange rate in 1993, it originally chose a managed and market demand-based exchange rate system instead of a fixed rate or a USD pegging system. However, as the currencies of neighboring countries were forced to depreciate significantly after the 1997 Asian Financial Crisis, the international community hoped that Renminbi would not depreciate, and the Chinese government also made a public commitment. So, the exchange rate of 1:8.27 was maintained from 1998 to July 2005, making the RMB exchange rate an unannounced, but de facto US dollar pegging system.

The post-1998 decade coincided with the period when years of China's drastic reform and opening-up program paid off. The most obvious manifestation is that productivity growth rate of China's exports surpassed that of the United States and other developed economies. This significant change of the real economy was in conflict with the "stable exchange rate" mechanism, because the almost unchanged exchange rate has made China's export products cheaper and cheaper under significantly improved productivity, thereby stimulating a robust global demand for China's products and driving China's export growth. As a result, China's trade surplus has increased significantly. The stable exchange rate, coupled with the opening-up policy, also stimulated the influx of foreign capital into China, resulting in a sustained double surplus not ever seen in the history of major economies. This opened a new channel for Renminbi issuance: all trade surpluses and foreign capital entering China are converted into RMB through the settlement of foreign exchange at China's banks. As the central bank keeps buying foreign currencies and continuously increasing the foreign exchange reserve of the country, it is also continuously issuing the base currency.

Therefore, SONG believes that "the exchange rate is the key link".[13] Because only by increasing the flexibility of the RMB exchange rate can China's balance its external and domestic demand, and avoid the potential danger of pushing up the aggregate demand by the too prosperous exports. He believes that special attention should be paid to the co-ordination between foreign-related policies and monetary policies. He suggests that the RMB be appreciated by 10%, or a policy combination be adopted to partially appreciate the RMB and adjust import and export duties at the same time so as to correct the imbalance between the major macro variables. Considering that China's foreign exchange reserves in 2003 were only $ 400 billion, and the annual trade surplus was $ 25.4 billion, and the CPI of that year was only 1.2%, I think SONG's research has valuable foresight.

---

[13]Song Guoqing (2005).

However, the mainstream opinions at that time were against RMB appreciation. In September 2003, Professor YU Yongding published an article to propose his disagreement with almost one-sided voice of opposing RMB appreciation from current media and economists.[14] YU is not proposing substantial RMB appreciation; instead, he proposes a managed floating exchange rate, which allows the RMB to appreciate slightly. YU clearly refuted all sorts of arguments against RMB appreciation. He examined the central bank's practice of buying lots of U.S. Treasury bonds and other USD-denominated assets while having to do cross hedging for the rapidly growing base currency, and argued that it seems that no country can do cross hedging operations long term without causing severe negative impact on the normal operation of its own currency system. To refute the popular interpretation of seeing the Japanese yen appreciation after the Plaza Accord in 1985 as the reason for Japan's asset bubbles and the deflationary crises, YU believes that internationally renowned economists, including McKinnon, have overlooked a key condition: Japan adopted an expansionary monetary policy in 1987. Germany also appreciated its currency in 1985, it did not take a similar move to ease its monetary policy, so it did not fall into a Japanese-style dilemma. This is a strong counter-evidence against the claim that "appreciation will inevitably lead to a trap, like what happened in Japan."

12.5 Macro Imbalance Undermines Foundation for China's Economic Growth

In fact, the proposal for a slight appreciation of the RMB was not accepted by the end of 2004. As a result, the aggregate demand was enhanced by wrong exchange rate, and the national economy started to see signs of "overheating". China's total economy was already very large, and the proportion of imports and exports in GDP is unprecedented for all major countries. Therefore, the call of stabilizing the exchange rate must be manifested somehow. So in July 2005, China announced to return to the "managed floating exchange rate" mechanism, but at this time, the very slight RMB appreciation against the US dollar was not enough to correct the growing macro imbalance; and what is worse, it created the new problem of more foreign capital entering China. That is to say, while the old double-surplus pressure has not been removed, the new pressure from hot money is added. As a result, "the trade surplus, FDI, and hot money have made China's currency liquidity flow like the rushing Yellow River."[15]

The cumulative changes in the currency landscape had to be reflected by the market. After 2004, China's urban residents experienced a sharp rise in real estate prices that were never seen in Chinese history. The Shanghai Stock Exchange Index rose from 1000 points to more than 6000 points in 2006. The stock market turnover in 2007 was five times that of the previous year. In the niche market, from antiques to

[14] Yu Yongding (2003).

[15] Zhou Qiren (2007).

calligraphy, from paintings to jewelry, from luxury goods to Pu'er tea, the prices have made one record after another – there are different reasons for all this events, but they share one thing in common: there was too much money. China's economy before 2007 was seen as "high growth and low inflation", which, of course, makes sense. Because inflation is generally defined by CPI, and China's average CPI from 2000 to 2006 was only 1.45% (the highest in 2004 was 3.9%). However, the currency-driven overall price rise has long taken place here and there, but it just didn't burst into the CPI until after August 2007, and those underestimating the importance of RMB exchange rate had to evade the topic.

Public opinions can be elusive. In 1997 when the international community, especially the developed countries, hoped that the RMB would not be depreciated, China made a commitment and honored it. Public opinions responded positively, and everyone was proud of China being a "responsible power". However, after 2003, as China's trade surplus increased, Japan, the United States, and other developed countries asked to appreciate RMB. The public sentiment was that China must not submit to international pressure. Anyone who votes for RMB appreciation is regarded as to yield to external pressure and as a traitor. Also conversely, anyone from the West who advocates that the RMB should not be appreciated is regarded as a true friend who safeguards China's interests. Such an unfathomable contrast, of course, cannot be explained by economics. By the time when inflation started its play in 2007, the public began to wonder "why RMB is appreciating outside China yet depreciating inside China?", it is the responsibility of economists to explain that the movements in both directions originated from the same economic force.

However, the dominant economic thinking since 2003 still focuses only on the price structure but ignores the general price level. Hence come such judgments as structural overheating, structural real estate bubble, structural stock market bubbles and structural price rise, and so on. Sure, structural problems forever exist in economic life, and naturally even more so for China's economy which is under transformation. However, the direct consequence of ignoring or evading the total amount of currency is the inability to fully leverage such tools as exchange rates and interest rates to regulate the total supply, and the government has to use more administrative orders, decrees and regulations, or even resort to direct control over the supply of key production factors (such as land) to impose direct intervention in certain products, certain industries or even certain companies. This only makes the structural problems worse, and shakes people's consensus and determination to solve specific economic problems through the market-oriented reform.

This is no trivial matter because it involves the fundamentals of China's economic growth. In recent years, many people at home and abroad believe that China's increased competitiveness in the international market is due to China's cheap labor. Since 2004, the author has been criticizing this view.[16] I simply ask back: 30 years ago, China's labor was even cheaper both in cities and in the countryside, why didn't we see "Made in China" across all global markets? I agree that it is the "cost advantage" that enables China's economy to make its way into the world market; yet in

[16]Zhou Qiren (2006: 7–23).

this cost advantage, what's most important is that China's institutional costs have been significantly reduced through reform and opening up, and that the incentives for Chinese people, enterprises and local governments have changed, turning cheap and originally poverty-stricken labor into China's competitiveness, and improving product quality through the improvement in the learning curve. In a nutshell, the improvement of China's competitiveness is driven by the decline of institutional costs. I have also noticed that the institutional costs, like other costs, will rise after falling. Therefore, only by adhering to reform and opening up and institutional innovation, can we continue to maintain the momentum of China's economic growth. From this perspective, the long-term price of increasing the micro-level administrative control to deal with the macro-imbalance, is to damage the foundation for China's economic growth.

Among all the opinions against RMB appreciation, Steven N. S. Cheung is unique.[17] As far as I am concerned, his point is that the problem with RMB is not about appreciation against the US dollar, but about de-pegging from the US dollar. However, before the de-pegging, we need to determine what should be the future anchor for RMB. In his view, in RMB's US dollar pegging or linking, the USD serves as the "nominal anchor", now to depeg, RMB would face the question of what should be the anchor. If we depeg without finding the anchor, RMB will face the risk of becoming an unguided missile. Cheung's suggestion is to peg RMB to a basket of currencies so that it will have its nominal anchor before de-pegging from USD. He also believes that China can considering to take a further step and release RMB to overseas so as to realize its potential advantage as a strong international currency.

From this perspective, Cheung's repeated statements against the appreciation of RMB is the opinion on exchange rate and monetary policy. However, no matter which set of commodities are selected as the anchor for RMB, it is inevitable to see RMB appreciated substantially against USD from the market price of 2003. The problem is, to identify a new anchor is much more difficult than to appreciate RMB under the current exchange rate regime, and therefore, it is more difficult to reach consensus. As to whether or not RMB should remain pegged to USD before this problem gets resolved depends on the actualities. Unfortunately, USD is not as strong as before. Pegging to the dollar without appreciation not only makes things difficult for the United States but also makes things worse and worse for China's own currency. At least by 2007, when signs of inflation re-emerged in China, it is practically impossible for RMB to de-peg from USD after changing its anchor, the only way is to accelerate appreciation within the existing foreign exchange framework. As to RMB internationalization, it will not be feasible until the RMB exchange rate roughly reflects market supply and demand. These days when lots of money from across the

[17]From May 23, 2003 when he began to publish "On Exchange Rate Strategy" (a series of 5 articles in total), to November 2007 when he wrote "The Dilemma of the RMB" (also a series of five articles in total), Cheung wrote a total of 50 articles on RMB exchange rate, all of which can be found in his SINA blog or SOHU blog.

world wants to enter China, if we release RMB to overseas, we still cannot prevent it from flowing back.[18]

At least by the end of 2007, China's economic situation clearly revealed the key of problem. Now China's foreign exchange reserve reached as high as US$ 1.5 trillion (not including the US$ 200 billion capital injection into China Investment Corp.), the trade surplus reached US $ 280 billion, and FDI to China reached US $ 300 billion. The rapid growing foreign exchange reserve faced the big risk of USD depreciation and social welfare losses, while accelerating inflation is worsening at home. Even if the central bank kept on hedging the currency, the proportion of "foreign exchange" in broad money supply (M3) still managed to increase to nearly 30 from 15% in 2003. In the first 11 months of 2007, M3 in China increased by 23.1% year-on-year.[19] Inflation, as a monetary phenomenon, finally emerged, and began to trigger the long-suppressed inflation expectations of the public, and repeatedly demonstrated that it was not driven by the cost rise of a handful of commodities.

By this moment the problem stay unresolved, but the scale has doubled. The US dollar is becoming weaker over the years. With the impact of the subprime mortgage crisis, the US economy has slowed down, China's export sectors face even more painful adjustment with the forced and accelerated RMB appreciation. In hindsight, had RMB appreciated by 10% in 2003, the price paid today should have been much smaller. But in the chess game of history, a move is a move, and you simply cannot go back. To avoid greater damage in the future, China needs to pull the plug and find answers from the excessive currency and the rampant liquidity to cope with increasing inflationary pressures.

To conclude, although CPI is a basic indicator for inflation, its structural analysis cannot help people understand the real cause of inflation. Inflation is not about any specific commodity, it is about money, namely the currency in circulation. When CPI rises, we need to find the cause and solution from the oversupply of money. The reason for China's current high inflation is also excessive currency issuance; but unlike the fiscal motives of a number of previous inflations in history, the main reason for the current excessive monetary supply is the distortion of the exchange rate mechanism. When inflation is already here, price control will not only be unable to curb it, but also undermine the foundation of China's economic growth with unjustified incremental institutional costs. To fight the inflation, we need to pull the plug to remove the root cause, namely to correct the exchange rate imbalance and tightly control the total supply of money.

[18]However from the institutional perspective, Professor Cheung's suggestion that China should choose a new currency anchor (standard) is of great value. Even though the proposed "a basket of currencies standard" faces technical and cognitive difficulties, his exploration into an impersonal currency issuance mechanism, just like what the Chicago monetarists and the Austrian school representatives have done, has far-reaching significance.

[19]The central bank issues central bank papers to hedge the excessive RMB base currency. First, the hedging cannot fully cover all the excess; second, the bank papers issued by the central bank cannot be fully seen as non-currency, since the central bank papers issued to monetary fund and insurance industry can be used in the market.

References

Bernanke, Ben S. et al. 2006. *Inflation Targeting: International Experience*, trans. Sun Gang, Qian Yong and Wang Yu. Sichuan province: The Press of Northeast University of Finance and Economics.

Bootle, R. 2004. *Inflation and Deflation*, trans. Liu Xiliang. Sichuan province: The Press of Southwest University of Finance and Economics.

Friedman, Milton. 2007. *Money Mischief: Episodes in Monetary History*, trans. An Jia. Beijing: Commercial Press

Guoqing, Song. 2005. Exchange Rate Is the Key. *Securities Market Weekly*, July 4.

Research Task Force of China Center for Economic Research (CCER) at Peking University. 2003. *Stepping out of Deflation and RMB Exchange Rate: A Summary*, September.

Skousen, Mark. 2006. *Vienna & Chicago: Friends or Foes?* trans. Yang Peilei. Shanghai: Shanghai People's Press.

Qiren, Zhou. 2006. Interpreting China's Economic Growth. *Take the Lamp to Examine the Sword*. Beijing: Peking University Press.

Qiren, Zhou. 2007. Unequivocally Opposing Inflation. *Economic Observer*, December 3.

von Hayek, Friedrich. 1997. *The Constitution of Liberty*, trans. Deng Zhenglai. Beijing: SDX Joint Publishing Company.

Yongding, Yu. 2003. Removing the Fright for RMB appreciation and Achieving the Transition to Balanced Economic Development. *International Economic Review* (9–10).

Chapter 13
System Cost and China's Economy

This paper aims to analyze China's economic growth through the concept of system cost which is the cost associated with the establishment, running and the changes of institutions. From 1978 to 2008, a significant reduction of system cost driven by reforms and opening up had helped China achieve an average 10% annual real GDP growth. However China's system cost has risen again over the past decade, evidenced by its higher than GDP growth in taxes and the fees, rent seeking, corruption and extravagant spendings in the public sector. China needs a series of a structure reforms that can again significantly reduce its system cost so as to achieve sustainable growth.

China's economy has long attracted global attention. However, people have divergent understanding, interpretation, and judgment of its success. This article is based on one perspective to join the discussion, with the central argument being that system cost is the key for the rapid growth of China's economy and its subsequent evolution.

13.1 The New Question: Interpreting Ups and Downs of China's Economy

Since the reforms and opening-up, China's economy has been growing rapidly for three decades. This phenomenon has been systematically reviewed by economists. In July 2008, Nobel laureate Prof. Ronald Coase, who was nearly 100-year-old at time, organized Conference on China's Economic Transformation at the University of Chicago to summarize China's experience with economic system reform. At the end of the year, the National Bureau of Statistics (NBS) issued an announcement

This article was published in *China Economic Quarterly* 16(3), 2017. The draft was first reviewed by WANG Dingding, XUE Zhaofeng, LU Feng, LIU Shouying, LI Lixing, WANG Min, WANG Yue, ZHANG Huiqiang, etc. with recommended revisions. Anonymous reviewers of *China Economic Quarterly* proposed some revisions. The author has given full consideration to all the comments and recommendations with appreciation. It is the author and not any other person to be responsible for the content of this paper.

Q. Zhou, *Property Rights and Changes in China*,
https://doi.org/10.1007/978-981-15-9885-2_13

that China's economic growth rate was 9.6% in 2008, although it was lower than the previous year, but still above the 30-year average since 1978. In the following year, China surpassed Japan to become the second-largest economy in the world. Then after another year, China became the world's largest exporter. In 2013, China became the world's largest trader. In 2014, the International Monetary Fund (IMF) announced that based on purchasing power parity, China's economic scale had overtaken the US, making China world's number one.[1]

Compared with the late 1970s, China's economy has made remarkable achievements, which also inspired academia to sum up China's success. After all, it was no incidental for such a large and populous country to achieve such miraculous results. On par with this economic miracle, there should be major academic establishment on China's economy. Therefore, roughly around 2008, people were no longer contented with just taking China as a case to verify existing economic theories; instead, they were determined to extract new theories and new thoughts from China's experience.[2]

However, economic theories may not always develop in tandem with economic achievements. When Adam Smith published *The Wealth of Nations* in 1776, it was only seven years after Watts invented the first single-acting steam engine, and at best, England was still in the early days of the industrial revolution. At that time, people could not perceive the blueprint depicted in *The Communist Manifesto* published 70-plus years later—"The bourgeoisie, during its rule of scarce one hundred years, has created more massive and more colossal productive forces than have all preceding generations together". In Adam Smith's era, the British economy had experienced only in a long period of slow growth. The vast majority of companies he saw at the time were still small, and there were only a few big companies like the East India Company with a royal charter, about which Smith was not upbeat. Meanwhile, the living standard of Britain seemed only mediocre, even lacking.[3]

It was under such economic basis that classical political economics which sufficed to influence the economic thinking for generations, was born. With this as a reference, even Adam Smith himself would be amazed at the 30 years of rapid growth of China's economy if he were alive today. It was only natural to expect an academic outcome that was commensurate with China's economic performance. But the problem is, the greater the ambition, the greater the challenges. Rightly starting from 2008,

[1]For economic growth rate in 2008 and the previous 30 years, see NBS of the People's Republic of China (2013: 45); for IMF figures, see America Usurped: China Becomes World's Largest Economy, (http://www.dailymail.co.uk/news/article-2785905/China-overtakes-U-S-world-s-largest-economy-IMF-says-economy-worth-17-6trillion-America-falls-second-place-time-1872.html).

[2]For example, Cheung announced in his unique style that "I never saw such a good institution in China." (See reports from http://news.ifeng.com/opinion/200809/0912.23_780811.Shtml). He also announced that he had decrypted the code of China's economic system (see *The Economic System of China*). For other publications on the China Model, see "Eyes on the Chinese model", on the Theory Channel of people.cn (http://theory.people.com.cn/GB/40557/149513/).

[3]In 1773 when Smith traveled a mere 410 miles from Edinburgh to London to publish his masterpiece, he had to take a public carriage, which operated only once a month, on a bumpy road for 10 to 15 days. Even worse, he had to sign his will before he went off because the journey was never safe (Ross 2010: 401).

China's economic growth presented some new changes. Although the high growth was sustained in 2009 and 2010 due to the imposition of strong stimulus policies, downward pressure eventually came up. In retrospect, China's GDP growth for the first quarter of 2007 converted to annual rate hit 15%, representing an unprecedented highest peak for an epical growth period. Just a few years later, the growth rate of the world's second-largest economy was slashed by more than a half.

This entails a new question, how to interpret the ups and downs of China's economy? The cause for the marvelous growth and the downturn can be dealt with and figured out separately. But if we are not complacent with this and hope to obtain a systematic understanding of the dramatic changes in China's economy from a succinct framework, we have to make more efforts. The text below starts with a core concept and attempts to expand the relevant analysis.

13.2 System Cost Implications

This concept is system cost. The "cost" as everyone is familiar with, is the price that any economic actor has to pay in order to obtain the benefit. Cost includes monetary or non-monetary, time, energy and spirit related indispensable efforts, abstracted as necessary expenditures in pursuit of any benefit, and it constitutes the most essential constraint on economic behaviors. However, for a long time in the past, the focus of business people, economists and experts on management was only the production cost, i.e. all the expenditures that have to occur in order to produce something. Only after the modern economy featured by mass production and high-volume transactions took shape, did the non-production costs start to attract attention. In 1937, Prof. Coase, a young scholar then, first proposed the concept of "transaction costs", as he found that to use the price mechanism for resource allocation itself is not cost free. Coase believes that it is because the transaction costs is positive that the market has the diversified enterprises (firms) and economic organizations, which has been overlooked by previous economics thinking. This plain discovery has changed the foundation of modern economics.[4]

Coincidentally, Pei-kang Chang, a young Chinese economist, put forward a concept of "pure commercial expenses"[5] in the 1930s when he was studying economic issues related to the War Against Japanese Aggression. He observed that the Chinese farmers in Hunan, Jiangxi and other provinces, were very poor, although the rice production costs was very low the rice from China's hinterland was unable to compete with the rice imported afar from Thailand in the grain markets in coastal cities such as Ningbo. After careful investigation, Pei-kang Chang found that the high cost of doing business was the problem. To sell grains from the producing hinterland to coastal cities, one had to overcome local separatism, excessive blackmailing by each checkpoint and all sorts of persistent problems, which came together to push the

[4]Coase (1937).

[5]Pei-kang Chang (1940).

otherwise-would-be competitive rice from the hinterland out of the coastal market. Hence his conclusion was, if the commercial channels were effectively improved to save the pure commercial expenses, China's wartime food supply would be improved. Given that he had no access at all to the aforementioned paper by Coase (1937), it is fair to say that a Chinese scholar had discovered on his own that there were other costs in addition to production costs.[6] This again shows that there is an opportunity for scholars to come up with a new concept to explain the observed anomalies when they rise up to the real world.

After years of silence, "transaction costs" finally caught the attention of the academic community and got interpreted further. In 1969, Kenneth J. Arrow, who later received the Nobel Prize in Economics, pointed out that transaction costs proposed by Coase is precisely "the costs of running the economic system".[7] He, therefore, linked up Coase's economic theorem with classical economics because scholars of Adam Smith's generation cared most about the operation of the economic system rather than isolated and sporadic economic activities. On the other hand, some of Coase's followers extended the concept of transaction costs into institutional costs.[8] For example, when Steven N.S. Cheung composed the entry for "Economic Organizations and Transaction Costs" for the New Palgrave Dictionary of Economics in 1987, he points out: "So defined, transaction costs may then be viewed as a spectrum of institutional costs including those of information, of negotiation, of drawing up and enforcing contracts, of delineating and policing property rights, of monitoring performance, and of changing institutional arrangements. In short, they comprise all those costs not directly incurred in the physical process of production."[9] It means that in addition to production costs, what needs to be paid is far more than the transaction costs in the narrow sense.[10]

In the real world, institutions are ubiquitous. People must follow specific property rights and contractual arrangements for all economic activities such as production, consumption, saving, and investment; and they all set up specific organizations and institutions, such as families, communities, enterprises, markets, currency systems, the legislation, taxation and policy making authorities, the government, and a series of surveillance departments. These interwoven organizations, organs and policies were not only spontaneously formed as a result of the voluntary choice by individuals, but were also built by the influence of the customs, popular ideas and

[6]Zhou Qiren (2006).

[7]Arrow (1969: 48).

[8]North (1990); Steven N.S. Cheung (1987).

[9]Steven N.S. Cheung (1987: 58).

[10]Take China for example. In the era of the planned economy, many behaviors and activities were enormously costly, although they may not be related to direct production or be regarded as transactions in the narrowest sense. These include: provinces and cities swapping allocated goods, local governments lobbying the central planning department for investment and construction projects, farmers trading products produced from their private land plot on the black market at the risk of "the capitalist tails being cut", and the movements one after another.

social enforcement.[11] Therefore, to advance further from transaction costs (or "pure commercial expenses") and institutional costs, we must shift the focus of our observation and research onto systematic institutions; in particular, we must follow how the socially enforced organizations and policies influence individuals' choices and, thus, economic operations.

System cost in this paper refers to a cost that must be paid in economic operations. A system is comprised of a series of institutions that are operated based on socially enforced property rights and contracts. Any resources consumed by the establishment, running, and change of the system constitute system cost. The nature of and changes in system cost have a huge impact on economic growth.

Compared with the concept of "transaction costs" in the narrow sense and the "pure commercial expenses", "system cost" cannot only be extended to the analysis of various non-market transaction behaviors, but also deepen the general interpretation of both market and non-market behaviors. Market transactions are usually seen as a combination of interest-guided voluntary choices and contracts, and therefore they do not involve those mandatory forces and mechanisms, including legal coercion. However, system cost is different. As a set of constraints to shape human behaviors in the real world, the socially coercive forces, including popular ideas, government power, and the derived policies—prohibitions or permissions, it is an indispensable element in the economic system from the very beginning. The observation and analysis of system cost involve state behavior and naturally the theory on the state. Unlike the institutional costs, system cost places the emphasis on the entire systematic institutions rather than a single policy or sporadic institutional arrangements; in particular, it focuses on the constraints of social-norm coercive forces itself that governs spontaneous and voluntary behaviors. Looking back, the narrow sense transaction costs and unitary institutional costs can be seen as part of, or special cases in system cost. Our cognition starts from local and special cases and moves on to the general abstraction.

13.3 The Secret of China's Miracle: Drastic Reduction of System Cost

The rapid economic growth in China was by no means a natural phenomenon. When China formulated the Sixth Five-Year Plan (1981–1985) in 1980, the average annual growth target was only set at 4%, with 5% as the stretch target.[12] Why did China set a target which was later regarded as underestimating its own potential at the start point of a rapid growth?

---

[11] Alchian (1987) pointed out that "socially enforced" is essential to property rights. After him, North (1990) introduced state behavior into the analysis of institutional changes.

[12] For the Sixth Five-Year Plan (1981–1985) for Economic and Social Development of the People's Republic of China, http://www.npc.gov.cn/wxzl/gongbao/1982-11/30/content_1478459.htm.

That is because, at that time, China's economy was facing a hurdle that was seemingly impossible to overcome. The biggest problem was how to feed the one billion people, of which 800 million were farmers. The farmers, accounting for the vast majority of the population, were destitute and unable to support industrial or urban development. So why was agriculture so backward and the farmers so poor? The answer lies in the formidable system obstacles: no matter how badly the government hoped to develop agricultural production and how eager the hundreds of millions of farmers were to improve their livelihood, the performance of the economic system simply was unsatisfactory and unable to open the valve to encourage more agricultural production.

What led to such a quagmire was not a single institution or a single policy, but rather the sum of systematic and interwoven ideas, institutional arrangements, and policy measures. First, the people's commune system featured by collective labor and egalitarian distribution. Although the system enjoyed, to some extent, the benefit from economy of scale, it was difficult to stimulate farmers' production enthusiasm because of the difficulties in the accurate measurement of the efforts and contributions from individual members. Not just that, the collective production model often suffered severe losses due to erroneous commands and arbitrary orders. Secondly, the establishment of collective ownership of rural land no longer needed to and did not allow to draw the line between rural households for land property rights. Thirdly, the unified purchase and marketing (sales) system (UPMS) essentially paralyzed the market mechanism, because the government regulated all the distribution of agricultural products by purchasing designated volumes at designated prices on the one hand and allocating the ration also at designated prices on the other. Finally, to maintain agricultural production, the state did not allow farmers to migrate and to freely transfer to higher-income non-agricultural sectors.

Under such circumstances, it is of no use even if you have abundant factors of production. Labor cannot be automatically converted into productive factors. The large population does not bring demographic dividends, but becomes a burden and hence leads to the strict birth control policy.[13] According to traditional analysis, fierce competition between producers leads to lower prices, which stimulate demand and, in turn, boost supply. However, this analysis ignores one point: excessively high system cost hinders the effective combination of productive factors and limits the output. As a result, China still suffered for a long time from short supply of agricultural products despite the ample production factors.[14] So the long-term coexistence of low production cost (the other side this is the poverty of farmers) and shortfall of agricultural products becomes a difficult hurdle for China's economic growth. Therefore, without careful analysis of system cost, it was impossible to understand the crux of the long-unsovable problems in China's economy.

[13]For an overview of the changes in population policies, see Zheng Zhenzhen (2012).

[14]In 1978, Deng Xiaoping summarized at the National Science Conference: "What is the status of our current production technology? Several hundred million people work in farming, yet the food problem is not truly solved."

The way China resolved these problems was system reform. Since the institutional obstacles were not isolated, but rather systematic self-contained, a multi-pronged solution was essential to crack it. The first move was a palliative policy: The government used its extremely scarce foreign exchange to increase grain imports so as to reduce the volume of unified purchase to alleviate the over-burdened agriculture, farmers and rural areas. Then the government used fiscal resources, which was then maintained by deficit, to increase the above-quota purchase prices so as to incentivize farmers to produce more at the margin. More importantly was the campaign to emancipate the mind and promote pragmatism, known by the famous phrase "Practice is the sole criterion for testing truth". Local governments, grass-root organizations, and farmers were encouraged to break the shackles of the original system and embrace bold reforms and innovations. In particular, when Anhui, Sichuan, and other provinces came up with and practiced the Household Responsibility System (HRS) in a bottom-up approach, the central government seized the opportunity to recognize the legitimacy of the spontaneous bottom-level reform with its political authority. As a result, in just a few years, in addition to a substantial yield increase, China's agriculture went through a progressive and holistic reform ranging from production, circulation and distribution, all the way to the land property rights system.[15]

In abstract, the operations costs of China's economic system i.e. the system cost, has been substantially reduced through the reform. In the rural reform, the actors to reduce system cost was firstly the rural households and the grass-root production brigades and teams; as the reform redefined the boundary for collective property rights and enabled the front-line parties choose the suitable system with lower operating cost without yielding to the dogmatically-designed but in reality inefficient old system. The local governments and the central government with the final decision-making power interacted actively with the grass-root practices, and eventually endorsed the legality of the reform although the reform policy was formulated with conflicts and compromises from time to time.

It is evident that the shortage and poverty compelled reform drastically reduced system costs, and thus translated abundant agricultural labor force into real productivity. Higher agricultural yield and farmers' income supported the growth of the national economy from both supply and demand sides. In retrospect, the history has substantiated the following conclusion: as the foundation laying ceremony, the rural reform surpasses the 4–5% national economic growth target set in the Sixth Five-Year Plan (1981–1986) and creates conditions for more rapid subsequent growth.

By the mid-1980s, China came to realize that it was not necessary to tie its 800 million farmers to agriculture and rural areas. Hundreds of millions of "surplus rural labors" began to migrate to more productive non-agricultural sectors and urban areas, constituting a solid foundation for China's rapid growth. However, to tap the potential for this wave of economic growth requires to break through bigger institutional barriers, including the national monopoly of industry and urban economic activities, and the legal ban on people hiring by the private sector including the self-employed, private partnerships and private enterprises. Given the circumstances of that time,

[15]For the internal logic of China's rural development driven by reform, see Zhou Qiren (1994).

these two obstacles were much harder than the recognition of HRS, because they touched the more systematic ideologies, laws, and customs. Fortunately, China had by then accumulated experience in gradual reform—allowing and encouraging pilots and trials, starting from local reform experiments, and eventually legitimizing the entire reform after the economic and social outcome from the new option became accepted by most people. Roughly by the 1990s, after a few rounds of ideological and political swings, the system of socialist market economy with Chinese characteristics was finally established.

13.4 The New Meaning for Comparative Advantage

Greater challenges followed. How to accommodate outbreak of China's labor and business force with a market? The way out was integrating with globalization process, and first of all, leveraging the markets of developed economies. This was also a practical choice because the later-prominent manufacturing capabilities of China were not endogenetic, and the capital, technology, and business models from developed countries had participated in its formation from the very beginning. It is logical for China, called "world factory" later, to rely on the global market to consume its huge productive force.

Trade data of the new era of economy was very impressive. China's export jumped from less than USD 10 billion in 1978 to more than USD 2 trillion in 2012, an increase of 210 times; the import from USD 10.8 billion to USD 1.8 trillion, an increase of 160-plus times; the foreign exchange reserves from USD 167 million to USD 3.3 trillion, an increase of nearly 20,000 times.[16] However, it is no easy job to understand this seismic change. Generally, the time-honored yet still fresh theory of comparative advantage is believed to be the best analytical framework for analyzing China's economic rise.[17] However, the prerequisite to apply this theory is to have massive trade between developed and developing countries. Then what is needed to awaken and then powerfully stimulate the potential comparative advantage?

To answer the question, the meaning of comparative advantage must be clarified. The comparative advantage is first of all about comparative costs, because the costs of production vary from one economic entity to another—from individuals, families, and regions, to countries. The absolute or comparative advantage is formed once products entering the market compared against each other. However, the comparison of the players is by far not just limited to production costs. In the real world, any production activity must be connected with a specific institutional structure and is

[16]NBS (2013: 224).

[17]The theory of comparative advantage was developed by David Ricardo to explain why there can be large trade volumes between developed countries and backward countries, which would be unlikely based on the theory of absolute advantage of Adam Smith. The key is "comparative advantage": although the developed economy has the absolute advantage over the developing economy across the board, the latter could concentrate on producing products with comparative advantage and then promote economic growth through international trade.

decisively affected by systematic institutional arrangements. Whether the production costs are high or low, and whether the potential comparative advantage is latent or real, or whether players can give rein to the potential cost advantage, are subject to the specific system rather than determined merely by the natural endowment.

China's experience is a telling example to educate us on the above difference. Before amazing the world with its trade data, China was a country with a backward economy and a large population, and the very low per capita income means a very competitive low labor cost.[18] Nevertheless, if the massive poverty-stricken low-cost labor is not put into effective production, there would be no products capable of participating global market competition, and hence no comparative advantage to speak of. Like what happens in physics, when the institutional frictions are too high to allow the flow of abundant human resources into production, much of the production activities simply cannot take place.

Needless to say, the potential low production costs will never automatically generate a comparative advantage. The key is whether the institutional constraints that hinder production activities can be removed or not. Unfortunately, the potential ultra-low production costs is often accompanied by extremely high system cost to impede economic operations, and as a result, the competitive potential cannot be realized. The large population, the heavier the burden, the employment for a large labor force were all problems back then. Then under such circumstances why China did not develop labor-intensive industries, it was because the ultra-low production costs are dragged by the extremely high system cost. More importantly, if the backward country does not open up and refuses to be compared with others at all, how could there be comparative advantage to speak of.

China's basic experience is nothing else. It is precisely through reform and opening up that the system cost has been greatly reduced. This is the prerequisite for economic growth. The key measures include breaking the country's administrative monopoly on industrial and other higher-yield sectors, embracing foreign investment, encouraging the development of private enterprises, giving up the state monopoly of international trade, reforming the foreign exchange system (especially substantially reducing the overvaluation of the local currency), continuously changing the import and export mechanism to fundamentally improve foreign trade services. All of these are indispensable tough battles in the reform. All in all, the goal is to dramatically cut down the prohibitive previous system cost and at the same time reduce the costs for Chinese people to learn advanced technology and managerial expertise. With this, China's potential production cost advantage has begun to be activated, with its export starting to gain momentum, and the world gradually sees the astounding comparative advantage of China's economy.

It seems that many popular viewpoints need to be re-examined. For example, "Cheap labor is the secret of China's rise". Just ask back: China's labor cost was even

[18]In 1978, China's agricultural population was 810 million yuan. The annual per capita net income was only 133.57 yuan. Previously, farmers' incomes were even lower. For example, in 1957, the figure was less than 73 yuan (Department of Planning, Ministry of Agriculture, Animal Husbandry and Fisheries 1983: 35, 523).

lower before the reform and opening up, why didn't we see any miracle? Another example is "Government regulation is the soul of the China model". Then in the Soviet model the government controls everything of the national economy, why it fails so badly that even the union country no longer exists? Even the popular view pinpointing "the Whole Nation System", it seems to me, does not hit the point. At the end of the day, does the Whole Nation System drive up the system operation costs, or does it greatly reduce the operation costs of the economic system through the reform and opening-up? In this paper I am arguing that the true China's experience lies in reducing the system cost and materializing China's comparative advantage in the global market through the reform and opening-up. To better understand and explain China's experience, it is necessary to have a broad understanding of the comparative advantage and include both system costs and production costs into the analysis framework.

13.5 The Cost Curve First Falls, then Rises

System costs is also a cost after all, so it follows the general law of cost behavior. According to economics theory, the curve for all costs will go down first and then upward. The traditional explanation for this is the diminishing marginal returns. As the scale of the economy expands, under a reasonable factor structure, the increase in the input of a certain factor will increase the output on the margin. At this point, the per-unit cost is reduced. However, beyond the reasonable critical point, further increasing this factor input will lead to diminishing incremental output; therefore, the cost curve bottoms out.

This analysis deepens the understanding of production costs. If other conditions remain unchanged, increasing labor input to a piece of farmland will increase the output, the same is true with more fertilizer. However, beyond the reasonable critical point, too much labor will only lead to idleness, and excessive fertilizer will burn the crops; the marginal return will go down and the cost curve will go up. However, the above analysis still ignores another question: even if the marginal production costs is still declining, would it be possible that there will be other costs at play as the scale gets bigger? And how will the output be changed in response to these other costs? This question was answered by Coase's discovery. When the product is delivered to the market and the consumer, transaction costs which is not related to direct production, such as marketing costs, will incur. Once the transaction costs moves beyond the technically reasonable point in the transaction structure, it may go up before the production cost. The analysis is in line with in-reality experience. When more agricultural or industrial products are produced, even if the marginal returns from production still goes up, it is likely that the marginal returns from transaction costs will go down because of excessive marketing expenses, for example. The real-world cost curve may turn around and go up again earlier than what is deduced by the blackboard economy which only sees the production but neglects the transaction.

However, even to add up the production costs and transaction costs is not enough to describe the whole picture of the cost behavior. In addition to apparent expenditures in the production and transaction process, such as labor, fertilizer, plant and equipment, marketing and other income-related cost behaviors, in the real economic process, players also have to pay a series of "involuntary expenditures", such as taxes and fees. They also have to take time and make efforts to deal with regulators or people with power, as well as disputes, conflicts, and damages related to property and products in the production and marketing process. Although the ratio between voluntary and involuntary expenditures is different from one economic system to another, the two of them exist across the board. Regrettably, unlike classical political economics, modern mainstream economics often ignores the analysis of the real-world involuntary expenditures.

The facts in China make us pay special attention to its system costs. They are not the costs that producers, consumers, or firms voluntarily pay so as to make a profit from the competition, but the systematic costs that the economic players have to bear even if they are not so willing to. These system costs are mandatory and not subject to market competition and bargaining. Therefore, they are less likely to be saved and may rise earlier and more significantly than production costs and transaction costs.

Let us look at a set of data. According to National Bureau of Statistics, between 1995 and 2012, China's nominal GDP increased from 6.07937 trillion yuan to 51.89421 trillion yuan, an increase of 8.5 times. That is obviously an extraordinary high-speed growth among major economies after WWII. However, inevitably China's high-speed growth came at a price or cost. Most people follow with interest whether or not the rapid labor cost growth had weakened the competitiveness of the manufacturing sector in China. However, we found that during the same period, the national wage growth was 8.7 times, which was almost equal to rather than much faster than the nominal GDP growth rate. What outpaced by far the economic growth during this period was the following: First, taxation, the total national tax revenue increased by 16.7 times, equivalent to 197% of the economic growth, or 192% of the total wage growth. Second, the non-tax fiscal revenue increased by 18.8 times, even faster than tax revenue growth. Third, the social security contribution increased by 28. 7 times. Fourth, the land transfer fee across the country increased by 64 times.[19]

All of the above items are the have-to-be-paid costs involved in the production of added value. The differences are: The total amount of wages occurs in the labor market and covers the country's human resources including most of the SOE workers, and the general practice is to adopt the labor contract system where the wages are determined by mutual agreement of the parties and it is governed by the supply and demand mechanism in the market. However, taxation and administrative service

[19]See NBS (2013: nominal GDP. 44; total amount of wages. 132; taxation 331: fiscal revenue, 328; social security contributions, 850); the land transfer fees amounted to 42 billion yuan in 1995 (including 2.4 billion yuan of make-up payment for previous land allocations, see *China Land Yearbook 1996:*60. The land transfer fees amounted to 2.69 trillion yuan in 2012 (See Land and Resources Statistical Yearbook 2013) and 4.28 trillion yuan in 2014 (See Ye Kai, *From 40 Billion to 4 Trillion—The History of Land Sales by Local Governments*, published by *China Business News*, August 29, 2016, http://finance.qq.com/a/20160829/036965.htm).

fees paid to government agencies are statutory burdens and mandatorily enforced. Individuals, families, and enterprises cannot pay less if they are unhappy with the administrative services, and it is difficult for tax payers to participate in tax legislation and setting the taxation rates. Social security is theoretically used for the assurance of future living expenses of contributors, and an integral part of labor costs in a broad sense. However, the amount of social security contribution, its operation, payment and other management are all performed only by government agencies per existing regulations, and are also legally mandatory. The last item, land transfer fee, is a unique economic operation cost of China under transformation, because under the current system, all the land for business operations in China is state-owned (including most of the land expropriated from rural collectives and converted to state ownership), and can only be leased to institutions and individuals by the government. Although there is a land lease market, but the government is the only party to control the land supply. Like other "markets" monopolized by the government or state-owned enterprises, there are always many demanders thus fierce competition with a sole supplier or only a few suppliers to prevent others from coming in. Therefore, the assets prices formed in such markets are, in essence, the rent of administrative power.[20]

Based on the above analysis, we can see that a significant feature of China's economic operation during the above observation period is that the growth of statutory or mandatory cost items is not only much faster than the economy growth but also by far exceeds the growth of other cost items that are governed by the market mechanism. It is a manifestation that the gradual reforms are still far from being fully in place, and it will inevitably affect the continued growth of the Chinese economy. In contrast to the early days reform, "liberating thoughts, decentralizing power and transferring benefits", the system cost has gradually turned around and recovered way faster than the rapid economic growth although it was once slashed as China materialized its comparative cost advantage and achieved high growth in the global market. The real situation is like a giant camel. Initially, the burden is relieved so that it can run faster; Yet while it is still running at high speed, more and more load is added and eventually it cannot run fast any more. This paper believes that as an economy establishing its foothold across the globe by comparative cost advantage, China's economy can be explained by the cut-down and re-climbing of system cost with regard to the changes in its trajectory of rapid growth.

13.6 Unquantifiable Institutional Friction

There are still some system costs that are difficult to be reflected by statistics. Observations indicate that in economic activities, the property rights delineation, contract

[20]This should serve as a caveat for transitional economies like China: special attention should be paid to the relationship between the resource allocation system and the income distribution system. Before power has been properly caged, the "charge" by the authority on a fast-growing economy may far exceed the sustainable level that the economy can afford.

disputes, new product development, market access, changes in scope of government monopoly, administrative litigation, and civil case trials all involve additional costs other than direct production costs. Although such broad transaction costs or system cost as defined in this paper also take place in mature market economies, these non-production-related costs are rather unique in a transitional economy like China and forms its own system. Based on several cases that the author has studied in recent years, this section will briefly discuss the nature of such costs.

The first case involved government monopoly over the telecommunications sector. The background was in the late 1990s when the rise of Internet provided a new opportunity for voice communications. Different from traditional telecommunications, the Internet-based voice communication (namely IP phone) does not need to exclusively occupy the expensive communication cable, but transfers massive voice packets with the same line, and thus can revolutionarily reduce communication charge. At the end of 1997, a private enterprise operated by CHEN Brothers in Mawei District, Fuzhou City, began to apply IP telephone to commercial activities and became very popular in the market. At that time, international calls were very expensive, ranging from 18 to 32 yuan per minute, but the IP phone provided by CHEN brothers only cost 6–9 yuan per minute. Naturally, their business was booming.

However, they were reported by the local telecommunications bureau to the police as engaging in "illegal business operations", and the district public security bureau sealed up their business venue, confiscated their equipment and limited their personal freedom. Later, they were released on bail pending trial after their family paid 50,000 yuan. The brothers filed an administrative litigation in the District Court and later appealed to the Fuzhou Intermediate People's Court. The President of Fuzhou Intermediate People's Court, Judge XU Yongdong, considered the case involved new technology, and asked the parties to provide expert witnesses to debate in court about the technical differences between IP telephone and traditional telecommunications. After the trial, Fuzhou Intermediate People's Court held that IP telephone did not fall within the scope of traditional telecommunications but belonged to a new business open to the private sector according to a State Council documents. On January 20, 1999, the Fuzhou Intermediate People's Court revoked the ruling of the Mawei District Court and ordered a retrial.[21]

Unfortunately, this well-founded 7,000-plus-word verdict was not duly respected. On January 21, 1999, the next day after the Fuzhou Intermediate People's Court issued the ruling, a division director of the Ministry of Industry and Information

---

[21] According to this, the Fuzhou Intermediate People's Court ruled that: "IP telephone is a new type communication business that is based on network technology and provided over Internet, and it falls into the scope of "computer information service business" described in the No. 55-1993 Circular of the State Council and in *Chinese Public Multimedia Communication Regulations*. The No. 55-1993 Circular of the State Council explicitly stipulates that "the computer information service business" is open to the private sector. Therefore, it is not a long-distance communication and international communication business under the exclusive operation of the post and telecommunications department as per No. 54-1990 Circular of the State Council, as claimed by the appellee Fuzhou Municipal Public Security Bureau Mawei District Branch." For the full text of the ruling, see http://bbs.cl14.net/thread-829885-1-1,html).

Technology (MIIT) declared publicly to the media that "the claim that 'IP telephone is not under the monopoly of telecommunication operation' is groundless." His basis is a "Notice" issued by MIIT, which stipulated that the "computer information network business" adopts the license system and "should temporarily not open telecom services such as telephone and fax." The director claimed that since the Notice clearly stipulates that the business "should temporarily not open to telecom services", then if someone uses IP telephone to operate long-distance telecommunications business, it is an illegal operation." He also disclosed the main ways to deal with such illegal activity as IP telephone: "If the scale is small, the administrative department will generally confiscate the illegal income and impose fines; if the scale reaches the threshold for crime, the case will be transferred to the judicial organ and dealt with as an illegal business operation according to Article 225 of Criminal Law. The relevant departments have investigated and handled many such cases in Guangdong and Shanghai, and some have been transferred to the judicial authorities." So it is clear, in the opinion of this director, a notice from his own administrative department is far more authoritative than the ruling of the Fuzhou Intermediate People's Court and the quoted State Council Circular, and it is beyond question and requires no judicial discussion.[22] Under such a "legal" atmosphere, the final verdict of the CHEN brothers' case went nowhere and became unknown to the public.[23]

The second case is the express delivery business by private sector that touched the cheese of the postal sector. With booming commercial activities, the demand for express delivery, such as for commercial documents, samples, and later prosperous e-commerce parcels, increases rapidly. In the 1990s, the Little Red Cap Express emerged in the private sector, and the top five international logistics companies such as FedEx also entered China market. However, they started and all faced this new problem: are non-postal service entities allowed to operate the express delivery? The postal department's answer was definitely negative, because the Postal Law of the People's Republic of China, adopted in the 1980s, clearly stated that the mail delivery business is operated by state monopoly. The new question is, can the old regulation automatically cover new businesses that did not exist when the old regulations were drafted? The position of the former Ministry of Posts and Telecommunications was that in order to protect citizens' freedom of communication, the business has to be exclusive to the postal service. Therefore, the focus of the dispute was shifted to whether the emerging express commercial package delivery fell into the category of the "mail".

The conflict of interest made it necessary to be particular about the wording. So, what is "mail"? The Rules for the Implementation of the Postal Law of the People's Republic of China formulated in 1990 (hereinafter referred as Rules) points out, "mail includes letters and postcards or other articles", and "letters refers to message

---

[22]Lao Rong, who provided expert testimony in the case of CHEN brothers in the Fuzhou Intermediate People's Court, recorded the case in detail. See http://laorong.blog.techweb.com.cn/archives/11.10.

[23]Xu Yongdong, a judge for eight years, later resigned and founded Tuowei Law Firm as Lead Partner (http://www.yearbooklawyer.com/sites/lawyer/detaiL20120727180134l547_c_10.html).

carrier in the form of sealed envelopes". By this definition, *Twenty-Four Histories, Das Capital, Encyclopedia Britannica* are all letters if they are sealed in envelopes. And additionally, what is "other articles with characteristics of a mail"? According to the Rules, they are "those carriers which transmit information by using such forms as symbols, images, or sounds". Considering possible different interpretations by different Chinese people for frequently used terms, the *Rules* specifically announced that the "specific content of the exclusive postal operation is subject to the interpretation by the Ministry of Posts and Telecommunications".

Even the after effects of the 911 terrorist attack in the United States added an episode to the extension of the monopoly of China's postal service. On November 15, 2001, to prevent the already reported anthrax virus in the US from spreading to China, the General Office of the State Council issued an urgent notice, requiring to "strengthen the management of postal services such as letters and printed materials to prevent anthrax spreading". On December 20, 2001, several competent authorities, including the State Post Bureau, jointly notified all enterprises that "need to handle the delivery of inbound and outbound letters and articles with the characters of letters", "should, within 60 days upon the issuance of this notice, go to the provincial postal department to handle the entrustment procedures." On February 4, 2002, the State Post Bureau issued a notice to the provincial postal department, the approval authority for entrustment applications, stating that "the scope of the postal entrustment is limited to the sending or delivery of inbound and outbound mails or articles with characters of letters with a weight of over 500 grams per item, or with the per-item charge above the state prescribed standard for express mail (of the same weight, to the same country/region). The nutshell of this seldom-seen awkward and lengthy sentence is that any mail with the weight of not exceeding 500 grams and the rate cheaper than the state postal bureau are not allowed to be entrusted (or delivered by private businesses). What is even more incredible is that the notice also made it clear that "the scope of the entrustment specified in the preceding paragraph does not include letters with the personal address of citizens and official documents of the party, government, military and other organs at or above the county level."! The author then commented that these unreasonable and inappropriate administrative controls only aim to protect the obsolete privileges of the postal department and have nothing to do with anthrax prevention.[24]

The third case is a strange story taking place in Dongguan. As a major coastal manufacturing city in the Pearl River Delta, the majority of the permanent population do not have the registered local permanent residence (called "Hukou" in Chinese), which resulted in severe short supply of local services. So lots of private enterprises came in, and their business included opening pharmacies. In March 2002, The Interim Regulations for the Establishment of Retail Pharmacies (hereinafter referred to as Regulations) announced the opening-up of the Guangdong's drug retail market. Investors from elsewhere swarmed into Dongguan with great enthusiasm. However, they soon found themselves running into an administrative wall that caused them bleeding. Starting from June 2001, the Dongguan Food and Drug Administration

[24]For more analysis, see Zhou Qiren (2002).

(FDA) began to implement a Regulation stipulating that any new pharmacy needs to be at least 500 ms from the nearest approved pharmacy by straight distance. Although the Regulation was abolished due to the intervention from the media and provincial leaders, this 500 meter hard requirement was implemented for a whole year. During this period, many investors spent lots of money on buying or renting store spaces, renovation, procurement, and labor costs, yet they could not open the store without the license simply because there was another pharmacy or drug counter within 500 meters, or there was a latecomer with connections. It is said that the officials of the local FDA drove a car to "accurately measure" the distance themselves. Even if it was only a few meters shy of 500 meters, the new store would not be approved. In fact, it is quite tricky to open stores in the market. There is no guarantee that you will not lose money even if you are the only store within a 10,000-meter radius. Likewise, you will not necessarily suffer a loss even if there are three stores within 50 meters. It should be the business of investors instead of the government to care about store layout; the job of the latter is to prevent fake drugs and fraud by supervision.

The above-mentioned cases seem to be trivial in China's fast-growing economy. However, only by deep diving can we clearly see the economic nature of the institutional friction encountered by China's economy. It is clear that in addition to direct production costs or direct service costs, economical operation has to pay for other expenses. The confiscated equipment, the bail money, the spending on the lawsuit and mental anguish in the CHEN brothers case, and the efforts to get lawful approval for express delivery and the pharmacy retail business, all belong to system costs which is studied by this paper. These "extra" costs can be prohibitive enough to prevent many business activities from happening at all.

Do not assume that as time goes on, these system costs that hinder innovation, investment, and employment will automatically decrease since these cases occurred at the beginning of the new century. Observations show that after China's economy freed itself from the previous round of deflation and regained a strong momentum at the beginning of the 21st century, "macro-control" preceded the deployment of the reform of "breaking administrative monopoly" and resulted in numerous unwarranted controls and administrative approvals. And this was why in 2012, the new administration once again emphasized on "decentralization and profit transfer" to ease the downward pressure on the economy. The new administration announced that it would clean up and abolish hundreds or maybe thousands of administrative approvals, most of which are not the legacy of the planned era but added to the economic operation one by one during the rapid growth period since the start of the new century. An iconic event may serve as an indirect evidence for the exorbitant system cost. China's telecom industry, which was supposed to open up as early as in the 1990s, is open only to a couple of central SOEs. Although some improvements have been made to the subscription fee and service quality, the whole sector is still widely criticized such that the Premier had to personally order it to increase the speed and reduce the charges for broadband.[25] However, the announcement from the

---

[25]"Premier Li Keqiang urged to increase the speed and reduce costs of broadband for three consecutive times," *Beijing Times*, May 14, 2015. Two years later, Premier LI Keqiang said in his government

higher level did not get automatically implemented since it involved the power and interests of departments.[26]

13.7 Economic Consequences of Corruption and Extravagance

In July 2008, in the paper presented to the Seminar in Commemoration of the 30th Anniversary of China's Reform moderated by Prof. Coase at the University of Chicago, the author not only explained what DENG Xiaoping did right since the reform and opening-up to bring China's economy to the world's attention, but also came up with a judgement: "During the decentralization reform, redefinition of rights, recognizing and encouraging private entrepreneurs, and large scale adoption of the price mechanism, corruption did not only come like a shadow, but also seemed to spread even faster than the pace of reform."[27] Revisiting this conclusion nine years later, I believe the only amendment that needs to be made is to delete the word "seemed to", which I had written at the time out of caution.

Indeed, as of today we still lack of systematic research based on solid facts, rigorous statistics, and scientific norms, on corruption in transitional China. However, the quick-responded and resolute new anti-corruption policy since the 18th CPC National Congress, and the facts disclosed in the publicly available anti-corruption notices, reports, news coverage, and relevant judicial proceeding documents[28] are sufficient to help us to come to this conclusion: the astonishing corruption in the transitional period cannot be simply explained by moral degradation of a handful of officials, nor generally regarded as the result of negligence at work or lax governance. On the contrary, the corruption during the transition is a systematic institutionalized corruption that is endogenous with the transformation.

In the above-mentioned paper, I also quoted Steven N.S. Cheung's economic theory to explain why China in transition is accompanied by severe corruption. The theory holds that two basic economic systems have been formed to resolve resource contention: one is to regulate and restrain people's behavior with hierarchical privilege to prevent the abuse of scarce resources; the other is to create freedom spaces for people to engage in economic activities by defining property rights so as to stimulate production, exchange, division of labor and co-operation. When the transition is made from the first economic system to the second one (i.e. the market

work report on March 5, 2017, that all domestic long-distance fees and roaming fees for mobile phones had to be abolished within the year, and the Internet access fees for SME dedicated lines and international long-distance telephone charges should be drastically reduced. (See the special telegram by Xinhua News Agency Beijing New Media).

[26]The controversy over online car-hailing since 2015 is just one of the many new telling cases.

[27]Zhou Qiren (2010: 25).

[28]For example, since 2013,Caixin.com has been publishing the "Anti-Corruption Weekly" column to cover major anti-corruption cases. It has produced a total of 130 editions so far.

economy), the original hierarchical privilege will inevitably strive for "power rents", resulting in rampant corruption, or even institutionalized corruption due to lack of the corresponding restriction mechanisms. This shows that "corruption is not only a concomitant of the early reform, but also can be a corrosive agent to disintegrate the public support, and even a deadly killer to terminate the reform. How the transition economy responds to institutionalized corruption is a grave challenge."[29]

The next thing to look at, is how the severe corruption affects China's economy. The popular approach seems to add up all incomes, including the illegal incomes of corrupt officials, easily obtain the total national income, and then discuss "economic growth" on this basis. However, it is precisely this no-longer-ignorable transformational corruption that reminds us of the need to make clear distinctions among incomes of different natures. Although the income from corruption is also part of the national income, it constitutes an obstacle to the sustained growth of production activities by other citizens, and should, therefore, be rightly regarded as a negative factor that drags down economic growth and undermines the international competitiveness of China's products.

Let us start with an abstracted simple phenomenon: in order to get extra extrajudicial benefits, the briber gives an authority official or a family member of the official for some kind of gain, large or small, and get some return from the bribees. Here we omit various possible motivations for the behavior—be it voluntary, premeditated, or acting on implied or explicit hints, or having to follow the unspoken rules, etc., and only focus on the chain impact on the economy from the bribery.

The first logical result is that the bribe pays off. Whether it is in the form of business facilitation or quicker approval, or special opportunities to acquire land or credit, to list on the stock market, or to get market access, as long as these returns still serve production activities, then compared to the "no bribe, no handling" scenario, the bribe pushes the project forward, the investment gets recovered, and more jobs and revenues are created. Within this context, individual corruption does serve as a lubricant for economic growth.

But the story does not stop here. Successful bribery of someone else that leads to winning in resource contention will trigger a chain of subsequent behavior: More business people will follow the example of the briber, and more officials will follow the bribe taker. Therefore, the second logical result occurs, namely the dynamic expansion of the bribery, which also constantly "educates" powerful departments and officials to realize that the public power in their hands has great personal economic value. As a result, rent-seeking becomes rampant and eventually escalates to rent-setting—departments and officials with power begin to proactively seek illegal personal gains by imposing costs on players in the market.[30] In terms of phenomenon, the corruption not only proliferates to batches and batches of officials from lucrative departments and large SOEs; severe corruption also takes place in such unprofitable agencies and institutes, such as the statistics bureaus, cultural

[29]Zhou Qiren (2008).

[30]Barzel defines the power as the ability to impose costs, see Barzel (2002: 10).

organizations, scientific research institutions, and universities. With the proliferation of the corrupt logic, corruption transcends the category of moral anomie among individual officials, and presents a malignant, systemic, and institutionalized situation. The economic implication of this step is that the more resources the corruption occupies, the less resources can be used to serve productive activities, and the ratio decreases.

Unless the anti-corruption is strong enough, the corruption proliferation will not stop. However, corruption, after all, is not morally "correct", plus severe corruption damages the foundation of the legitimacy of state power and will eventually be investigated and punished; therefore, no matter how rampant corruption is, it will always try to hide under the radar and pay extra costs to avoid getting caught. Let us make it clear, all system costs associated with the attack on and defense against the corruption are non-productive—this is also the fourth-step logical consequence of corruption. If the corruption costs that hinder economic growth are also seen as part of national income and incorrectly regarded as components of the rapid growth, it is impossible to judge if the usually recognized "economic miracle" is inflated or not. Ironically, anti-corruption in the context of its proliferation is sometimes criticized for "harming economic growth".

Therefore, our conclusion is that although isolated corruption can somewhat lubricate the economic operation and generate certain objective productive effect; yet when corruption becomes common and institutionalized, it quickly devours the healthy cells of the economy like cancer; therefore, it is a deadly enemy of sustained growth. It is not difficult to understand why no economy with serious corruption problems in today's world can achieve sustained growth. On the other hand, we can testify that the proliferated corruption parasitical on fast growth will continuously erode the foundation of economic growth and social justice, impair the motivation for innovation especially entrepreneurship, and eventually drag down the pace of growth and put the economy back to stagnation.

Extravagance enveloped officialdom also has complex impacts on economic growth, but it is even more difficult to quantify than corruption. We just estimate out of intuition that the impact of extravagance on the economy is far bigger than corruption. Generally speaking, extravagance, including the breathtaking ostentations and enjoyments that cost tons of public money, does not convert public resource into private interests, it is usually limited to incumbent officials as their treatment, and cannot be turned into the officials' private property which they can still enjoy after retirement. Therefore, extravagance spending is not only listed in accounting as public expenditure, but also perceived as "necessary" payment to enhance social cohesion, build the image, increase people's sense of identity, and encourage low-paying officials to work hard.

Government spending cannot be seen as naturally having the positive value of boosting demand. Some people might ask: aren't all the above-standard accommodations, fleets, meals, and other extravagant public spendings converted into purchase orders in the market? Aren't they continually generating demand for raw materials, energy, parts, equipment, and services and thus contributing to employment, revenue, and taxation? All the visible extravagance is more than just "boosting economic growth", it is part of economic growth by itself!

However, the economic source of extravagance has exposed its counter-growth nature. In the context of payment by government taxes and fees for the extravagance, it is not difficult for us to find that it is the too fast growth of taxes and fees that constitutes the financial foundation for the extravagance. As mentioned before, the taxes and fees growth rate itself which doubled the nominal economic growth is a manifestation of rising system cost for economic operation and increased burden for the growth. Apart from the already too fast growing taxes and fees, the business world provides financial support for all sorts of extravagance spendings, be it voluntary or imposed, and we see this as an even bigger extra burden. Under these circumstances, the extravagance has made public service which should be provided by the public power more and more expensive. Based on the economic logic, if more taxes and fees must be paid for every piece of incremental value added, then once this goes beyond a certain tolerable threshold, the willingness to engage in production, creation, and investment is bound to decline. In a nutshell, the logical result of extravagance is similar to corruption, and the true face of the fast-climbing spendings to suppress economic growth will eventually be unveiled.

13.8 Conclusion: System Cost Is Vital

System cost defined in this paper refer to the cost brought to economic operations by the systematic institution. They include not only transaction costs or pure commercial expenses—the original and enlightening discovery of our academic forerunners, but also the costs imposed on the parties through a series of institutions in the market and non-market environment, including taxes, fees, regulations, approvals, legal restrictions and prohibitions, as well as the expenditures on ideology, public opinion, public policy debates, and political competition in the hope of changing these variables. Mandatory costs are common because any economic activity must involve the state and its agents. Where property rights are protected (which in itself is the result of state action), and resource utilization is based on voluntary choices, the implementation of all kinds of contracts, in fact, always involves legitimate coercive force which provides services in the process. In the case of the command economy with direct resources allocation by the state, the coercive force is born in the administrative and economic complex that integrates the government and the enterprise, and the system cost directly constitutes the operating costs of the economic system. In either case, the state coercion is involved in economic operations, and economic growth has to pay system cost. The world of zero system cost is but a utopia.

The transition from a planned command economy to a market economy is a systematic change, where a series of institutional changes takes place and affect the operation of the economic system. As system variables are at the more prominent and central position in the transitional economy, the system cost—beyond direct production costs and narrow transaction costs, is easier to enter the horizon of transitional economy researchers. Understanding and interpreting the various phenomena of a transitional economy, such as the driver of reform, resistance and friction, the sudden release of potential productivity, and the ups and downs of the long-term economy, cannot be possible without analysis of system cost. The rule of thumb is that if the must-be-paid cost per unit output is low, the economic growth rate will be high, and vice versa. To understand this point, the only thing needed is to appropriately extend the usually-seen production costs and transaction costs into system cost which encompass mandatory elements.

China's economy provides a rare case. The embarrassing pre-reform poverty also means that the direct production costs was meager, indicating that China's economy had great potential in comparative cost advantage. The problem to be solved is to drastically reduce the system cost. To this end, it is necessary to break the hard shell of the original system. The reform and opening-up has achieved this mission. Through a series of institutional reform—changes in concepts, in law, in systemic policy design and organizational arrangements—China's potential comparative advantage has been materialized and made its way into the global market, thereby changing the trajectory of operation of the economic system and its performance to create a miracle of rapid growth. Therefore, the primary clue to understand China's experience is nothing else but precisely the operation costs of economic system significantly reduced by a series of institutional reform.

However, the great achievements by China, albeit changing the world economic landscape, cannot change, and it is impossible to change the cold economic rules. The cost curve goes down first and then up again, and the system cost even rises more steeply in the high-speed economic growth. As people have noticed, along with the high speed economic growth, the once drastically reduced system cost comes back up again, which is reflected in growth of the taxes, fees, and various statutory burdens which outpaces the economic growth, the stacked layers and layer of administrative approvals, the rampant rent-seeking, and the absence of necessary market supervision in parallel with overstepping administrative regulation. All these constituent factors for system cost are synthesized to lead to a negative result: the per unit output has to bear the increasingly higher cost, compromising the comparative advantage of China's economy in the world, and dragging down China's economic growth which has been driven by its cost advantage. The situation is very clear: to reverse the steep upward trend of system cost through comprehensive and deepened reform is the indispensable prerequisite for sustainable growth of China's economy.

References

Alchain, A. 1987. Property Rights. In *The New Palgrave A Dictionary of Economics*, ed. John Eatwell, Murray Milgate, and Peter Newman, 1031–1034. London: The Macmillan Press Limited and The Stockton Press.

Arrow, K. J. 1969. The Organization of Economic Activity: Issues Pertinent to the Choice of Market versus Non-Market Allocation. In *The Analysis and Evaluation of Public Expenditures: The*

PBB-System, Joint Economic Committee, 91st Cong., 1st Sess., 1. Washington, DC: Government Printing Office.

Barzel, Yoram. 2002. *Theory of the State: Economic Rights, Legal Rights, and the Scope of the State*. Cambridge: Cambridge University Press.

Chang, Pei-kang. 1940. *Grains Distribution and Sales in Zhejiang*. The Commercial Press.

Cheung, Steven N. S. 1987. Economic Organization and Transaction Costs. In *The New Palgrave: A Dictionary of Economics*, Vol. 2, 55–58. Palgrave Macmillan. For Chinese text, see Economic Organizations and Transaction Costs" by Cheung, published in *The New Palgrave Dictionary of Economics,* Vol. 2, Economic Science Press, 1996: 58–60.

Cheung, Steven N.S. 2009. *The Economic System of China*. Beijing: Citic Press.

Coase, R.H. 1937. The Nature of the Firm. *Economica* 4 (2): 386–405.

National Statistics Bureau of PRC. 2013. *China Statistical Yearbook 2013*. China Statistics Press.

North, Douglass C. (1990). *Institutions, Institutional Change and Economic Performance*. Cambridge: Cambridge University Press.

Qiren, Zhou. 1994. China's Rural Reform: The Evolution of the Relation Between Government and Property Rights. *China Social Sciences Quarterly (Hong Kong)*, Summer Issue, August 15.

Qiren, Zhou. 2002. The Right to Play with Wording", "The Irrelevant Anthrax", "The Situation of Express Mail Market and its Upper Layer". *Income Is a Series of Event*, Peking University Press.

Qiren, Zhou. 2005. Market Competition Is a Right, "From IP Telephone to 3G". *Take the Lamp to Examine the Sword–Observing the Big Era of Economy,* Peking University Press.

Qiren, Zhou. 2006. Attending Pei-kang Chang's Lectures. *Income Is a Series of Events*, Peking University Press, 11–14

Qiren, Zhou. 2008. What Deng Xiaoping Did Right. *What China Did Right*, Peking University Press 2010, 10–27.

Ross, Ian Simpson. 2010. *The Life of Adam Smith*. 2nd ed. Oxford: Oxford University Press.

The Planning Department of the Ministry of Agriculture, Animal-Husbandry and Fisheries. 1983. *Agriculture Economic Information.*

Xiaoping, Deng. 1983. *Selected Works of DENG Xiaoping,* Vol. 2. Copenhagen: The People's Press.

Zhenzhen, Zheng. 2012. A Review of China's Population Policy and Its Future Directions, china.com.cn on July 12. http://www.china.com.cn/guoqing/2012-07/12/content_25890510.htm.

The manufacturer's authorised representative in the EU is Springer
Nature Customer Service Centre GmbH, Europaplatz 3, 69115 Heidelberg,
Germany. If you have any concerns regarding our products, please
contact ProductSafety@springernature.com

Printed and bound by CPI Group (UK) Ltd, Croydon, CR0 4YY
30/09/2026
02225246-0013